AMERICAN NATURE

Our Intriguing Land and Wildlife

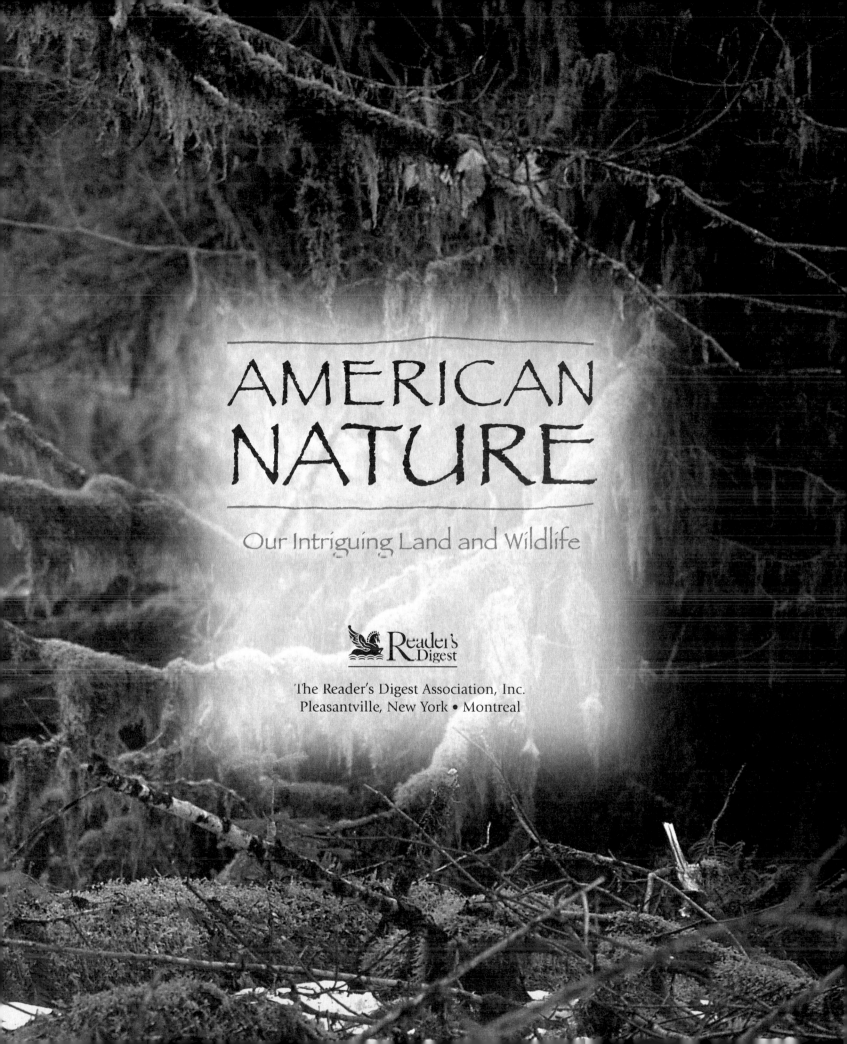

AMERICAN NATURE

Our Intriguing Land and Wildlife

Reader's Digest

The Reader's Digest Association, Inc.
Pleasantville, New York • Montreal

READER'S DIGEST GENERAL BOOKS

**Editor-in-Chief,
Books and Home Entertainment**
Barbara J. Morgan

Editor, U.S. General Books
David Palmer

Executive Editor
Gayla Visalli

Managing Editor
Christopher Cavanaugh

The credits and acknowledgments that appear on pages 326–327 are hereby made a part of this copyright page.

Copyright © 1997 The Reader's Digest Association, Inc.
Copyright © 1997 The Reader's Digest Association (Canada) Ltd.
Copyright © 1997 Reader's Digest Association Far East Ltd.
Philippine Copyright 1997 Reader's Digest Association Far East Ltd.

Library of Congress Cataloging in Publication Data

American nature: our intriguing land and wildlife.
     p.   cm.
  Includes index.
  ISBN 0-89577-948-X
   1. Natural history—North America. I. Reader's Digest Association.
QH102.A53 1997
508.7—dc20   96-38413

Reader's Digest and the Pegasus logo are registered trademarks of The Reader's Digest Association, Inc.
Printed in the United States of America
Address any comments about AMERICAN NATURE: OUR INTRIGUING LAND AND WILDLIFE
to Editor, U.S. General Books, c/o Customer Service, Reader's Digest, Pleasantville, NY 10570.
To order additional copies of AMERICAN NATURE: OUR INTRIGUING LAND AND WILDLIFE, call 1-800-846-2100.

Front matter and part opener photos: *p. 1, burrowing owl; pp. 2–3, Roosevelt elk; p. 5, Yosemite Falls, CA (top), river otter kits (bottom); pp. 6, 8–9, Canada geese; pp. 7 (top), 152–153, old-growth forest, Vancouver Island, British Columbia; pp. 7 (bottom), 214–215, waves breaking on Pacific Coast.*

AMERICAN NATURE
Our Intriguing Land and Wildlife

STAFF

Project Editor
Sharon Fass Yates

Project Art Editor
Kenneth Chaya

Senior Research Editor
Maymay Quey Lin

Editor
Thomas A. Ranieri

Senior Associate Art Editors
Martha Grossman
Irene Ledwith

Associate Editor
Richard M. Mazurek

Associate Art Editor
Andrew Ploski

Editorial Assistant
Valerie Sylvester

CONTRIBUTORS

Editor
Edward S. Barnard

Consultants
Robert E. Budliger
Director of Environmental Education (retired)
New York State Department of
Environmental Conservation
*(Part 1: America's Amazing Animals
and Part 3: Living Landscapes of America)*

A. Wayne Cahilly
Manager of the Arboretum and Grounds
New York Botanical Garden
(Part 2: America's Bountiful Plants)

Writers
Spider Barbour
Janine M. Benyus
Robert M. Brown
John Calderazzo
Justin Cronin
Jerry Dennis
Edward Duensing
Dwight Holing
Patrick Huyghe
Les Line
John Hanson Mitchell
Edward R. Ricciuti
William G. Scheller
Gary Soucie
Ann O. Squire
Scott Weidensaul (chief)
Christina M. Wilsdon

Art Production Associate
Peter Gargiulo

Picture Editors
At Carousel Research, Inc.:
Laurie Platt Winfrey
Fay Torres-yap

Picture Researchers
At Carousel Research, Inc.:
Van Bucher
Leslie Mangold
Robin Sand

Illustrators
Dolores R. Santoliquido
Drew-Brook-Cormack Associates
Robert Villani

Copy Editor
Mel Minter

Proofreader
Virginia Croft

Indexer
Northwind Editorial Services

Special thanks to

Nancy Bent
Assistant Librarian, Brookfield Zoo, Brookfield, IL

Dr. David H. Griffing
Director of Education, Paleontological Research Institution
Ithaca, NY

Michael J. Mac
Biological Resources Division, U.S. Geological Survey, Reston, VA

Harold A. Vanasse
Meteorological Consultant

Elizabeth Walsh, Ph.D.
Dept. of Biological Services, University of Texas at El Paso, TX

AMERICAN NATURE
Our Intriguing Land and Wildlife

CONTENTS

Part One
AMERICA'S AMAZING ANIMALS

Part Two
OUR BOUNTIFUL PLANTS

Part Three
LIVING LANDSCAPES OF AMERICA

AMERICA'S AMAZING ANIMALS

Animal Champions *America's record breakers*

What is our heaviest flying bird?

Ranging from 20 to 38 pounds, the trumpeter swan (seen year-round in parts of Montana, Oregon, and Wyoming) is not only the heaviest flying bird in North America, but the largest swan in the world as well. Flying is a labor-intensive activity for any bird, and hefty birds like this one must fly faster than lighter ones just to stay airborne. For the trumpeter

➤ *One of nature's greatest comeback stories is that of the trumpeter swan, which by 1912 had nearly vanished but now numbers in the thousands. The bird seems to herald its triumph over extinction every time it issues one of its trombonelike honks—the product of an elongated windpipe that extends into the bird's body.*

swan, simply taking off from the ground requires Herculean effort. It builds up the speed necessary for liftoff by running across the surface of the water while flapping its wings with all its might. Touching down is equally tricky. To avoid a crash landing, the big bird must gauge its descent carefully as it glides toward earth. If the runway is a lake, the trumpeter thrusts its wide, webbed feet forward and skis across the water to break for a stop.

In the eyes of earthbound viewers, however, the flight of the trumpeter swan seems anything but arduous. When a flock of these surprisingly graceful birds swirls skyward like a snowstorm in reverse, their resonant bugling seems only to celebrate the glory of taking to the air on beating wings.

Is there one invertebrate that dwarfs all the others?

Eyes the size of basketballs gaze from the head of a giant squid, a deep-sea creature so elusive that scientists have never actually seen one in its natural habitat. Our knowledge of this enormous mollusk (kin to cuttlefishes and octopuses) has been gleaned primarily from dead specimens that have washed ashore, been hauled up in fishing nets, or been pulled from the stomachs of sperm whales. The largest of their kind are estimated to weigh over two tons and measure up to 70 feet long; much of this length consists of a pair of long, thin tentacles that, armed with sharp-edged suckers, stretch out to seize fish and crustaceans.

Nautical lore is rife with tales of epic battles between sailors and squids, their squirming arms dragging boats beneath the waves. The animal's chief adversary, however, is the sperm whale. The dark hides of these creatures are often scarred with circles carved by the squid's rasping suckers—marks that bear mute testimony to furious struggles in the inky depths of the ocean. Researchers are now probing this realm in submersibles and with robots to learn more about the secret life of squids and to explore their mysterious lairs.

Which animal reigns supreme in size?

A blue whale starts life as all animals do—as a single cell, an egg too small for the eye to see. But once fertilized by a sperm cell, it grows at a rate unrivaled by any creature. In only 11 months this speck of life becomes a three-ton baby. Over the next seven months, it will gain an incredible 200 pounds per day.

As an adult, a blue whale measures between 80 and 110 feet and weighs between 135 and 190 tons, dwarfing the biggest dinosaurs ever to roam the earth. This girth grows even greater when the animal's pleated throat widens to swallow a mouthful of krill. Up to four tons of these creatures fill its stomach each day. Visitors to the Gulf of St. Lawrence can sometimes spy blue whales stocking up on food in early fall as they prepare for migration.

Among land mammals, which one is the biggest?

One look at the largest set of bison horns on record is all you need to fathom the enormity of its owner. On view at Yellowstone National Park, these massive specimens—measuring 23½ inches long, with a spread of 35⅜ inches—once belonged to a creature that stood some six feet tall at the peak of its hump and weighed perhaps more than a ton. Americans often refer to the bison as a buffalo, but true buffalo, which have no humps, are found only in Asia and Africa. The two subspecies that inhabit North America are the plains bison, which once roamed the Great Plains in vast numbers, and the larger and darker wood bison, which resides in northern Alberta and the Northwest Territories of Canada.

For their size bison are surprisingly fleet-footed, maintaining speeds of up to 35 miles per hour for as long as half an hour. Not only can they flee for many miles without showing signs of fatigue, but they can outrun teams of horses and outlast relays of good saddle horses. Seen grazing, these gargantuans might appear lazy, but anyone who has viewed them in action can attest to the fact that a galloping herd of bison is a true force of nature.

Which adult insect has the shortest life span?

An adult mayfly's time on earth is so limited—a few hours, a few days at most—that the insect must devote its entire life to reproduction, not even taking time out to eat. Prior to this ephemeral existence, however, a mayfly spends from several months to two years as a nymph, molting many times before emerging from a lake or pond. A second-to-last molt transforms it into a form unique to mayflies, complete with wings but covered in a drab skin. This cloak is shed to reveal a glistening adult, ready to live its short life to the fullest.

What is the largest fish?

Though it measures up to 60 feet long, the whale shark is one of the most harmless creatures in the sea. Slow-moving, it feeds on plankton, which it filters through its sievelike gills. Cruising near the surface, this amiable shark lives in warm oceans throughout the world and travels as far north as New York.

The skull of a bison is so thick that it could flatten a rifle bullet fired from 10 yards away (without any apparent damage to the animal), and so large that it serves as a snow plow during winter grazing.

A gentle giant if ever there was one, the whale shark (which can weigh up to 20 tons and has a five-foot-wide mouth studded with hundreds of raspy, tiny teeth) is so tame that it doesn't even mind when divers hitch a ride by grabbing its dorsal fin.

What are the largest and smallest meat eaters?

If you took a single claw of the Kodiak bear, it would provide more than enough space to cradle a pygmy shrew, North America's smallest mammal. An animal that weighs less than a book of matches and measures just over three inches long may not sound like much of a predator, but the pygmy shrew is a tireless hunter. Though it may not appear threatening, earthworms and grasshoppers would beg to differ. This short-legged, long-snouted meat eater moves so fast in its quest for food that its heart rate can reach 1,000 beats per minute. Hunting in all hours and all seasons, a pygmy shrew must find and devour the equivalent of its body weight every 24 hours just to stay alive.

The Kodiak bear, which can weigh up to 1,700 pounds, doesn't need to search out food so intensely. Nevertheless, it's an enthusiastic eater. Named for its habitat (an archipelago off the coast of Alaska), it dines mainly on mice, marmots, and ground squirrels but is not above such lighter delicacies as berries and succulent marsh plants. Its favorite fare, however, is the fat Pacific salmon, which swims upstream during midsummer to spawn.

Sometimes as many as 70 or 80 Kodiaks will congregate beside the rapids, awaiting the arrival of salmon. Most catch their prey by belly-flopping on a fish, pinning it down on the river bottom. Others simply sit down in the water, wait for the fish to swim by, and paw one with lightning speed. The bear often eats its meal on the spot, tossing away the head and gill cage, then turning its attention to the next victim. A safe distance away, youngsters watch to see how it's done.

Is the biggest spider also the most dangerous?

Huge, hairy spiders that attack people are mainly the stuff of horror movies. In reality a desert tarantula would much rather sink its fangs into insects and small reptiles. With thick legs that span four inches and a heavy body almost three inches long, this bristly, brown spider is North America's largest. Surprisingly, the female is even bigger than the more nimble male, with an abdomen the size of a walnut.

A tarantula kills its enemies with chilling efficiency. After it has subdued its prey by pouncing on it, the animal sinks its fangs into it, injecting a fast-acting venom. Pinning down its victim, the tarantula keeps its fangs inserted in order to digest the internal contents, sucking them through the fangs into its gut. Even ruthless killers, however, have rivals, and the one this creature fears is the tarantula hawk wasp, a two-inch-long predator that also paralyzes its victim with venom. After dragging the tarantula into a burrow, the wasp lays an egg on its body, seals the tomb, and flies away. The larva that hatches feeds on the living tarantula, growing as its host slowly dies.

Some 200,000 times larger than a pygmy shrew (inset), the Kodiak bear is the undisputed lord of its realm. When sniffing the winds for trouble, a full-grown bruin may rise 10 feet in the air.

Of all "creepy crawlies" the tarantula has the worst reputation—and the most undeserved. When under attack, it usually flings its fine hairs at the assailant. For humans, its bite is no worse than a bee sting.

Of all reptiles, which one is the leading heavyweight?

Black skin studded with bony plates covers the back of the world's largest turtle, the aptly named leatherback. This marine reptile, which weighs anywhere from 600 to 1,600 pounds, crawls ashore on beaches in Florida and elsewhere for one purpose only: to lay eggs. The rest of its life is spent at sea, where the seven-foot-long turtle rows with flippers that may span a width greater than its length. Seven ridges run down its back, serving as keels that streamline its shape; five more stripe the underside of its almond-shaped body.

Oddly, the mainstay of this giant's diet is one of the sea's most insubstantial creatures—the jellyfish. Notched jaws help the leatherback seize its slimy prey; spines in its mouth and throat ensure that it slips into the turtle's gut. Leatherbacks can venture deeper than any other sea turtle, plunging more than 3,000 feet below the surface to a realm frequented by sperm whales, elephant seals, and other deep-sea divers.

What is our tallest bird?

Striding on slim black legs, a whooping crane patrols a marsh near its nest. Suddenly alarmed, the regal white bird bugles a cry that can be heard two miles away—a sound emanating from a windpipe that's often a bit longer than the bird is tall. A 4¼ foot tall whooper may possess a windpipe nearly 5 feet long, almost half of it coiled within the bird's breast.

The whooping crane, North America's tallest bird, is perfectly constructed to wade into marshes and ponds. Long legs hoist its body above deep water, enabling the bird to keep its feathers dry. The crane's slim, supple neck twists like a snake as it grubs with a long, pointed beak for creatures buried in mud. Not surprisingly, the American flamingo and sandhill crane—birds that hold their heads nearly as high as the whooper—are also long-legged waders.

Which bird takes the prize for speed?

Dropping like a thunderbolt from an altitude of 3,000 feet, a peregrine falcon can plunge at a speed of up to 200 miles per hour. It is supremely adapted for such a feat, with slim,

sharply pointed wings swept back like a jet fighter's, smooth feathers slicked tightly over its body to further streamline its form, baffles in its nostrils that redirect the air rushing in, and eyes that can quickly adjust focus as the bird rockets toward its victim.

Where can you find the best natural insulator?

Along the seacoasts of northern Alaska and Canada, where stocky ducks known as eiders congregate to breed, piercing gusts of wind are a harsh fact of life. But eiders are well equipped to brave such adversity, for their feathers offer nature's finest insulating material. An eider mom lines her nest with it to incubate her eggs and shield them from the cold. Plucking the gray down tucked beneath her brown-and-black breast plumage, she pads her nest to swaddle her clutch. Air trapped inside the puffy quilt not only keeps out the chill but retains the warmth generated by the vigilant mother bird. After hatching, ducklings don't enjoy their cozy nest for long; their mother swiftly leads them toward the water.

➤ Having swum thousands of miles to a warm nesting ground, this female leatherback (which usually mates every other year) hauls herself ashore, where she will dig a hole with her hind flippers and lay 80 to 100 round white eggs.

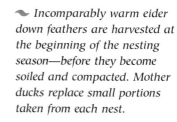

➤ Incomparably warm eider down feathers are harvested at the beginning of the nesting season—before they become soiled and compacted. Mother ducks replace small portions taken from each nest.

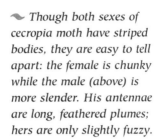

What is the widest wing span of any insect?

Cecropia moths fly on wings that span up to six inches as they sail above fields, through forests, and around suburban lampposts of North America east of the Rockies. These broad wings are dusty brown, edged with rust and white; dark spots mark the forewings and white crescents grace the hindwings. The female's wingspan is often slightly wider than the male's.

The cecropia shares much of its range with the polyphemus moth, which flaps russet wings that spread a scant quarter-inch shy of the cecropia's span. Other wide-winged fliers include the orange-and-gray regal moth and the sage-green luna moth. All start life as fat green caterpillars, the regal moth being the biggest at nearly six inches in length. Next to this red-horned monster, the cecropia moth's knobby, four-inch caterpillar seems almost cuddly.

~ Though both sexes of cecropia moth have striped bodies, they are easy to tell apart: the female is chunky while the male (above) is more slender. His antennae are long, feathered plumes; hers are only slightly fuzzy.

~ True to its name, the indigo snake is a sleek, black beauty. The eastern variety, found in Florida and Georgia, is a gleaming blue-black; that of Texas is a browner shade of black.

Of all mammals, which one has the tiniest newborns?

A litter of 20 Virginia opossum babies weighs barely half an ounce and can fit in the palm of your hand. After gestating for a mere 13 days, each jellybean-size embryo comes into the world as a blind, deaf infant equipped with strong forearms for grappling its way across its mother's furry belly and into her pouch. This two-inch journey is a survival of the fittest. A few may die en route, and the survivors play a life-and-death game of musical chairs as they clamber to secure one of the 13 teats inside the pouch. The winners are permitted to suckle and grow for the next several weeks as their mother ferries them about. This arrangement frees the female to forage far and wide instead of sticking close to a nest. Two litters may be born to a female opossum in just nine months. She can start reproducing when she's six months old, but she's unlikely to enjoy more than two summers because opossums rarely live more than two years. A high rate of reproduction, however, ensures a constant supply of these creatures, North America's only pouched mammals.

~ Two months from now these baby opossums will crawl out of their mother's pouch and ride on her back until they're on their own.

Why is our longest snake also one of our most ruthless?

A mere inch or two distinguishes the indigo snake of the Southeast as North America's longest. Some 8½ feet long, this reptile barely edges out such contenders as the black rat snake and the coachwhip. A connoisseur of small animals, the indigo doesn't hesitate to pursue its prey

underground. Finding a young tortoise tucked inside a burrow or mice huddled in a tunnel, this ingenious predator offers them no escape. It simply presses them against the sides of these constricted spaces and seizes them with its jaws.

How strong is the strongest natural fiber?

If a textile company wanted to manufacture a fabric made from the strongest natural fiber, it would undoubtedly award its contract to the golden silk spider, which spins its three-foot-wide webs in the southeastern United States. A web of spider silk—as sturdy as the toughest nylon, though much more elastic—is strong enough to trap small birds or knock a person's hat off. It can't be used commercially, however, because these spiders are so predatory toward each other that they can't be reared in captivity.

Pumas have been known to vault 20 feet into the air, a distance they cover easily when bounding across the land in pursuit of prey or to clear obstacles.

If an animal could earn a gold medal for high jumping, which one would win it?

Anyone who has ever seen a house cat spring to the top of a refrigerator will not be surprised that its distant cousin, the puma, is a champion leaper, able to jump from 12 to 15 feet straight up into a tree. The lowest estimate of the puma's ability puts it on a par with a kangaroo's best effort; although the Australian hopper is the uncontested leader in the broad jump, none has been known to top 12 feet straight up. Among wild cats pumas have the longest hind legs in relation to their forelegs. These muscular limbs provide them with the power they need to propel themselves upward. The puma can tackle larger prey better than any other big cat. A 150-pound male, for example, can conquer an elk that outweighs it six to eight times. Known by a variety of other names (among them cougar, panther, and mountain lion), the puma is believed to be the most widely distributed carnivore in the Western Hemisphere.

Living Quarters *Nests, burrows, hives, and other dwelling places*

~ *Champion diggers, badgers prey on burrowing rodents by excavating their burrows with incredible speed. When surprised out in the open by a predator such as a wolf or dog, a badger can dig a hole and disappear from sight in seconds.*

~ *Though capable of digging its own den, the burrowing owl (above) often prefers to occupy a burrow abandoned by prairie dogs. At the age of four to five weeks, red fox pups (right) begin to poke their heads out of the den their parents appropriated from a ground-hog. By six weeks, they will start venturing outside.*

Where do badgers live?

Named for the distinctive badge of white fur that runs back from the bridge of its nose, the badger lives in American grasslands from the Mexican border to Ohio and California and north to the Canadian prairies. Resembling a fur rug, this incredible burrower conceals beneath its loose-fitting skin powerful muscles, which drive front legs tipped with long, sharp claws.

Whether its purpose is to find food (mainly ground squirrels and other rodents), refuge from heat or cold, or protection from an enemy, a badger can tunnel through hard-packed soil with ease. For shelter, it burrows six to eight feet below the surface, sometimes boring a tunnel 20 to 30 feet long that slopes down to a main chamber and then leads up to two or more exits. During the summer a badger may use up to 50 widely scattered dens, but when winter snow restricts its wanderings, it will occupy just one or two dens and remain underground for weeks at a time, living off accumulated body fat.

Do all burrowers dig their own dens?

Badgers, ground squirrels, and other burrowing animals provide ready-made dwellings for all sorts of interlopers. Coyotes, for example, often take over abandoned burrows and, after a little remodeling, move right in.

Existing burrows also serve as secure nesting sites for puffins, storm petrels, and other seabirds that go underground during the breeding season. Burrows sometimes shelter so many animals that they take on the air of tenements. When gopher tortoises dig their roomy dens, frogs, snakes, and a host of other uninvited guests are likely to arrive.

More often, however, a burrow is inhabited by a series of occupants that move in one after the other. Prairie dogs, for instance, donate their dwellings to their offspring before relocating. A scientist observing a woodchuck burrow once recorded an astonishingly high turnover of tenants—first came a cottontail, followed by a skunk, a raccoon, and finally a red fox that made the hole its home.

Why do birds build so many different types of nests?

Just as each type of bird has its characteristic song, personality, and appearance, it also has its own unique nesting habits. Endowed with a remarkable instinct, each kind of bird builds exactly the right sort of nest for its particular family—without ever having to learn how. Scientists, in fact, can usually identify the builder of a nest by its location, materials, and design. The most common type is the cup-shaped nest, like the robin's, which allows birds to scan the horizon for danger. But a host of other varieties reflect nature's infinite flair for creativity.

The simplest nests may be nothing more than shallow depressions in the ground, such as those made by sandpipers, or piles of sticks in the treetops, like the ones built by many birds of prey. The northern oriole, in contrast, constructs one of the most elaborate—a beautiful, intricately woven basket of plant fibers hung from the tips of branches.

Nests vary not only in complexity but also in size and shape. A hummingbird's home, for example, is no bigger than half a walnut shell, while a bald eagle's may be a two-ton masterpiece that has grown larger with each consecutive breeding season. Some birds, such as wrens, build dome-shaped domiciles that shield them from the elements. Others, including murres, dovekies, and boobies, build no nests at all, laying their eggs on rocks or bare ground.

Other nests are individually tailored to specific building sites. The belted kingfisher digs a tunnel into an earthen bank and lays its eggs in a pitch-dark chamber at the end. Woodpeckers use their powerful beaks to chisel out cavities in trees. Some aquatic birds, including grebes, build nests that float on the water, usually anchoring them to tall weeds.

A few species—barn swallows, house sparrows, and chimney swifts, for example—place their nests on existing man-made structures, showing just how ingenious some birds can be. One of the cleverest—or laziest—of all is the cowbird, which manages to do without its own nest. By laying its egg in the nest of another bird, it enlists a couple of total strangers to serve as foster parents for its offspring.

➤ *Cliff swallows, famed for returning each spring to the California mission of San Juan Capistrano, are master masons. Males bring mud pellets to nesting sites; females construct gourd-shaped nests, cementing them to cliffs, bluffs, trees, and the walls of buildings.*

➤ *Whether it nests on the ground or atop a tree 100 feet tall, the great blue heron uses the same building materials—sticks that are arranged into a platform and then lined with twigs, mosses, grasses, and leaves. Older nests three or four feet across may be occupied year after year; sometimes dozens of nests will fill a single tree.*

How many beavers live in a lodge?

The beaver, it's been said, was the world's first engineer, and its dam-building feats are legendary. One structure in New Hampshire, the work of generations of beavers, was 4,000 feet long. But North America's biggest rodent also is a pretty fair architect. Consider the lodge that is a beaver clan's refuge when the world is locked in ice and snow. The weather-tight dome of mud and sticks might rise eight feet above the surrounding pond's water level and measure 40 feet in width, although most lodges are somewhat smaller. The hollowed-out living quarters are six to eight feet wide and at least two feet high, with a dry sleeping platform a few inches above the chamber's main floor, where plunge holes lead to a submerged food supply.

Back in 1807, John Colter, a famous trapper and frontier guide, escaped from pursuing Indians by diving into a beaver pond, squeezing through a water-filled tunnel, and hiding in the lodge. Presumably the inhabitants were busy elsewhere, but in winter his cramped asylum would have held anywhere from six to a dozen beavers—an adult pair, kits from the previous spring's litter, two or three yearlings, and perhaps older offspring who had been unable to start colonies of their own and returned home.

For weeks on end during the winter, beavers huddle together on mattresses of shredded bark, assiduously grooming one another's fur, their collective body heat warming their lodges.

Rodents, of course, have a reputation for being vicious when crowded. But a Canadian scientist who cut a window in the back of a lodge saw little aggression. A growl, shove, or stare quickly resolved any dispute over sleeping space or a choice aspen branch pulled from the larder.

➤ Two beavers, one playfully hitching a ride, swim into an underwater tunnel leading to their lodge's (inset) snug and dry living chamber. Beavers use tons of sticks, small logs, and earth to build their predator-proof dwellings. Mud plastered in the cracks will freeze solid in winter.

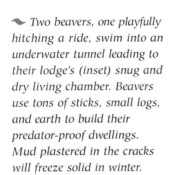

Quick-change artists extraordinaire, hermit crabs can switch the snail shells they wear over their unarmored abdomens for new ones in the blink of an eye. Once inside their recycled homes, hermit crabs are almost impossible to dislodge. Rasps on their tails anchor them firmly in place.

Why does the hermit crab keep changing homes?

Hiding its soft, unprotected abdomen inside an empty snail shell and guarding the entrance with powerful claws, a hermit crab has a nearly impregnable shelter, but one that it will eventually outgrow. Even so, hermit crabs seem to change shells much more often than their growing bodies would demand.

In fact, watching a hermit crab try on several new shells in the course of a single day, it's hard to avoid the conclusion that the crab is endlessly searching for the perfect fit. When the crab spots a likely contender (scientists believe they watch for large shapes that differ from the color of the background), it carefully turns the shell over, reaching inside with its long walking legs to explore for debris or other inhabitants. If the size is about right, the hermit crab makes a lightning-fast switch, sliding out of the original shell and backing with incredible speed and agility into the new home.

If it fits well after several exits and entries, the new shell may be adopted on the spot, and the old home unceremoniously abandoned. Often, however, the new shell turns out to be a bit too large or small, and the crab makes another quick change back to its former lodging. Where shells are abundant, the crabs can afford to be choosy, but in places with a skimpy supply, fights may break out between hermit crabs over prime specimens, and many of the crabs must either drag oversize shells or make do with cramped homes that leave them dangerously exposed.

━ *With wing feathers spread and tail fanned, an osprey alights on its bulky nest atop a dead tree. An osprey pair will return for decades to the same site, adding bits of debris until their agglomeration of sticks and driftwood weighs a half ton or more.*

chosen sites have to be able to support them. Because such sites are relatively hard to locate and the nests take more effort to construct, large birds such as ospreys and bald eagles tend to reuse their nests for years, refurbishing them annually with additional branches and grasses.

These nests may also be passed on from generation to generation. As a result, some become enormous. Over time the nest of a bald eagle, for example, may get to weigh two tons and measure as much as 20 feet deep and more than nine feet across.

How does the worm get into the apple?

"Worms wind their way into our sweetest flowers," wrote the poet William Cowper, who might have been thinking about apple blossoms and the fruit they bear. Insecticides have reduced their presence in supermarket fruit, but apple "worms"—actually the larvae of codling moths—have been finding their way into apples as long as apples have been with us.

The ancestors of most modern apple trees in North America probably came to Europe during the Middle Ages from central Asian orchards in Kazakhstan, along the old Silk Route. About 300 years ago, English settlers imported seedlings to this continent, and with them, no doubt, came the larvae of the codling moth.

A pinkish-white codling moth larva literally grows up inside the apple as it develops. In the spring the grayish moth will lay a tiny yellow egg within the apple blossom. As the flower's ovary develops into a young, or "codling," apple and then into a larger, mature fruit, the larva, already inside, grows with it. By summer the larva may tunnel its way out and transform into a pupa and then an adult moth, only to lay another egg, this time on the apple's surface. The newly hatched larva will tunnel its way in from there. Before the era of pesticides, apple eaters and pie cooks commonly found codling moth larvae in apples and simply pared out the bad sections. However, modern-day consumers, most of whom live far from farms and apple orchards, are intolerant of even small blemishes. Apples are now regularly sprayed with pesticides, and few worms survive the process.

Do birds return to the same nest each year?

Most birds are strongly attached to their nesting grounds. Large-bodied species such as golden eagles and red-shouldered hawks that tend to mate for life typically return to the same spot year after year and very often even use the same nest. Many small birds build new nests each year, if not in the same location, then within just a few hundred feet.

The reason for this difference is simple. For many songbirds, such as robins and red-winged blackbirds, there is no lack of suitable nesting sites. They can build a home just about anywhere. You'll find them in shrubs, in trees, on the ground, even in light fixtures. These nests are not designed to last, however, and usually break apart or fall down during the winter.

For large birds, however, the number of potential nesting sites is at a premium. Their nests have to be big and sturdy, which means that

What is so special about a honeybee comb?

Created with almost mechanical precision, the waxen, six-sided cells of a honeybee comb are among the most economical designs in the natural world. Round chambers, like those made by many other insects, would inevitably waste both space and wax.

Each flat-sided hexagonal cell shares its walls with six neighboring cells, with no unused space between. (Square or triangular cells would also eliminate gaps but would be weaker and require more wax.) With hexagons bees are able to create the greatest number of cells with the least wax to support the most weight. Combs consist of vertically hung, double-sided sheets of cells, each holding honey or bee larvae securely inside.

Worker bees, guided by instinct and using only their bodies as measuring sticks, build cells of amazing uniformity. The bees gather wax scales from their abdominal glands, chew them to softness, then build up the cell walls heavily, and finish by shaving them to their proper $1/3000$-of-an-inch thickness. Each bee constantly checks its work by pressing against the wax and judging the amount of give. It's a stunningly accurate system: the thickness of comb walls rarely varies by more than $8/100,000$ of an inch.

☙ *Clustering on a comb inside a hollow tree (inset), worker honeybees feed tiny white larvae hatched from single eggs laid by the queen in each cell. The combs in an average hive contain a total of about 100,000 cells made from two to three pounds of wax.*

Multilayered
shell

Comb

How do bald-faced hornets build their paper nests?

~ One of the most elaborate paper structures in nature, a hornet nest develops over a summer, beginning as a single comb with less than a dozen hexagonal egg cells. By summer's end it may become a four- to six-story apartment house with hundreds of cells (see diagram). These small chambers are arranged in combs suspended from a central stalk and enclosed by a multilayered paper shell a foot or so in diameter.

Shaped like an irregular globe, the gray mass of a hornet nest is the product of hundreds of insects, working ceaselessly with nothing more than old wood and saliva.

Hornets and their close relations, the paper wasps, get their raw material from weathered wood—the silvery trunks of dead trees, aging fence posts, patio decks, even unpainted bluebird boxes. The hornet uses its powerful jaws to scrape away a thin layer of wood fibers, mixing it with saliva to form a gooey pulp. Spread out in a thin band along the lower edge of the nest, it quickly dries to a tough paper.

Nests are not reused from one year to the next. The queen hornet, the only member of the colony to survive the winter, picks a new location in spring—usually the underside of a tree branch or the eaves of a house. Here she builds a small, round nest suspended by a tough stalk of paper. Inside she constructs a few egg cells, in which she raises the first of hundreds of offspring.

Paper wasp nests remain simple, but as summer passes, a hornet nest becomes more and more elaborate as workers build dozens of additional six-sided egg cells, similar in shape to those in a honeybee comb, and add new layers to the outer walls. By autumn the nest may be larger than a football, containing up to half a dozen saucer-size combs of egg cells connected by a central trunk and enclosed in several layers of paper. Air between the layers acts as insulation, and the single opening at the bottom discourages enemies from entering—although few if any predators are likely to risk the ferocious stings of hornet workers.

Why do sticklebacks and sunfish build nests?

Nature has a way of seeing to the young, but most often it's the female of any species that assumes the lion's share of child care duties. Not so with sticklebacks and sunfish. The males of these fish families—among the most abundant in North America—are some of the most devoted single parents found anywhere.

Cast your eyes among the shallows of any river or pond from New England to Florida during late spring, and you are likely to see dark, saucerlike shapes in the water. These depressions, scooped by the fanning tails of male sunfish, are bursting with eggs—perhaps as many as 30,000—and it's the male that watches over them, keeping the nest clean, protected, and bathed with fresh water. Even after the eggs have hatched, the male stays close by, herding the fry in a tightly knit school during the first, crucial weeks of life.

Like the male sunfish, the male stickleback is a fascinating example of parental role reversal, but his nests are even more elaborate and part of a complex courtship and mating practice that has intrigued scientists for decades. As high-strung as a hummingbird and as pugnacious as any prizefighter, this testy little fish—usually about three inches long—begins the spring spawning season by donning an ascot of bright orange pigment on his throat and belly and selecting a quiet spot in the shallows to build a nest. Using a gluelike secretion from a gland near his kidneys, he binds sticks, twigs, and other aquatic debris together. Some stickleback nests resemble barrels or tunnels; others are more like bird nests, anchored to reeds or some other stationary object. His marriage bed thus readied, the male sallies forth in search of mates, darting frenetically around a prospective partner to express his interest. If she fails to get the message, he may resort to brute force, biting her fins or poking her with his sharp dorsal spines to herd her into his nest. Their romance is brief; once she's laid her clutch, the male chases her out and repeats the process until his nest is full of eggs. So keen is the competition for breeding rights among male sticklebacks that they frequently attack each other's nests, and sometimes an immature male will drop his colors and infiltrate another male's nursery to fertilize the eggs—a practice aptly known as cuckolding.

➤ *After a spring color change from greenish gray to vibrant orange and blue, the male three-spined stickleback builds a nest, using secretions from a gland near his kidneys to glue together plant matter.*

➤ *Having completed his nest, the stickleback male leads a female to the entrance. Should she be reluctant to enter, he will nip her tail fins and threaten her with sharp dorsal spines held erect.*

➤ *Once the female deposits 15 to 25 eggs and departs, the male enters the nest to discharge his sperm. Then he'll emerge, search for another female, and repeat the process.*

Group Life Schools, colonies, packs, and herds

Are all fish in a school related?

Whether it's a dozen, a thousand, or even a million fish swimming side by side, fish in a school are no more related to one another than students at a local school. A few might be siblings, but most are not. Usually schooling fish are all the same species, but not always. About one-fourth of the world's fish school, but there is no common denominator. Some school only as juveniles, a few only during the mating season. Others school all their lives.

But why school at all? Since fish in a school usually all look alike, the reason seems largely a matter of defense. Predators are known to target stragglers or any individual that looks a bit different. But if each fish in a school looks and moves like all the others, none is singled out. By presenting a predator with a mass of nearly identical individuals, fish in a school find safety in numbers.

It's likely that schools of larger predatory species, as well as multi-species schools, hang together more for feeding than for defense. Schooling tuna, for example, hunt cooperatively in the open sea. So do mackerel. Some fish converge into schools only during courtship, facilitating the process of mating.

One of the most amazing characteristics of fish in a school is the nearly uniform distance each fish maintains from another. As a fish travels, it leaves vortices, or little whirlpools, behind on either side. Any fish that gets too close will find itself in an adverse current. But just outside this vortex is a favorable current that makes swimming easier. No wonder, then, that schooling fish position themselves one vortex-width apart.

However, these positions are not static. Whenever a school changes course, fish on the flank find themselves in front, and those previously in the vanguard become the flank.

The vortices may also help explain how schools manage to move together in such spectacular harmony. Fish have an array of sensors along the sides of their bodies that help them "read" the vortices of their neighbors. With this lateral sense—and normal vision, of course—fish are able to maintain speed and spacing as well as follow directional changes. It's a good thing, too, since schools perform their amazing synchronized ballets without a leader!

How can termites bring a house down?

One tiny bite at a time. That's why it may take two decades for a colony of termites to destroy a home. It requires millions of subterranean termites working as a team, of course, but teamwork comes naturally to these social insects, and their extremely fecund queens provide the required numbers. But only some of the queens' offspring are directly responsible for the estimated half-billion dollars' worth of property damage caused by termites in the United States each year. The culprits aren't the reproductive termites that leave the nest to form other colonies or the large-jawed soldiers. The destructive critters are the workers, which provide regurgitated food for the community and just happen to devour such things as dead trees, fence posts, and entire homes in the process.

The tiny, white, blind workers enter a home through cracks in the foundation as small as $1/32$ of an inch. They commute from their moist underground colonies to the nearest available source of wood via long, quarter-inch-wide mud tubes. The workers feed on the wood frame and walls of a house until even thick beams become little more than hollow shells.

While termites harvest the wood, chewing it up into pulp, it's the microscopic organisms in their guts that digest this cellulose stew. Without their diminutive bacterial companions, termites could not live up to their fearsome reputation as agents of silent and invisible destruction.

⬥ Schooling jack mackerel flash their silvery sides in waters off California. The size of fish in a school remains fairly constant. Smaller and larger fish break away to form their own schools.

Why do birds live in colonies?

The most famous bird colony in North America is a flat topped chunk of granite 40 miles off the northeast coast of Newfoundland. Funk Island is only 50 acres in size, but in the summer it is home to over a million common murres, black-and-white seabirds that stand upright like penguins and lay their single eggs on bare rock.

Few people aside from the occasional scientist land on Funk Island, because it is a seabird sanctuary. "It is a spectacle powerful enough to numb the senses and create lasting disbelief," wrote one visitor. He had been warned by an old fisherman that "a man could go mad on the Funks," and indeed he was disoriented by the incessant roar of the nesting murres and especially by the overwhelming smell of rotting eggs, dead chicks, uneaten fish, and tons of guano.

To varying degrees the phenomenon can be found in any large colony of seabirds or waterbirds, such as gannets, puffins, gulls, terns, cormorants, pelicans, herons, ibises, and wood storks. Noise and death are constants.

While such places are uninviting to most humans, colonial nesting offers a number of avian benefits. In the case of seabirds, there is safety not only in the remoteness of their breeding islands but also in numbers. The odds that a particular murre's egg will be taken by a gull or the chick will be lost to a predator like a peregrine falcon are smaller when there are thousands of other nests packed together. (Nests on the outer edge of the colony are the most vulnerable.)

Terns rout such egg-snatching intruders as crows and gulls by mobbing them. Squadrons of herring gulls patrol Atlantic puffin colonies intent on hijacking bill-loads of fish destined for puffin chicks. The puffins, however, have devised a strategy against piracy: After fishing, they circle until the sky is full of birds carrying fish. A synchronized landing swamps the gulls, substantially reducing any one puffin's risk of being robbed.

One of the more unusual reasons for colonial nesting was reported from Alaska's Wrangell Island, where small groups of snow geese lay their eggs close to the nests of snowy owls. The owls are a fierce enemy of Arctic foxes, which in turn are a major predator on waterfowl nests, especially during years of lemming shortages. By nesting alongside one hunter, then, snow geese protect themselves from another.

Densely packed at more than 200 birds to the acre, gannets incubate their eggs in a colony on Bonaventure Island off Quebec's Gaspé Peninsula. Gannets always return to the same ancestral nesting sites, never switching as cormorants and terns sometimes do. This site and several others in the Canadian maritime provinces have been occupied by gannets for 1,000 years or more.

Snapping and snarling, wolf pack members jostle for position at a carcass. The alpha male usually has the privilege of dining on the choicest portion of a kill. Other high-ranking individuals get less desirable places at the table. If there isn't room for all to feed at once, subordinates must wait until dominant animals have had their fill. An adult wolf can eat more than 10 pounds of meat at a sitting. A wolf's stomach capacity must be large because several days may pass before the pack makes another substantial kill.

Who's in charge of a wolf pack?

As in many traditional American families, Pop is the boss, and everyone knows it. Except when Mom is, and then everyone knows that, too. The typical wolf pack usually includes the parents, their immediate offspring, and sometimes aunts and uncles.

The leader of the pack—whom biologists call the alpha male—is the family patriarch, the undisputed leader, enforcer, and dispenser of favors. The alpha male and his consort, the alpha female, usually mate for life and are typically the only wolves in the pack that breed. Both alphas, male and female, lift a leg to urinate, but all the lesser animals, whatever their gender, squat. When the occasion calls for it, the alpha female will boss her mate around. If the alpha male isn't dominant enough, she might take an equal or even dominant role.

Wolf packs are cohesive cooperatives in which all the members know their roles within the pecking order. Even when howling, the wolves within a pack sing their own parts; polyphony, not unison howling, is the rule. Under the alphas are the "biders," young wolves biding their time until they split off and form their own packs or take over when an alpha dies or gets too old to defend his authority. The lowlier members are the pack's babysitters and playful court jesters. Young pups enjoy a special, pampered position in the pack, but once the winsomeness of babyhood wanes, they too must toe the line.

Wolf packs may contain as few as two wolves or as many as 30, depending on the food supply. The larger or more numerous the prey, the larger the pack. In the lower 48 states, wolf packs typically contain 5 to 10 wolves.

The alpha male is responsible for scent marking the edges of the pack's territory. On frequent boundary patrols, he stops every quarter mile or so to plant No Trespassing signs by urinating on stumps, logs, and rocks. Other pack members, following him single file, often wait in line to do the same. By maintaining scent stations, the alpha puts wolves from adjacent territories on notice that trespassers will be prosecuted.

A pack's territory is usually on the order of 50 to 150 square miles, depending upon food availability. In good deer country, however, a pack's territory may be only 30 square miles; in the Arctic, as large as 1,000. When food is scarce, territorial expansion often results in border conflicts, which may be fought to the death.

Wintering elk paw through light snow to graze on last season's grass in Yellowstone National Park. After the fall rutting season, several harem bands, each consisting of about two dozen females and calves led by a stag, joined together to form this herd of 120 or more. In spring the herd will split up as hinds move off to bear calves, and stags join bachelor bands.

Why do certain mammals live in herds while others are solitary?

If you are a large, grazing mammal such as a musk ox, it makes sense to associate with other members of your species. An animal in a group is less likely to get killed than a single animal when a wolf pack shows up, as it inevitably does in the harsh world of the Arctic tundra. There is safety in numbers, as the old adage has it.

By contrast, if you are a large meat-eating predator such as a polar bear, it makes sense to work alone. A solitary, stalking bear is less likely than a group of bears to scare away a wary ringed seal at a breathing hole in the pack ice.

Many large grazing mammals form herds. These vary in size from small bands of less than a dozen bighorn sheep nimbly jumping from

rock to rock on steep Rocky Mountain slopes to loosely organized groups of 25 or more elks grazing in foothill pastures to huge aggregations of over 100,000 caribous roaming over the Alaskan tundra. These immense herds are usually trailed by wolf packs. As long as the caribous stay together, they are safe from wolves, but if one drops back from the others—a mother with a newborn calf, for example, or an aging, slow-moving individual—the wolves close in.

Although most big-hoofed mammals such as deer live in herds, and many large predators such as mountain lions hunt alone, there are exceptions to the rule. One of our biggest grazers, the moose, is solitary, and our most notorious predator, the wolf, hunts in packs.

Why do ants enslave other ants?

It is ironic that of all the living things inhabiting this planet, one of the creatures least resembling humans in appearance and biology, the ant, most resembles humans in its social organization. Ants, it has been suggested, live in a perfect society—a perfect feudal society. They have a rigid social hierarchy, organizing themselves into castes of workers, drones, soldiers, and queens. They make war. They practice agriculture. They keep the ant equivalent of cattle (aphids, which they milk for their honeydew), and they practice slavery.

Several hundred ant species are known to make slaves of other ants, but the most common are a group known as amazons, which occur throughout the world. Amazon ants rely on scouts to locate the colonies of ants they intend to raid for slaves. Having located a nest of potential slaves, the soldier scout (all soldiers are females; thus the common name *amazon*) will return to her colony, laying down a scent trail as she goes. Thus informed of a possible source of slaves, an army assembles and sallies forth. Soldiers of some amazon species are led to the nest by the scout. Other species navigate along the scent trail laid down by the scout. Once at the enemy colony, the raiders gather and then charge in, dispersing the protectors. Some amazons have large cutting mandibles with which they kill any defenders that rise up to protect the nest. One species of slave raider practices the equivalent of gas warfare, spraying the nest and causing the inhabitants to disperse. This spray carries chemicals that signal alarm; roused by the spray, the defenders rush out of the nest to attack the enemy, when in fact the enemy is already within the fortress.

The raiders are actually after the nest's young, not the adult ants. After all the defenders are dispersed or killed, the warrior amazons carry the white, cocoon-covered pupae back to their own colony, where a new brood of servants will shortly hatch. These kidnapped ants are essentially unaware of their status. They go about their appointed duties as if they were back home with their own species.

Slave making among the amazons is so ingrained that they have lost the ability to do anything but fight and make raids. In fact they are so specialized they are incapable of even feeding themselves and are entirely dependent on their captives. The slaves construct the nests the amazons live in. They collect food, feed their masters, and care for amazon young. Meanwhile the masters, like knights of old, remain at home in the castle until called upon by a scout to undertake another raid.

Can animals recognize their kin?

One of the most chaotic places on earth is a great gabbling colony of seabirds such as common terns. The young always seem to be desperately hungry and the din is overwhelming. Somehow parents coming back with food after a fishing expedition must find their young in this cacophonous crowd. The way they do this is related to the racket. To us all baby terns look alike and sound the same. In fact, each chick

A female northern sea lion lifts up her pup by the scruff of its neck while a bull bellows behind her. A sea lion mother can easily pick her baby out of a pod of pups by its distinctive bark and scent.

has a distinct voice. A returning parent knows its kin by sound and proffers a fish only to its own.

Other animals besides seabirds can also pick out relatives in a crowd. Honeybees distinguish between the odors of sisters and half-sisters and are less likely to fight full sisters. Tadpoles cluster with siblings, perceiving them by smell. Spadefoot toad tadpoles gobble up smaller tadpoles but spit out brothers and sisters. Salamanders detect eggs of first cousins by taste and avoid eating them. Mice, squirrels, and many other mammals recognize their kin by scent.

Communal birds and mammals clearly benefit by knowing their own. Otherwise parents might care for others' young, leaving kin to die, and not pass on their genes. For animals like bees and frogs, recognizing one's relatives has advantages, too. By not fighting or devouring one another, they perpetuate the dynasty.

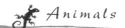

Denizens of the Dark *Cave creatures and night stalkers*

is to gather more light so that the animal can see clearly even at low levels of illumination. Light enters its eye through the cornea and passes through to the retina, where the image is registered by the animal's brain. But in order for the animal to see, a certain amount of light is needed to stimulate light-sensitive cells. The tapetum collects this light, then reflects it back to the retina. Without this ability many animals would not be able to go about their business in the dark.

You can make a pretty good guess at the identity of the animal behind the shining eyes without actually seeing it. A group of eyes is more than likely a herd of deer. A slow-moving pair is probably an opossum, while a quick-moving set often belongs to a raccoon. If you don't drive, you can witness the same effect by shining a flashlight at your cat's eyes in a dark room.

Can owls hunt in complete darkness?

Silent in flight and endowed with incredibly keen hearing and vision, owls are the stealth bombers of the animal world. So supremely adapted for nighttime hunting are these creatures, that they make other nocturnal prowlers seem comparatively inept. Unlike those of other birds, the flight feathers of owls are serrated, or fringed, along the forward edge. This softens the sound of their flight, enabling them to swoop in and snatch prey almost before being detected. The rest of the owl's plumage is unusually soft, also serving to cushion the subtle acoustics of flight. Because owls patrol the same territories night after night, they become intimately familiar with the landscape. In other words, a mouse doesn't have to make much sound or movement to attract an owl's attention.

Renowned for their solemn, spooky mien, owls have large eyes that face forward, an arrangement that's rare even among predatory birds. This gives them binocular vision and the resultant depth perception necessary to judge distances with almost pinpoint accuracy. These fast-focusing eyes are also equipped with a mirror-like membrane that lets them sample extremely dim light twice, and a dense concentration of light-sensitive cells in the retina. While owls may not be able to see everything in total

Piercing the darkness with an eerie yellowish white glow, the eyes of a gray wolf reflect light from afar. Such colors vary according to the visual pigment in the animal's photoreceptors. A rabbit's eyes, for example, shine red, an antelope's white, a cat's golden, a raccoon's yellow, and a bullfrog's green.

Why do some animals' eyes shine in the dark?

If you take a slow drive at night on a back-country road, you'll probably spot at least one pair of glimmering eyes that appear mysteriously in the dark woods, then suddenly vanish when the headlights point in another direction. Many nocturnal animals have a mirrorlike layer called the tapetum behind the sensitive cells of the retina. The purpose of this reflective surface

darkness, they can see what other nocturnal predators might miss.

An owl's ears (not to be confused with the tufts that are sometimes called ears) are mere holes in the head beneath the fluffy feathers—but what holes they are. Partly because most owls have asymmetrically shaped ear holes, one ear detects a sound ever so slightly before the other one does. This helps the owl to gauge not only its direction, but its distance as well.

Even among owls, the barn owl is a nocturnal wonder, capable of locating prey by sound alone and capturing it in total darkness, though it may be hiding under snow or vegetative cover. The heart-shaped facial ruff that gives this haunting creature such a baleful look also serves to augment its hearing. The concave, stiff-feathered ruff functions as a reflector, funneling sounds toward the ears. The result: a barn owl can locate the source of a sound to within 1.5 degrees of its actual location, both horizontally and vertically—more precisely than any other species of animal ever tested.

Do animals that live in perpetual darkness have the ability to see?

Shrouded by eternal darkness, the bowels of a cave are as still as death, the air stirring only, perhaps, when bat wings swirl into the night. Bats, of course, can come and go at will. But some inhabitants of caves are permanent residents, due largely to the fact that they're blind. Caves harbor salamanders, fish, crayfish, millipedes, flatworms, and myriad other creatures without eyes—or, at least, eyes that see. Although this deficiency would doom them on the surface, below ground it is immaterial, because even the keenest eyes cannot see in total darkness. Senses other than vision kick in, leveling the playing field between the sightless and their sighted com-

petitors. Northern cavefish, for example, feel their way around inky waters with supersensitive nipplelike bumps on their skin, allowing them to pinpoint the location of predators and prey.

Cavefish and most other blind cave dwellers lack not only functional eyes, but also the colors that help other animals hide and identify mates. Appropriately for creatures of such an eerie abode, they are as pale as ghosts. No matter, though. Where vision doesn't count, neither does color. Many unseeing, pallid denizens of darkness have relatives above ground that have normal sight and coloration, as did their ancestors before they left the sunlit surface for the subterranean realm. Over countless generations sight and color were gradually shed as excess baggage, worthless in a netherworld that is as dark as dark can be.

Why do bats come out at night?

Except for a few nectar-eating bats that live along the Mexican border, all of the 40 or so species found in the continental United States are insect eaters. Since many more insects are airborne at night than during the day, that's when bats go to work. With the skies practically all to themselves, these fabled creatures—our only true flying mammals—excel at their trade. Using built-in sonar, bats can locate, pursue, and capture their prey in half a second, making it possible for them to consume as many as 600 mosquito-size insects in the course of one evening. Like anyone who works the night shift, bats use the daylight hours to rest. Retreating to a cave, attic, hollow tree, or other dark, secluded spot, they roost upside-down—either alone or in groups, depending on the species—in preparation for another night of labor.

➤ *By bouncing high-pitched sound waves off a nearby object and allowing the echoes to be registered by their large ears, bats can determine not only the object's size and shape but its distance as well. So precise is this process, called echolocation, that some flying bats can detect and avoid something as fine as a single strand of hair.*

➤ *An endangered species, the Texas blind salamander is a typical cave dweller, with a ghostly pale body and eyes buried so deeply beneath its skin that they appear to be no more than tiny dark dots.*

On the Move *How animals get around*

◣ *The biggest of all fish, the whale shark grows up to 45 feet long. Despite its immense size, it is one of the least dangerous sharks. It feeds by swimming along placidly, mouth open, raking specks of animal plankton from the water with its gill plates.*

Do all sharks need to swim constantly?

A relationship is like a shark, Woody Allen quipped in the movie *Annie Hall.* "It has to constantly move forward or it dies." The notion that sharks must swim all the time may inspire good comedy, but it's not true of all species—one of many misconceptions about these widely misunderstood creatures. The 110 or so species in North America range in size from six-inch midgets to the 12-ton whale shark, the largest animal on earth after whales themselves. Some, like the tiger shark, fit the shape of our nightmares: sleek gray missiles with triangular dorsal fins that slice ominously above the water. Others shatter the stereotype: the angel shark, for example, which looks like a pancake with a tail.

Sharks also vary in their need for movement. A few species, such as the black-tipped shark, rest by floating suspended for hours. Others, like the nurse shark, are even less dynamic: lying torpidly on the sea floor, it moves only to snatch easy food, like a passing squid.

The species that roam the deep realms of the sea, however, are restless wanderers. To keep from sinking and to force oxygen-rich water into their gills, they must swim constantly. (Other fish don't face these problems because they have an air-filled "swim bladder" for buoyancy and are able to pump water to their gills even when still.) Though continuous motion requires enormous energy, these sharks are superbly adapted for the task. They "sleep" by periodically lowering their metabolism. Moreover, they are equipped with flattened heads, powerful tails, and dorsal fins tapered like the wings of an airplane to give them lift. Despite their reputation as man-eaters, only a handful of species ever attack humans, and then only rarely. Usually, the assault results in a single, seldom fatal bite, after which the shark seems as much in a hurry to flee as the terrified victim.

How do slugs and snails move around with only one foot?

Slugs and snails raise drooling to a high art. As they search for a feast of leaves, these backyard laggards slide along at a pace only slightly faster than continental drift, laying down a never-ending ribbon of slime that protects their squishy bodies from sharp rocks and twigs. With two antennae poking up like a victory sign, a snail uses this mucus to ooze over bumpy soil or hang on to the underside of a rocky ledge. Drooling from the front of a retractable foot that is the longest part of its body, the snail literally rows along the surface of its own slime using microscopic hairs. It combines these leisurely rhythms with equally slow contractions of the foot itself, whose thousands of sinuses and interconnected blood chambers allow it to contract in back and then stretch out in front, over and over again. Now and then, a rippling wave of motion runs up one side of the foot, then up the other, creating a curious shuffling or lurching motion that resembles a poor imitation of Frankenstein's monster.

How does such a slowpoke manage to evade its predators? About all a snail can outcrawl is a rock, so when it's harassed by birds and large horseflies, it simply curls up in its hard, gorgeous shell. Once a year, when it withdraws into itself to retreat from winter, it finds one more use for all that drool: a slimy coat that gradually hardens over the opening where its foot was, forming a second shell that keeps it safe and sound until spring.

Do any birds fly backward?

A bird should not be able to fly backward any more than an airplane should be able to fly without an engine or propellers. Birds take flight by forcing air downward and backward with their wings. Although some can soar or even hover for a few seconds, to fly backward or sideways, or to hover with ease, a bird would need to be a sort of miniature helicopter. Yet hummingbirds, America's smallest birds, can perform all these feats as well as flying upside down. In a blur of iridescent greens, purples, or reds, a hummingbird can speed by in forward flight, then brake in midair to probe its needle-like beak into a flower for a sip of nectar. Its wings beating so fast that they resemble gossamer, the bird will back out of the flower and sidle over to the next blossom.

The wings of these adroit little birds rotate rapidly at the shoulder, tilting to force air forward and down on the downstroke, but also backward and down on what should be the upstroke. By adjusting the tilt, they can hover or move in any direction. Aided by a powerful breast muscle that is proportionally four times larger than that of a chicken and a metabolism that is 10 times faster than that of a human sprinter, some hummers can beat their wings 1,000 times in the span required to read this sentence.

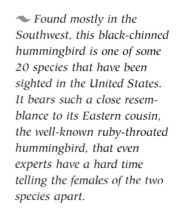

~ *Found mostly in the Southwest, this black-chinned hummingbird is one of some 20 species that have been sighted in the United States. It bears such a close resemblance to its Eastern cousin, the well-known ruby-throated hummingbird, that even experts have a hard time telling the females of the two species apart.*

~ *A snail's pace is decidedly slow—about one inch per minute—but what the creature lacks in speed it makes up in versatility. On rough surfaces the mucus secreted by this land snail reduces friction, while on smooth surfaces it increases traction.*

Why does a cat as small as the lynx have such large paws?

Stalking a red fox across snow-covered terrain, a lynx springs into action with astonishing speed. The fox makes a valiant attempt to outrun its pursuer, but it doesn't stand a chance. Though not nearly as fast or agile as the fox, the lynx has one crucial advantage: large, heavily furred feet

A lynx's broad, thickly furred feet enable it to bound across lightly crusted snow. Even in fresh, fluffy snow, the animal's paws will sink only an inch or two.

that function like snowshoes. As the fox tries to flee, it keeps sinking into the snow, while the lynx (though it may weigh twice as much) manages to tread softly on the surface.

The saucer-size feet that make this mobility possible are a perfect example of nature's flair for problem-solving. Wherever lynxes live, snow covers the ground for several months a year—difficult conditions to pursue prey. However, lynxes have developed paws that are broad and so completely covered with fur that it grows between their toes, making the paws, in effect, webbed. Thus, by distributing its weight over a larger area, this expert stalker can move around more easily in soft snow than small-footed animals can. In addition, these out-size paws serve as ideal "launching pads" for the lunging attacks that are a trademark of this stealthy creature.

There is one animal, however, that proves a worthy opponent for even the nimble-footed lynx. With a touch of irony only nature could provide, the lynx's primary quarry just happens to be an animal that also has heavily furred feet, the aptly named snowshoe hare. Since both predator and prey are equally endowed and can run at about the same speed, any match between the two would certainly qualify as an evenly handicapped race.

How can birds fly for long periods without flapping their wings?

Spiraling ever upward on still wings, a vulture soars effortlessly overhead, in seeming defiance of the law of gravity. Like an airplane's wings, a bird's are more curved on top than they are underneath. This forces air to go over their wings faster and farther—and to thin out, thereby reducing the air pressure that pushes down on the wings. The higher pressure underneath lifts the bird into the air. All of this works, however, only if the bird is flying fast enough to offset the effects of gravity. While soaring birds are aided by their large wings, they are hindered by the fact that such broad wings create a certain amount of drag. As a result, these birds must rely on updrafts to stay aloft. Hills and mountain ridges deflect winds upward, allowing birds to practice what is known as slope soaring. In a different process called thermal soaring, birds also take advantage of air currents that are created as heat rises from the earth and mixes with cooler air.

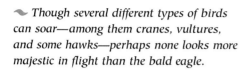

Gliders of the Night Forest

Chipmunk-size, with large, sensitive eyes for good night vision, flying squirrels are creatures of the forest canopy. As dusk falls, they emerge from their dens in old woodpecker holes ready to forage for nuts, seeds, and insects. Facing downward, they spring fearlessly into the air, spreading all four legs apart to stretch out loose flaps of skin on their flanks like parachutes. Sailing silently, they maneuver skillfully around branches, using their tails as rudders. A glide from one tree to another can cover a horizontal distance of 150 feet or more. Flying squirrels are extremely agile in trees but relatively clumsy on the ground. Highly sociable, they often feed in groups, and as many as 20 individuals may den together in winter. Although flying squirrels outnumber their kin in many Eastern and Western forests, these handsome creatures are seldom seen because of their nocturnal habits.

Though several different types of birds can soar—among them cranes, vultures, and some hawks—perhaps none looks more majestic in flight than the bald eagle.

Among land birds, the best soarers—turkey vultures, golden eagles, and California condors (which can cruise up to 60 miles without once flapping their wings)—enhance their ability to glide by spreading their primary feathers. This reduces the wingtip turbulence of their broad wings. The air slots between the primary feathers turn each one into a miniature, low-drag wing. Seabirds rely mostly on winds deflected upward by waves, just as they would be by earthen hills, only not as high or as fast. Seabirds must therefore soar closer to the surface, riding upward on the deflected winds until they stall out, then plummeting toward the water until they catch another updraft.

Which animal has a built-in sail?

Nature's windsurfer extraordinaire is a three-inch long organism called a by-the-wind-sailor, or velella. Though it looks like a jellyfish at a quick glance, the by-the-wind-sailor is actually a colony of tiny polyps suspended below a translucent, gas-filled float. Some of these polyps have a single purpose, such as feeding, self-defense, or reproduction. Cruising the warm oceans of the world in numbers beyond imagination, these creatures are usually encountered only when hundreds of them are blown ashore, as they are in springtime along the coasts of California and Oregon. Equipped with a triangular "sail" of gelatinous material set at a permanent angle—some are cocked to the right, others to the left—the by-the-wind-sailor moves around by taking advantage of prevailing winds and ocean currents. In other words, it has absolutely no control over where it's going.

A close relative of the by-the-wind-sailor, the Portuguese man-of-war, is also endowed with a natural sail: an inflatable ridge attached to a foot-long balloon-shaped float. As perilous as it is pretty, the man-of-war drifts on the surface of warm waters, giving no hint whatsoever of the danger that belies its beauty. The animal uses its 50-foot-long tentacles, which are covered with powerful stingers, to secure food and protect itself from enemies. Its sting—as potent as that of a bee or wasp—is dangerous to humans even when the creature is found dead along the shore, but the stingers of the by-the-wind sailor are harmful only to the tiny animals it feeds on.

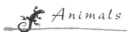

Is there a bird that can actually walk on water?

Not exactly. But there are several birds that give a pretty good impression of being able to do so. One is the Wilson's storm-petrel, a seabird found in abundance off the Atlantic Coast. To snatch tiny squid and other small animals from the water, it hovers like a kite with its wings held upward and its long, slender legs dangling. Watching this sooty brown bird patter along the wavetops with its webbed feet, one could easily believe it is walking on water—hence the name petrel, which is derived from St. Peter's miraculous feat. Wilson's storm-petrel is believed to be the most abundant bird on earth. It nests in loose colonies in burrows and rock crevices along the shores of Antarctica, where on a single group of islands, the South Shetlands, the species' breeding population is estimated at 1 million pairs.

A bird that creates a similar illusion in a different manner is the purple gallinule of Everglades National Park and other Southern wetlands. One of the world's most colorful water birds, it strides over lily pads and other floating aquatic plants on long, unwebbed toes. The purple gallinule is also famous for its intricate nest of cattail blades, with a sloping runway to the pond where it hunts insects, spiders, and small frogs.

Do any birds "fly" under water?

Ducks, terns, pelicans, and many other birds can dive and even swim under water to feed, but none can match the aquatic feats of the American dipper, or water ouzel, a chunky gray land bird that, ironically, spends much of its time in water. Its search for food leads the dipper to fast-flowing streams and rivers, where it periodically performs deep knee bends—hence the name dipper—before plunging under water. Once on the river bottom, the bird in effect flies.

➤ *Supporting its weight on exceptionally long toes, the purple gallinule is one of the few birds able to walk on lily pads, which it uses as a kind of floating stepping-stone.*

Angling its body against the current to help it stay submerged (which it can do for up to half a minute), the dipper propels itself forward by beating its short wings. All the while, the bird steadies itself by repeatedly grasping the muddy floor with its sharp claws. Using this unconventional but highly effective method of locomotion, the bird probes for snails, flatworms, insect larvae, and other favorite foods.

Even streams that are too deep and swift for humans to wade through don't daunt the dipper, which can dive as deep as 20 feet. Thanks to oil glands (which keep its thick, downy plumage dry) and an eyelidlike membrane (which protects its eyes), the dipper can venture where other birds can't. Though they are found throughout our Western mountains, dippers are seldom seen flying over land, and even then only for short distances. They usually build their domelike, mossy nests alongside rushing, tumbling waters and often nest behind waterfalls, flying through the cascading water to escape predators.

Why don't spiders get stuck in their own webs?

Orb-weaving spiders are well acquainted with their territory because they create it, and they do so using two types of silk. In building webs, spiders first spin out nonsticky silk threads in a radiating pattern, not unlike the spokes of a bicycle wheel. On these they superimpose a spiral of sticky threads designed to trap their prey. Spiders spend most of their time on the nonsticky hub of the web, using the spokes of the frame to maneuver around.

If a spider enters the adhesive spiral—which it does only in response to prey—it never gets trapped in its own snares. The protein and sugar compound that forms the "glue" is concentrated in microscopic parcels along the threads, so they're not uniformly sticky. The spider uses ultrasensitive hairs to freely tiptoe across even the stickiest portions of a thread. Caught unawares by the spider's ingeniously designed and virtually invisible deathtrap, the prey touches so many sticky nodules at once that it becomes fastened securely in place. On the way to its meal, the spider itself may occasionally get stuck on a few nodules, but the creature is strong enough to easily extricate itself.

Don't be fooled by the delicate beauty of this dew-bejeweled spider web. Its silk is so strong that ounce for ounce, it can bear as much lengthwise stress as steel.

How do millipedes coordinate all those limbs?

The vast majority of a millipede's dozens of legs are used purely for locomotion, but a few perform double duty by serving as sex organs.

Despite their names, millipedes have nowhere near a thousand legs; most of the 600 or so species found in North America have from 20 to 200 limbs. Yet moving even a couple of dozen limbs requires amazing coordination, so it's a good thing that millipedes—relatives of the first spiders on the planet—have had about 400 million years to learn their steps. When your enemies include scorpions and stinging ants, you can't afford to trip up, so a millipede must keep a tight rein on its own parade.

Millipedes that inhabit the red rock country of Arizona or Utah push above ground after a sweet-smelling rain to cool their heels—all two or three hundred of them. Then because their shell-like bodies shrivel up easily in the desert sun, they hustle back into the moist, dark earth before the oven of the desert turns to high. Like most of the world's 8,000-odd species of millipedes, their 100 or more segments, or rings, are each outfitted with two pairs of legs (as opposed to centipedes, which have one pair per ring). When it's time to march, nerve impulses race through neurons in each ring, firing one leg after another. From back to front the limbs snap into rippling motion like a line of chorus dancers. Without missing a step, millipedes can shift through three distinct gears almost instantaneously. In first, a power gear, a few legs swing forward while the rest push back. In second gear, the body gets up on its toes, some legs kicking forward, some back, and some simply dangling. Finally comes overdrive, an up-tempo pace of about one yard per minute—not bad for the miniature Rockettes of the invertebrate world.

Which sea dwellers use jet propulsion?

The jet aces of the sea are the missile- or torpedo-shaped squids, which propel themselves by taking in water and rapidly purging it through a built-in siphon. Other jet-setting sea creatures—cuttlefishes, octopuses, and nautiluses—are far less streamlined than squids and not nearly as fast. But then again, they don't need to be; they spend less time swimming and more time basking on the ocean floor. Octopuses usually crawl around on their tentacles, using jet propulsion only over short distances. Jellyfishes and related freshwater medusas move around considerably more sedately, pumping water by very slowly opening and closing their bell-shaped bodies.

But for sheer comic relief,

Unlike a squid, which can propel itself at 20 miles per hour, this giant Pacific octopus moves in short bursts to get out of harm's way. It also escapes its foes by ejecting a screen of black ink.

➤ *After leaving the Dry Tortugas (shown here), sooty terns spend virtually their entire lives in the air, almost never alighting on land or water. When not nesting, they may wander hundreds of miles from their breeding grounds, but they always find their way back with the aid of a remarkable homing instinct.*

perhaps no creature can compete with the scallop. As it jets across the sea floor by rapidly opening and closing its shells, the scallop is reminiscent of one of those chattering-teeth windup toys. A squadron of them blasting by is a sight no diver will soon forget. File clams also clap their shells to get around. But other clams and oysters lead more sedentary lives, using their built-in propellers only to blow sand out of the way as they dig with their feet.

What do seabirds drink when they travel over the ocean?

Water, water, everywhere, nor any drop to drink." The dilemma of Samuel Taylor Coleridge's ancient mariner is also shared by seabirds, because for them as well as for humans, too much salt can be just as bad as too little. Unlike mammals, whose bodies produce poisonous urea that must be diluted, birds have kidneys that produce nonpoisonous uric acid that doesn't need to be diluted. This saves them lots of water.

Seabirds take in salt water every time they preen their feathers, swallow food, or drink seawater to slake their thirst. But a highly developed gland located between their beak and eyes enables them to filter the excess salt from their bloodstream and then expel it through their nostrils in a concentrated solution. Thus birds are able to conserve what little freshwater they do get. This process explains how birds such as the sooty tern can survive. Young sooties raised on the

aptly named Dry Tortugas, located off the southwest coast of Florida, wander at sea for three years or longer before returning to the virtually waterless islands as adults. But thanks to their wonderful adaptation, they need not a drop of freshwater during their entire lives.

How do animals climb cliffs that are nearly vertical?

The rocky, precipitous realm above the timberline is the domain of two species of wild sheep and a goat that is really an antelope. In the Colorado Rockies, bighorn rams plunge down nearly vertical chutes, hurtling from niche to niche in what can best be described as a semi-controlled fall. In the Coast Mountains of British Columbia, mountain goat nannies deliver their kids on knife-edged pinnacles. Within hours the youngsters can negotiate steep trails. Both of these sure-footed creatures are capable of such fancy footwork because their hooves are equipped with rubbery pads that provide traction. Moreover, the sheep have independently movable toes that can dig into the smallest of crevices. But accidents do happen, and falls and avalanches are a major cause of mortality among these high-living beasts.

➤ *Mountain goats (below) are cautious climbers, slowly checking for the next foothold. But bighorn and Dall's sheep clatter over jagged cliffs with reckless abandon.*

How do feathers help birds fly?

One of nature's most amazing inventions, the feather is truly a masterpiece of design, combining exquisite form and multiple functions in one magnificent package. Comprised of keratin (the same material that makes up human nails and the scales of reptiles), feathers are not quite as light as a famous cliché would have us believe. In fact, a bird's feathers may weigh twice as much as its bony skeleton—and the larger the bird, the more each of its feathers weighs. The feathers of a bird's plumage are replaced about once a year in a process called molting and become more abundant as the winter approaches. A white-throated sparrow, for example, may have 1,500 feathers in summer, but as many as 2,500 in winter.

The feather, quite literally, makes the bird, distinguishing it from all other animals. On either side of its central shaft, or quill, spring 100 or so tiny filaments, or barbs. Each of these is similarly fringed with another 100 or so smaller filaments called barbules. On feathers used in flight, these barbules bear tiny hooks that join together neighboring filaments to produce a continuous vane. The quill of the flight feather does not run down the center, however, but off

to the side facing the incoming air. If flight feathers were not reinforced near their leading edge in this fashion, they would twist or buckle in the wind and the bird would lose control. The rest of the bird's outer contour feathers are arranged on its head and body in such a way that they minimize drag, streamlining the bird in flight.

For some birds, feathers are as useful underwater as they are in the air. Cormorants and anhingas, for example, are very capable underwater swimmers despite the fact that they have heavy bodies. When their contour feathers get soaked, trapping very little air, their buoyancy is reduced and they are able to pursue fish without the need for an aerial dive. Afterward, however, they must climb out of the water and stretch out their wings to dry them in the sun.

Such antics would not be possible without the underlayer of downy feathers that keeps birds warm. Since the barbules of such feathers have no hooks, their stems fluff out in different directions, trapping layers of air that maintain the bird's body temperature between 104°F and 109°F. As anyone who uses a down quilt can attest, these feathers are superb insulators against the cold.

Do flying fish really fly?

If you sail off the coast of Florida or southern California, you might see what resembles a blue and silver bird with scales sailing alongside you at eye level. Look closer and you'll notice that it's a flying fish—a misnomer, really, since this and similar fish don't actually fly but glide, thanks to long, fanned-out pectoral fins that act like the wings of a glider.

An open-ocean surface feeder, the fish makes an enticing meal for larger fish that whoosh up on it from below, so it's equipped for fast take-offs. Accelerating underwater, a flying fish angles up through the surface and snaps open its fins. Its tail, which has not yet left the water, now waggles back and forth at a rate of about 50 times per second, thrusting the fish into the air at a speed of 30 to 40 miles per hour. Without flapping its fins, this bird of a fish can soar for 3 to 15 seconds—enough time to elude larger fish, but also enough time for a lucky seal or dolphin to snatch one out of the air. A snappy breeze can keep the fish airborne for a minute or more, covering a distance of perhaps half a mile. Sometimes a flying fish hops across the ocean, dipping its blur of a tail into the water to pick up speed and lift or even to change direction.

Is it true that sea anemones stay put for life?

With their delicate, translucent tentacles waving in the ocean currents like the flowers for which they are named, sea anemones look very much like plants, but they are animals, closely related to corals. Unlike corals, however, which are permanently cemented into their stony colonies, anemones have the ability to move from place to place.

Not that they move quickly. After having drifted on currents for weeks after birth, the juveniles finally settle down by using a suction cup–like disk at their base to attach themselves to rocks and other solid objects. There they can move around at the less than heartstopping pace of one or two inches per hour.

Anemones may take a more acrobatic approach to move-ment, however. Though some species crawl, others swim with their tentacles, and a few even perform a sort of slow-motion somersault. But the most resourceful strategy of all may be hitch-hiking. Several types of anemones live on shells inhabited by hermit crabs, and are often placed there by the crabs themselves. One species of Hawaiian crab sticks a small anemone on each claw, brandishing the living weapons at would-be attackers.

How fast is a grizzly bear?

Faster than we are. In a sprint a grizzly can do 30 miles per hour. With luck, a human might briefly be able to do 28, which doesn't bode well should one of them start chasing one of us. While such attacks are rare, people have been killed (and eaten) by these ferocious and impetuous beasts, whose scientific name, *Ursus arctos horribilis*, strongly suggests that we keep our distance.

So how do these large, lumbering creatures manage to be so swift? To start with, bears are quadrupeds, which gives them an inherent advantage over bipeds like us. Since they can gallop, bears can achieve far more momentum than we can with our bipedal striding. As they drag themselves forward with their front paws, bears gather their body into a compressed ball. Then their back legs drive down, their back straightens out, and they push off with their legs. This sort of lunging and gliding resembles a spring uncoiling and allows them to move quickly.

◆ *Like many of its kin, the rose anemone has limited mobility, but it can move around enough to find a good feeding ground—usually a place where currents bring a fresh supply of tiny animals that can be captured by its stinging tentacles.*

◆ *Weighing more than 1,600 pounds, a grizzly bear—the world's largest flesh-eating land mammal—is astonishingly swift for its size. Its speed comes, in part, from its strength. Some 300 pounds of muscle are concentrated in the animal's shoulders, back, and buttocks, enabling it to deliver more force to its limbs than a human can.*

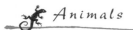

Sensational Senses
Seeing, touching, smelling, and hearing

~ *Since birds see color differently from humans, we don't know if the bright plumage of this male scarlet tanager appears as red to other birds as it does to us. But we do know that such gaudy garb plays a vital role in courtship, as when the tanager fluffs its fiery feathers to impress females. Color is equally important to the honeybee (right), which is attracted to blossoms that we perceive as yellow, blue, or purple.*

Do animals see in color?

Most animals—birds, mammals, reptiles, amphibians, fishes, and insects—have color vision. But with the exception of Old World primates (gorillas and chimpanzees, for example), an animal's perception of things is not the same as a human's, for the natural world is painted with a very different palette of colors. Our sight is based on three primary colors: red, blue, and green. Most other mammals use a two-color system based on red and green; in other words, they're blue blind. (Deep-sea fish, however, see countless shades of blue—the dominant color of their world.) The color vision of birds seems to be based on four or five primary colors, depending on the species.

Some animals can perceive colors we can't. Bees, butterflies, and other insects, for example, are not able to identify red, but they can see ultraviolet—a color that is beyond the blue end of the visible light spectrum. Though such a color is invisible to us, it apparently screams out to insects. Honeybees, for example, can navigate through a sea of flowers because the petals have spots visible only to ultraviolet-sensitive eyes. These markings, known as honey guides, usually radiate from the center of the flower and direct the bee—like lanes on an airport runway—in its final approach to the flower's nectar and pollen. Interestingly, creatures that see ultraviolet are often adorned with this distinctive color themselves. One example is the luna moth. Males and females look pale green to human eyes, but both genders of the insect perceive males as darker than females.

How well do seals and sea lions see under water?

The big brown eyes of seals and sea lions that give them their puppylike appeal play a critical role in helping these marine mammals hunt for food. Because a seal's eyes are larger in proportion to its body than human eyes are to ours, they are capable of capturing more light. While our eyes do not focus properly under water, those of seals are equipped with large, spherical lenses that can focus retinal images sharply. Seal retinas also differ from ours in that

Under water the California sea lion (an eared seal found all along the Pacific coast) has remarkably keen vision, but on land it does not see nearly as well. The animal's eyes, which lack tear ducts, would dry out in the air were it not for a fluid that keeps them moist and gives them their weepy look.

Six of the wolf spider's eight eyes serve as motion detectors, resolving data into one single overlapping image. The pair in the center of the front row play a unique role: they process sunlight, allowing the spider to navigate.

they are far more densely concentrated with rods—receptors used to detect dim light. Behind these rods are shiny cells that reflect light back to the rods. In the open ocean under the bright light of day, seals can spot prey at depths of more than half a mile. Even under cloudy skies in relatively clear coastal waters, they can find small prey, such as herring or sardines, at some 650 feet down. Perhaps most amazing of all, in clear water on a moonlit night, a seal can detect a moving object when as far as 1,500 feet below the surface—a depth at which a human being would not even be able to see his hand in front of his face during the day, much less at night.

Why do some spiders need more than one pair of eyes?

Having eyes in back of your head is useful not only on city streets but in the wild as well. Take the eight-eyed spider, for example, which can see straight ahead, to the right, to the left, above, and behind—all without moving an eyeball. A spider with panoramic vision can remain still while targeting its prey, and since even the slightest movement can cause quarry to flee, this ability offers a distinct advantage during hunting.

The precise arrangement of a spider's eyes is one of the features that distinguish one species from another. For example, the wolf spider, when viewed head-on, has a front row of four small eyes and a back row of four slightly larger ones. But some spiders are not so well-endowed. Most nocturnal and cave-dwelling species make do with only six eyes, having no need for the pair their eight-eyed cousins use to orient themselves in sunlight. Such spiders rely more on vibrations—as all spiders do to some extent—to determine the size, nature, and position of their prey. A few other spiders that make the dark their home have but four, or just two, motion-detecting eyes. But this fixation with numbers is quite beside the point for one species of wolf spider found in Hawaii. Because its members spend their entire lives in hardened lava tubes, they have no eyes at all.

Why are whiskers so important?

Ask any bald man and he will tell you that he bumps his head more often than he did when he had a full head of hair. The reason? Hair gives advance warning of an object that one's skull is about to encounter. Far more sensitive than normal hairs are the whiskers that grow on the snouts of many mammals. Whiskers play a major role, for example, in the cat-and-mouse game. Both of these creatures use them to feel their way around in the dark and to maneuver through tight spots.

Perhaps the ultimate whiskers are those sported by the magnif-icently mustachioed walrus, which can manipulate its remarkably strong and flexible snout hairs as if they were fingers. Walruses swim in plankton-clouded Arctic waters, feeding on clams, mussels, and other invertebrates inhabiting the muddy ocean floor. Questing for a meal, a walrus swims head-down, its snout skimming the bottom. As it probes the mud for edibles, the walrus uses its whiskers to sort out hard-shelled creatures from the soft-bodied ones it feeds on, such as starfish.

Only mammals have true whiskers, but a few species of birds have bristly feathers that approx-imate them. Like the mustache of the walrus, the pseudowhiskers on either side of the whip-poorwill's gaping mouth are also a device for gathering food; the bird uses them to net flying insects from the air. For animals that are equipped with whiskers, trying to survive with-out them would be a close shave indeed.

What's so special about the nose of a star-nosed mole?

In a word—tentacles. Pink and quivering, 22 of them blossom from the tip of the star-nosed mole's snout like the petals of a flower. The result is not only one of the most bizarre-look-ing noses in the animal kingdom, but one of the most useful. As a touch-sensitive tool, it gives its owner an unrivaled ability to locate insects, worms, and other prey. In addition to the tenta-cles that jut out from the animal's nose, whiskers sprout from the sides of its snout and its feet, allowing the mole to sense even the most minute movements of prey, either underground or under-water. When digging for edibles, the mole folds its tentacles over its nostrils to prevent dirt from entering the nasal passages.

Although the star-nosed mole has its family's characteristic appearance—sausage-shaped body, pinprick eyes, and ears hidden beneath thick water-repellent fur—its forefeet are smaller than those of most moles. This is a hint that it spends less time dig-ging than hunting on the surface. Unlike most of its relatives, which are soli-tary, star-nosed moles reside in loose colonies, and pairs stay together for much of the year.

By day the whippoorwill may sleep on a bough, but at night it hunts flying insects, snaring them in midair with the aid of its whiskers.

Despite the prominence of its proboscis, the star-nosed mole has only a mediocre sense of smell. For feeding and orientation, it relies heavily on its fleshy feelers, known as Eimer organs, which are extremely sensitive to touch.

Why do some insects wear perfume?

Just as humans wear fragrances to attract members of the opposite sex, many species of insects—including moths, butterflies, bees, wasps, and aphids—advertise their availability with natural perfumes known as pheromones. Nature's equivalent of a love potion, these powerful chemicals come in two varieties: attractants, usually emitted by the female to lure a mate, and aphrodisiacs, used by males at close range. Some attractants are so potent that even minute amounts can work their magic over great distances. Thanks to special sense organs on his antennae, the male cecropia moth, for example, can detect the attractant pheromone of the female from several miles away, even though the female emits less than one hundred-millionth of an ounce. When a suitor approaches for a rendezvous, he too may apply a dash of cologne to get things rolling. Using two brushlike appendages on his belly called hairpencils, the male pokes and prods his prospective partner, bathing her in his unique sexual scent—a form of insect foreplay.

Among nesting insects, pheromones may play an even larger role. The so-called "queen substance" secreted by a queen honeybee is tantamount to her highness's royal signature. When licked from her body and passed along to the rest of the hive, this powerful pheromone enables members of the hive to recognize their queen, tells them when to swarm and forage, and inhibits them from rearing any new queens to challenge her authority—a chemical reminder of who's in charge.

How do creatures "see" with their antennae?

For a host of insects and crustaceans, antennae are the principal organs with which they sense their world. While these lower creatures can't actually see with their antennae, they

Using scent receptors on its feathery feelers, a male luna moth can mate often during its two-week lifespan.

do have highly evolved senses of smell, taste, touch, and hearing. Unlike mammals, which develop a separate appendage for each newly acquired awareness, some of these creatures use their antennae to do it all.

Smell is a vital sense for most, and its detectors are located on the antennae. Bees use them to find the sweet smell of success: the nourishing nectar of flowers. Likewise, mosquitoes employ them to follow a trail of carbon dioxide to their next mammalian victim. Shrimp use their antennae to "taste" leftover particles of food that have been shed in the water by other diners. Male mosquitoes "hear" with tiny pits located on their antennae, which can detect whining females up to a quarter of a mile away.

For ants, which use their antennae to smell, touch, taste, and hear, these sense organs are veritable jacks-of-all-trades. When an ant is active, its antennae are almost constantly in motion. Ants secrete various chemicals that say, in effect, "Alert!" or "Food's over here, guys" or "Relax, I'm your neighbor," and they read such messages with their antennae. If these organs were removed, ants that would normally fight one another to the death would become downright docile, feeding together peacefully.

Another animal that puts its antennae to good use is the spiny lobster. Sitting in ambush with its long appendages extended into the water, it waves them to smell and taste for approaching victims, such as small snails and various scavengers. Snails divide the jobs of smell and taste between two pairs of antennae: one that's waved in the air to pick up a scent and another that's dipped into each new find to test its merits.

By congregating in groups of 10 or more, spiny lobsters are better able to protect themselves from predators. If one does approach, it will be swatted and raked by their saw-toothed antennae.

Which animals use sonar?

The trick of painting an unseen world with sound and reconstructing its shape from the returning echoes—a hunting and navigation technique that is known as echolocation or biosonar—is surprisingly widespread in nature. Bats and toothed whales have raised this skill to its highest level, but several other groups of mammals, as well as a handful of tropical birds, also make use of it. Because the study of biosonar is relatively new, however, the total number of animals that employ it is not yet known.

To echolocate successfully, an animal does not rely on reflections of random noise. Rather, it must generate its own continuous cascade of sound, precisely pitched and timed to create the best echo picture. A big brown bat hunting over a Midwestern meadow, for example, uses its larynx to produce a string of calls (inaudible to humans) that are broadcast into the night air. As the sound waves bounce off objects, the returning echoes are detected by the bat's remarkably sensitive ears, which can distinguish the softer echoes from the much louder blasts of outgoing

greater distances. But instead of using its vocal chords, a dolphin produces sounds with its head—literally. Its clicks and whistles originate in air sacs located in the soft tissues around the blowhole. These sounds pass through the melon (a large pocket of fat on the forehead), which focuses and amplifies them like a megaphone.

Although not as renowned for this skill as bats and dolphins are, shrews also use biosonar. Much of their time is spent investigating mouse tunnels and burrows, and short-tailed shrews, among others, use ultrasonic vocalizations to navigate through the darkness ahead. Seals may also employ echolocation, perhaps explaining why even blind ones can survive in the wild.

How do fish swim in tight schools without touching one another?

Herring, anchovies, mullets, and other schooling fish swim in a precisely choreographed unison that would be the envy of Esther Williams and her corps of synchronized swimmers. At first glance it seems an odd way to go. Bunched up like that, a school of fish would appear to make a bigger and better target. But for smaller fish in open waters, it's actually the best strategy. When a predator charges the school, it's confronted with a wall of shimmering eyes and silvery bodies that surrounds it, confusing its sense of direction. For a successful attack the predator needs to focus on a single fish, but this becomes virtually impossible when the school numbers in the thousands.

To achieve such perfect harmony, schooling fish use their vision as well as a unique instinct called "the sense of distant touch." Along both sides of the fish run horizontal lines of pores. Under them is a canal lined with ultrasensitive hairlike cells that enable the animal to "feel" the turbulence of its neighbors' tail beats and swim just beyond it.

One-quarter of all fish school as adults. Although haddock, Atlantic cod, and groupers gather together to spawn, they never achieve the impressive teamwork of herring or anchovies. But even they can make mistakes. Occasionally, one may turn right when the others head left. And if the school is under attack, those that are out of step may pay the ultimate price for their lack of discipline.

Bottlenose dolphins, shown here in the waters off Hawaii, are star performers in more ways than one. By echolocation alone, a blindfolded bottlenose can differentiate between two plates of the same size and shape—one made from copper, the other from aluminum.

sound. The real wizardry, however, takes place within the bat's brain, which instantaneously analyzes the time lapse between sounds and echoes, along with the echoes' strength, to create a mental map of the bat's surroundings. The accuracy of echolocation is astounding: many insect-eating bats can determine the size, shape, and texture of flying insects from echoes alone.

In a sense, toothed whales, such as dolphins, have an easier job, for water, which is denser than air, carries sound waves faster and farther, allowing aquatic practitioners to echolocate over

— *Birds are among the most reliable weather forecasters in the animal kingdom. When a storm is nearing, migrating ducks and geese (above) often take flight, while gulls and robins remain on the ground. Waterfowl also move out very rapidly with approaching cold fronts, which may freeze up their resting areas.*

Can animals predict weather?

Meteorologists often scoff at the notion that animals can do their job, but farmers are not so quick to discount the claim. Although hard scientific data is not easy to come by, eyewitness evidence abounds. As a storm approaches, ants have been reported to build tiny dikes at the entrance to their tunnels, and prairie dogs cover their doorways with clumps of grass. Horses, some say, bunch together, while cows and goats seek lower ground. Many a homeowner has noticed that just before a front moves in, there's a lot more activity than usual at the backyard bird feeder.

Such curious behavior has given rise to all kinds of weather wisdom. "If a rooster crows when he goes to bed," goes one adage, "he'll wake up with a wet head." "When spiders weave their webs by noon," insists another, "fine weather is coming soon." These proverbs may be rooted in science as much as folklore. Most animals are highly sensitive to atmospheric changes in temperature, air pressure, air density, and humidity. Moreover, their acute hearing enables them to hear distant thunder long before we can. Nevertheless, as one scientist warns, "One restless filly does not a forecast make."

Why do woodpeckers peck?

The woodpecker pecked out a little round hole," goes an old nursery rhyme, "and made him a house in a telephone pole." Home building, though, isn't the only reason woodpeckers are such diligent drillers. Often heard echoing through the forest, their resonant *rat-a-tat* may also be a kind of dinner bell, for many woodpeckers bore holes in the bark of a tree to feed on insects, which they extract with their long, sticky tongues. Woodpeckers also use their drumming the way other birds use song: to stake out territory, to attract a mate, and to "talk" to one another as they breed and raise their young.

In late winter male red-headed woodpeckers select their breeding sites and waste no time announcing their presence. There are 20 or so species in the United States, but this one is notable for its aggressive pursuit of nesting sites. Clinging to trees with their sharp claws and propping themselves in place with their stiff tails, they jackhammer away at a rate of some 20 beats per *second*, sending a signal to males and females alike. To potential rivals it says, "No trespassing!" Females, however, interpret it as a sort of serenade. They may even select a mate according to the tone of his taps; a distinctively hollow "dead wood" sound, for example, suggests that a male has found a prime nesting site, making him an all but irresistible prospect.

Once they become partners, the pair may go house hunting together. When the male finds a suitable tree trunk, he asks his mate's opinion by drumming on the spot. If she approves, she taps in response, and after a lively exchange, excavation begins. If she doesn't tap, it means the site is unacceptable—a silent but unequivocal message that the male must keep searching.

How do mammals say "keep out"?

Whether scraped into the ground, sprayed on rocks, or molded in mud, No Trespassing signs of various kinds are used by most mammals to define their territories. Endowed with an olfactory sense that is perhaps hundreds of times more discerning than our own, most wild land mammals use scent in some form as a marker and can speak volumes simply by leaving behind a dab of this or a squirt of that. Almost any body fluid will do, but the ones most commonly used are urine and glandular secretions. Bobcats, for example, spray urine on trees and rocks, then scrape nearby soil to mark the spot. This enables other bobcats to determine the age, sex, and breeding condition of the sprayer, and perhaps even its social standing.

Why use scent? Odor is a silent signpost, revealing a great deal of information without giving away the animal's location, as a call or song might do; this is especially important for mammals that are relentlessly preyed upon by others. What's more, scent lingers

in the air long after the animal has moved on, telegraphing its unmistakable message to any nose that can interpret it.

Meadow voles, for example, spray urine on their feet. Short-tailed weasels, which use the vole scent trails to hunt them, lay down odor flags of their own, dragging their hindquarters along the ground to smear musk from their anal glands. Weasels, like most mammals, pay strict attention to such markers, avoiding the territory of another individual of the same gender.

Just as the vole leaves smelly footprints, so does the white-tailed deer; the source is not urine, however, but scent glands between the toes. During mating season a buck will augment this aroma with scent glands on his forehead and around his eyes to mark overhanging vegetation. These "buck scrapes" attract does and also discourage would-be rivals.

The prodigious pounding responsible for these tree holes—made by pileated woodpeckers in search of carpenter ants—doesn't result in injury because the bird is equipped with a superior shock absorption system: a thick skull, strong neck muscles, and a sturdy, chisel like bill.

Scent-marking every 250 yards or so, wolves may return to a site every few weeks to renew their message. Five months later these scents may still be discernible.

All Kinds of Communication · How animals talk to each other

Why do birds sing?

Despite the musings of poets down through the centuries, birds do not sing to enliven the summer's day or because they are filled with joy, like William Blake's "Merry, merry sparrow." However lovely the sound, a bird's melody is very serious business indeed.

When a red-eyed vireo darts through the kelly green leaves of a May forest, dropping its wheedling notes into the shadows below, it has two purposes: to proclaim a territory and to attract a mate. During the spring and summer breeding season, when most avian singing occurs, birds devote an extraordinary amount of time to the activity; one red-eyed vireo sang 22,197 times in the course of a single day! Little wonder the species was once known as "the preacher bird."

Singing often acts as a vocal boundary marker, permitting a bird to scribe the edges of its territory, even through thick vegetation. Only when another bird ignores the auditory signposts does a fight erupt, so singing saves both time and energy. Song also lets a male alert females of his availability, as when a male black-throated blue warbler croons his signature "I-am-so-lay-*zee*."

Although singing is an overwhelmingly male activity, it is not an exclusively masculine one. Female cardinals often sing a whispered echo of their mate's tune, while pairs of gray-cheeked thrushes belt out duets, tossing their tumbling notes to and fro.

Avian vocalization also serves an additional purpose: identification. Song allows a bird to distinguish the species of the singer, preventing confusion during mating. It can even help identify individuals. Many birds improvise on their species' general theme, singing subtle variations that allow the sharp ears of their mates or offspring to recognize them from afar. The same is true for neighbors. An unfamiliar song will rivet a territorial male, who expects—often correctly—that a newcomer may be looking to acquire a home by force.

Birds generally sing from high, conspicuous perches—the better to be seen and heard. A male robin may repeatedly travel a circuit around and through his territory, singing from established vantage points—the top of a backyard maple or the peak of a garage roof. Where there are few perches—on the prairie, for instance, or in the desert—birds often sing on the wing. Male bobolinks pour out their bubbling songs while sailing over meadows on fast-buzzing wings, and in the southern Plains and Southwest, Cassin's sparrows launch themselves straight up from yuccas or cacti, then drift to earth on outstretched wings while trilling. The effect is exquisite, like musical jacks-in-the-box endlessly popping up through the desert morning.

Why do crickets make such a racket?

As late summer cools into autumn, the lengthening nights echo with the song of the insect world's greatest fiddler—the male cricket. Rubbing together his forewings, each ridged with a hundred or more tiny triangular teeth, this miniature musician produces a raspy tune, called stridulation, that can be heard as far away as a mile.

Monotonous as it may sound to us, this song is sweet music to the ears of the female cricket. Her "ears," actually air-filled bubbles halfway down her front legs, are sensitive to only one sound: the song pitch of her own species. This song is split up into short, repetitive bursts, called "syllables," which make up the cricket's familiar chirp. It is with such chirps resonating throughout her rigid body that the female moves unerringly toward a calling mate.

The male cricket, however, is not just a johnny-one-note. By varying the rhythm of his chirps, he changes their meaning. When a female approaches within a few inches, the cricket switches to a softer "courtship call" intended

🐦 *Two red-winged blackbirds face off with blazing epaulets backed by a harsh defensive whistle. Although aggressively territorial, these birds rarely resort to violence, relying instead on visual and verbal displays to do battle.*

🐦 *To distinguish the songs of field crickets from those of grasshoppers, simply try to hum along. Crickets call with a distinct musical tone, which can be hummed, while grasshopper song is a pitchless buzz.*

to woo only her. Some chirps signal aggression toward rival males, and others alarm, hushing all the crickets within earshot—useful if their chorus has attracted listeners with predatory, rather than romantic, intentions.

Do whales really "sing" to each other?

Many whale species make sounds, but the humpback, with its large flippers, wide pluming blows, and virtuoso vocal range, is clearly the Pavarotti of the underwater world.

Singing primarily in the warm waters of their winter breeding grounds, male humpbacks produce an eerie repertoire of groans, yelps, squeaks, and growls, intended, it seems, to attract a mate. But these haunting calls are not simply love songs: they also serve to ward off rival suitors, averting the bruising tussles that erupt when these 40-ton behemoths square off over a female.

Each song is a complex musical composition, consisting of as many as 10 stylistic "themes" sung in a specific sequence. Individual songs generally last fewer than 30 minutes, but a whale may repeat a tune for 22 hours or more at a stretch. All the humpbacks in a given population sing the exact same song, and as the breeding season progresses, they make changes to its structure. As phrases are shortened, dropped, or replaced, all the local whales adopt the variations immediately. The singing ends with the breeding season, but the humpbacks will recall the tune precisely the following winter despite the intervening months of silence.

To remember their epic songs, humpbacks may be using rhymes, just like the storytellers of old. Whales seem to repeat particular sounds at regular intervals in successive themes, particularly in their most complex songs. This has led some whale admirers to hypothesize that these songs represent the "oral history" of the humpback.

⬎ The powerful bond between a female humpback and her calf is eloquently expressed through nonverbal communication. A humpback mother is in almost constant physical contact with her offspring—nuzzling, coaxing, or caressing with her long pectoral fins—for the 11 months the calf nurses.

Why do mockingbirds mimic other birds?

Song mimicry has always posed a bit of a puzzle to ornithologists. Almost all male birds use song to attract females, but these musical suitors cannot succeed unless potential mates recognize their species-specific melodies. By appropriating the songs of dozens of other birds, a habitual mimic like the northern mockingbird would seem to defeat its own efforts.

As authentic as these avian impersonations may sound to human ears, however, female mockingbirds are not so easily fooled. The pitch and tempo often differ from those of the original, but even more telling is the seeming gusto with which a male mockingbird goes about his singing. Rapidly cycling through a succession of 30 or more songs, he makes it simple for a female to tell the difference.

In fact, as a male mockingbird develops a wide repertoire, he actually enhances his ability to woo a mate. Research has shown that female mockingbirds are more attracted to males with a wide selection of songs. Since it takes time for a male mockingbird to learn an array of calls, the females may simply be using their ears to find a more mature and experienced mate.

The vocal agility of mockingbirds is remarkable; one mocker whistled through the songs of

~ A school of blue-striped grunts—named for the sound made when they grind together the teeth located in their throats—can be heard as well as seen as they slip through the waters off the Florida Keys.

~ Listeners attuned to avian arias can identify mimics by song alone. A mockingbird (right) repeats each tune six times or more, a brown thrasher just twice, and a catbird only once.

55 species in just one hour, and individual repertoires of more than 150 songs have been documented. Mockingbirds also borrow freely from the nonavian world, including barking dogs, gray treefrogs, or even a squeaky wheelbarrow.

Do fish make sounds?

Jacques Cousteau may have called it "the silent world," but sonar operators say the sea sounds more like the dinful deep. Just ask any angler who's ever caught a pigfish, croaker, or drum, and you'll learn about the sounds fish make. But the roster of rowdies doesn't end with those so noisily named. Seahorses, ocean sunfish, clownfish, and countless others add to the clamor in ways variously described as beeps, groans, growls, honks, hoots, whistles, and even "the dragging of heavy chains."

Fish lack vocal cords, but collectively they employ a formidable arsenal of noisemaking mechanisms. A herring may bark, hiss, or squeak by expelling gas from its swim bladder. Squirrelfish and porkfish grate their teeth, and still others, like the triggerfish, rub fin spines, bones, or other skeletal parts against one another. Many of these sounds seem to relate to alarm and mating.

Most fish sounds are not very loud, but a few true noisemakers—like midshipmen and other toadfishes—use their resonant swim bladders as natural amplifiers. Likened to a foghorn or the drone of a B-17 bomber, the mating call of a single toadfish has been measured at more than 100 decibels—louder than the roar of traffic on an interstate highway.

Does a songbird always sing the same tune?

Some birdsongs are so distinctive and familiar that we can usually identify the singer, but that's not to say that birds have a limited vocal range. The fact is that many birds are versatile crooners, with dozens, even hundreds, of songs in their repertoire—some of them subtle variations of an old standard, others completely different melodies.

Ironically, birds are not born knowing which song to sing, but must hear males of their species in order to learn the right notes. As a bird ages, it is believed to pick up new melodic elements from its neighbors. A bird may also have dozens of other vocalizations—flight chirps for staying in contact with the migrating flock, alarm squeals when a predator is sighted, and various calls signaling aggression, courtship, recognition between parent and offspring, and so on. Most birds have between 6 and 12 simple calls as well as several complex song types. With the exception of mimics, songbirds have basic melodies that are nearly universal among their species—such as the creaky "ok-a-leee" of a red-winged blackbird or the high notes and trill of a song sparrow.

One of the greatest champions of versatility is the male brown thrasher, a virtuoso mimic who can belt out more than 3,000 different numbers. Not all songbirds are quite as accomplished, however. A single male Carolina wren may sing more than 40 versions, while sedge and marsh wrens may sing more than 100. Then there is the white-throated sparrow which sings but one song, the plaintive "oh sweet Canada-Canada-Canada" that is the signature call of the Northern forests.

Melodic variations creep across territorial borders as males appropriate song elements from their neighbors, sometimes even changing their tunes entirely to match those of males in adjoining territories. Some songbirds even tailor their performance to their audience. The male chestnut-sided warbler, for instance, sings two variations of its "please please pleased to meetcha" call—an accented form that females find most appealing and an unaccented form used to ward off rival suitors.

Because songs are learned, dialects are fairly common among songbirds, especially those whose populations are widely scattered. They may persist through many bird generations, as a decades-old white-crowned sparrow dialect has done in California. In New England, common yellow-throats now sing four- or five-note songs—a tide of musical innovation that swallowed the three-note versions they favored prior to the 1920s.

Why are red squirrels so noisy?

Most small woodland animals avoid drawing attention to themselves, but not the red squirrel. Active just after sunrise and just before sunset, these vocal rodents often scold trespassers with harsh, strident calls. Their incessant bickering arises not from alarm but from strong territorial instincts. Red squirrels are unusually aggressive in defending their home range—often one to eight acres of mixed hardwood and conifer forest dotted with middens, the large caches of pine cones these tenacious rodents gather for the winter.

An intruder is first warned off with a buzzing, agitated call, punctuated by jerks of the flattened tail and foot stomps. If that message is ignored, the defender will launch a blistering frontal assault, sometimes routing squirrels several times its size. But this is not merely bad temper; the red squirrel must defend its carefully gathered caches of seeds and nuts from plundering, or it may face starvation over the harsh winter.

Just as a bird's song can peacefully establish its territory, a red squirrel's noisy calls deter physical encounters by clearly defining boundaries for its neighbors. When one red squirrel begins to chatter, all the others within earshot may join in—a noisy but effective form of backwoods diplomacy.

❧ *From dawn to dusk, the staccato chatter of the red squirrel—as subtle as a jackhammer—echoes through the forests of Canada as well as those of the Appalachian and Rocky mountains.*

❧ *Often described as dreamy or insectlike, the favored call of the Savannah sparrow (left) is a lisping "tip, tip, tip seeee saaaay."*

~ *Always on the lookout for danger, a hoary marmot stands on its hind legs atop a rocky ledge, scanning its mountain domain. If an eagle or a hawk is circling overhead, the marmot will watch with more than passing interest. Should the bird fold its wings in preparation for a dive, the marmot will whistle to warn other marmots in the vicinity and scurry into its burrow.*

How do animals alert others of danger?

On any given summer day, the vast stillness of the high Rockies may be pierced suddenly with a shrill whistle, the alarm call of the hoary marmot. Similarly, the deep silence of an Eastern forest may be shattered by warning calls: the scream of a blue jay, the triple caw of a crow, the short descending whistles sounded by chipmunks just before they dive for cover, or the scolding chatter of a red squirrel. In the often hazardous wild, the animals that sound off the best alarms and respond to them the fastest are usually the most likely to survive.

This is especially true for social animals like the marmot, a look-alike relative of the woodchuck, which inhabits the mountain meadows of the West and lives in burrows. Marmots feed in grassy meadows and often post a sentinel while they are out in the open. If a predator appears, the sentinel will sound its warning whistle, which can be heard as much as a mile away. All the marmots in the area then dive for the cover of their burrows, and the predator is foiled.

Geese use the same strategy. If a dog or a person appears on the shore of a pond or at the edge of a field where geese are feeding, one or two will give a specific alarm call, and then the entire flock will begin to call. In fact, geese are so alert to danger, that the Romans used them as sentries.

Most animal alarms are vocal, part of a large vocabulary of sounds and calls that critters use to communicate with one another. Loons, for example, have a wide range of calls, but one of them, a brief tremolo-like cry, is a specific signal of warning and defense. Seals also use a special call to communicate danger. White-tailed deer, surprised in the forest by an intruder, will sometimes give a short, barklike warning scream.

In many cases these vocal warning signals are accompanied by telltale actions. Loons will ride up on their tails and flap their wings when they give their warning call. Deer will stamp their hooves—sometimes without even barking—and red squirrels and gray squirrels shake their tails while they sound their warning chatters.

Other animals rely entirely on body language or nonvocal techniques to serve as warnings. Beavers, for example, slap their tails on the water when they sense danger. Of course, some animals do just the opposite: they warn you of their presence, the rattlesnake being a prime example.

When does a worker bee dance?

A worker bee performs a remarkable soft-shoe routine whenever she returns to her hive after finding new nectar or pollen. The successful scout first shares news of her discovery by disgorging a drop of nectar or bit of pollen, a sort of free sample, so to speak, to drum up interest. When curious workers circle her, she begins to dance on the honeycomb's vertical surface.

Her dance pattern resembles a squashed figure eight with the center line acting as a pointer to tell other bees how far from the left or right of the sun's bearing they must fly to reach the food. For purposes of her dance, she locates the sun as if it were directly above the comb, regardless of where it hangs in the sky.

As the bee walks the center line, she waggles her body to indicate distance from the hive: the greater it is, the faster the waggling. If the food source is out near the fringes of the area the hive patrols, the scout may gyrate her abdomen faster than a hula dancer wiggles her hips. (For distances less than 100 yards, the bee walks without waggling.) The speed at which she circles also indicates how far away her discovery is; the slower she circles, the longer the distance.

If the colony is reluctant to follow the scout's advice, the usually brief dance may instead last hours, during which time the sun's bearing changes. As she dances, the bee adjusts her "map" to account for the passage of time.

The honeybee's dance routines are accurate and reliable, and humans can even learn to read them. But what makes these dances remarkable among animal "languages" is the bees' ability to transfer physical information to symbolic form.

How do ants talk to each other?

The ways of the ant are said to be wise, but given their small brains and short life spans, the word *resourceful* better describes these amazing insects. This is especially true when it comes to how they communicate the 20 or so signals that form their basic "vocabulary."

You name it and ants use it in "talking" with their nest mates. There's sound, of course. If a colony is threatened, an ant may rap its body against the nest wall or chirp by rubbing body parts together to signal alarm. Ants also use motion, touch, and taste to convey intentions. After a scout finds a food source, she returns to her nest and attempts to recruit workers by wiggling from side to side, tapping a nest mate with her antennae or forelegs, or letting other workers taste disgorged food. But the ants' most effective means of communication involves smell.

Chemicals called pheromones trigger an ant's olfactory apparatus much as perfumes do ours, and help workers recognize fellow workers, mark trails to food sources, and alert the colony to danger. Though humans cannot detect pheromones without instruments, ants are so acutely sensitive to them that minute amounts convey a world of information. A scent trail may indicate not only the presence of a food source, but its location, quantity, and quality as well. So potent are these communicative chemicals that just a milligram of pheromone—about the amount found in one ant colony—would be enough to make a scent trail nearly 80,000 miles long.

A honeybee's dance (diagram) serves as a treasure map for her fellow workers. The straight center line of this bee's figure-eight pattern points directly up the honeycomb, which means that the food she has found lies on the same bearing from the hive as the sun. If the straight line were tilted so many degrees to the right or left, the food would be located on a bearing the same number of degrees to the right or left of the sun's position.

Tapping and stroking one another when they meet, worker ants use receptors in their antennae to smell pheromones, chemicals that are secreted by their bodies and help them tell friend from foe.

Why are tails so telling?

An animal's tail may be located at the opposite end of its body from its mouth, but it's no less valuable a tool for communication. In many cases an individual will use its tail to signal others of danger. Slapped hard against the water with a pistollike crack, for example, a

Like a furry flag, the tail of a white-tailed deer flies at full mast, signaling that the animal is disturbed by a sight, smell, or sound. As deer race through woodlands, the sight of these bouncing strips of white fur makes it easier for the group to stay together.

beaver's flat tail alerts every animal within earshot of an imminent threat. The tail of a white-tailed deer, which is dark on top and white underneath, serves a similar purpose. Fleeing from an enemy, the animal flips up its tail to warn other members of the herd that danger is nearby. The beauty of this two-colored tail is that it functions as an on-again, off-again alarm system. As soon as the tail is lowered, the white vanishes, allowing the deer to once again blend in with its surroundings.

Among wild canines, the position, fullness, and movement of the tail announces its owner's social standing. In a wolf pack the dominant, or alpha, male will carry his bushy tail at a stiff upward angle, flaunting it as a badge of authority. If he challenges a subordinate, his tail may arch even higher. The lower-ranking wolf, on the other hand, will show submission by flattening its own tail and tucking it between its hind legs.

A gray squirrel's tail—a vital counterbalance as it careens through the treetops—also does double duty as a semaphore flag, lashing in sync with its owner's chittering. With equal eloquence the tail expresses gentle greetings between mother and offspring or florid courtship advances by amorous males.

Undoubtedly, the most unmistakable message conveyed by an animal tail is that of a skunk. All four species, including the widespread striped skunk, raise their black-and-white plumes in warning—a threat backed up by a pungent chemical defense that any intruder ignores at great peril.

How do dolphins communicate?

With a hiss, a whistle, and an occasional Bronx cheer—or so the underwater language of dolphins may sound to us. The highly gregarious dolphin is the chatterbox of the underwater world. Bottlenose dolphins, for example, are among the most vocal of mammals, using a medley of expressive, variably pitched squeals and whistles to communicate with one another. One might denote sexual arousal, while another signals distress, and still another anger. There may even be whistle dialects. For instance, an alarm call that scatters one pod of dolphins will have no effect on another. But most tantalizing of all are the "signature" whistles that may be the equivalent of names. When dolphins swim together, more than half the sounds they produce seem to be for the purpose of identification.

Whether dolphins can convey more complex messages than these is not known. Certainly the clicking sounds that make up a large part of their vocal repertoire are more related to their highly efficient sonar system than to communication. Using its characteristic clicking sounds, a bottlenose dolphin can identify an object as small as three inches in diameter from as far away as 400 yards.

Do prairie dogs kiss?

They do, but sometimes a kiss is not a kiss. Some 400 million prairie dogs once inhabited the Great Plains of North America, but during the past century these rabbit-size rodents were broadly exterminated because they were thought—incorrectly—to compete with cattle for grass. They now survive only in small, isolated colonies, or towns, found in parks and wildlife refuges. A town is inhabited by as many as 1,000 prairie dogs and is divided into tightly knit communities called coteries, each of which has about 30 members and up to 100 interconnected burrows. At each burrow a sentry is posted. Standing upright or sitting on its haunches, the lookout uses the mound beside its burrow entrance like a front porch to get a good view of what's going on. At the sight or sound of anything unusual, the sentry becomes the town crier, barking out an alarm that specifies not only the type of intruder—be it a badger, hawk, or coyote—but also its size.

During the breeding season each coterie keeps very much to itself, defending its boundaries even against other prairie dogs. At other times, when life is more relaxed, these highly sociable creatures may stroll about town, wandering into one

another's territory. When two of them meet, they stand upright, forepaws touching, and put their mouths together as if exchanging a rather reserved kiss. They may then inspect one another's anal glands to see if they are part of the same social group. If they are, they'll groom each other, kiss again—this time open-mouthed—or move off to graze together. If they turn out to be strangers, however, they'll either separate quietly or whirl apart to begin a fight, each one trying to bury the other under a mound of kicked-up dirt.

➤ *To human ears, the rapid-fire clicks of a dolphin may sound like a rusty hinge or a ducklike quack. So vocally versatile are these chatty creatures, that they've convinced some humans—from Aristotle on down—that they should even be able to communicate with us.*

➤ *It is not unusual for a prairie dog pup to kiss its mother. Between unrelated individuals, gestures such as smooching, hugging, and nuzzling are used to reinforce social bonds and are signs of recognition rather than affection.*

Feeding in the Wild
How birds, bears, butterflies, and others eat

~ A male eastern bluebird hesitates before deciding which squawking youngster to feed the grubs he has caught. Once the young have left the nest, the male bluebird teaches them to forage on their own. Bluebirds eat crickets, grasshoppers, beetles, and other insects, as well as wild fruits and berries.

Is it correct to say that birds "eat like birds"?

No, birds have ravenous appetites—not because they're gluttons, but because it's the only way to stay alive.

A chickadee, for example, must maintain a body temperature of about 104° F. To keep such a miniature blast-furnace fueled, the chickadee must forage constantly, eating 30 percent of its weight in seeds, berries, and insects a day.

Winter is particularly hard on small birds. The laws of physics are against them; tiny animals have less heat-retaining body mass compared to heat-dissipating surface area than larger animals, so they need more energy to maintain their internal temperature. A biologist studying white-winged crossbills in Canada estimated that each of these birds must eat a spruce seed every seven seconds from dawn to dusk in order to stay alive.

Hummingbirds must feed even more voraciously. They feed on sugar-rich nectar (plus insects) every few minutes all day long. To keep up with a hummer, a human would have to drink twice his or her weight every day—hardly the image of someone "eating like a bird."

If a sponge has no mouth, how can it eat?

Though mistaken for plants, sponges are actually primitive animals. Unselective particle feeders, they function like pool filters, drawing in water through tiny openings dotting their surfaces. This water passes into chambers lined with cells equipped with whiplike flagella, which create minute currents. These cells sweep up microscopic plants and animals, either digesting them or passing them on to other cells, and gently move the water out through larger pores.

Most sponges stay put, but some hitch rides. A sponge found off Florida, for instance, attaches

itself to the shells of snails and hermit crabs. By being taken for a ride, the sponge increases its opportunities for obtaining food and oxygen. The crabs and snails benefit too because their hitchhiking companions help camouflage them from predators.

~ Found in coastal waters around Florida, vase sponges grow up to two feet wide and three feet tall. Filter feeders, sponges must pump a ton of water through their networks of pores and chambers to gain an ounce of weight.

Do animals ever use tools to get food?

The appealing, button-nosed face of the sea otter belies the strength of its jaws and sharp teeth, which easily crack apart crabs, snap urchins in two, and crunch through most shells. This clever mammal has even been observed using its teeth to slit open soda-pop cans found underwater, then eating the tiny octopuses hiding inside. But when its built-in tools are foiled by its prey, this sleek, velvety mammal employs stones as hammers and anvils to get its meals.

A baseball-size stone fits the bill when a sea otter attempts to wrest an abalone from an underwater rock. The otter can pry loose most shellfish with its teeth and claws, but an abalone's mighty grip is not so easily broken; its muscular foot is designed to clench rocks so firmly that waves and currents can't dislodge it. However, the implacable force of the ocean is one thing; the persistence of a hungry sea otter is another. Grasping its heavy stone, the otter hammers away at the abalone until the stubborn shellfish relaxes its hold. The otter's labor is rewarded with a meal that provides up to two pounds of meat.

When thick-shelled mussels and clams are on the menu, the otter, afloat on its back, smashes its catch against a stone anvil lying on its belly. This task, too, requires great effort. Biologists observing one otter's mealtime workout found that the animal pounded 2,237 times to crack apart 54 mussels! When a sea otter finds a good stone, it tends to reuse it, even tucking the favorite tool into a pouchy armpit for safekeeping as it dives for another course.

Using its tummy as a table, a sea otter slams a clam in its paw against a rock to break open the shell. Each day a sea otter must consume about a quarter of its body weight in crabs, clams, snails, mussels, abalones, and sea urchins.

Is there anything that a grizzly won't eat?

As the naturalist John Muir once observed, to a grizzly bear "almost everything is food except granite." Animals of every size, from ants to moose and whales (if you count beached leviathans), make up half or more of its diet, but when high-protein animal food is in short supply, a grizzly will eat anything edible in its neighborhood. The list of plants whose seeds, fruits, foliage, flower heads, stems, roots, or tubers are eaten by North American grizzlies certainly exceeds 200 species.

Nor is griz persnickety. The smell of a ripe carcass or a garbage dump is an irresistible magnet. Twenty-three grizzlies were once counted feeding on bison remains in Yellowstone National Park. At such crowded feasts, a reasonable decorum is maintained by an ursine social hierarchy. When over 100 grizzlies congregate on Alaska's McNeil River every June to fatten up on spawning salmon below a 300-foot waterfall, the bosses are 1,000-pound battle-tested males, but sows with cubs take little guff. Further down the social ladder and farther downstream at poorer fishing sites are younger males, who clearly know their place in the clawing order.

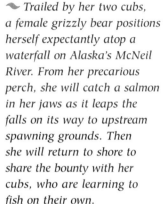

Trailed by her two cubs, a female grizzly bear positions herself expectantly atop a waterfall on Alaska's McNeil River. From her precarious perch, she will catch a salmon in her jaws as it leaps the falls on its way to upstream spawning grounds. Then she will return to shore to share the bounty with her cubs, who are learning to fish on their own.

How much time do animals spend feeding themselves?

Most animals spend the majority of their time looking for something to eat, but few are as hard pressed as shrews, which do little else besides scour their surroundings for sustenance. Shrews, some of which weigh only as much as a dime, are furry bundles of nervous energy that live life in high gear and in seemingly constant agitation. Their tiny hearts can palpitate at a rate of 1,200 beats per minute when they are excited or alarmed. Virtual eating machines, shrews need so much food to fuel their hyperactive bodies, they must feed every three hours day and night. The amount of insects, earthworms, and other small creatures that a shrew can consume in a single day is comparable to a 150-pound person wolfing down 300 pounds of food during the same period.

Although not every animal is as hard pressed as the shrew to find food, getting enough to eat is a continual struggle for all. How much food an animal needs can depend on external conditions, such as changes in the weather. (During the winter, when birds such as sparrows crowd up at a backyard feeder, you can bet that a storm is coming.) Songbirds must maintain body tem-

peratures of over 100°F. When cold air moves in, birds need more food to stoke their internal furnaces, which is why they find an enormous boon at backyard feeders, especially when snow on the ground makes it difficult to peck for seeds and insects. Frigid temperatures create a critical situation for small birds, which lose body heat more quickly. A titmouse, for example, will chill more quickly than a wild turkey. To keep its body warm in freezing weather, a titmouse may eat as much as a third of its body weight in a day.

Unlike birds and mammals, reptiles cannot regulate their body heat but, instead, depend on the temperature of their surroundings. Because reptiles do not burn food to produce heat, they generally eat less. A bullsnake, for instance, can do quite well on a meal of a rodent or two per month. Throughout much of North America, winter air temperatures are too cold for snakes to be active, so they slide into crevices, caves, and burrows, where temperatures are higher than above ground, and hibernate, not eating at all.

Preparation to reproduce can also cause feeding to cease in a number of creatures. American eels travel 1,000 miles from continental waters to their breeding grounds in the Sargasso Sea, south of Bermuda, an arduous year-long trek during which they consume not a bite. After reproducing, they expire. Similarly, Pacific salmon fast as they migrate from the ocean to spawning sites far up rivers and streams in western North America. After spawning, their task of producing another generation done, the salmon, like the eels, expire.

How does a sow put her piglets on a feeding schedule?

One of the first decisions that human parents must make is whether or not to feed their baby on demand. For most mammals the subject isn't debatable. Wild boars and barnyard porkers, for example, allow their young to suckle on demand right after birth but quickly establish time intervals between meals.

Although she can nurse a dozen piglets at once, a sow usually gives birth to from four to eight. Milk flows from as many of the sow's teats as she has young. Even then, some teats generate more milk than others, so newborns fight for the best places. Once the piglets have each claimed a teat, the sow lets them nurse until they doze. Later, when the piglets hear the sow snorting,

~ *Seven piglets suckle contentedly on a sow's top row of teats. Two others suckle on the bottom row, while the one on the left grunts with displeasure at being squeezed out of the feeding lineup.*

they fasten onto a teat and swill down milk for about a minute until the sow stops the flow. Then, about a half an hour later, she sounds the dinner bell again. Over a period of three months, she extends the time between feedings to two hours. This process encourages the piglets to sample adult food in between nursing times and nudges them toward independence.

How does a squirrel lay away food for the winter?

In the course of an autumn, one gray squirrel may store hundreds, even thousands of acorns in its territory, burying each one individually an inch or two deep. A vital resource, the nuts provide much of the squirrel's food for the next six months. Because white oak acorns germinate soon after they hit the ground, the squirrel nips off their tips, killing the embryos to ensure they won't sprout before being eaten.

Scientists believe a squirrel uses both its keen sense of smell and a sharp memory to locate its nut stashes even under deep, crusted snow. Few buried nuts go unrecovered. Squirrels even engage in petty theft if they see another's acorn being buried. As if aware of potential thievery, gray squirrels will pretend to bury a nut if they think they're being watched, then carry it away for secret burial. Squirrels view humans as possible thieves, too, for they will fake a burial if they know people are watching them.

~ *A red squirrel may spend days in midsummer industriously cutting cones from conifers, dropping them to the forest floor, and then collecting them into caches (inset).*

Searching with sensitive paws for suet and seeds, a hungry raccoon raids a bird feeder. Raccoons love sweet corn when they can get it, but these versatile eaters will down nearly anything from seeds and berries to cray-fish and frogs. Favorite haunts are stream banks and pond edges.

What makes raccoons so curious?

Words like *curious* and *clever* seem just right for raccoons. These masked bandits are famous for figuring out how to break into latched camp coolers and burglarize pest-proof garbage cans that foil most other animals. When raccoons amble along the shoreline of a pond or river, they peer into muskrat holes, sniff at unfamiliar objects, and probe beneath rocks and logs like mischievous children. In fact, one of the distinctive characteristics of raccoons is that they seem to be curious about everything. But is it curiosity? Or is such a label a case of anthropomorphism—our tendency to attribute peculiarly human qualities to animals?

Raccoons share their inquisitive nature with a few other mammals, notably wolves, monkeys, apes, and humans. All are opportunistic and omnivorous feeders that depend for survival on persistence, patience, and luck. Omnivorous animals are likely to find food almost anywhere, which means a curious individual ready to investigate every new possibility is more likely to stay well fed and healthy than one that depends on only a few set patterns of behavior. By sticking its nose where it doesn't belong and pawing around in every nook and cranny, a raccoon is rewarded with meals such as earthworms, snails, and birds' eggs that less inquisitive animals would never locate.

Finding such hidden treasures requires special equipment. Raccoons have evolved sensitive and remarkably nimble forepaws ideal for manipulating small objects and exploring in hard-to-reach places. Indeed, the Algonquian Indians, from whom we borrowed our word *raccoon*, called the animal *arakun*, "he who scratches with his hands."

Raccoons in captivity are often observed "washing" their food — dousing it in water before eating it and sometimes dipping it repeatedly. This is probably not a sign of fastidiousness. Since raccoons are accustomed to finding much of their food in shallow water, some biologists have suggested that they may prefer their food to be wet. Also, the skin on the raccoon's forepaws becomes softer and more pliable when moist, increasing their sensitivity to the food and other objects they handle. It may be that wetting their paws increases the pleasure raccoons get from manipulating food and rolling smooth objects back and forth between their paws. Whatever the reason for this ritual, it is certainly one of the most curious habits of this curious creature.

Do insects have teeth?

If you've been bitten by a horsefly, you probably think it had choppers the size of its namesake's, but insects don't have teeth. They have mouthparts that vary according to diet.

An insect that sucks juices, such as a horsefly, bed bug, or mosquito, has mouthparts forming a piercing proboscis that usually consists of three to six needlelike stylets enclosed by a sheath. When the insect bites, the sheath folds out of the way, and the stylets penetrate the skin.

A plant-eating insect such as a grasshopper has jaws for chewing. On either side of its gullet are pincerlike mandibles. In many chewing species the insides of the mandibles are as close to teeth as an insect gets. In front are raised, incisor-like cusps, while in the rear are flatter structures similar to molars. Predatory insects such as praying mantises sport shearing cusps. Grasshoppers and other leaf eaters have lower ridges for grinding. One or two pairs of feeler-like appendages behind the mandibles test for edibility and help to hold the food.

Grasping a blade of grass with its front legs, a short-horned grasshopper chews down the end with its two mandibles, mouthparts with grinding surfaces that move from side to side.

How does a woodpecker detect food through solid wood?

Sharp eyes and ears may be just as vital to a woodpecker as a sharp beak. Downy woodpeckers, for example, patiently examine cracks and crevices in trees, looking for insect cocoons, spiders, and beetles hiding inside. Pileated woodpeckers—the crested, crow-size "log cocks" of mature forests may use visual clues such as sawdust piles to locate carpenter ant colonies that they uncover in dead trees.

Although evidence is sparse, ornithologists have long assumed that woodpeckers can find insects by listening for them. Wood-boring beetles and ants make sounds that are sometimes audible to humans, and so they undoubtedly can be heard by birds as well. Woodpeckers frequently peck on house shingles to get at masses of cluster flies underneath, probably attracted by buzzing sounds. Some experts believe that hairy woodpeckers may actually feel for insects by driving their bills into wood and then holding stock-still to sense vibrations.

Woodpeckers may also locate certain boring and tunneling insects by analyzing the noise of their own pecking. A dead tree trunk undermined by beetle larvae or carpenter ants sounds different from an undamaged one when pecked.

However it locates its food, the woodpecker is well-equipped to excavate it. Using its powerful bill as a chisel to make a hole, the woodpecker then brings its extraordinarily long tongue into play. The tongue of the flicker, or golden-winged woodpecker, for example, is attached to an extensible, cartilaginous bone, which divides at the back of the throat and passes around both sides of the windpipe. Then it travels up and over the skull and down to an anchoring point near a nostril. When the flicker fully stretches out its tongue, the slender, white tip can dart two or three inches beyond its beak into a decaying log on the ground or an anthill to impale grubs or ants on its sticky tip.

➤ *A female pileated woodpecker prepares to feed her young regurgitated insects. Females build new nesting cavities each year, then lay three or four eggs by early May. Cavities are large enough for adults to move freely—10 to 24 inches deep and 7 to 8 inches wide.*

How does a snake swallow such large meals?

🐍 *A Texas rat snake swallows a wood duck egg larger than its head with astonishing ease. Gastric juices will dissolve the egg's shell as it passes through the digestive tract. Because a snake's jaws are loosely connected to the skull, their gape is limited only by the elasticity of the mouth's soft tissues. The brain is enclosed in bone to protect it from over-size and still-struggling meals.*

Although its victims are much bigger round than its closed mouth is wide, a rat snake can easily swallow a fat rat after squeezing the rodent to death. This North American constrictor readily slithers up trees and barn rafters to pursue its quarry. Racers can also climb but are more likely to remain on the ground as they hunt mice and other small creatures. Both species frequently gulp down meals bigger than their heads.

The ability of many snakes to swallow large animals is due to the flexible construction of their jaws. The bones of a snake's upper jaw aren't rigidly fixed to its skull. This flexibility is true of the lower jaw, too. The two sides of the jaw are attached only by an elastic cord so that they can spread as the snake devours its food. Luckily, the jaws can't unhinge, and their loose attachment to the skull permits a snake to achieve a gape of about 130 degrees—nearly four times wider than a human's biggest yawn.

As a snake engulfs its prey, its curved teeth hook into the meal. Moving first one side of both the upper and lower jaws and then the opposite side, just as a person hauls in a rope by pulling first with one hand and then with the other, a snake "crawls" over its food. Strong muscular contractions finish the job as the reptile's skin stretches to welcome the unlucky victim.

How do butterflies sip nectar?

Butterflies sip nectar much the same way children drink milk shakes—with a straw, gusto, and a lot of sucking.

For the world's 17,000 butterfly species, the straw is actually a specialized feeding tube called a proboscis. Located under the head and tightly coiled like a watch spring when not in use, this elephant trunk–like appendage allows butterflies to reach deep inside flowers.

Butterflies rely on a finely tuned system of senses to find nectar. Their antennae are used for smelling, and chemical receptors on their legs become stimulated when they get close to the sugary substance. When that happens, the butterfly uncoils its prehensile proboscis, composed of several elongated mouthparts forming a tube, and drives it into the flower, pumping its head up and down. If the insect strikes liquid gold, another chemical reactor located on the tip of the proboscis triggers a powerful head pump that uses muscles and air sacs to draw the flower's nectar up the food tube.

Although all butterflies use their proboscises to eat, not all feed on flowers. Some sip nutrients from rotting fruit; others prefer the honeydew secreted by aphids; and still others favor animal urine or fluids in animal carcasses.

Zebra longwing butterflies, which live in the southeastern United States, use their proboscises to scrape pollen off the anthers of passion vine flowers. These colorful butterflies then mix the tiny pollen balls with regurgitated juices to create an amazing liquid meal that has a higher concentration of the essential ingredients needed for butterfly survival than does ordinary nectar. Giving new meaning to the term "Breakfast of Champions," the pollen the zebras consume is credited by scientists with making these butterflies among the longest-lived in the world.

➤ *Agitating its coiled proboscis, a zebra butterfly mixes stomach juices with pollen from flower anthers. Once the tacky grains are liquefied, the butterfly will draw the protein broth up its proboscis. Most adult butterflies feed exclusively on nectar and live only about 10 days. On their high-protein diet, zebras can survive six months or more.*

Do bats really suck blood?

Of the world's nearly 1,000 species of bats, only three are blood eaters. Most eat insects, fruits, flowers, or nectar; a few hunt birds, small rodents, and fish. Vampire bats prefer to dine on the blood of cattle and other domestic animals, seldom biting human beings. The three species live in Central and South America. Only one, the hairy-legged vampire, has ever been reported in the United States. It was seen in a Texas railroad tunnel near the Mexican border.

Only about three inches long, vampire bats creep daintily over their sleeping hosts on the heels of their hands. Finding a sparsely haired spot, the vampire bat bites with sharp, chisel-like incisor teeth and begins lapping with its tongue. An anticoagulant in the vampire's saliva keeps the blood from clotting. In a half hour or less, when its belly is full and its weight has almost doubled, the sated bat will fly back to its roost, often being replaced at the wound by another.

➤ *A vampire bat settles on the belly of a sleeping pig. After licking its feeding spot to soften the skin, it makes a tiny puncture and begins lapping blood. A vampire bat often returns to the same farm animal night after night. The tiny, three-inch creature can consume over six gallons of blood a year—enough to drain three human beings.*

Hunting
Jaws, claws, bills, webs, pouches, and packs

Why do some animals prefer to hunt at night?

Of the proverbial thousand eyes of the night, many belong to predators. They hunt after sunset because that's when multitudes of the creatures they prey upon are active, similarly engaged in the quest for food. Like musicians who work the club circuit, a vast number of animals snooze during the day and earn their living on the night shift. Three-quarters of the world's 4,000 species of mammals, for example, are nocturnal, as are half of the 2,500 different kinds of snakes. Only a few insects—notably bees, wasps, and butterflies—are diurnal, and amphibians tend to shun the sun because it desiccates their bodies.

According to one school of scientific thought, most mammals are active at night because their primal ancestors hid from marauding dinosaurs during daylight. (A modern-day example may be the Virginia opossum, which does its foraging at night not only to consume the nocturnal insects and frogs it dearly loves to eat, but perhaps to avoid hawks, which need daylight in order to see their prey.) Over time, the thinking goes, these ancient mammals came to rely on heightened senses of touch, hearing, and smell as alternatives to vision—qualities that are shared by most nocturnal mammals today. A raccoon, for instance, has such sensitive handlike paws that it could probably pluck a frog, clam, or crayfish from the water even if it were blindfolded. Moreover, hearing and smell are more effective at night because once the wind dies down, background noise decreases and scents linger.

Whether or not an animal is active at night may simply depend on where it lives. Snakes that inhabit cooler climates tend to hunt by day because chilly evening temperatures make them sluggish. Under the sizzling desert sun, however, snakes are in danger of being cooked alive,

◆ *Notorious for their nighttime raids, raccoons are the masked bandits of the animal world. On the prowl from dusk to dawn, these omnivorous creatures reach their peak feeding activity before midnight, sometimes feasting on the smorgasbord of leftovers found inside suburban trash cans.*

so they begin prowling as dusk cools the sands. Rattlesnakes are particularly well adapted for nighttime hunting, with organs in their heads that sense the warmth of nearby small rodents.

Hunting at night also helps some animals avoid competition for food and lets them double up on the same feeding ground without rubbing shoulders. Both robins and woodcocks search for worms in fields and meadows, but robins do it by sunlight, and woodcocks by moonlight. A hungry robin locates worms with its keen eyesight, while a woodcock probes the soil, feeling for them with the sensitive, flexible tip of its long bill—a method that works as well in darkness as in daylight. Often, nocturnal hunters and the creatures they stalk share similar adaptations for nighttime survival. Both kit foxes and the kangaroo rats they feed on, for example, have prodigious external ears designed to scoop up sounds made by other animals. Whether the fox eats or the rat survives often depends on which one hears the other first.

What is the one creature a porcupine fears?

Clad in more than 30,000 needle-sharp quills, a porcupine would seem to be a nearly invincible foe, and it certainly acts that way. Porcupines show little fear of any animal, and just one swish of that barb-studded tail is enough to make even a grizzly bear give ground. There is one creature, however, that can penetrate the porcupine's defenses: a fox-size weasel known as a fisher. Lithe and agile, this North Woods hunter feeds on a wide variety of birds and small mammals, even snacking on fruits and nuts on occasion, but it has a particular fondness for porcupines.

Legend has it that the fisher flips the porcupine over and attacks its quill-less underside. This is not the case, however. When a fisher takes on a porcupine, it makes a daring frontal assault, darting through the lightning-fast lashes of the porcupine's tail to bite its face and nose. Only when the huge rodent is dead does the fisher concentrate on the unprotected belly, carefully rolling back the skin as it feeds.

Despite its speed and agility, the fisher is

~ *Encountering its favorite prey—a porcupine—on a tree, a fisher will try to corner the animal at the end of a branch, but the porcupine is safe as long as it keeps its quill-covered back to the enemy.*

a stoop. Folding its wings, the bird drops—feet extended forward—in a nearly vertical plunge to the ground and soars back up with, say, a squirming meadow vole in its talons. To pinpoint such tiny prey from high altitudes, the hawk relies on its famously keen eyesight. Most raptors—as birds of prey are called—have visual acuity far beyond that of humans, but the frequently cited claim that a hawk can see as well as a person looking through eight-power binoculars is misleading. Hawks do not have greatly magnified vision; they have abundant receptor cells in their retinas, enabling them to discriminate detail at far greater distances than humans.

Scientists now believe that hawks and other raptors can see detail about two or three times better than people. What's more, they apparently detect a greater range of light, including near-ultraviolet wavelengths that are invisible to us. Thanks to special oil droplets in their receptor cells that enhance contrast, raptors are particularly adept at spotting objects against green or blue backgrounds—precisely those found in the wild. With its forward-facing eyes fixed on its prey, the hawk also benefits from superb depth perception. During its high-speed dive, special muscles around the eyes instantaneously change the curvature of the lenses, keeping the target in perfect focus right up to the moment of strike.

inevitably punctured by quills, especially around its muzzle. Most predators would die from a mouthful of porcupine quills, which work their way deeper and deeper into the body. But the fisher has an amazing tolerance for quills, most of which are diverted to a layer of fat beneath the skin. Remarkably, even those that pierce internal organs seem to do no harm. Overall, the risks are small and the payoff large, for a porcupine may provide the fisher with enough food for a month.

How does a hawk high in the air find and snatch prey far below?

Wheeling in a boundless blue summer sky, a red-tailed hawk surveys the scene hundreds of feet below. Once a potential meal has been sighted, the hawk zeroes in for an attack, usually in the form of a steep dive known as

~ *A red-tailed hawk may eye its prey while soaring or hovering, but more often it employs a different hunting strategy. Perched for hours atop a tree, telephone pole, or haystack, it may suddenly glide and swoop down upon its target, seizing the animal with its viselike talons and then tearing it apart with its powerful hooked beak.*

Do all spiders spin webs?

Though silk webs are a hallmark of spiders, not every species uses them to hunt. Instead, many spiders rely on speed, ambush, and deceit—even trap doors—to procure a meal. For example, the wolf spider, like its mammalian namesake, uses speed and agility to run down insects and other small invertebrates. Commonly seen in woodlands, fields, and backyards, this nimble creature is identifiable by its gray-brown hairy body, which usually sports black-and-white stripes. One of its relatives, the fishing spider, employs a similar chase-and-grab technique on the water, skimming over the surface of ponds and lakes at night, capturing insects and even tiny fishes and tadpoles.

Many other spiders hunt without the benefit of webs, though they may use them for shelter. In gardens crab spiders often hide among the petals of the daisies or sunflowers, where they change colors to match their surroundings. With infinite patience the crab spider waits, motionless, for a hover fly, bee, or butterfly to land on the flower.

Perhaps the most remarkable group to forsake webs are the jumping spiders, so active and brilliantly colored that they have been nicknamed the hummingbirds of the spider world. Rotund, short-legged creatures with a jerky, mechanical gait, they number nearly 300 species in North America alone. Iridescent scales cover part or all of this spider's body, lending it an almost tropical appearance. Unlike most of their relatives, jumping spiders are active by day and therefore easy to identify. A jumper on the prowl moves cautiously, in short hops and careful steps, until it is within range of its prey (generally 3 or 4 inches, although some can jump as far as 10 inches).

As their name implies, so-called trap-door spiders, found in the southern states and along the Pacific coast, use a hunting strategy that's considerably more passive but equally effective. In essence, they wait in their cozy silk-lined tunnels until a meal arrives at their doorstep. Using special comblike rakes on its jaw, the trap-door spider digs a burrow in loose soil, concealing itself in a silken underground chamber. Through the top it cuts a circular opening that's hinged at one side. Waiting patiently for the delicate footfalls of an approaching beetle or other insect, the spider simply pops out of its ambuscade,

The trap-door spider uses its venom not only to paralyze its victim, but to predigest it or preserve it for later consumption.

These silken tightropes (top left) were formed when a spider wafted them from one tree to another. Though one would expect them to sag, they remain taut because they were tightened by the spider. The jumping spider (above) has only one chance to pounce on its prey. But thanks to its multiple eyes, which enable it to calculate the exact position of a target, it often succeeds.

Why do jellyfish have tentacles?

In one Sherlock Holmes story, the great detective probes the death of a schoolteacher killed while swimming in the ocean. Finding the culprit stranded in a tide pool, he triumphantly shouts: "Behold the lion's mane!" The creature in question is a jellyfish—not just any jellyfish, but one of the largest of its clan, with tentacles that extend more than 100 feet. Ninety-five percent water, these primitive marine animals have no brain, no blood, and no backbone, which explains why one scientist has playfully dubbed them "Jell-O with a mouth."

Outside of fiction it's unlikely that even a jellyfish the size of a lion's mane could be hazardous to a healthy human. Nonetheless, their tentacles deliver a fearsome zap. Despite their value as defensive weapons, tentacles are primarily used for hunting small fish, crustaceans, and other animals. Each stinger is a tiny, hollow thread housed in an oval capsule, where it is bathed in venom. When an object touches the jellyfish's delicate hairlike trigger, the capsule's lid opens, the stinger shoots out, and—if it penetrates the prey—a dose of venom is injected. Once immobilized, the victim is hauled into the jellyfish's mouth, which lies beneath its gelatinous, bell-shaped body.

then drags its victim below ground to feed on it.

Though spiders such as the orb weaver can create platter-size webs, many kinds of spiders don't spin webs at all. Yet they still produce silk for a dozen other purposes. This strongest of all natural fibers is used to encase egg masses, to form a protective canopy over newly hatched young, and to provide a safety line when prey is pursued. In winter many northern spiders create silken hibernation cocoons beneath slabs of bark. A courting male also has a use for silk. He spins a tiny web and deposits a drop of sperm on it. Wrapping the drop in the silk, he carries it in the hollow tip of a small, leglike appendage, ready to insert the precious cargo into a female's abdomen—unless she happens to eat him first.

~ *A master of camouflage, the crab spider (shown here in its white phase) has a flair for changing color. Like its namesake, the crab spider can even walk sideways—a distinct advantage when hunting.*

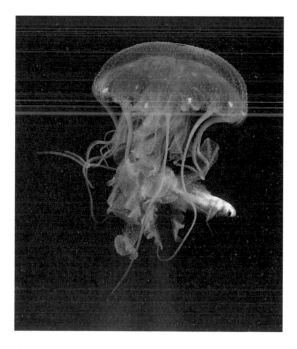

~ *Accustomed to pursuing small prey, some types of jellyfish have tentacles that deliver such a light sting that it can't be felt by sensitive human skin.*

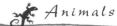

~ *Caught in the act, a bobcat displays its conquest: a snowshoe hare. Named for its short, stubby tail, this versatile hunter literally goes for the jugular (see inset), pulverizing the throat of its victim in a matter of seconds.*

Do all cats use the same hunting technique?

Who hasn't watched a pet tabby trying to sneak up on a robin, usually in vain? Stalk and pounce—that's the modus operandi of hunting felines, be they wild or domestic. Cats depend on their keen vision and hearing to locate prey, and the idea is to get as close as possible before making a final dash to nab the unsuspecting victim. Bobcats, however, often employ a different strategy: they simply wait for their meal to come to them. In winter, for instance, they'll crouch for so long in their so-called "hunting beds" that clumps of their fur actually get frozen to the packed snow.

Ambush is an especially good tactic if your favorite food happens to be cottontail rabbits.

These animals are usually plentiful, have small home ranges, and tend to hop along well-traveled lanes through brushy fields and forests. Any bunny that bounces within a few feet of a bobcat's boundary is almost guaranteed to have a short life expectancy. The lives of these two animals are so closely intertwined, in fact, that when Idaho's cottontail population declined, bobcats continued to hunt the scarce survivors even though equally edible black-tailed jackrabbits outnumbered their cousins 9 to 1. Instead of jackrabbits, birds and rodents made up the temporary shortage.

Even on those occasions when they do stalk prey, bobcats exhibit extraordinary patience and stealth. One individual in Louisiana, for example, reportedly took 13 minutes to creep forward three feet before finally snatching its meal.

Which fish use rods and lures to catch their food?

If the key to being a successful fisherman is to think like a fish, then perhaps the key to being a successful fish is to think like a fisherman. Several varieties do just that, outsmarting their quarry by using their very own versions of rods and lures—movable appendages that they twitch and wiggle to entice would-be victims within easy reach of their gaping jaws. The goosefish, for example, which gets its name because it sometimes forgoes a diet of fish and gulps down geese and seabirds instead, has a maw so large that a two-foot-long specimen can swallow a cod of the same size. Atop the goosefish's snout stands a long, movable spine—actually a modification of the dorsal fin—tipped with a leaflike tab of skin. When a potential meal approaches, the goosefish (sold in markets as monkfish) dangles the bait in front of its mouth and twitches it so that it resembles a tiny fish, worm, or crustacean. If the other fish makes the mistake of going for the meal, it becomes one instead.

Even more complete anglers are relatives of the goosefish called—not coincidentally—anglerfish. Denizens of deep water, anglerfish have a dorsal spine that ends in a lure shaped like a bulb. On some species the spine is so flexible that it can be whipped around like a fly line. More-

over, anglerfish living in the lightless depths of the ocean have lures that resemble bulbs in every sense of the word. Bacteria that inhabit these bulbs cause them to shine with living light, which attracts prey.

Do animals use their tongues for more than tasting?

A snake may have a forked tongue, but there's nothing deceitful about the way it's used. Contrary to popular belief, a snake uses its tongue not to sting, but to gather information about its surroundings—specifically, whether or not food is available. The tongue of a snake, as well as those of many lizards, picks up particles of scent and transfers them to two chambers in the roof of its mouth, where cells determine the location of a nearby animal and whether or not it is edible.

While a snake uses its tongue to find prey, other animals rely on their tongues to capture food. To a grasshopper or fly, the tongue of a frog or toad can be a lethal weapon. As sticky as flypaper, it is attached at the front of the lower jaw and, at rest, folds to the rear. Once an insect has been targeted, the tongue goes into action with dazzling speed. Infinitely faster than a person could ever swing a fly swatter, it flips over and shoots out of the mouth, sometimes reaching twice its normal length. The tip curls upward around the prey and folds back into the rear of the mouth. A quick contraction of the throat muscles is all it takes to send the meal down the gullet. Another deadly tongue lies in the mouth of the alligator snapping turtle. The wiggly tip of its tongue looks just like a worm—a delectable tidbit for fish. Lying on the bottom of lakes and rivers with its massive jaws wide open, the turtle activates its bait. Fish that go for a nibble soon find out, much to their misfortune, how quickly the worm turns.

~ *In addition to a tongue that helps it smell, the garter snake is equipped with other valuable hunting aids: fixed, unblinking eyes that enable it to focus on moving objects, internal ears that can detect low-frequency sounds, and a highly sensitive body that can feel vibrations transmitted through the ground.*

~ *A goosefish appears to be all head—and its head appears to be all mouth. So large is this orifice that its sudden opening creates enough suction to help draw in food. An insatiable eater, it can consume half its own weight in one bite.*

🐟 *Pelican chicks use their mother's pouch as a kind of soup bowl, dipping into it for a meal of partially digested fish. If the chick is too small to reach, however, the mother will simply dribble the smelly mess onto the webs of her feet.*

How do pelicans use their pouches?

A wonderful bird is the pelican, / His bill will hold more than his belican." This fanciful rhyme from a modern verse is no exaggeration. The prominent pouch of a white pelican (one of only two species found in North America, the other being the brown pelican) can hold nearly three gallons of water—more than twice the capacity of its stomach.

A pelican uses its pouch, first and foremost, as a fishing net. The white pelican, which forages in flocks of up to 100 birds, dips its enormous bill into the water, expands the fleshy lower half like a balloon, then scoops up schooling fish. Rather than carrying its catch back to the nest, the pelican tilts its head, drains the pouch, and swallows the fish whole. The brown pelican, on the other hand, hunts more aggressively. Flying over a body of water, it spots a fish near the surface, folds its wing into a V-shape, then dives toward it headfirst from a height of 50 feet or more. Thanks to air sacs that give it buoyancy, the bird bobs to the surface in an instant, emerging with a prize tucked away securely in its pouch.

On hot summer days a pelican may even use its pouch to cool off, opening its gape and rapidly fluttering its pouch to dissipate body heat. Not surprisingly, a pelican must keep its multipurpose pouch in tip-top shape. Hence, the bird performs a painstaking regimen of elaborate stretching exercises—such as pointing its head skyward and backward—that would be daunting to even the most disciplined athlete.

Do all killer whales use the same method of finding food?

How a killer whale hunts depends entirely on whether it's a resident of the territory or a traveler passing through. For example, in the Pacific Northwest, off the coast of Washington State, resident killer whales stake out well-defined ranges where they feed exclusively on salmon. They may pursue their prey either individually or in groups. When using the latter approach, they corral the fish and then converge on them like wolves. During these highly coordinated attacks, resident killer whales constantly "talk" to their cohorts, frequently using sonar clicks to help single out a victim, and a mix of screams, whistles, and pulsing sounds to communicate with one another.

By contrast, traveling killer whales—free-ranging nomads that cruise far and wide—disdain fish. They prefer bigger game: seals, sea lions, porpoises, even other whales. More solitary by nature, they often travel alone or in teams of two or three. Unlike residents, traveling killer whales seldom communicate during the hunt and—except for perhaps a click or two—don't use sonar to locate their prey, since marine mammals (their food of choice) might be alerted by the sound.

🐟 *In the waters off the southeast coast of Alaska, a killer whale unleashes its power on a Dall's porpoise. This fierce hunter will even lunge ashore to snatch a seal, killing it with a series of body blows or, sometimes, a single bite.*

Why do wolves hunt in packs?

Predatory animals aren't looking for a fair fight. Survival smiles on surer things. Predators either hunt alone and pick on smaller animals or hunt in packs so that they can gang up on larger prey. Because nature has dealt the wolf a habitat of forests, plains, and tundra populated by large herbivores (including moose, deer, elks, caribous, musk oxen, and formerly, bison), it is by necessity a pack animal. A lone wolf wouldn't have much luck hunting these animals; they're either too quick and wary or too big and strong. Given the fact that their prey is so challenging to conquer, wolves must pursue food relentlessly, traveling as much as eight hours a day in search of a meal. Yet despite their tenaciousness, they sometimes go for days, even weeks, without a kill.

Once predator and prey finally eyeball one another, the war games begin. If a herd is fresh and takes off at full tilt (often faster than wolves can run), the wolf pack will dog the herd until it tires of running. Darting in and out of the herd, provoking individual members to move about, the wolves size them up, looking for weak candidates: the elderly and the very young, the sick and the injured. Once a target has been chosen, the wolves usually attack its haunches, knocking the animal off its feet if possible. They then use their powerful jaws and sharp teeth to dispatch the victim in short order, often feasting on it where it fell. A famished wolf may devour up to 20 pounds of meat, bones, and hide in one meal, leaving little for scavengers. If hungry cubs and "babysitters" are waiting back at the den, a few lowly members of the pack have the duty of trotting home and disgorging some of what they've eaten.

As soon as wolves abandon one kill, they search for another. The moose, their largest and most formidable prey, is shown here with a pack in hot pursuit (inset). Its fate will depend largely on whether it is healthy and confident enough to stand its ground if attacked.

Animal Defenses *Tricks and techniques for survival*

🐟 *A hover fly (left) and a yellow jacket meet face to face. By wearing black-and-yellow warning colors, the harmless hover fly mimics the appearance of the stinging insect and thus discourages birds and other potential enemies from making it a meal.*

Are mimicry and camouflage the same thing?

In the animal kingdom mimicry and camouflage are different, deceptive means to the same end: surviving long enough to produce offspring. Camouflaged animals evade their enemies by matching their background: brown birds on twiggy nests, green lizards on leaves, fish with dark backs and silvery bellies, which help conceal them when seen from above or below.

A few animals even use bold patterns for camouflage. They don't disappear into the background, but spots, stripes, and other marks break up their outlines. Predators may notice them but can't identify them as prey. Even reef fish with gaudy colors and markings may be well camouflaged among corals from predatory fish that don't see colors the same way we do.

🐟 *A black spotted moth resting on a granite ledge in Mt. Rainier National Park shows how bold markings can be the best camouflage on the right background.*

Animals that are big, ferocious, toxic, or terrible-tasting have less need for camouflage. Many small but well-armed or noxious creatures flaunt their presence—as if to say, "Look but don't touch." Protected by their powerful scent, skunks can afford to wear bold blacks and whites in a world of greens, browns, and grays. Foul-tasting black-and-orange monarch butterflies can flaunt their beautiful colors.

However, not every animal wearing warning colors is poisonous, bad-tasting, or malodorous. Several completely innocuous creatures sport black-and-yellow or black-and-orange patterns. This kind of misrepresentation is called mimicry. Not as widespread as camouflage, mimicry occurs most frequently among insects. The viceroy, for example, is a good-tasting butterfly, but it looks so much like a toxic monarch that predators can't tell them apart. Hover flies and some other stingerless insects masquerade in the warning stripes of bees and wasps.

Other animal mimics employ a variety of ruses besides adopting lethal looks. The giant swallowtail butterfly produces caterpillars that look less like bird food than bird droppings. Sphinx moths, also known as hummingbird which fly with wings slightly uptilted, strikingly resemble turkey vultures and may be mistaken for these harmless carrion-eating birds by rodents, toads, and other small animals. Some creatures even use mimicry to attract prey. Fireflies can imitate the mating flashes of other species, luring those males to their deaths.

Why do chipmunks have stripes?

S mall mammals such as chipmunks live in a tough world. A host of predators is out to get them—foxes, owls, hawks, snakes, weasels, coyotes, cats, and even bears. Chipmunks have developed some clever tricks to survive. They scamper very quickly over short distances, never range far from their holes, and create several entrances to their burrows just to make sure they have places to hide nearby. But their best protection is their distinctive coloration and patterning.

Perpetually vigilant, the chipmunk will run for its burrow at the slightest hint of danger. It never leaves telltale piles at the entrances; instead, it carries the dirt a distance away in its cheek pouches.

If you look carefully at a chipmunk, you'll notice that it has a white throat, white underbelly, and a back marked by a series of white stripes outlined in black on a gray and reddish brown background. These colors seem conspicuous, but they actually help the chipmunk blend into the habitat in which it lives: the forest floor.

The white throat, the light underbelly, and back markings also help to disguise the chipmunk by breaking up the shape predators see. Instead of looking at a solid outline of an animal, enemies glimpse only a broken form, a moving patch of light on an amorphous brown background, similar to the dappling on the forest floor. In fact, what the predator probably spots first is the raised tail. A chipmunk, unlike a squirrel, runs with its tail aloft, so that if an enemy does strike, it's more apt to get a mouthful of fur than a meal.

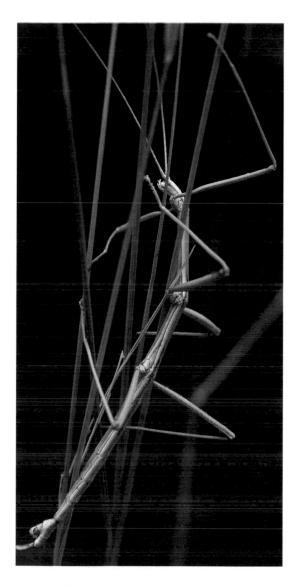

A walking stick hangs motionless by its legs during the day, mimicking twigs. At night when insect-eating birds sleep, it will feed on foliage.

moths, closely resemble their tiny namesakes. (Hummingbirds are so fast and agile, predators don't bother with them.) When plovers and other ground-nesting birds are menaced, they hunker down and skitter off on a "mouse run," leading enemies away from their broods—behavioral mimicry.

Potential victims are not the only ones to use camouflage and mimicry. Guileful hunters wear subtle browns and grays, not necessarily to protect themselves but to make stalking of prey easier. In winter, when arctic and varying hares and ptarmigans turn white, so do two of their predators: arctic foxes and weasels. Zone-tailed hawks,

Galloping gracefully across Wyoming's High Plains, these pronghorn antelopes can easily maintain a steady pace of 35 to 40 miles per hour for three or four miles before tiring. No large predators—not even wolves or mountain lions— can keep up with them.

Which fleet-footed animals leave danger in the dust?

On the open plains, where stunted trees cower in the lee of hills and a predator's sharp eye can roam the horizon unhindered, there is little safety in stealth and camouflage. Speed is the primary strategy many animals adopt in order to survive.

Only the prairie wind outruns the pronghorn. Not a true antelope but the lone member of a uniquely American family, this long-legged grazer of shortgrass prairies and deserts is built for speed. Its gallop is rather "the rapid flight of birds than the motion of quadrupeds," Meriwether Lewis and William Clark wrote after they encountered pronghorns in Montana in 1805.

Padded hooves and thickened leg bones protect the pronghorn from uneven terrain, and an oversize windpipe funnels oxygen to its unusually large lungs and heart. The fastest land animal in North America, a pronghorn is capable of sprinting more than 50 miles per hour. That is nearly twice as fast as its quickest predator, the

run punctuated by leaps that may span 15 feet. However, it can't sustain this speed for more than a few hundred yards. Antelope jackrabbits, found only in the Arizona deserts, are even faster, hitting speeds of 40 miles per hour.

Why is it so hard to swat a fly?

Here you are, hulking over the picnic spread as you watch a pesky fly. With a rolled newspaper clutched in your hand, you try to calculate where to aim, when to swing, and how to avoid upsetting the pitcher of lemonade. And there's the villain on the pickle jar, its enormous compound eyes seeing equally well in virtually all directions at once, each of its 8,000 eye facets sending messages to a brain that is many times more dedicated to things visual than your own. Calculations computed and error-checked, you swing. *Whap!* There go the fly and the lemonade, one buzzing off to the nearest sandwich, the other flooding the bowl of Aunt Fanny's famous potato salad.

Besides being able to see the newspaper coming long before it approached, the fly could react faster than you could correct your swing. Flies take in moving images 10 times faster than humans can and react to visual signals 5 times faster. You might have had a better chance (that is, any chance at all) wielding a fly swatter that was full of holes and wouldn't have pushed such a hurricane of air ahead of it.

The fine hairs covering the fly are pressure sensors. They are "hard-wired" via the largest, fastest nerve in its body to a set of muscles dedicated to jump-starting its wings, an arrangement that wastes no time processing signals in the brain. When the fly first sensed trouble (whether with its eyes or pressure cells), the alarm response immediately triggered the large muscles of its middle legs to pop the insect straight up into the air. As soon as the hairs under its body lost contact with the pickle jar, the wing muscles were automatically fired into motion. With the fly's big eyes and tiny brain, it was really no contest at all.

coyote, a surprising excess with an explanation that may lie buried in Ice Age history. Until the end of the last glaciation 12,000 years ago, pronghorns were prey for the now-extinct American cheetah, which presumably ran as fast as its surviving African relative. Experts believe the pronghorn's speed is a relic of its cheetah-fleeing past.

Speed is also the survival tactic of choice for smaller runners. The black-tailed jackrabbit of the West relies first on camouflage, but when trouble gets too close for comfort, the rangy hare explodes into a ground-eating 35-mile-per-hour

➤ *As a housefly buzzes off, its wing muscles are supplied with blood 14 times more rapidly than they were at rest. Flies flap their wings 2 to 3 times faster than hummingbirds—almost 20 times faster than the quickest movements of any human athlete.*

A muzzle full of quills has taught this Siberian husky pup a lesson he will never forget: porcupines are better left alone. From the rear a threatened porcupine (inset) looks like a solid mass of quills, but the barbs are thickest on the back and tail and entirely absent from the underside.

What makes porcupine quills so dangerous?

A porcupine bristles with tens of thousands of quills, but even one can be a deadly weapon, thanks to its unique construction.

Although a porcupine cannot throw its quills, these greatly modified hairs are only loosely attached to the rodent's skin and easily pull free when they puncture the hide of an enemy. Each quill measures two to five inches long and is needle-sharp. The half-inch or so nearest the tip is shingled with tiny, overlapping scales, which serve as microscopic barbs, anchoring the quill so firmly in flesh that a pair of pliers may be needed to remove it.

What's worse, once in place, a quill's tip expands slightly as it absorbs moisture from the surrounding tissue, and a victim's muscle movements pull the quill deeper and deeper into the body at a rate of an inch a day. Quills can migrate deep into the abdomen, puncturing vital organs with fatal results, or they may reappear through the skin, many inches from their original entry point. (One punctured biologist patiently tracked a quill as it traveled under the skin from his bicep to his forearm, where it exited without damage.) Surprisingly, infection is rarely a problem, for the quills contain a fatty acid that seems to curb bacterial growth.

Do skunks spray other skunks?

Given the fact that skunks can spray an enemy from a distance of a dozen feet or more and score a direct hit, you might expect that a donnybrook between two of them would be a very odoriferous affair. Not so. It is extremely rare for one skunk to let loose at another, and such an engagement probably would be a miscalculation. A skunk reserves its spray for large predators, using it as a last resort when its life is on the line. Only a very confused, terribly rattled skunk would pull the trigger on its own kind. Skunks are also very tolerant of one another and seldom quarrel. When they do, the fight is broken off as soon as one of them begins to get the worst of it.

It would be counterproductive for a skunk to waste its chemical weaponry on another skunk. The anal glands that produce the spray hold only enough ammunition for a few blasts at one time. This is why skunks call their shots carefully and generally fire off only one round per battle. Usually, however, a single hit is all it takes to send a predator running, its eyes burning and temporarily blinded. After that the unhappy culprit will give animals bearing vivid white-and-black colors a wide berth.

At least one hunter, however, seems not to fear the skunk's battle flag. Great horned owls routinely prey on skunks, and it is not unusual for these birds to smell like—well—a skunk.

How do slow-moving animals protect themselves?

If you can't run from danger, then the next best thing is to hide—in a shell, out of sight, or behind a chemical screen. These are strategies that many of nature's slowest animals use every day.

A turtle's shell is perhaps the most famous defense for slowpokes, although many freshwater turtles such as cooters, sliders, and painted turtles are really quite agile, and the largest sea turtles can swim several miles per hour. Terrestrial turtles, on the other hand, depend entirely on the protection offered by their shells, retracting their legs and head when predators find them. Most turtle shells are rigid, but the lower plates of several species are hinged, allowing them to close like a drawbridge.

Many mollusks, such as snails, take an almost identical approach, although the shell design is much different. As the soft-bodied animal grows, its shelter grows along with it as it secretes addi-

tional material around the lip of the shell. When disturbed, or when the climate becomes dangerously dry, the snail withdraws into its shell, sealing the opening with an oval plate called the operculum. Mollusk shells might seem impervious, but they are not—and other mollusks are often the culprits. An inch-long snail known as the oyster drill, common along the northeast coast, uses its filelike tongue to rasp a neat hole through the shell of a young oyster, then sucks the soft flesh out.

One of the best ways to avoid trouble is not to go out at all. Many small caterpillars—a favorite food of birds like warblers—live inside the leaves they eat, creating a camouflaged pantry. The caterpillar of the cherry leaf roller selects a black cherry leaf, nips holes in the central rib to weaken it, and rolls the tip back into a tube, anchoring it with silk. Then the larva can eat in peace, safe in its green hideaway.

Pill bugs, gray crustaceans that live on land and are common under old boards and logs, roll up into almost perfect balls when threatened, protecting their soft bellies beneath tough, overlapping scales. If that doesn't work, they may spray attackers with a potent chemical deterrent contained in glands near their tails.

In fact, chemical defenses are quite common among nature's smaller slow-movers. When disturbed, millipedes secrete bad-smelling chemicals; blister beetles exude an unpleasant liquid from their legs that causes blisters; and water skaters produce a substance from the tips of their abdomens that breaks the surface tension of water, allowing them to scoot rapidly over a pond's surface—safely away from predators.

⬿ *Land-dwelling relatives of crabs and lobsters, pill bugs live in damp leaf litter. To protect themselves from predators, they roll up into balls with their armorlike back plates facing outward.*

Why do fawns have spots?

Without their 300 or so spots, fawns would be easy prey for wolves, wolverines, pumas, bears, and even golden eagles. Wobbly-legged at birth and innocent of the wily ways of the world, fawns must hide from predators. In order to survive, adult deer rely on their acute senses, bounding agility, and outright speed to evade predators. Until they develop these defenses, young deer rely on the protective coloration of their white-spotted brown coats, an instinctive tendency to remain motionless when trouble nears, and for the first week or two of their lives, an almost complete lack of telltale odor.

Because they must be able to hunt in dim light, most predators have eyes that are extraordinarily sensitive to motion but poorly suited to distinguishing colors, details, or even shapes. Wolves' eyes can discern subtle differences in shapes, but even these master hunters have a difficult time spotting dappled, scentless fawns hunkered down and motionless among leaves, twigs, grass, and rocks.

Like white-tailed and mule deer fawns, elks are also spotted at birth. Only the largest members of the deer family (moose and caribou) are born without spotted coats. These animals, however, have other means of protection. Moose calves, while almost helpless at birth, grow very rapidly—faster than any other large American mammals—and moose cows are big and fierce enough to defend their young even from grizzly bears. Caribou calves can keep up with the herd within a day or two of birth, outrunning wolves and other predators across the tundra.

⬿ *Instinctively freezing at the first sign of danger, a pair of white-tailed deer fawns look up from grazing on the lush, late-summer vegetation growing along the banks of a Montana stream. These fawns will soon molt out of their dappled coats and don a somber grayish brown for winter. Twins are most common among white-tailed deer, but a doe may bear only a single fawn or triplets or even quadruplets.*

⟩ *When startled, a nine-banded armadillo can shoot straight up into the air. This extraordinary bit of acrobatics wins the armadillo an extra few seconds to escape when danger threatens. Originally residents of Central and South America, armadillos trundled into the United States from Mexico in the late 1800s.*

When does an armadillo leap straight up?

A wild armadillo busily grubbing for insects steadfastly ignores human observers. Let a dog crash onto the scene, however, and the "dillo" may explode three feet into the air like a toy snake from a can before running for its life, zigzagging to dodge its pursuer. Finally, it scoots into one of the many burrows veining its territory or stops to dig a new one, pelting the dog with dirt. Wedged firmly into its tunnel, the armadillo endures the frustrated dog's attempts to grasp its slippery hide and yank it back out.

Although clad in armor, the armadillo is far from invincible. Its bony carapace does enable the armadillo to thwart predators by darting into thick, prickly brush patches, but it's not tough enough to withstand the crushing fangs of a cougar or coyote. Nor can a nine-banded armadillo roll into a ball like its three-banded South American cousin. Even its pogo-stick leap is of no avail against its main modern-day killer: the car. After avoiding a car's wheels, a startled armadillo will often leap up and strike the undercarriage.

How can a horned lizard squirt blood from its eyelids?

Squat and prickly, a horned lizard is a difficult meal to swallow, and an animal that manages to down one successfully could risk a serious case of indigestion. The lizard gives fair warning of its unappetizing texture by inflating its body, turning itself into a miniature blimp studded with spikes. If this fails to dissuade an enemy, the "horny toad" then tilts to display its formidable array of horns and spines.

⟩ *An eyelid with a telltale crimson glaze indicates that this horned lizard has recently squirted blood from a pore above its eye to repel a fox or other potential predator.*

Inexperienced foxes or coyotes who ignore this show of bravado are likely to be blasted by the lizard's last line of defense: a javelin of blood, shot from one of its eyes, that can hit a target a surprising three feet away. An agitated horned lizard produces this eruption by constricting muscles that impede blood flow out of its head. As its blood pressure rises, blood shoots from an opening in the lid.

Zoo keepers and others who handle horned lizards rarely see them eject blood, even when

provoked. Dogs, however, readily spur the lizards to spray. The spiky creatures seem to reserve the ruddy blast for predatory mammals at least the size of a cat. Oddly, the lizards don't let fly at roadrunners, which regularly gulp them down. Just how the blood irritates the skin or disgusts the senses of mammals remains a mystery.

Horned lizards rely primarily on their camouflage to shield them from enemies. Their pebbly coloration and flat, fringed bodies help them disappear against the background of the Western deserts and dry grasslands in which they dwell.

How do octopuses and squids evade their enemies?

These quick-change artists of the deep have no peers in the animal kingdom. At the first sign of trouble, an octopus or squid will in a wink alter its color—to ghostly white, perhaps, or ominous black. Sometimes one startling change is enough to scare off such would-be predators as seals, sharks, dolphins, swordfish, and killer whales. If it isn't, another amazing permutation is in order—to virtually transparent nothingness for free-swimming squids, to wrinkled brown or maybe rough brick red for bottom-dwelling octopuses. One Florida octopus can even make one half of its body one color and the other half another color.

These instant costume substitutions are made possible by special skin cells containing pigments or chemicals that produce a variety of colors plus whitish colorlessness, iridescence, or eerily glowing bioluminescence. Octopuses also have muscles that vary their skin's surface texture.

If color change and camouflage aren't enough to end the threat, the octopus or squid can dig deeper into its bag of tricks. First, it will spew a dark cloud of ink into the water. Both decoy and smoke screen, the cloud contains enough scent to divert a predator while, unseen, the cephalopod squirts water out of its siphon, jet-propelling itself away from the scene. A squid will sometimes briefly flash its bioluminescent cells before blasting off, attracting a predator's attention to where the squid was but now isn't. A deep-sea squid, living in perpetually dark waters where black ink clouds would be of no benefit, squirts luminous ink when threatened, then retreats with lights dimmed. The luminous cloud continues sparkling long after the perpetrator has vanished.

The Ringneck's Ruse

The ringneck snake may get its name from its head, but it gets its reputation from its tail. The "ring" refers to the red or yellow collar sported by these woodland inhabitants. Though dull-colored on top, its underside is yellow or orange and red.

The ringneck's two-tone skin has a purely practical purpose. When zeroing in for the kill, predators tend to attack the head of their prey, where the greatest possible damage can be inflicted with one strike. A threatened ringneck snake curls up the end of its tail, flaunting its bright underside to divert attention from its head. Sometimes, it even rolls onto its back. Since red, yellow, and orange are nature's shorthand for "I taste bad," most would-be attackers take the hint and give up.

For those that persist, the ringneck has a second line of defense. The beleaguered snake emits a foul musk from glands in its anus. In any case, this is one yellow-belly that stands up to its enemies.

~ *Unrivaled master of camouflage, the octopus can change its colors almost instantaneously to suit its mood or to match its background—from the deep greenish browns of seaweed to brilliant blood crimson to the mottled blues and grays of a coral reef.*

❧ *Bold markings similar to its parents' provide good camouflage for a killdeer chick as it forages among the pebbles of a California beach. Killdeer frequently build their simple, inconspicuous nests—usually little more than slight depressions lined with bits of grass—on gravelly areas along beaches and roads. The young leave the nest soon after hatching and search for insects with their parents. The name* killdeer *is a phonetic imitation of the bird's call.*

Does a bold pattern help or hinder an animal?

While it's easy to see how the mottled plumage of a ruffed grouse or the cryptic bands of brown on a copperhead's back help these animals to hide, the strongly contrasting pattern of the killdeer would seem to be a distinct disadvantage. Its brown back is retiring enough, but its gleaming white breast is crossed by two heavy slashes of black, and there are stark patches of white on the forehead and around the eyes.

Far from standing out, though, this unlikely pattern actually helps the killdeer fade from sight. It is a dramatic example of what biologists call disruptive coloration—the same principle that military planners use when they paint heavy blobs and streaks on tanks and other equipment. The markings break up the outline of the bird's body, making it appear to be a jumble of unrelated forms and not something a predator would want to chase. Several other plovers, including the small semipalmated plover, rely on similar patterns. Even their downy chicks, fresh out of the egg, are covered with swirls and patches of buff, black, and white, which allow them to disappear among the pebbles and shells of a beach. (Disruptive coloration is most effective in open country, where bright sunlight produces harsh shadows.)

Other animals use colors and patterns to make themselves as obvious as possible. Venomous or toxic creatures advertise this fact through warning coloration—the red, yellow, and black bands of a deadly coral snake, the yellow-and-black pattern of many bees and wasps, and the toxic orange skin of the salamander known as the red eft. Many butterflies try to keep an eye on danger: fake eyespots formed by rings of yellow or white may fool a bird or lizard into thinking it, too, is being sized up by a dangerous hunter. What's more, predators often attack the heads of their victims, and a quick grab for a false eye may leave the hunter with a scrap of wing, and the butterfly tattered but alive.

Other butterflies and moths combine camouflage and bright colors. Resting on the trunk of a tree, an underwing moth banks on the excellent camouflage of its upper wings. But if a bird comes too close, the moth suddenly flashes its hidden lower wings, striped with red, orange, or yellow. The unexpected flash of color often startles the bird just long enough to allow the insect to escape.

Are opossums the only animals that "play 'possum"?

No sprint champion, a Virginia opossum faced with imminent danger will hiss loudly and emit a foul-smelling liquid. If this tactic fails, the opossum will topple over with eyes glazed and mouth open, its tongue lolling lifelessly. No other American mammals do this, but the hognose snake engages in similar antics.

Normally shy and retiring, and so docile it seldom bites even when handled, the hognose snake responds with a melodramatic flourish when threatened. Flattening its head and neck cobralike, the harmless, toad-eating snake hisses ominously and may lunge with open mouth as if striking. If bogus bellicosity doesn't send trespassers scurrying, the hognose snake will go into convulsive tremors, turn belly-up, and dangle its tongue loosely from a mouth spread wide. It's quite a death act, except that if you turn a hognose snake right-side-up, it will roll over again and resume a deathlike posture.

Why do musk oxen huddle together?

Whipped by freezing winds and blanketed in ice and snow, the tundra of Alaska and Canada is an inhospitable land in winter. Yet this region is the year-round home of musk oxen, the shaggy beasts so evocative of the Ice Age. Musk oxen actually seek out exposed areas where winter winds sweep away snow and make foraging easier. Long, dark coats with thick, fluffy underlayers of wool keep them warm even when the temperature plunges to almost –70°F.

Although winter's harsh conditions usually claim a few musk oxen's lives, their main enemy is the wolf. While a 700-pound bull with a helmet of horns is not easy prey, a pack of wolves can in fact kill a solitary male. What the wolves seek ardently are the soft-eyed calves; what they often find is a united front of horns and hooves. Bulls and cows crowd into a circle facing out, the calves bundled securely between them or in the circle's center. They may also back up against a cliff wall, horns out and calves behind. If the wolves press their attack, a bull may lunge out of formation and swipe at them. Any wolf hooked on a horn is flung into the air, then trampled.

When humans are predators, however, this strategy backfires. Musk oxen lining up for battle become targets in a shooting gallery. Years of persecution pushed the great beasts close to extinction by the early 1900s. Since then, musk oxen have rebounded thanks to protective laws, careful management, and release programs.

Feigning death, a hognose snake lies belly-up, with mouth gaping comically and tongue hanging limp. The hognose snake apparently thinks a dead snake is an upside-down snake. Once the coast is clear, however, it flips over and beats a hasty retreat.

Musk ox bulls, cows, and three calves circle in a united front against predators. If this maneuver isn't enough to ward off danger, the adults will squeeze the calves into the circle's center, and the dominant bull will charge any interlopers daring to approach the herd for a closer look.

Turf Wars *Trespassers, beware!*

How do birds protect their home turf?

To keep interlopers out of their territories, birds use everything from gentle reminders to aggravated assault. In most cases mere melodies are enough to ward off intruders. Songs are the most common form of territorial defense, and they are often backed up by threatening actions. Robins, for example, will greet uninvited guests by crouching, lifting their tails, and sprinting toward them. Other birds don't even wait for outsiders to approach. Red-winged blackbirds flash their crimson-and-yellow shoulder patches, and loggerhead shrikes flutter their white-marked wings—No Trespassing signs that are easily seen from a distance.

Territorial defense is usually used against birds of the same species. Birds have evolved habitat preferences, food choices, and foraging techniques that are largely unique to their species. A pair of American robins will willingly share a backyard with a pair of cardinals because the two species rarely compete for the same resources. Another pair of robins, however, would pose serious competition and would be quickly driven out. While males usually provide the most aggressive territorial defense, females can be surprisingly pugnacious. Among cardinals and American goldfinches, for example, males and females take on only those rivals from their own gender. In a match between birds of the same species, the invader almost always loses, perhaps because the resident has a home-court advantage or perhaps because it has a greater incentive to fight harder. For example, when a male warbler chases a trespassing neighbor across the invisible border between their home ranges, the tables are instantly turned, and the trespasser suddenly becomes the defender.

Nesting areas aren't the only territories defended by birds. Hummingbirds chase other hummers away from good nectar sources, and terns protect their exclusive feeding grounds. Although sanderlings will stake out a stretch of beach, they will defend it only if there's a certain amount of food available. Too little food simply isn't worth the effort, and too much makes competition unnecessary.

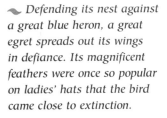

~ *Defending its nest against a great blue heron, a great egret spreads out its wings in defiance. Its magnificent feathers were once so popular on ladies' hats that the bird came close to extinction.*

Why don't bighorn sheep get hurt when they head-butt?

Bighorn jousts are an unforgettable sight to behold. One minute, two closely matched males may be sharing the same grazing space, seemingly unaware of each other. The next minute, they become dueling gladiators. Standing up on their rear legs with front hooves held high, they suddenly lock gazes and start to race toward each other at full steam. In the blink of an eye, their bodies drop (adding the force of gravity to the charge), their heads flick forward, and their horns meet with a resounding crack that can be heard more than a mile away. In such feats of strength, the two opponents may achieve a combined speed of 45 miles per hour. Though mildly dazed, they'll often go back to feeding as if nothing happened, but something has: the winner—whichever one didn't back down—is first in line for the females.

Despite the ferocity of such clashes, these males are able to escape injury because their skulls have two cross-connected layers that sandwich a number of large cavities. The horn's inner core, honeycombed in structure, is sheathed in a soft, bony material. All these features add up to one of nature's best shock absorbers. According to one account, two combatants collided 48 times in one day, with no ill effects other than blunted horns, broken noses, and quite possibly, splitting headaches.

What's the difference between horns and antlers?

Though the terms are often used interchangeably, horns and antlers are not the same. Horns, such as those found on mountain goats and bighorn sheep, grow continuously throughout the animal's life and are never shed. Antlers, such as the enormous racks grown on elks, moose, and caribous, are shed annually.

Hoofed animals (also known as ungulates) use horns and antlers like hats to attract the opposite sex, like lances to ward off predators, or like dueling swords to settle disputes. As hats, horns and antlers are quite popular with the ladies, since a large set indicates that the male is robust enough to compete for forage. As lances, horns and antlers can be lethal weapons. Even a pack of wolves may not challenge a healthy moose if the animal flaunts its antlers. As dueling swords, horns and antlers work in different ways. Horned animals, like mountain goats, use their short needle-sharp horns to settle boundary disputes, but for animals with antlers, this isn't very practical. They generally live in more open areas where a wounded animal would quickly attract predators, putting all at risk. Thus elks, deer, moose, and caribous lock antlers in usually bloodless wrestling matches.

➤ *Most duels between bighorn rams—like this encounter in Yellowstone National Park—are simple one-butt affairs, but some can last up to 25 hours.*

➤ *Weighing as much as 70 pounds, the rack of a mature bull moose requires as much energy to grow as a female invests in rearing a calf.*

Do insects have territories?

Though the sight of black swallowtail butterflies fluttering atop a grassy hilltop may seem peaceful enough, it represents one of the most intense territorial wars in the insect world. Among the largest butterflies in North America, the male black swallowtail (named for the two tail-like appendages at the base of its yellow-and-orange spotted wings) makes his springtime debut with one thing in mind: real estate. While waiting for females to emerge (usually three days later), he claims his turf, favoring the highest point in an open field. The stakes are large: without a patch of air to call his own, no female will approach him. So pugnacious is this charmer that virtually any dark shape that comes along—birds, dogs, even people—will be met by a blistering aerial assault.

Among butterflies the black swallowtail is not alone in his warlike ways. In fact, many types of insects have a fierce territorial instinct and will aggressively guard the ground or sky they call home. Male crickets vying for the same turf, for example, will try to outsing their rivals. Failing

➤ *With two pairs of rigid wings providing speed and maneuverability, the white-tailed dragonfly is well equipped to defend its turf.*

that, they resort to lashing one another with their antennae until one retreats. Male dragonflies (nicknamed "mosquito hawks" for their favorite food) exhibit some of the most spectacular displays of ritualized territorial struggle, as much dance as dogfight. When one male encroaches on another's hunting grounds (usually about 15 square yards over a pond or stream), the two chase each other in turn, zinging back and forth like a tennis ball. Rarely do they come to blows, which seems to be the point—sooner or later one will give up, and both can get back to business.

How do animals defend their territories?

When a bear scratches a tree trunk, it isn't to sharpen its claws but to mark its territory. A bear stakes its claim on an area by using its claws and teeth to gouge deep cuts into a tree. Another bear may challenge that claim by carving its own name, so to speak, into the bark. If the would-be usurper leaves scratches that are higher up on the tree trunk, the original tenant may vacate the premises, allowing the newcomer to move right in. Such a ritual is, in effect, the wildlife equivalent of a playground slam-dunk competition—whoever reaches the highest wins.

Animals use various methods (some nonviolent, others literally a matter of fang and claw) to mark and defend their territories. Most often, though, territorial wars are waged with sensory weapons. Two male short-horned grasshoppers contesting a territory will go sonic and engage in a battle of songs, droning and buzzing at each other until one of them finally tires and abandons the field. Bobcats, wapitis, and white-tailed deer go the chemical route, urinating repeatedly at designated spots to leave behind their scent. Sometimes a territorial signpost can send more than one signal. A bobcat's scent may ward off a potential rival or attract a mate. Either way, everybody gets the message.

➤ *A white-tailed buck sniffs a branch to find out whether the territory belongs to another buck. Adults have a strong, musky aroma, but their young are scentless—a natural defense against predators.*

What sparks animal rivalries?

The drive to reproduce is at the heart of nearly all conflicts between animals of the same species, and confrontations over breeding privileges provoke some of the most dramatic clashes in the natural world. When autumn paints the aspens yellow across the Rockies, for example, bull elks come into the rut—the annual mating season. Weighing 1,000 pounds or more, an adult may swagger beneath six-foot-long antlers, each sporting a half-dozen or more tines. Gathering a harem of cow elks, the bull defends them against rival suitors; he'll tangle with encroaching males when necessary but relies mostly on intimidation.

Younger males with smaller racks are easily routed, but if the herd bull is confronted by an interloper of equal size and strength, a fight may erupt. First, however, the opponents strut side by side, flaunting their enormous headgear like crowns. Suddenly they spin around and lock antlers, legs straining as they push mightily. The long, curved tines of the antlers sometimes cause severe injuries, accounting for the deaths of about 5 percent of the brawling males each year.

The rutting contests of bull moose are even more impressive—in part because the moose is

the world's largest deer, reaching up to 1,800 pounds and standing seven feet tall at the shoulder. Its vast, palmate rack, which may also span seven feet, figures prominently in elaborate brush-thrashing displays, which only occasionally lead to pitched combat.

Some of the fiercest battles occur among male seals and sea lions. Northern elephant seal bulls, guarding harems of 40 or 50 cows along the California coast, try to intimidate rivals with stares, bellows, and even body slams; when that fails, the 2½-ton bulls go chest to chest, inflicting bloody but rarely fatal bites. Breeding fights are not limited to mammals, of course. Male snapping turtles engage in rolling, muddy tussles in the shallow water of the ponds they inhabit, and male smallmouth bass spar with each other for the opportunity to fertilize a female's eggs, then defend the dish-shaped depression where they are laid.

↖ *Walruses use their tusks not only to defend themselves against polar bears but also to assert their dominance over rivals.*

↖ *Sparring between bucks is common among arctic hares (the biggest species in North America) prior to their mating season in early spring.*

Wooing in the Wild *Dances, serenades, and other courtship rituals*

Do animals mate for life?

Till death do us part is a promise that applies to few animals (including humans, cynics might add), but a select number of birds and mammals take the vow very seriously indeed. To these devoted partners, monogamy of the kind known by biologists as "long-term pair bonding" is the commitment of a lifetime and has distinct advantages for the survival of their offspring.

Mating for life is rare in the animal kingdom because in most species the males try to mate with as many females as possible in an instinctive effort to maximize their chances of reproducing. Sometimes, though, it makes better sense to stay with a single mate rather than play the field. One such circumstance is when females are scarce, and a great deal of effort is required to find new mates. Another is when the young are more likely to survive if both parents help in the challenging and time-consuming job of incubating, feeding, and protecting them.

Although long-term bonds are known to exist among several North American mammals, such as wolves, coyotes, foxes, and beavers, one must look to the skies to find our true monogamists: the birds.

Of all vertebrates, birds are the most consistently faithful to their mates, with nearly 90 percent of our species practicing some form of monogamy. Most birds, however, stay together only long enough to build a nest, incubate eggs, and feed their young; then they find new mates when it is time to nest again. Only a few species mate for life: the bald eagle, Canada goose, mute swan, tundra swan, and raven, among others. For these large birds the search for new mates over a large territory can be a long, exhausting process. So once they are mated, they tend to stick together.

For centuries stories have been told of eagles, geese, swans, and wolves that spend months or even years mourning the loss of their mates. Nevertheless, it is the urge to breed, not to grieve, that wins out, as successive pairings of bald eagles in New York State readily proved. The first male died, and the next year the female returned to her nest with a younger male. After successfully breeding, the female died, but her widower was soon seen paired with a new mate. Still, tales of lifelong mourning persist, perhaps revealing something about human attitudes toward monogamy. Divorce statistics to the contrary, we just can't resist a good love story.

Which animals keep harems?

Images of voluptuous luxury attend the word *harem*, but for male animals who keep harems, leisure is out of the question. Their breeding season is a time of constant vigilance, a tug-of-war between attending to females and challenging rival males.

Northern elephant seals clearly demonstrate the trials of the harem lifestyle. In early December bulls haul themselves onto a few Californian beaches, a month before the cows will arrive. They spend this time threatening and thrashing each other to determine dominance. The massive animals inflate their pendulous noses as they roar challenges at rivals. If this impressive display fails to dampen a foe's zeal, a battle ensues. The two-ton fighters slam their hefty bodies together, wrestling sumo-style and biting until the waves run red with their blood. By the time the cows join them, the bulls have established a pecking order. A top bull, or beach master, roams among a harem of up to 50 cows, mating with receptive females, ever ready to respond to their shrieks of outrage when low-ranking males approach them.

Inland, the American elk of Western mountain regions heralds the mating season with shrill whistles. Bulls shake majestic antlers at each other and bugle loudly as they compete for

~ *In a sensitive show of affection between lifelong partners, a pair of wolves sniff, nuzzle, rub, and grab each others' snouts just prior to mating.*

herds of cows. Once established as harem master, a bull elk must still confront other males who challenge him, and intercept any females eloping with a handsome stranger. By season's end the harem master is spent. He parts company with his bevy of wives and funnels what is left of his energy into surviving the winter.

Are there any marine animals that leave the sea to spawn?

In California the still of a spring evening is shattered as a moonlit beach begins to churn under a wriggling blanket of silver fish. Along Delaware Bay a balmy May night ticks with the clatter of thousands of horseshoe crabs scrabbling over each other on the shore. Each tumultuous scene is a mating frenzy, a riot of reproduction dictated by the ebb and flow of the tide.

The fish that flood California's beaches every two weeks from March to August are small, cylindrical creatures called grunion. They wash ashore a few days after the highest tides of the month, which attend each new or full moon. Females burrow their tails into the sand to lay eggs, which the males then fertilize. Afterward, the grunions cease struggling against the ocean's pull and flow back to sea. In another two weeks the surf will again hit the highest tidal line and sweep the newly hatched grunions into the ocean, too.

Horseshoe crabs crawl ashore during high tides in May and June. Males crowd the beach first, forming a scuttling carpet that may blacken the shore for more than a mile. The teakettle-size females trundle ashore next and are immediately engulfed by amorous males. After spawning, both parents return to the sea.

Over a million horseshoe crabs may throng the beach in breeding season as well as tens of thousands of migrating seabirds. These migrants consume tons of crab eggs as they fuel up for the remainder of their northward journey. In California, the grunions' breeding orgy also inspires a feeding frenzy: holders of fishing licenses may, during certain periods, catch as many grunions as they like, but only what they can grasp with their bare hands.

With a thunderous roar an elephant seal bull asserts supremacy over his domain. Between dueling with other males and mating, this 4,000-pound beach master will not pause to eat until the last cow slips back into the sea at season's end.

Having come ashore to spawn, a female grunion deposits her eggs at water's edge as circling males vie to fertilize them.

Why do ruffed grouse drum?

On a soft spring morning, when the plump, russet wood thrushes are singing their flutelike songs, a male ruffed grouse hops up onto a fallen log. Standing upright, his wide, banded tail flayed behind him, he begins to beat his wings—slowly at first, each flap making a muffled whump, then rapidly increasing to a whir, like an old engine sputtering to life and dying again seconds later. Like the thrush's melodic song, the drumming display of a male grouse serves two purposes: territorial defense and a way to attract a mate. Although ruffed grouse drum year-round, the activity reaches a peak during the spring mating season.

The bird usually selects an old, toppled log—though a rock or hummock will do in a pinch—in an area of forest with good visibility at ground level. If the drumming attracts a female, the grouse switches to visual display. Fanning his tail and drooping his wings, he completes the seduction with a show of black feathers raised around his head and the fleshy combs above his eyes glowing an orangy red.

Controversy long surrounded the mechanics of the grouse's drumming sound; some people thought it smacked the log with its wings or beak or clapped its wings together. High-speed motion pictures finally revealed the surprising answer: during its five- to six-second drumroll, the grouse's cupped wings flap forward and up, compressing air and creating a string of 50 or more tiny sonic booms.

➤ *To avoid being blown over backward by its own whirring wings, the ruffed grouse braces against a log with its tail and claws.*

Do animals ever change sex?

Change is constant in nature; mountains erode to plains, meadows mature to forests. Even gender, while it may seem permanent to humans, is subject to reversal; many animals change sex as casually as a bird replaces a feather, and in much less time. Nowhere is this truer than on a coral reef, where many of the most common fish—groupers, sea bass, parrotfish, and wrasses—can switch from female to male in a matter of hours. Some of the parasitic crustaceans these fish carry are capable of the same trick, as are shrimp.

Scientists call these gender-bending creatures "sequential hermaphrodites," because one set of gonads shrinks to insignificance when the other grows. (By contrast, "simultaneous hermaphrodites," such as land snails and earthworms, possess functioning male and female organs at the same time.) Along the Gulf coast and Florida's Atlantic coast, the blue-headed wrasse performs this reproductive sleight-of-hand easily. As it grows, a slender, yellowish female wrasse can mate with the dominant male on the reef, but when she gets large enough, she may switch sexes—and thus have the opportunity to mate with an entire harem, vastly increasing the number of her offspring. In fact, many female reef fish, particularly the largest in a group, will jump gender if males are in short supply: researchers once removed 58 male sea bass from a reef community, and 57 females changed sex, starting with the biggest.

What causes oysters to mate at the same time?

When a number of women in a circle of friends become pregnant at the same time, some wag is bound to remark, "There must be something in the water!" For edible oysters living along North America's coasts, this quip is no joke: there is indeed something in the water that stimulates an entire bed of the mollusks to spawn

➤ *All oysters are born as males. Amazingly, they can change their gender and may do so several times over the course of their lives.*

simultaneously. That "something" is a blend of hormones and ocean temperature.

A water temperature of about 68°F induces male oysters to spawn. As the sperm disperse, they emit chemicals that spur female oysters to release their eggs. From 10 to 100 million minuscule eggs gush from each female as the storm of fertilization progresses.

Such mating en masse may seem extravagant, but it is necessary if the oysters are to overcome their many predators, ranging from sea stars and hungry humans to that most appropriately named seabird, the oystercatcher.

Why does a narwhal need a tusk?

Spiraling to a delicate taper, the narwhal's hollow nine-foot tusk has excited speculation since the 11th century, when it was thought to be the magical spike of the unicorn. In fact, it is a specialized tooth, one of two that grow from the upper jaw of the male narwhal (the other tooth usually remains tiny, although double-spired whales have been seen). Scientists originally believed the tusk was too brittle for combat and theorized that it was used in ritual displays, to poke holes in the ice, spear fish, or even to

radiate excess body heat. In recent years, however, experts have concluded that it really is a weapon, noting that males with the largest, heaviest tusks—presumably the dominant bulls—also have the greatest amount of scarring on their heads from battles over mates. What's more, photographers and biologists have seen males crossing tusks like duelists ceremoniously touching sabers before a fight.

Narwhals, which reach a body length of 15 feet, live farther north than any other mammal in the world, inhabiting the Arctic Ocean from the pole to the islands north of Hudson Bay. Living in small family pods of a dozen or so, these brownish whales cruise the frigid waters hunting for fish and squid, but they gather each year by the thousands to migrate to their wintering grounds west of Greenland, where wind and ocean currents keep the pack ice at bay. If they need to break open a breathing hole, they do so with their round heads—not their tusks.

➤ Narwhals (top) are gregarious animals that socialize in groups as large as 2,000. Interactions between these exotic sea dwellers are not always peaceful, however, as this pair of sparring males (inset) can attest.

A Shark's Savage Embrace

It might look like the result of an overactive appetite, but when a male nurse shark chomps down on a female's fin, it is the urge to mate, not to eat, that drives him. Normally mild-mannered, these reef dwellers are anything but when it comes to breeding. The male first captures his reluctant partner by "inhaling" one of her pectoral fins. Then, with the thrashing female locked firmly in his jaws, he tows her to deeper waters to mate.

What do male birds do to impress females?

Grebes often incorporate gift giving into their courtship dances. Dipping their heads below the water, they gather offerings of moss or weeds for their intended.

For much of the year, the sage grouse is a modest, chunky bird whose grayish brown and black plumage normally camouflages it well on sagebrush-dotted plains. During the spring mating season, however, the male of the species turns into a flamboyant performer eager to advertise his presence with odd sounds and bizarre movements. Gathering to flaunt their finery, the males strut their stuff on a traditional "parade ground" called a lek. As many as 400 grouse may gather for this annual exhibition. Each male stakes out a small section of the lek, with dominant birds claiming the center. Ruffling their fluffy boas of white feathers, spreading their wings, and fanning their stiff, pointed tails, the birds strut proudly, both to intimidate other males and to attract females that enter the lek. Each male also inflates a pair of bulbous yellow air sacs on his neck, which wobble as he pumps air in and out to produce loud popping noises.

A male may spend several hours a day on the lek, but the female pays only one brief visit. After inspecting the swaggering suitors, she mates with her choice, usually selecting a fine fellow established on the central plaza. She then sets off on her own to nest and raise her young.

Other grouse also court hens with elaborate displays. Greater prairie chickens swell bright orange sacs on their necks, filling the air with booming calls as they stomp and circle on ancient lek grounds. In a swath extending from Alaska across central Canada to the Great Lakes, sharp-tailed grouse gather in grasslands and forest openings to shudder their wings, erect their tails, stamp their feet, and pirouette—all in the hope of wooing a potential mate.

Some native American peoples were so inspired by the stamping, shaking, bobbing, and posturing of grouse that they incorporated these movements into their own dances. Others emulated the graceful ballet of the whooping crane. Nearly five feet tall and clad in brilliant white plumage, this highly endangered crane is North America's tallest bird. After bowing to its partner, a whooper bounds three feet into the air and flaps its massive wings, inspiring its mate to leap and prance in kind. The ecstatic display seems to both celebrate and cement the lifelong bond that unites these graceful performers.

Why do seahorses dance?

The union of two seahorses begins with a delicate ballet performed in an underwater meadow of seaweed and eelgrass. Each fish brightens visibly as it nears its partner, trading its subdued gray or brown for a brighter hue; some species even don a gaudy red or orange. Both the male and female wind their tails around a single stalk of grass and gracefully circle their tiny maypole, letting go only to waft side by side toward another hitching post. This spinning and strolling continues until the male bows deeply to his mate. His gallant gesture, repeated many times, signals that he is ready to accept the female's eggs, for it is he who will incubate them.

After three days of courtship, the female strains her body toward the ocean surface, giving notice to her partner that her eggs are now ripe. The diminutive dobbins then float upward together. A slender organ called an ovipositor extends from the female into the slit of the male's brood pouch, and she swiftly lays her eggs. The male fertilizes the eggs as they pour into his pouch, which has grown thick and spongy in preparation for their arrival.

A female does not desert her mate during his "pregnancy." She stops by each day to engage in a brief reprisal of the mating dance with her big-bellied beau. Most likely, however, the male will be alone when the hatchlings spew from his convulsing pouch—a process that can go on for a day or more. Then the pair will soon mate again, beginning a new family as their herd of youngsters drifts away.

How do porcupines mate?

Very, very carefully, goes the usual explanation. But contrary to folk tales and ribald jokes, porcupines encounter no more hazards in mating than other mammals. They do not face each other with the wariness of warriors armed for combat, nor do they couple stomach to stomach to avoid prickly quills. The truth is, when a female porcupine is receptive to the advances of a male, she is scarcely armed at all. She relaxes her quills and lays them flat, arches her tail forward, and elevates her hindquarters to make it easy—and safe—for the male to approach.

One reason porcupine love is the subject of myths is because so few people have observed it. A female porcupine is sexually receptive for only 8 to 12 hours during a single day each year. Under ordinary circumstances both males and females are solitary animals, rarely seeking each other's company. But in the days before a female

enters estrus, males may follow her patiently, announcing their interest with a repertoire of grunts, moans, and coughs. The suitors may also rise on their hind legs and stagger around in a blatant effort to capture the female's attention. If she shows interest in a suitor, he will chase her and wrestle with her before mating. After coupling, the female drives the male off with aggressive hisses. Then, armed with her 30,000 dangerously barbed quills, she goes on her usual solitary way.

➤ *The gentle mating dance of these seahorses signifies a lifelong bond rather than a chance meeting. Only the death of a partner will separate a mated pair of these steadfastly monogamous ocean dwellers.*

➤ *Although encounters between courting porcupines are peaceful (below), the same cannot be said for competing suitors. During the breeding season, males do battle with tooth, claw, and quill in sometimes fatal contests over available females.*

Do walruses really sing?

A buck-toothed, bristle-faced, warty walrus bull with bloodshot eyes doesn't depend on rugged good looks to compete in the mating game. Instead, he sets the chilly waters of northern seas throbbing with song. The pulsing pattern he belts out intimidates rival males, though its effect on the cows has yet to be determined.

A singing walrus produces his underwater volley of loud knocks and soft taps for several minutes, starting or finishing with a ringing sound often likened to pealing church bells. How the bull makes these sounds is unknown, but he may be clicking his tongue to create pulses that resonate in his inflatable throat pouch. The wrinkly warbler then rises to the surface to breathe deeply and emit a few noisy thumps and whistles before diving to repeat his song.

Dominant bulls laying claim to a group of females seem to be the only singers. Any lowly male who dares to utter a few notes, whether he is part of a herd or a skulking intruder, is quickly silenced by his superiors. A mere flaunting of tusks usually suffices to stifle would-be performers, but fights occasionally break out.

All walruses in a given area sing the same rigidly structured song, yet there are always some variations. Young males may clumsily flub their lines, and experienced bulls occasionally add personal flourishes by altering their opening or closing phrases. It's often just enough to make individual singers instantly identifiable to researchers, if not to other walruses.

Why do most animals breed in certain seasons?

Breeding seasons are usually timed so the young are born when the weather is temperate and food abundant; imagine a young cottontail trying to find a meal in a blizzard or a bluebird foraging for insects in the bitter chill of November. Among mammals a long gestation period and infancy helps set the breeding schedule. For example, it takes about 6½ months for a white-tailed deer embryo to develop prior to birth and another 6 months for the fawn to grow to independence. By mating in autumn, the deer

↝ *After long dives in frigid waters, walruses come ashore to bask in the sunshine. Dominant herd members often crowd to the center, where they can best conserve heat.*

ensure their fawns will be born the following spring, with the summer and fall to grow and learn the skills of survival.

An animal's environment also determines its breeding season. Wood frogs, which inhabit shady woodlands from Maine to Alaska, spawn explosively in early spring, allowing their tadpoles to develop before the summer sun dries up their puddles of snowmelt. Fish often take a cue from the water temperature; when it hits about 60° F, largemouth bass and bluegills begin to court, the males luring big, egg-laden females to circular nests in the weedy shallows.

One animal that ignores the general rule about breeding in balmy weather is the great horned owl. This powerful hunter begins courtship in early winter, and the one to three eggs are usually laid in the icy depths of February, when even brief exposure to the cold can kill them. Despite this danger the owl chicks benefit from their head start when they leave the nest in late spring, learning to hunt at a time when the woods are full of vulnerable young prey.

Why do fireflies light up?

Not flies at all, the soft-bodied beetles known as fireflies make the summer twilight sparkle. While the constellations of dancing lights may look random to us, they are actually very precise signals from the flying males to females hidden on the ground. In fact, each species—there are more than 130 in North America alone—puts on its own unique show. One common variety flashes nine times in rapid succession while fly-

ing a level course; another repeatedly emits a single blink while dipping and rising in flight, painting glowing fish hooks against the darkness. Some only display for a short time just after sunset, while others go on long after full dark has settled in. Even the color of the flash varies among species—from clear yellow to greenish white or orange.

In a single meadow or backyard in the East (where fireflies are most common), several dozen species may take to the air at once. Somehow, a female firefly is able to sift through the confusion of twinkling lights and spot her species' signal. She answers with her own pattern of blinks, and the male zeros in to mate. While most fireflies flash in courtship, the females of a few species also light up to eat. One kind can imitate the blinking patterns of four other varieties of fireflies, tricking unrelated males into thinking they have found a mate. When an unsuspecting suitor lands, she overcomes and consumes him.

In one area in the Great Smoky Mountains of Tennessee, fireflies even synchronize their flashes, a phenomenon previously known only in Southeast Asia. Blinking in rapid bursts, they create waves of light that ripple along the hillsides.

The remarkable chemicals that make these light shows possible are luciferin and luciferase. Combined with oxygen in the firefly's abdomen, they create light with virtually no heat. In contrast, an incandescent light bulb squanders more than 97 percent of its energy as heat. Although scientists have long studied this super-efficient light system, they have yet to find a practical way to reproduce its cold fire.

Spawning from May to August in Eastern lakes and streams, pumpkinseed sunfish construct colonies of closely packed nests in shallow, plant-rich water. As in other sunfish species, it is the male of this pair who guards the eggs as they develop and hatch.

A little goes a long way when it comes to the firefly's built-in beacon. The glow of a single courting male is intense enough to enable a person to read a newspaper.

Raising the Young Caring for pups, cubs, kits, and hatchlings

How do sea otters keep their pups from floating away?

Unique among mammals, California sea otter pups are our original water babies. Born in the water, they spend nearly their entire first year either floating on their backs or riding on the chests of their floating mothers atop the open sea. Thanks to fluffy fur that traps air between their hairs, and large lungs that function like built-in flotation devices, these animals are virtually unsinkable from birth.

This great buoyancy allows pups to float on their own for six or more hours a day—an essential measure of independence, since their mothers must hunt often for sea urchins, abalone, and other types of shellfish. (Animals that live in cold water have a high metabolism to keep warm, so adult sea otters must eat the equivalent of 25 percent of their own body weight each day—6 to 20 pounds, depending on the individual's size.)

When the weather is calm and the currents are weak, mothers leave their babies floating on their own in open water. During strong swells, however, the young are placed in clear areas between kelp fronds to keep them from drifting off. In stormy weather mothers use seaweed to tether pups to their floating nurseries.

Why are so many mammals born blind and helpless?

There are vast differences in the ages at which young animals are ready to face life. The antelope-like pronghorn, which needs near-instant mobility to survive in a world teeming with cougars, coyotes, and other predators, runs with the herd just a week after birth. Yet for a variety of reasons, many other mammals experience a prolonged infancy.

Consider the opossum, America's lone marsupial (pouched mammal). Baby opossums arrive bean-size, hairless, and helpless because female marsupials lack a placenta, the sac that nurtures an embryo within its mother's womb. Instead, females have an external pouch, where the barely formed infants can suckle their way to viability, though first they must haul themselves into it on their stubby forelegs.

North America's bears—black, polar, and grizzly—all have placentas but still give birth to tiny infants. A 1,200-pound adult Alaskan brown bear (a grizzly) begins life as a mere one-pounder. Birthing cubs that look like four-legged gumdrops is actually a boon to the mother bear: she doesn't have the encumbrance of carrying large fetuses. Since bruins offer no protection to pregnant females, this is a decided advantage.

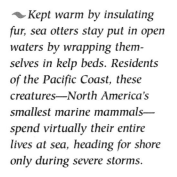

➤ *Kept warm by insulating fur, sea otters stay put in open waters by wrapping themselves in kelp beds. Residents of the Pacific Coast, these creatures—North America's smallest marine mammals— spend virtually their entire lives at sea, heading for shore only during severe storms.*

What makes ducklings so obedient to their mother?

Anyone who's ever tried to round up a handful of unruly youngsters can only marvel at a mother duck's ability to discipline her troops. Ducklings are adored for their habit of playing follow the leader, but they fall in line not out of choice but instinct. About 13 hours after they have pecked their way out of their eggshells, ducklings "tune in" to the world around them. During the next few hours, they become fixated on the first large, moving object they see—an attachment called imprinting. In the wild this is usually their mother, since other creatures are driven away by the time of hatching. Mistakes, however, do happen, and chicks will occasionally bond with an adult from the wrong species, jeopardizing their survival. Once imprinting has occurred, the ducklings faithfully follow their leader wherever she goes, though this response begins to wane as they mature.

How do alligators safeguard their eggs?

Though a female alligator may not look particularly maternal to human eyes, she actually is. Unlike most reptiles, which simply leave their eggs—or in some cases, fully formed young—in surroundings conducive to their survival, the alligator is a model mother.

Prior to laying her eggs, the alligator spends several days scooping up muck and vegetation in her powerful jaws and depositing them in a heap at the water's edge, where they will be fashioned into a nest about two feet high and five feet across. Periodically, she packs down the pile and moistens it with water that drips from her body after a swim. Once the nest has been completed, she mounts the top and, with her hind feet, digs a hole measuring about one foot wide by one foot deep. With her hind legs straddling the hole and her tail lifted, she lays up to five dozen eggs, then covers them with vegetation. But even then her work is far from done. For two months, as the eggs incubate, she guards the nest, warding off intruders by hissing at them with her jaws agape or—if they venture too close—charging at them. When the young hatch, they utter squeaky grunts that alert the female. This prompts her to bite open the nest, which enables them to emerge.

The moment their mother issues a loud danger call, these ducklings will quickly fall into formation, queuing up behind her.

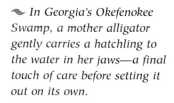

In Georgia's Okefenokee Swamp, a mother alligator gently carries a hatchling to the water in her jaws—a final touch of care before setting it out on its own.

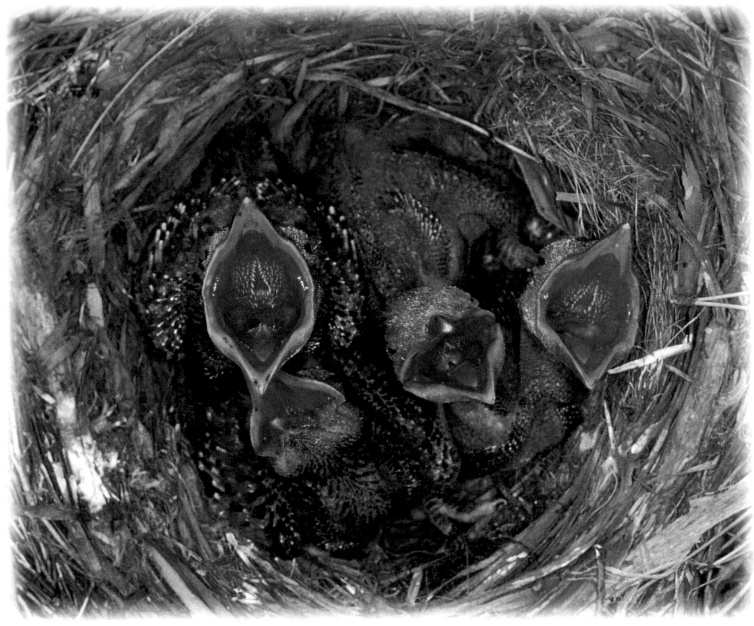

Fiery mouths agape, crow nestlings clamor for a meal as their mother approaches with a tidbit. Rather than trying to remember which chicks have been fed, the mother pokes randomly into an open beak. If the morsel isn't gulped down quickly, it's a sign that the youngster is full, which prompts the mother to pluck it out and pop it into another open beak.

Why is the inside of a bird's mouth so brightly colored?

On North Atlantic islands off the Canadian coast, where such largely black-and-white ocean birds as puffins, razorbills, guillemots, kittiwakes, and gannets return each summer to raise their young, the flash of a strikingly colored open mouth, or gape, commands immediate attention. The color of the gape varies—yellow in the Atlantic puffin and razorbill, red in the black guillemot and black-footed kittiwake, black in the gannet. However, the parental message it conveys is always the same: "Get off my turf."

In these crowded colonies, nesting space is at a premium, with the territory of a breeding pair limited to just a few square feet. When a neighbor steps over the invisible fence that separates one piece of property from another, posing a perceived threat to the occupant's eggs or chicks, the trespasser is sure to be greeted by a wide-open bill. In fact, in burrow areas puffins often engage in so-called gape contests. If the defender's silent roar fails to make the intruder back off, a fierce fight may ensue.

In the case of other birds, such as cormorants, a conspicuous mouth serves a different purpose: it makes a better target for feeding chicks, which thrust their heads into their parents' bills. Among nestling songbirds the role is reversed. The young birds' cavernous, brightly hued mouths make it easier for a parent to stuff them with food.

How do baby whales nurse underwater without drowning?

Within hours of birth, a baby whale begins to feed. Its mother, tilting her belly toward the infant, offers her newborn a nipple that protrudes from a mammary slit. The calf quickly grasps the nipple in the tip of its jaws, then wraps its tongue around it to form a kind of straw. This action stimulates the mother's mammary muscles to shoot a stream of milk into the infant's mouth. Because newborns instinctively know how to swallow without breathing, the infant can do this without the risk of drowning.

Unlike most newborn mammals, whales can't nurse for long periods; they need to surface for air regularly. When they start out, baby whales nurse for no more than a minute and a half. As they grow older—and better able to hold their breath—they nurse for several minutes at a time. (The world record is held by right whale yearlings, which can suckle for up to eight minutes.)

Because a newborn whale gets all its nutrition from its mother's milk during the first few months of life, the fluid must be high in fat and calories. The milk of a gray whale, for example, is roughly 50 percent fat—many times richer than cow's milk. Blue whale infants are so well nourished by their mother's milk that they grow by as much as 200 pounds in a day.

Why do mammals lick their young?

With the exception of ice cream cones and lollipops, people generally frown upon licking. But among less civilized mammals, licking is alive and well—as a means of investigating, communicating, and simply getting things done.

A wolf pup's first experience after birth is, most likely, being licked all over by its mother. This initial tongue bath serves a variety of purposes. It cleans the infant, provides comfort and reassurance, and helps mother and baby bond to each other by scent. Most important, that first good licking has the same effect as an obstetrician's slap on a newborn's rear: it encourages the pup to fill its lungs with air and begin breathing on its own.

The benefits don't stop there, however. Like many other mammals, wolf pups are completely helpless at birth—unable to see, hear, wag their tails, or even urinate and defecate on their own. By licking her pups, the mother stimulates their involuntary reflexes. This encourages the pups to relieve themselves in the wild and keeps the den clean and odor-free. Indeed, a spotless home is important for survival, since most predators find food by following their noses.

Some mammals, such as goats, actually label their offspring by licking them. This distinctive fragrance can be a valuable means of identifcation when the time comes for mom to pick her own baby out of a field full of kids.

The killer whale weans its young after 14 to 18 weeks, but the duration of nursing varies widely from one species to another. Fin, blue, and gray whales stop nursing after seven months, while right whales have been known to suckle—in rare cases—for as long as 15 years.

By nuzzling up to its mother's mouth, this wolf pup reinforces its familial bond and communicates that it's hungry. The mother will respond by regurgitating semiliquid food.

Are babysitters ever used in the animal kingdom?

Every busy mother needs some time to herself once in a while, and pronghorns are no exception. But unlike human mothers, who often face the dilemma of getting a babysitter on short notice, pronghorn mothers never have to worry about this problem. Like many animals, they use a system whereby another member of the group—an adult female, in most cases—keeps an eye on the kids while mom is away. This caretaking custom begins when the fawns are about two weeks old, at which point they and their mothers join together in bands called nursery groups. Although a substitute mother may have offspring of her own to tend to, she is often put in charge of as many as a dozen frisky youngsters at one time. Why or how a particular female is chosen for this extra duty is a bit of a mystery, especially since the females in a group may not even be related. (Among wolves the criteria are more obvious because the members of a pack are close kin, consisting of parents and several generations of offspring.)

Though equally effective, the form of babysitting favored by terns is considerably more haphazard. Terns nest on the ground in large colonies crammed with ever-hungry chicks. To keep themselves and their young well fed, adults must carry out repeated fishing expeditions. Nevertheless, some members of the colony are always left behind to protect the homestead.

Which bird makes the best father?

By and large, the animal kingdom is not the place to look for examples of fatherly dedication. The natural world is rife with males that at best ignore and at worst threaten their offspring. Yet some notable exceptions do exist. One is the Wilson's phalarope, a long-legged, needle-billed relative of the sandpiper. Bred on North American prairie wetlands, this bird winters in South America. It spends most of its time feeding on the surface of small ponds and bays, spinning about like a twirling top. Like his Canadian cousins, the red and northern phalaropes, the male Wilson's phalarope is passive in

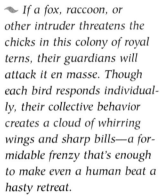

If a fox, raccoon, or other intruder threatens the chicks in this colony of royal terns, their guardians will attack it en masse. Though each bird responds individually, their collective behavior creates a cloud of whirring wings and sharp bills—a formidable frenzy that's enough to make even a human beat a hasty retreat.

courtship, during which he may be pursued by two or more females. But in his subsequent role as a father, he is a dutiful partner.

Among this species it is not uncommon for a female to have two mates and two nestfuls of eggs at the same time. The male may help the female in piecing together their home (typically a grass-lined hollow in a concealed marshland spot), or she may be the sole nest builder. But in what is surely one of the most unconventional sex role reversals in nature, it is the father that guards each nest and incubates its eggs. When the nestlings hatch some 20 days later, the male continues his surrogate role, rearing the youngsters without any help from his mate. He is soon enough at liberty, however, for the chicks gain independence in two or three weeks.

Why are animals so playful?

When a mustang colt kicks up its heels or black bear cubs stage a rollicking wrestling match, they are not just horsing around. Though some animals, such as river otters, frolic simply because they feel good or want to let off steam, play has a more significant role. For the young such antics provide practice for the activities they'll have to engage in as adults—hunting, courting, escaping enemies, and otherwise interacting with members of their own kind. In short, play is serious business. It not only stimulates the senses but builds the strength and endurance necessary for survival in the wild.

Generally, the more intelligent the animal, the more likely it is to engage in romping. Mammals, for instance, tend to have intricate patterns of play and spend more time in sporting activities than other creatures, particularly when they're young. Wolf cubs, cougar cubs, and pronghorn fawns may spend most of their waking hours having fun, always under the watchful eyes of adults. The rough-and-tumble grappling between wolf cubs enables them to establish a pecking order within their ranks, which later eases them into the hierarchy that governs the pack as a whole. Moreover, the cubs bond with one another, establishing a camaraderie that will cement the pack's solidarity in the future.

When a cougar cub pounces on a windblown leaf or waits in ambush for a litter mate, it's rehearsing tactics that, once refined, will enable it to stalk and bring down a deer. While juvenile predators are learning to hunt, the creatures they

stalk are honing their skills of evasion, though certainly not deliberately. When young pronghorns race across the landscape with wild abandon in wide circles, they are developing flight behavior that may one day save their lives.

Play also awakens the reproductive instinct. Often, submissive and dominant postures assumed by young animals correspond to those taken by adults during mating. When only a few weeks old, pronghorn males will lower their heads in a game of push and shove, just like adult bucks do when they joust for the right to mate with females. By and large, those animals that dominate the playing field turn out to be winners in the game of life.

Black bear cubs, among the most intelligent and curious of all mammals, practice their climbing skills. When they reach maturity, this prowess will prove invaluable for feeding.

How do unhatched chicks breathe inside their shells?

A chick in its shell is a little bit like an astronaut in a space capsule: protected from the harsh world outside, yet utterly dependent on its miniature environment for survival. An egg is one of nature's greatest marvels of engineering, supplying everything the growing chick could need or want: food, air, and a suit of armor to shield it from life's unrelenting hard knocks. The chick's food comes, of course, from the egg yolk, and the value of the protective shell is obvious. But just how does the chick breathe inside that impervious little package?

Despite its sturdiness an eggshell is actually porous, allowing oxygen and other gases to flow in and out. Air entering the egg is absorbed by a thin membrane that lines the inner surface of the shell. This membrane, rich in blood vessels, acts as a "lung" for the growing embryo.

As the chick matures, its respiratory demands increase. When the specialized membrane can no longer keep up with the chick's need for oxygen, it's time for the bird to hatch. A buildup of carbon dioxide inside the egg causes a sharp twitch in the "hatching muscle" at the nape of the bird's neck. As the chick's head jerks back, its beak smashes upward into the shell. This happens again and again until, finally, the chick breaks through the weakened shell.

➤ *With little fanfare two ring-necked pheasants make their debut in the world. They are able to peck their way out because of the shell's unique properties. Made of bullet-shaped crystals packed tightly together like stones in an arch, the shell becomes stronger as pressure is applied from the outside, but weaker when it's exerted from within.*

Are songbirds born knowing the tunes they sing?

Like human children who learn their first language from their parents, most songbirds develop their melodies by imitation. Baby songbirds, like human infants, are tutored in the cradle. The big difference is that only their fathers (and later in life, other neighborhood males) are role models, since females usually don't sing. Every time the father brings food to his offspring, he belts out a tune. Once they leave the nest, the young males endlessly rehearse it, quietly at first and then progressively louder. One researcher compared their earliest attempts at singing to the babble of a toddler, but eventually the sounds begin to resemble adult songs.

Except for a few species of mimics, such as mockingbirds and catbirds, songbirds can't learn a foreign language. Built-in constraints prevent a song sparrow from imitating the medley of an indigo bunting, for example, or a rose-breasted grosbeak from adopting the flute song of a wood thrush. If a male bird were to learn the wrong song, it would never find a mate and would never be able to defend its territory against intruders of its kind. One group of songbirds, the flycatchers, have relatively simple vocalizations that are encoded in their genes. For example, eastern phoebes reared in a laboratory developed normal "fee-be" songs even though they never heard another phoebe sing. By contrast, white-crowned sparrows raised under similar conditions did not develop their characteristic melodies. The brains of flycatchers lack the circuitry necessary for learning songs.

➤ *A virtuoso performer, the male song sparrow boasts up to 20 different melodies, with 1,000 or so variations.*

Do animals teach their young how to hunt?

Only mammals truly educate their young on how to find, stalk, and kill their prey. The ones that provide the most comprehensive education are carnivores, particularly foxes, raccoons, and otters. Theirs is a time-consuming task, but they have pupils that any teacher would envy. Born with a hunter's instinct, young animals are eager students, burning with the desire to search and destroy because it is branded into their genes. Moreover, some youngsters possess innate behavior patterns and reflexes—neck biting, leaping high, crawling low to the ground—that can be polished by their parents and perfected by practice. As soon as a red fox pup is strong enough to toddle out of its den, for example, it will pounce upon insects, trying to pin them to the ground between its forepaws so it can deliver a lethal bite. By following the example of its parents, the pup will eventually learn how to target a field mouse with astonishing speed and accuracy, though it often misses.

Foxes whet their pups' appetite for a predatory lifestyle one step at a time. First they bring food to the den. Then, when the pups become mobile, they leave it near the entrance. After that they hide a carcass (a rabbit or grouse, perhaps) several feet away, encouraging the cubs to use their senses to track it down. Gradually the adults drop food farther and farther away from the den, encouraging their young to venture out into the world beyond the burrow or hollow log where they were born. As they grow stronger, the pups accompany their parents on nocturnal hunting expeditions, exercising those senses that make them among the canniest of all hunters.

The North American river otter is faced with a double challenge. A mother must teach her young not only to catch slippery fish and frogs but to do so in the water, which her offspring are not particularly fond of. First she catches a fish or frog and takes it to the water's edge, where she shows the animal to her kits. Alert and inquisitive, they are entranced by the wriggling item on display. Then she releases it into shallow water, prompting the kits to charge after it in a wild, splashing pursuit. After myriad repetitions the game turns deadly serious. By the time they are eight months old, the young otters disperse in search of hunting waters of their own.

To raccoons trees are nothing less than the staff of life, providing dens where they are often born, nooks where they usually hibernate, and playpens where they learn to climb and fish. Tutored by their mothers in the warm months, youngsters enter their first winter well trained for life in the wild.

Cycles of Life *From newborns to adults*

A fine example of a sea star's regenerative powers, this misshapen individual is actually a severed arm in the process of sprouting four new ones. When its arms are fully grown, the sea star will look exactly like others of its kind. A sea star does not have a brain—only nerve cords running down each arm and a ring of nerve tissue surrounding the central mouth.

What animals can grow new body parts?

Fishermen who harvest stone crabs in waters off the southern Atlantic and Gulf coasts return their catch to the water after removing one marketable claw from each crab. Stone crabs (and other crabs as well) can grow new claws, assuring fishermen of a continuing supply.

Regeneration of body parts can help some creatures not only survive but also reproduce. A flatworm that loses its head or tail can sprout a new one, and a sponge can quickly replace a missing chunk—and in each case the scrap that has parted company with its owner can grow into a brand-new individual. (Unlike Humpty-Dumpty, a sponge can put itself together again even after being passed through a sieve!) A sea star's ability to grow new arms is legendary, but a detached arm can also grow into a new sea star. Until this fact was understood, some shellfish growers tried to rid oyster beds of sea stars by cutting them up and tossing pieces back into the sea, unwittingly multiplying the creatures they wanted to eliminate.

During regeneration, an animal's cells increase and differentiate just as if the creature were growing from scratch. Most higher animal forms cannot replace their more complicated tissues and organs. The creatures that can are usually lower forms without backbones. Some lizards, however, can reconstruct their tails, and salamanders can restore both tails and limbs. Sometimes, though, regeneration goes awry, producing a salamander with no tail and five limbs or a flatworm with a head at each end.

🐾 *Sporting impressive five-point antlers, a white-tailed deer buck looks up from his task of rubbing them against branches to scrape off their "velvet," now hanging in tatters. Antler size depends on age and nutrition.*

🐾 *The American alligator is the longest lived of the crocodilians, an ancient order of reptiles that includes crocodiles, caimans, and alligators. Alligators can live as long as 66 years, but crocodiles seldom survive more than 25. Like other reptiles alligators continue growing throughout their lives although the pace slows down as their age advances. The largest alligator on record was a Louisiana specimen measuring 19 feet 2 inches from the tip of its snout to the end of its massive tail.*

How do deer grow antlers every year?

The antlers that sprout like topsy from the heads of male deer each spring are created by explosive bone-cell growth. This wildfire cellular proliferation mirrors the multiplication of malignant bone cancer cells—except that the antler cells' progress is stringently controlled and results not in tumors but in headdresses of elaborate, pointed complexity. Antlers grow faster than any other bones except those of developing embryos. The cells that manufacture antlers surge upward and outward from a skin-covered ridge above the deer's brow. They are supplied with blood from the skull via a covering of soft skin called velvet. As fall approaches, the bone at the base of the antlers becomes so dense that blood flow ceases. The velvet dries, and the males scrape it off on trees.

Antlers are fully grown by the onset of rut, the time when male deer duel others over females. At rut's end antlers weaken at their bases, breaking off when they strike branches and rocks. It would seem, therefore, that the role of antlers is sexual. There is a rub, however. Female caribou have antlers, leaving scientists to ponder whether or not these bony crowns have another role, which humans haven't yet fathomed.

Which animals live the longest time?

Humans occasionally live more than 120 years, longer than any other mammals. Only a few whales, as far as we know, approach this age: fin whales may eke out 116 years, killer whales about 90. Among birds, parrots and swans enjoy life spans exceeding 70 years.

Most of the longest-living animals are amphibians or reptiles. Alligators can live 66 years; snapping turtles have been kept alive for 59 years. Box turtles, which usually measure around six inches, can live more than twice as long: one plodded on for 129 years. In fact, box turtles can outlive all but the oldest tortoises, some of which have survived over 150 years.

One invertebrate has a lifespan that challenges the tortoise's. The quahog, an Atlantic coast clam with a hard, rounded shell, may live about 150 years. Other invertebrates of note include lobsters, the longest-living crustaceans, which get bigger as they age. Since 35-pounders are about 50 years old, the largest lobster ever caught (off Long Island), weighing 44½ pounds, must have been older.

When it comes to longevity, though, colonial invertebrates are in a different league. Sea anemones, for example, have lived nearly 100 years without any signs of aging. Sponges have not only amazing powers of regeneration but also no apparent life span limits. They are, as far as we can tell, immortal.

With the ends of their abdomens linked, a pair of cecropia moths begins the mating process. The male (right) will pass a packet of sperm to the female during the time they're attached, usually one to six hours.

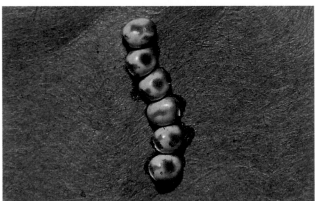

Once the female's eggs are fertilized by the male, she lays them on a tree or bush, gluing them in place with a sticky substance exuded from a duct in her abdomen. Each egg is about as big as a rounded pencil tip.

After a tiny black larva chews its way out of an egg, it feeds voraciously, molts four times, and eventually becomes a green giant (right) more than three inches long and thousands of times larger than it was upon hatching.

Having just emerged from her spun-silk cocoon, a female cecropia moth pumps fluid into her wings to expand them to their full size. Soon males will appear, attracted by her scent from as far away as a mile or two.

How does a caterpillar become a butterfly or moth?

"Everything is in a state of metamorphosis," wrote the Roman philosopher Marcus Aurelius, and butterflies and moths are a marvelous case in point. While the growth of fish, birds, and mammals is largely a matter of gradual increase in size and strength, the life cycles of butterflies and moths, and many other insects as well, are punctuated by a succession of completely separate stages—egg, larva, pupa, and adult. A visitor from Mars would be unlikely to see much connection between a creeping, leaf-munching caterpillar and a flitting, nectar-sipping butterfly or moth. Yet one becomes the other through an incredible process called metamorphosis.

The strange, double life of a butterfly or a moth begins in the egg at the very earliest stages of an embryo's development. Shortly after cells start dividing in the fertilized egg, a wave of complex chemical compounds spreads from an area in the embryo where the adult insect's thorax will eventually develop. These chemical messengers program certain cells for roles they will play in the larva's life. A second wave programs other cells for roles they will play in the insect's pupal and adult stages. Held in check by hormones, these "imaginal" cell clusters, as the cells destined to be a pupa and then an adult are called, remain for the time being in a state of dormancy, but the larval cells develop rapidly. Soon a fully formed but tiny caterpillar eats a hole in the eggshell and struggles out.

The caterpillar is essentially a food-processing machine that eats everything in sight, starting with its own abandoned eggshell. As it devours the leaves of the plant on which its egg was laid, its body swells, pushing against the walls of its tight outer skin. Eventually the skin splits, and a larger caterpillar steps out. Molting occurs four or five times during the caterpillar's life, and with each molt it nearly doubles in size. The larval body cells don't actually multiply; they inflate like so many balloons.

Just before its last molt, the caterpillar stops feeding and spins a cocoon of silk around itself or ties itself to a twig with a silk belt. Hormones that have been delaying the growth of the imaginal cells stop flowing. The caterpillar sheds its skin for the last time and becomes a pupa.

The term *pupa* comes from the Latin for "doll," and indeed, the pupae of most insects appear so doll-like and inert that perhaps *mummy* would be a better word. It is, however, the business of life, not the stillness of death, that fills the silent pupal cartridge. Inside, larval tissues are breaking down into a sort of cellular soup, providing raw materials for the imaginal cells, which are beginning to divide at a furious rate. The caterpillar's body along with its chewing mouthparts, stubby feet, silk-spinning glands, and leaf-processing digestive organs dissolves as the coiled, nectar-drinking proboscis, reproductive system, long limbs, sensitive antennae, and magnificent wings of a butterfly or moth develop.

Once the adult is completely formed, the pupal case cracks. The winged insect emerges, unfolds its damp wings, and allows them to dry in the air. A larval eating machine has been miraculously transformed into one of nature's most exquisite creations, a butterfly or moth. Totally dedicated to reproduction, it will rendezvous with a mate to fertilize eggs for the next generation, then die.

What happens when lobsters get too big for their shells?

When an American lobster is born, it is the size of a mosquito. That's an unpromising beginning for a creature that can reach a length of two feet or more and weigh over 40 pounds. Along with luck at avoiding predators and traps, a lobster needs quite a few changes in outerwear to be able to grow anywhere near that size.

Crustaceans such as lobsters and blue crabs lack internal skeletons like those of vertebrate mammals. A lobster wears its "skeleton" on the outside in the form of its hard shell. As a lobster grows, its body exerts increasing pressure on that rigid external armor until the shell splits, and the lobster wriggles free. All the while, a new shell has been forming under the old one. It remains soft for about a week while the lobster grows. During that time the animal is defenseless and avoids venturing from its hiding place to hunt for food, but it does eat. Using its claws to break up its discarded shell, it nibbles on the pieces and thus takes in calcium to help harden the new shell.

By the end of its first year, a lobster has molted 10 times but is still only two inches long. Even at the age of six, the creature weighs just a pound. Growth continues at a slower pace, finally tapering off so that an older lobster sheds its skin but once a year—that is, if it has avoided that picturesque but deadly predator the lobsterman.

How do tadpoles become frogs?

When tadpoles first hatch from their eggs, they don't look much like frogs—just minuscule globules with tiny whiplike tails. Look closely enough, though, and you can see beady little eyes, round, rasplike mouths, and feathery external gills. In short order tadpoles become egg shaped, with long flattened tails, their growing bodies covering the gills in the process. As tadpoles continue developing, their tails shorten, and they sprout hind legs and then front legs. Their mouths also enlarge rapidly as they switch their cuisine from algae scraped off submerged surfaces such as rocks and leaves to live insects.

Inside and unseen, lungs slowly replace gills, and long, coiled intestines necessary for strictly vegetarian diets shorten. This process of change from egg to larva to adult, called metamorphosis, also occurs among insects, crabs, and many other marine invertebrates.

Most frogs lay hundreds, even thousands, of jelly-coated eggs that are fertilized after being laid. Depending upon species and conditions, the eggs hatch into tadpoles 40 hours or up to 30 days later. The tadpoles become froglets in 12 days to three years—unless they become toadlets. (Scientists make no clear distinction between frogs and toads, but those that have shorter legs and drier, bumpier skins and that spend more time on land are usually called toads.)

Frogs and most toads lay their eggs in the shallow waters of bogs, ponds, ditches, and stream edges. A few toad species lay their eggs in puddles during rainy periods. The tadpoles develop rapidly within their eggs and hatch out as tiny toadlets. The white-lipped frog found only in the Rio Grande valley lays its eggs in puddles and then whips the gelatinous eggs and puddle water into a frothy mass. The hatching tadpoles live in their foamy nest until it rains again; then they writhe and wriggle the slimy mess to the nearest standing water, where they will transform into frogs. In drought years many puddle-laying toads don't breed at all.

~ Straddling worlds, two leopard frogs in the process of changing from tadpoles into adults rest on submerged tree leaves at a pond's edge. The one on the right has fairly well developed hind legs but no front legs yet, still feeds on algae, and breathes with gills. The one on the left has nearly transformed into a frog and needs only to reabsorb the remainder of its tail.

Why are mice so small?

"A wee, sleekin, cow'rin, tim'rous beastie" was poet Robert Burns' disparaging description of a mouse. Because they are relatively small and defenseless, mice are preyed upon by a legion of birds, reptiles, and other mammals, from shrews to bears. Because their bodies have proportionately more surface area from which to lose heat than those of larger mammals, mice must eat constantly to compensate for lost calories, consuming a third of their body weight daily—the equivalent of a 150-pound man eating 50 pounds of food every 24 hours.

Life for mice, then, is a never-ending struggle to eat enough and to avoid being eaten. Their diminutive size forces mice to live their lives in high gear, eating, breathing, and reproducing at a pace much faster than the animals that prey upon them. The very speed and intensity of their lives, however, are what ensure their survival.

Mice multiply so fast that they are the most numerous and widespread of all mammals, sometimes reaching population densities as high as 400 or more per acre. A female mouse begins to breed when she is only six weeks old. She may have six or seven litters of from four to seven young each in her short life of 10 to 20 months. If all these offspring were to breed in turn, one female could be responsible for as many as a quarter million mice born during her lifetime.

For mice the compensation for being small is that their bodily processes, including reproductive rates, run much faster than those of larger mammals. The amazing fecundity of mice outweighs the disadvantages of being pursued by hoards of predators and needing to eat all the time. Although small size may dictate a short and frantic appearance in nature's drama for a mouse, it guarantees a long and successful engagement for mousekind.

Are there animals that never stop growing?

If track and field stars possessed the skeletons of reptiles and amphibians, the record books might have to be rewritten. Unlike mammals these creatures have no unsurpassable upper limit to the sizes they can reach—and the reason for this lies in their bones.

All of our amphibian and reptile species, ranging from bullfrogs to garter snakes to American crocodiles,

A deer mouse nibbles on a carrot. Although primarily a seed eater, this omnivorous rodent consumes almost anything edible, from tender buds and leaves to insects of all kinds. Among the most widespread of North American mice, it lives from the dry grasslands of Mexico northward to the dark coniferous forests of Canada.

A bullfrog may live 20 years and reach nearly a foot in length, not including its equally long legs. Bullfrogs, like other amphibians and reptiles, continue growing throughout their lifetimes, although the pace slows considerably as they get older.

share an important skeletal trait. Their bones lack epiphyses, the "caps" that form at the ends of long bones in mammals and birds and which are joined to the bones themselves by cartilage during the animal's early development. When the epiphyses fuse with the main parts of the bones in early adulthood, maximum growth (though not weight, as most of us learn) is determined.

With no epiphyses to act as stop signs for skeletal growth, there are no theoretical limits to amphibian or reptilian size. But "theoretical" is the key word. There's a good reason why we don't live in a world of 50-foot rattlesnakes and bullfrogs the size of dairy cows. As these creatures age, their growth slows. Snakes, for example, grow quickly until they are sexually mature, at the age of two to five years. After that their growth tapers off.

The notoriously bad-tempered alligator snapping turtle of the southern United States can occasionally exceed two feet in length and weigh 200 pounds—but that would be one very old turtle, alive and lucky for decades. Ultimately it is time, not bone structure, that stops reptiles and amphibians in their tracks. As one biologist puts it, "They just die before they get larger than what we'd call ordinary."

How many eggs does an animal lay at once?

Sneaking quietly into her newly completed nest at dawn, a female robin lays a single pale blue egg in the mud-and-grass cup, then steals away again. She will return every morning for several days, depositing one egg each time until her clutch of four or five is complete. An oyster, on the other hand, takes a wholesale approach to reproduction, pumping microscopic eggs into the water by the millions.

The number of eggs a female animal usually lays at once depends in part on the size of the eggs. The smaller the eggs, the greater the number laid, and the less of an investment a mother has in each of her potential offspring. Mackerel, which simply release their fertilized spawn to the mercy of the ocean currents, will lay up to 50,000 poppy-seed-size eggs, and a cod up to 9 million. Frogs and toads produce gelatin-covered eggs by the thousands, each much smaller than a pea. A one-pound female box turtle will lay about 80 leathery-shelled eggs in a nest

dug in sunny ground, while a 1,000-pound sea turtle will drop about 100, the size and shape of Ping-Pong balls.

Almost all birds lay one egg every 24 hours or so, but the total depends on the species. Waterfowl and game birds, which face a host of natural enemies, compensate with big families—up to 28 eggs in the case of a bobwhite. Raptors, on the other hand, face fewer perils and have smaller families. Bald eagles average two eggs. California condors have a glacial reproductive rate—roughly one chick every two and a half years.

Why do birds molt their feathers?

Feathers, like clothes, wear out—only a lot faster than a pair of jeans. Wing and tail feathers in particular can become so tattered from brushing against foliage, branches, and the ground that a bird's flight performance is affected. Bright colors fade from exposure to sun and weather.

Because of such wear, birds replace some or all of their plumage at least once a year, and species that live in northern latitudes add extra feathers in late summer and early fall to help them stay warm in winter. Ptarmigans, hardy grouse that use their feathers for camouflage, have three sets of feathers to match seasonal changes in their Arctic and alpine habitats: white in winter, mottled brown in summer, and a transitional fall molt.

Flight feathers on the wings and tail usually are shed slowly and in pairs, one on each side, to preserve a bird's aerodynamic balance. Waterfowl, however, lose all of their flight feathers at the end of the breeding season. For several weeks ducks and geese are flightless but not helpless, since they can swim or dive to escape enemies. The males, moreover, temporarily molt into a coat of drab feathers and adopt the female's furtive manners. Some male songbirds, among them the scarlet tanager, bobolink, American goldfinch, and various warblers, also lose their colors after nesting. Until late winter, when a partial molt restores their courtship garb, birds of both sexes, all ages, and sometimes different species look very much alike, creating consternation and confusion among birders tracking fall migration flights.

➤ *Looking decidedly worse for wear, this male scarlet tanager is losing his handsome courtship plumage. After the fall molt is completed, he will be a dull green above and yellow below. His once resplendent scarlet and black markings are the most vivid of any American songbird's.*

Conquering the Cold *How animals survive winter woes*

Do bears truly hibernate?

While bears have long been associated with hibernation, theirs is not the deep sleep of such true hibernators as woodchucks, yellow-bellied marmots, and some species of ground squirrels. Rather, it's more like a long winter's nap.

A bear prepares for winter by putting on an extra layer of fat during summer and fall. When the days grow short and temperatures drop, a bear gets sleepy. Its head begins to droop, and its movements slow. Finally, the bear seeks out someplace warm and cozy. Grizzly bears make their own dens by digging a tunnel or deep burrow into the earth, while black bears look for a hollow tree trunk or a cave.

Once inside, a bear curls up on its side and slips into a state of torpor. Its heart rate slows from the usual rate of 40 to 50 beats per minute to as low as 10 or 12. During its stay in the den, a bear neither eats, drinks, urinates, nor defecates. Not all activity comes to a halt, however. A pregnant female gives birth in midwinter and suckles her cubs in the den until spring.

Bears are the only large mammals that become dormant in winter, but their lethargy never reaches the level of smaller hibernators, and their body temperature doesn't fall as dramatically. A sleeping bear can wake up fast if provoked, giving rise to the saying, "Careful, he's a real bear when you wake him."

➤ *Her cubs safely out of sight, a female black bear peers sleepily from her winter den. Unless she feels threatened, she will resume dozing until spring, when water from melted snow may well force her and the cubs to vacate their snug, underground cavity. Female black bears have from one to five squirrel-size cubs in January or February and nurse them for a month or two after leaving their winter dens.*

Why do some whales go to warm waters to bear their young?

The need to seek out a more nurturing climate for newborns is the reason behind the great whale migrations between the icy feeding grounds in the polar regions and the warm breeding grounds nearer the equator.

Expectant California gray whale females lead the way in the longest whale migration of all. Starting in late summer, they leave the food-rich Bering Sea and make their way down 5,000 miles of coastline to Baja, California, where in February they give birth in the warm and protective waters of shallow coastal lagoons. Full-grown males soon follow, and immature whales of both sexes bring up the rear.

Warm water is vital to the survival of baby whales. Much smaller than their parents, they have more surface area in relation to their volume than adults and lose heat much faster. They also lack the thick insulating layer of blubber that their mothers and fathers possess. If they were born in the frigid waters up north, the calves would quickly lose too much heat and die.

For these reasons nursing cows and calves are the last to leave Baja when the herds begin the second half of their 10,000-mile journey—the return trip north in spring. When they do travel, mothers and young stick to routes that take them through the warmest waters. Because seawater temperatures are usually higher near the coast, migrating California gray whales can often be seen swimming close to shore.

How do small birds survive harsh winters?

In the dead of winter, when Canada's vast coniferous forests are buried in snow and temperatures plunge far below zero, white-winged crossbills often are busy doing what other birds do only in summer: nesting and raising young.

Many North American songbirds, of course, flee in autumn to the tropics, where they feast on insects and ripe fruit. But the mostly seed-eating species that stay behind—crossbills, evening grosbeaks, purple finches, pine siskins, and others—have few problems coping with cold or deep snow so long as they are well nourished and have a sheltered place to sleep. They just need to find enough food during the short daylight period to replace the energy burned the previous night—and to build a reserve for the long, dark hours of the night ahead. A bird that goes to sleep hungry will die if its body temperature drops too low.

In years when there is a bumper seed crop, crossbills will breed year-round, even in January. These plump finches use their crossing upper and lower bills to force apart spruce cone scales so that they can remove the seeds with their tongue. They eat as many as 3,000 kernels a day.

In the case of the common redpoll, a frost-and-strawberry finch that lives at the edge of the tundra where winter nights are the longest and coldest, the bird stuffs a special storage pouch in its esophagus with high-caloric birch seeds just before dark. The food is digested while the redpoll sleeps, like fuel flowing to an automatic furnace. "Little redpolls can survive at –60°F if they have plenty of food," a scientist reported. Some years, however, catastrophic seed crop failures occur, causing spectacular mass movements, or "irruptions," of redpolls and other boreal birds to areas far south of their usual haunts.

To deal with changing winter weather conditions, songbirds use a repertoire of survival tricks. Chickadees lower their body temperature at night, significantly reducing their food demands. In daytime, resting birds shiver to increase heat production, and on sunny days they perch behind windbreaks and soak up solar radiation. Stay-at-home species such as cardinals also wear additional feathers in winter. They fluff their extra-thick plumage when they are roosting at night to create an insulating air layer and tuck in their beaks to breathe the warmed air.

Sheltered sleeping places are critical for wintering birds. Cardinals, tree sparrows, and juncos take refuge in dense evergreens at night; chickadees, nuthatches, and woodpeckers sleep in tree cavities; bluebirds pack together in nest boxes; and snow buntings in Alaska plunge into snowbanks, where the temperature two feet down can be 40 degrees warmer than it is at the surface.

Fluffing up his feathers to create insulating air spaces, a male cardinal perches on the ice-glazed branches of a crab-apple tree. Songbirds such as cardinals have more feathers per ounce of body weight than larger birds to compensate for their tendency to lose heat faster. They also wear from 10 to more than 20 percent more feathers in winter than in summer.

Two nearly half-grown polar bear cubs snuggle with their mother during a snow-storm. Only two pounds, blind, and nearly hairless at birth in December, polar bear cubs spend the first three months with their mother in a snug snowbank den, warmed by her body heat. When they emerge from this cozy maternity ward in early spring, they have dense coats of fur to protect them from the Arctic chill.

What land animals can brave the cold the best?

Unlike humans, animals can't just pull on sweaters and coats when the temperature plummets, so many of them have developed remarkable adaptations that let them forage, hunt, and even sleep through some of the most hostile weather on earth.

Caribous are protected from subzero Arctic temperatures by thick winter coats consisting of long guard hairs and fine, crinkly underfur. Even their noses and ears are covered by dense fur, and tufts of hair growing between their toes shield their fleshy footpads from the frozen tundra.

Like caribous, arctic foxes rely on dense fur to protect them from the polar cold. These small, white foxes can snooze in the snow at −50° F. Hair-covered paws and unusually stubby ears give off little precious body heat, and a luxuriant coat of fur traps insulating air. Scientists have found that an arctic fox can maintain its normal body temperature for an hour even in a labora-tory deep freeze set at −144° F!

Only one other land animal besides the arctic fox has what it takes to venture out in the win-ter darkness on the frigid ice pack surrounding the North Pole: the polar bear. These lumbering giants are double-wrapped against far-below-zero temperatures by four inches of blubber and heavy fur with six-inch hollow guard hairs, which channel solar heat to the bears' dark skin, add buoyancy when the bear swims, and shed water rapidly when it emerges from the sea. On land the polar bear's dense undercoat insulates it so effectively that there isn't even enough body heat given off to be visible on infrared film.

The polar bear's large size is an advantage, too. With more bulk in relation to its surface area than smaller bears of temperate and tropical lands, a polar bear tends to lose less heat from its skin. But the nomadic bruin pays a price for its ability to retain heat. Even at a slow trot, its body temperature can soar, which is why polar bears are seldom in a hurry.

Which creatures use "antifreeze"?

When exposed to very low temperatures, the water in an animal's blood and tissues tends to freeze, with death being the unfortunate result. Some animals, however, have evolved a way of surviving even the coldest winters by using a natural antifreeze remarkably like the green liquid some drivers pour in their automobiles' radiators.

Many insects, including field crickets and woolly bear caterpillars, start manufacturing a substance called glycerol in fall as the weather turns cooler. Glycerol is similar to glycol, or car antifreeze. When their cells are permeated with this fluid, these creatures can spend the winter in a supercooled (but not frozen) state. With the coming of spring, the insects warm up, and glycerol production is suspended.

Some other animals actually freeze solid during cold weather. Tree frogs, spring peepers, and wood frogs all spend the winter under moss or leaf litter, where temperatures can fluctuate across a wide range. While their cells are protected by the same antifreeze insects use, much of the fluid outside the cells freezes hard as a rock during hibernation. The term *spring thaw* has special meaning for these amphibians, which literally thaw out and come back to life when warm weather finally arrives again.

How do seals and walruses keep warm in Arctic waters?

Fat, fur, and nifty thermoregulation tricks keep seals and walruses warm in the frigid northern waters of Alaska and Canada.

The ringed seal, the smallest seal in North America, lives on the Arctic ice. An envelope of blubber, a very poor heat conductor, prevents its body warmth from escaping into the frigid waters of the Arctic Ocean. In late autumn 40 percent of a ringed seal's weight of 150 to 175 pounds is blubber. In early summer, however, when it is basking in the midnight sun and fasting, the layer of blubber melts to about 23 percent of its body weight.

An old male walrus may weigh as much as 3,000 pounds, with heat-retaining blubber accounting for a third of this bulk. His body has only a scant covering of hair, but its thick, wrinkled hide is an extra buffer against cold currents as he roots out clams, crabs, and other ocean-bottom food.

In contrast, the northern fur seal of the Pribilof Islands in the Bering Sea has no blubber at all; its luxurious, waterproof fur traps a cushion of warm air and furnishes protection in waters as cold as 30° F. Its large flippers, however, are not fur covered; heat loss is reduced by a network of blood vessels running side by side. Cool blood in veins leaving the flippers is warmed by fresh, arterial blood flowing in adjacent arteries.

➤ *With her newborn pup dozing behind her, a female harp seal peers from a breathing hole in the Arctic ice pack. Although the pup lacks heat-retaining blubber and would quickly die in the icy water, its thick, white coat keeps it sufficiently warm as it lies on the ice. Nursing on its mother's fat-rich milk, the pup will gain over five pounds a day during its first nine days.*

A woodchuck emerges tentatively from its burrow on a mild afternoon in early spring. True hibernators, woodchucks do not store food but depend on an ample layer of fat to get them through the winter. As they sleep, they slowly burn away this fat, losing from 17 to more than 50 percent of their body weight by spring.

How do hibernating animals know when to wake up?

A hibernating animal such as a snake, a bat, a ground squirrel, or a turtle has a built-in alarm clock—the hypothalamus—that tells it when it's time to go to sleep or time to rise. Located deep within the brain beneath the cerebral hemispheres, the hypothalamus is a nerve center that functions somewhat like a thermostat. It reacts when the weather grows cold by triggering a slowdown in an animal's metabolic rate. Breathing slows and body temperature falls. The animal lapses into a dormant state, living off stored fat for weeks or even months.

With the onset of spring, the hypothalamus senses the change in temperature and triggers the animal's heating system. The rise in body temperature coincides with an increase in heart rate, respiratory rate, and oxygen consumption.

For most animals the process of awaking from winter sleep is rapid and involves sudden and great increases in bodily activity. The heartbeat of a woodchuck, for example, will jump from 4 or 5 beats per minute to 200 times per minute within two hours. Despite months in hibernation, a thirteen-lined ground squirrel takes only about an hour to wake up once the heating process starts. Brown bats are even speedier: they're ready to fly within 15 minutes!

How do butterflies survive cold northern winters?

Butterflies dancing through falling snow! What a wonderful sight it would be!" With these words a Japanese poet painted long ago a dream of delicate beauty. Such a dance, however, would be one of death for the butterflies, which survive winter either by taking cover or by escaping the season's icy grip.

The vivid orange-and-black monarchs migrate to warmer climates, but most butterflies must wait out the chill by hibernating under flaps of bark or in crevices of walls and buildings. Sheltered from cold and protected by a natural antifreeze that prevents their cells from freezing and rupturing, these sleeping beauties draw on stored fat for their reduced energy needs. This strategy works for the mourning cloak, though sunny days may lure it from its cozy nook to spread its yellow-rimmed purple-brown wings.

Many butterflies hibernate as chrysalises, tiny purses of life that wait for spring before bursting open like buds. Camouflage shields them from sharp-eyed birds: the tiger swallowtail, so conspicuous as a yellow-and-black adult, resembles a bit of wood as it dangles from a twig, and the brown chrysalises of the little spring azure butterfly seem to vanish in the leaf litter.

Butterflies may also endure the season as caterpillars or even eggs. The great spangled fritillary, the color of fire and ash as an adult, finds a cozy niche to hide in after hatching as a caterpillar and eating its eggshell in autumn. Viceroy caterpillars make tubular sleeping bags by rolling up leaves and binding them to twigs with silk. In Arctic regions some species ride out two winters as crawlers before earning their wings.

How do frogs breathe when hibernating underwater?

When days grow short and nights get cold, animals leave town, prepare for winter, or simply close up shop. Robins fly south to wait out the weather in tropical warmth; squirrels store nuts and seeds to sustain them until spring. Other animals, including frogs and toads, sleep the winter away.

Ready to hibernate, a bullfrog swims to the bottom of a pond, where it burrows into the soft mud. There it will remain, motionless and barely alive, until spring's balmy temperatures telegraph a wake-up call.

In warm weather frogs must breathe to survive, but when the mercury dips below 40° F, they develop an amazing ability to take in oxygen without breathing. The frog's skin is permeable and contains a network of fine capillaries that pick up oxygen from the water and transfer it to the bloodstream. Waste products such as carbon dioxide diffuse out of the skin the same way. By "breathing" through its skin in winter, a frog gives its respiratory system a vacation. In fact, a frog can make it through several months of hibernation without using its lungs at all.

Which animals store food for the winter?

Humans aren't the only members of the animal kingdom that believe in saving for a rainy day. Hundreds of species of insects, birds, and mammals put food away to help them make it through the winter.

By storing food, animals avoid having to migrate or hibernate or hunt for food when pickings are slim and the weather is at its worst. By having a good supply on hand when their hungry young are born, animals also help to ensure the survival of their species.

When it comes to storing food, squirrels are among the biggest hoarders. Red squirrels, for example, store their favorite delicacy, white spruce cones, in piles called middens. A single midden typically contains two to four bushels of cones—anywhere from 13,000 to more than 30,000 cones. Flying squirrels don't stint when making deposits to the food bank, either. Biologists estimate that a single flying squirrel may sock away 15,000 nuts during harvest season.

Chipmunks take food storage to even greater heights. Like stereotypical misers who distrust banks, chipmunks stuff their mattresses with food, piling up nuts and grains so high that their leaf- and grass-covered beds nearly touch the ceilings of their basketball-size sleeping chambers.

Other small mammals store food, too. Kangaroo rats and pocket mice transport seeds in cheek pockets. Pikas, which resemble guinea pigs, create "haystacks" in mountain meadows in late summer. When the piles of stems and leaves dry, the rodents carry several pieces in their mouths at a time to burrows, for use in winter.

Rodents sometimes become stored food themselves. Foxes and wolves bury mice and other prey in shallow caches. Saw-whet, great horned, and boreal owls have found a clever way to turn their winter catch into frozen dinners. They drape freshly caught rodents over tree limbs, allowing them to freeze, thus preserving them for future use. When the owls grow hungry, they simply thaw the frozen meals by sitting on them and incubating them like eggs.

An acorn woodpecker (top) perches on an oak trunk amid a stash of acorns. Common in Western states, this woodpecker digs holes in tree bark and stores an acorn in each one for retrieval in winter. *Its cheek pouches bulging, a chipmunk (above) carries two acorns to its burrow, where it may store up to six quarts of food for winter.*

Beating the Heat *Strategies for keeping cool*

Do animals perspire?

As the mercury rises, people become perspiration factories. Hundreds of tiny sweat glands spring into action, producing a watery liquid whose evaporation quickly cools the body. Sweating is fine for humans because they have relatively little body hair, but furred and feathered creatures need a more effective cooling system, since even those animals that do have sweat glands don't have nearly enough to cool them off. During the dog days of summer, the chief coping strategy used by animals is panting—quickly breathing in air through the nose and exhaling warm air through the mouth. As air flows over the maze of moisture-covered surfaces inside the nose, it cools them by evaporation. Further evaporation takes place each time the animal exhales, as air streams over its moist tongue. Animals with long noses and large tongues, such as wolves and foxes, have the most efficient cooling systems of all.

Can desert animals survive without water?

Water may be the elixir of life, but when it comes to drinking, some desert animals just say no—or so it seems. While no animal can live without replacing the fluids lost through normal activity, some quench their thirst by pulling moisture practically out of thin air.

The quintessential teetotaler is the kangaroo rat, which manages to survive in the withering desert without drinking a single drop of water. By scurrying around at night, the rodent protects itself from heat and sunlight. Gathering seeds, the animal stuffs them into its bulging cheek pouches, then stores them in a tiny underground den. The water content of these seeds and the by-products of digestion combine to treat the diner to a one-dish meal of food and beverage. Water loss is prevented by the rat's nasal passages, which squeeze moisture from each tiny exhalation and send it back into the animal's body. Thanks to its efficient kidneys, which excrete a highly concentrated form of urine, this creature makes optimum use of the small amount of fluid in its body.

For some desert animals the minuscule amounts of water provided by morning dew are all that's needed to satisfy their modest requirement for moisture. Carnivores often get adequate liquid from the body fluids of their prey, while herbivores rely on the juices of succulent plants. One of the best examples of such moisture misers is the chuckwalla, a prehistoric-looking lizard that "drinks" almost entirely through the leaves, buds, and flowers it consumes. Once ingested, this liquid is stored in the form of lymphatic fluid.

The unusually large ears of this Kansas jackrabbit, nearly twice as long as those of its Alaskan cousin, serve as a built-in cooling system in hot weather. When temperatures soar, more blood flows to the rabbit's ears, which are equipped with a vast network of veins. As the skin becomes warm and flushed, excess body heat dissipates into the surrounding air. Settlers of the Southwest dubbed the animal "jackass rabbit" (later shortened to jackrabbit), but its lean, lanky body and long legs are the hallmarks of a hare.

How do birds cool off?

To appreciate what it must be like for a bird to keep cool in hot weather, imagine going for a walk in midafternoon on a sunny day in August—wearing a down coat. Feathers furnish the best insulation nature can provide, which is great news for birds during the winter but a bit of a problem in summer.

For most birds the solution lies as close as their feet. Lacking feathery insulation, their feet and legs lose heat rapidly, giving birds a natural cooling system. Just as we can cool off quickly by taking a dip, birds can do so by wading in water, which chills their legs and feet more than four times faster than air.

Other strategies for chilling out include panting, ruffling feathers, and most important, staying out of direct sunlight. Songbirds, for example, take a siesta in shady trees during the hottest hours of the day. Gulls and other birds that nest out in the open employ a different strategy. Throughout the day these birds keep turning to face the sun, ensuring that only their white, reflective plumage gets the full force of its rays. The cleverest trick of all for beating the heat may be the one used by California gull chicks: they simply stand in the shadows of their parents.

What do desert toads do to escape the summer heat?

When alarmed, the spadefoot toad wiggles backward into the soil while digging furiously with a horny knob on each of its hind feet and—in a jiffy—disappears into the earth. The toad's burrowing skills not only help it evade predators, but enable it to survive in conditions that few other amphibians can tolerate. In the desert, temperatures over 100°F are lethal to most amphibians, which quickly shrivel up in hot, dry air because they get moisture by absorbing it through their skin rather than by drinking. Spadefoot toads, however, are unique in that their relatively thick skin is neither as moist as a frog's nor as dry as a toad's. They spend most of their lives in underground burrows (where the temperature is lower and the moisture level higher), thus cutting down on water loss and gaining an edge in their arid habitat.

No toad adapts to the whims of the desert better than the spadefoot. If the humidity drops even a few percentage points, this resourceful creature will drive itself deep into the soil, sometimes as far as a dozen feet below the surface. When a toad stays underground for a long time, its metabolism slows down so much that the animal requires hardly any nourishment, oxygen, or moisture. Some spadefoots stay this way for 90 percent of their lives, surfacing only during short, heavy rains, when they gather in droves at puddles to reproduce in rapid-fire fashion. While most frogs and toads take weeks or even months to evolve from egg to adult, some spadefoots complete this process in just a couple of weeks. By the time the puddles in which they were born and bred have evaporated, they are able to breathe. Then, after feeding for several days, they vanish into the shelter of the cool, moist earth.

Like vultures, wood storks use a radical method of cooling off when water isn't available for wading: they squirt liquid excrement on their bare legs.

The spadefoot toad conserves water by spending much of its time several feet beneath the broiling surface of the Sonoran desert, where it lounges in relative coolness. In summer, however, the subtle vibrations of thunder or raindrops coax it out to breed. Soaking in rain-fed pools or in mud, the animal absorbs water through the thin skin of its lower surface.

Mysteries of Migration *Birds, herds, and more*

How do migrating animals return to the same place every year?

Some birds have the uncanny ability to find their way across the globe, often traveling with pinpoint accuracy to their summer and winter homes. In one study red knots (banded for identification) were found nesting in the same Arctic hollows and feeding on the same Argentine mudflats year after year. Hoary bats return from the Gulf states to within a few hundred yards of their capture in Ontario.

Although several towns have capitalized on the unflagging fidelity of certain species—most notably the cliff swallows of San Juan Capistrano, California, and the turkey vultures of Hinckley, Ohio—individual birds can also be astonishingly faithful, reappearing to nest in the same wood lots, perhaps even the same tree. Like a person who can maneuver safely through his own darkened living room, a bird familiar with its surroundings can navigate more easily. It knows the best feeding areas, the safest spots to nest, and the quickest escape routes. Small wonder that the older and more experienced the bird, the more likely it is to return to the same place each year.

Youngsters, on the other hand, usually head for the far horizon. In one study more than half of the adult tree swallows observed came back to their territories in subsequent years, but fewer than 2 percent of their chicks did. Juvenile dispersal is common among most animals, for it helps species colonize new areas while reducing the chances of inbreeding.

🦋 *Western monarchs roost at Natural Bridges State Park in California. As caterpillars they feed safely on poisonous milkweed, which protects them from being eaten by birds and other predators.*

Memories of local landmarks may help returning birds find their territories, but monarch butterflies operate solely on an instinctive map. The itinerary of America's most populous—and popular—species of butterfly, the monarch, remained somewhat of a mystery until fairly recently. No one knew exactly where they stayed in the winter months after heading south by the millions (at speeds of up to 75 miles per hour in supporting winds). One day in early 1975, a Toronto scientist named Fred Urquhart, intrigued by a tip that monarchs had been spotted during the winter months in the Mexican highlands, climbed 9,000 feet into Mexico's Sierra Madre. There he found a type of fir tree he had never before seen, one completely covered with a curious black-and-orange coloration that occasionally moved in slow waves, even when no wind was blowing.

Suddenly, Urquhart knew what he had found: monarch butterflies from half a continent away had found a winter refuge. Chilly enough to keep them in partial hibernation, the high altitude of the mountains preserves their body fat, fueling their return trip back north in the spring. Urquhart had discovered the missing piece of the puzzle. Relying on some inner navigational impulse, millions of monarchs head every fall for several small areas in the Sierra Madre that provide hibernation room for all. Then, with winter on the wane and the sun gradually warming up their bodies, the butterflies turn north. Whoever gave the monarch its name was wise indeed, for it commands widespread admiration for its grace and majesty.

Interestingly, the monarch is a generational migrant: no single butterfly completes the entire 2,500-mile marathon. Those born in late summer head south in autumn, migrating from the eastern United States and Canada to converge on fewer than a dozen tiny fir groves in the Mexican highlands—a stunning feat of navigation. They depart in March, but most die in the Gulf states after laying their eggs, leaving the next generation to finish the trip north across the eastern half of the continent. These soon die as well, and in fall their offspring's offspring begin the cycle anew—drawn back to a place known only to their great-great-grandparents.

What do animals do to prepare for migration?

They eat—voraciously. Although migrants face many dangers on their journeys, perhaps none is greater than the risk of running out of energy before the trip is complete. So in the weeks leading up to departure, they start feasting. Many North American songbirds that must travel to Central and South America each year, such as the gray catbird, switch in autumn from a high-protein diet of insects to a high-fat diet of berries and other fruits. Not just any fruit will do, however. The birds target dogwood, spicebush, and sassafras, whose fruits contain up to 35 percent lipids—the perfect fuel. In the weeks before migration, sandpipers and other shorebirds may double their body weight, stretching their skin like overinflated balloons.

Because migrants burn so much energy, refueling stops may be critical. Some kinds of shorebirds, which travel tens of thousands of miles each year, vault from one feeding spot to another. But timing is crucial. Around the end of May, just as more than 1½ million migrating shorebirds descend upon the region, horseshoe crabs jam the beaches of the Delaware Bay to lay their eggs. Having flown without rest from South America, the birds feast on the tiny, pale green eggs, laying on enough fat to carry them the rest of the way to their Arctic nesting grounds.

At the other end of the scale is the Swainson's hawk, which travels from the northern Plains in huge flocks each autumn, journeying as much as 5,000 miles to Argentina. The hawks are believed to fast during much of their migration, perhaps because it would be difficult for these grassland raptors to hunt in the dense forests of Central America. If this is true, it makes an already remarkable migration simply astounding.

Is every migration an extended journey?

Traveling from one pole to the other, crossing and recrossing the Atlantic in a giant figure eight, the arctic tern is the undisputed champion of migration, racking up some 22,000 frequent flyer miles each year. Other North American birds travel almost as far. The bristle-thighed curlew, for example, travels from Alaska to Polynesia and back. Not every migration is an odyssey, though. Some animals—including some species of birds, such as wild turkeys—cover distances of only a few hundred yards. Each spring, frogs and toads travel to and from their breeding ponds in a matter of hours or even minutes.

Northern birds that are normally sedentary or that migrate only short distances may flock south in years when their food supply is inadequate; bird watchers eagerly wait for such "finch winters" to bring a wealth of siskins, grosbeaks, and other boreal finches. When lemming populations plummet in the Arctic (an event that occurs about once every four years), the ghostly snowy owls that feed on them may wander as far south as the Gulf states to find mice instead.

For mountain animals, including bighorn sheep and the large jay known as Clark's nutcracker, escaping the woes of winter means traveling only a few miles downhill to a more temperate climate. Oddly, though, at a time of year when many other species are moving downhill, the blue grouse of the Rockies is heading in the other direction. When snow arrives, the grouse migrates on foot from the lowlands up to the conifer forests, where there are spruce and fir needles aplenty to satisfy its winter diet.

A crustacean conga line? Not exactly. These spiny lobsters—having depleted their local food supply—gather together in the weeks leading up to migration. By marching across the sea floor in single file, they can shield each other's vulnerable abdomens from lurking predators.

Though a far cry from the legendary journeys taken by arctic terns, the relatively short trek made by wild turkeys from their summer range to their winter range is also an example of migration.

Which reptiles migrate?

Looking like windup toys with outsize limbs, newly hatched green turtles scrabble out of their sandy nests, down the beach, and into the ocean. Two to three decades later, when they've reached sexual maturity and are seized by the urge to procreate, they will return with pinpoint accuracy to the very same shore. Guided perhaps by scent or by some mysterious magnetic faculty, the green turtles that cruise the warm seas of the world cross vast expanses of open water as they migrate between feeding and breeding grounds.

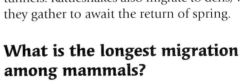

The southeastern shores of Florida beckon a small number of green turtles home to breed. Mating takes place in the water; then the female crawls ashore to deposit her eggs—a heartbreakingly laborious effort. The paddle-shaped flippers and broad shell that enable the four-foot-long reptile to glide gracefully in the water are, unfortunately, ill suited for maneuvering on land. Weeping salty tears and sighing heavily, she lumbers up the beach to a point just above the high-tide mark, where she scoops out a bowl with her hind flippers and fills it with about 100 golf-ball-size eggs. After burying them, she returns to sea, leaving in her wake a tractor-tread furrow through the sand.

Loggerhead turtles also migrate to breeding grounds. Those that winter off the coast of Florida may swim as far north as Virginia Beach to lay their eggs, while others head for shores along the Gulf of Mexico. Unlike their vegetarian cousins, loggerheads prey on a wide assortment of sea creatures, devouring everything from sponges to the highly venomous Portuguese man-of-war.

Though most land-based reptiles are homebodies, desert tortoises do migrate from summer feeding grounds to winter tunnels. Rattlesnakes also migrate to dens, where they gather to await the return of spring.

What is the longest migration among mammals?

On land, the barren ground caribou of the Arctic take top honors as long-distance travelers. These gray-brown deer migrate hundreds of miles between summer and winter ranges, with some herds making round trips of up to 1,600 miles. In July the animals begin

their time-honored move south, following ancient trails carved into soil and rock by previous generations of caribou. The scraping and scratching of their hooves, together with the clicking of their tendons against anklebones, gives this march an almost musical quality. After spending the winter sheltered in the coniferous forests of Canada and Alaska, the caribou head north to the wide expanse of the tundra to birth their calves and feed on the lush vegetation of the brief growing season.

For sheer distance no migrating land mammal rivals the gray whale. In fall these 40-ton giants begin their 6,000-mile journey from the fertile feeding grounds of Alaska's seas to the warm lagoons of Baja, California. After months of feasting on crustaceans dredged from the northern sea floor, the whales—thick with blubber—are prepared to fast as they steam south. Youngsters may dawdle along the way, but pregnant cows have a single-minded purpose: to complete the seven-week trip and give birth in the shallow waters of the sheltered lagoons. At winter's end the whales turn their barnacle-covered heads northward again.

Gray whales swim close to shore, affording whale watchers along the Pacific Coast a good chance of spotting them. Patience may yield a glimpse of the great beast's frothy spout or, for those who are lucky, the stirring sight of a breaching whale as it heaves three-quarters of its body out of the water, then crashes sideways with a mighty splash.

Do all birds use the same means of navigation?

To human eyes the air seems empty and featureless, but to a migrating bird it hums with navigational clues—both visible and invisible. A bird on the wing faces two problems: orientation and navigation. An American redstart in the Yucatán, for example, must first pinpoint its location in the world, then determine a course that will take it back to an aspen thicket in Maine. On the familiar ground of its home territory, the bird's memory of landmarks is believed to be an important factor. But during migration the guideposts are largely instinctive, and not every bird uses the same techniques.

Birds that fly at night, including warblers, orioles, thrushes, and most other songbirds, orient themselves according to the setting sun and the

constellations. Those that travel by day—hawks, swallows, jays, and hummingbirds, among others—use the position of the rising sun as well as major landscape features, such as mountain ranges, river valleys, and coastlines. Nonvisual clues may also play a role in navigation. Birds seem to have an extraordinarily sensitive internal compass that is finely attuned to the earth's weak magnetic field. One recent theory suggests that birds may even be able to see this magnetic field by detecting its effects on polarized sunlight. Although most birds are thought to have little or no sense of smell, storm-petrels and other seabirds find their nests each night by sniffing them out. Whether scent plays a role in migration, however, is still unknown.

Migrating birds, such as this Baltimore oriole, may capitalize on their ability to hear ultra-low-frequency sound waves, which carry thousands of miles. Flying down the middle of North America, a bird may be able to chart its course by hearing the roar of the Atlantic in one ear and the moan of Rocky Mountain winds in the other.

Reaching speeds of up to 45 miles per hour, a flock of Canada geese slices the sky with its familiar arrowlike formation. While this shape has become synonymous with Canada geese, these birds actually fly in various configurations—a straight line, a double or triple arrow, even a random jumble.

Why do Canada geese fly in a V formation?

It is the very symbol of the wild: the V formation of Canada geese, honking musically as they cross the sky every spring and fall. But why the arrow shape? It's long been assumed that Canada geese and other large migrating birds arrange themselves into a V-shaped pattern because of its aerodynamic advantages. The wings of a bird in flight create a downwash and an upwash of air, with most of the upwash concentrated behind and just beyond the tips of the wings. A bird that follows in this upwashing air is lifted slightly, encountering less drag than it would if it flew solo. With the exception of the trailblazing bird in the lead, all the members of the flock should gain an advantage from the bird ahead, thus saving energy during long flights.

The V formation is efficient, however, only if the birds fly within about one-quarter wingspan of one another and position themselves with their wings slightly overlapped. Since geese in a flock are seldom that close or spaced apart that precisely, the purpose of the formation remains a mystery. It could be that geese organize themselves in echelons simply because the arrangement allows each bird to see clearly, avoid collisions with its neighbors, and stay securely within the flock.

How do salmon find their home rivers?

After years of swimming and feeding in the ocean, a salmon heads for the very spot from which it hatched: a patch of gravel in a fast-flowing stream far inland. Logjams, water-falls, and dams may block the way, but none can deter these determined fish. Pulled by the ancient urge to migrate upstream and spawn, a salmon bursts from the water, clearing one hurdle after another with heroic 12-foot leaps.

While a primal tug may motivate salmon, scent is the lure that guides them. Salmon are able to locate their birthplace—within yards—by smelling the unique odor of the stream's soil and vegetation. That something so subtle can summon a salmon home is amazing enough. Yet some scientists believe the fish may also be able to detect chemicals released into the water by a previous generation that had struggled against the currents of the same river.

Swimming across the ocean to the mouths of rivers, Pacific salmon cover daunting distances. By the time it thrashes into a northwestern stream, a chinook salmon may have logged over 2,000 miles. Inevitably, such grueling journeys take a toll. The fish die soon after spawning, providing a feast for scavengers. Atlantic salmon, however, often survive the rigors of migration. They drift back to the sea to feed and renew their strength for their next upstream journey.

What signals birds to migrate?

Nature's precision timepiece, the sun, sets the biological clock not only for birds but for virtually all living things. The waxing and waning of daylight through the seasons govern every-thing from the timing of repro-duction to the molting of feathers. The ratio of sunlight to darkness also tells a bird when it's time to migrate. As spring approaches, daylight lasts longer, triggering physiological changes in the bird. Within the span of two weeks or so, it develops an enormous appetite, resulting in a buildup of needed fat reserves for the trip north.

Yet birds do not set off blindly. These natural-born meteorologists judge the weather to fine-tune the timing of their departure. Unseasonably cold weather will delay northbound migration in spring, as will abnormally warm weather in the fall. Robins, among others, ride the coattails of the spring thaw line as it creeps north across the continent and uncovers worm-rich lawns. In autumn, songbirds wait for the falling barome-ter and northerly tailwinds of a cold front to push them along, while in spring, when many must cross the open waters of the Gulf of Mex-ico, they rely on the warm southerly flow of high pressure off the Atlantic coast for a lift.

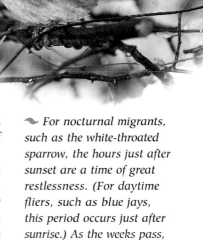

For nocturnal migrants, such as the white-throated sparrow, the hours just after sunset are a time of great restlessness. (For daytime fliers, such as blue jays, this period occurs just after sunrise.) As the weeks pass, the agitation grows until the bird can wait no longer to migrate.

In the clear waters of the Adams River in British Columbia, hordes of sockeye salmon return to their birth-place. Despite their vast numbers, these fish spawn in a relatively small area. In one nearby streambed, half a million salmon teemed in 269 acres of water.

Poisonous Animals *Secrets of chemical warfare*

Are black widows our most dangerous spiders?

One unexpected benefit from the invention of indoor plumbing was a decline in black widow spider bites. This glossy, inky-black spider, with its trademark red hourglass on the abdomen, has a fondness for dark nooks—such as the gloomy holes of old outhouses. Today most people bitten by this spider, North America's most venomous, are attacked while placing unsuspecting hands under picnic tables or into stacks of firewood, piles of trash, or other sheltered spaces where it lurks. The spider injects tiny amounts of a virulent toxin that attacks the nervous system. This venom is particularly potent to humans, producing severe abdominal cramps sometimes mistaken for appendicitis. Fortunately, the minuscule dose rarely results in death, and only about three fatalities are recorded each year.

In much of the southern and central United States, a greater hazard is the brown recluse spider. While not as venomous as the black widow, the spindly legged recluse is often found in and around the home—in basements, closets, and other dark, undisturbed areas—and its bite produces a festering ulcer that may grow for months, leading to gangrene if it is left untreated. Also known as the fiddlehead spider for the distinctive violin-shaped marking on its carapace, the recluse is creeping its way to colder climes and has been found as far north as Maine and the Great Lakes states.

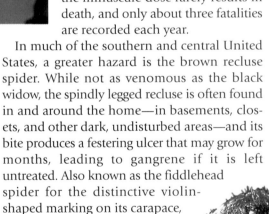

◆ *Despite its fearsome reputation the infamous black widow is, at best, a reluctant villain. Unless protecting her eggs, the widow usually prefers to flee from an adversary rather than inflict her deadly bite.*

What insects inflict the most painful stings?

Harvester ants, fire ants, and Southern paper wasps are all worthy contenders for the title King of Sting, but the tarantula hawk often tops entomologists' lists as North America's most painful stinging insect. Only the velvet ant, however, has earned the nickname "cow killer" for its ferocious wallop. Bristling with dense, brilliant red, orange, or white fur, these fuzzy, wingless wasps pack an impressive arsenal: an excruciatingly painful venom delivered via a stinger that can reach nearly half the length of its inch-long body.

Unlike a honeybee's barbed stinger, which can be used only once (it tears loose in the target mortally wounding the bee in the process), the smooth-shafted weapons of wasps such as the velvet ant and the tarantula hawk can be plunged into a victim repeatedly, compounding the suffering. Aside from the pain and swelling they cause, these venoms can trigger severe allergic reactions and, in the case of highly sensitive individuals, even result in death.

Despite legend the sting of the velvet ant is rarely fatal—even to cows. For most victims the pain fades within a few hours, though the memory it leaves may last a lifetime.

◆ *While the wingless female velvet ant (right) delivers a sting rumored to be strong enough to kill a cow, the winged male has no stinger and can be handled without fear of injury.*

Which sea creatures are the most venomous?

Though a jellyfish is 96 percent water, the remaining 4 percent can make life mighty unpleasant for any poor soul who happens to bump against it—especially if the swimmer tangles with the sticky, purplish tentacles of the Portuguese man-of-war, a jellyfish relative and one of the most potent stingers in North American waters. Actually a colony of organisms rather than a single animal, the man-of-war catches the sea breeze with its blue, football-size float, trailing 50- to 100-foot-long tentacles embedded with millions of venomous barbs. Although the slightest brush with these microscopic harpoons can result in crippling pain, muscle cramps, and paralysis, the man-of-war's deadly reputation is undeserved: the only documented death from its sting came as a result of a heart attack, not directly from the venom.

More dangerous are sea wasps—small, glassy jellyfish with boxy, inch-wide bells and short tentacles—found along the southern Atlantic and Gulf shores. Sea wasps are easy to miss, and their potentially fatal stings are often attributed

to the man-of-war. Sea nettles, another type of jellyfish, drape long tentacles behind a saucer-size disc, their painful stings threatening swimmers as far north as Cape Cod. A similar hazard is the lion's mane, the world's largest jellyfish. Ranging from Alaska to Southern California in the Pacific, and Maine to Florida in the Atlantic, this majestic creature grows a bell up to 10 feet across, with tentacles more than 120 feet long.

Other poisonous animals abound in the ocean, particularly in the warm waters off Florida's Atlantic coast, the Gulf coast, and California, where stings, barbs, and spines are a common defense against predators. Long-spined black urchins protect themselves with foot-long, venom-coated needles that can cause stinging and swelling. The spiny dogfish, a shark common along both coasts, injects a mild poison through barbs at the base of its dorsal fins, a tactic also used by several saltwater catfish. Found along the Pacific and Florida coasts, the scorpionfish, which looks more like a barnacle-ridden lump of stone than its landlocked namesake, lives up to its fearsome moniker with spines that can deliver a potent sting that's not soon forgotten.

➤ *Stingrays sometimes lay hidden on the sandy sea bottom, posing a poisonous threat to those who invade their shallow-water habitat. Each ray is armed with a long, wickedly serrated spine sheathed in a sack of venom. Should an unfortunate wader step on a hidden ray, the otherwise docile fish lashes out with its vicious weapon. The spine can embed itself in a leg or foot, tearing through its sheath and flooding the jagged wound with toxin. Although extremely painful, such attacks are rarely fatal.*

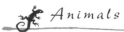

What are North America's most dangerous snakes?

Our continent is home to 22 species of venomous snakes, and determining which ones are the most dangerous is no simple task. A small, mildly venomous species that bites the torso of a young child may be more life-threatening than a larger, more potently poisonous snake that bites the ankle of an adult. The outcome of a snakebite depends on several important variables, which can combine in countless ways: the size, condition, and temperament of the snake; the age and physical condition of the victim; what part of the body is bitten; whether the venom enters a muscle or a vein; the speed and quality of medical attention provided; and most important, the amount of venom injected.

Moreover, the venom itself varies in toxicity from species to species; an untreated bite from a copperhead is rarely fatal for an adult, while an equal dose of cottonmouth venom is a much more serious concern. Coral snakes have exceedingly poisonous venom, but they are so reluctant to bite that many 19th-century naturalists thought them nonvenomous. All these factors notwithstanding, three species stand out as especially dangerous to humans: eastern and western diamondback rattlesnakes and the Mojave rattler.

At up to eight feet long, the eastern diamondback is the largest venomous reptile in North America. At home in the pine and palmetto flatlands along the Southeast coastal plain and Florida, this boldly patterned giant is coming into increasing contact with humans as its habitat shrinks. The smaller western diamondback slithers across a wide swath from Texas to southeastern California; it is responsible for most of the 12 to 15 snakebite deaths reported each year. Both diamondbacks are fairly aggressive when cornered and are capable of injecting very large doses of highly toxic venom.

Like the western diamondback, the Mojave rattlesnake dwells in the high desert from west Texas to southern California. While neither as large nor as common as the diamondback, the Mojave's bite packs a powerful punch, combining the tissue-destroying properties of pit viper venom with toxins that attack the nervous system. The venom of the Mojave rattlesnake is up to 10 times as potent as that of the diamondback, but fortunately the Mojave rarely bites people. In fact, about two-thirds of the snakebites reported each year in the United States involve people trying to catch, kill, or handle venomous snakes. Because snakes rarely bite unless they're cornered or provoked, avoiding a confrontation is often as easy as walking away.

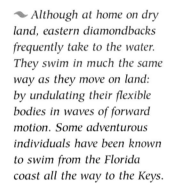

Although at home on dry land, eastern diamondbacks frequently take to the water. They swim in much the same way as they move on land: by undulating their flexible bodies in waves of forward motion. Some adventurous individuals have been known to swim from the Florida coast all the way to the Keys.

What keeps a bombardier beetle from exploding?

When a bombardier beetle gets so angry that it comes to a boil, it keeps itself together by blowing off a little steam—literally. These peculiar creatures, half an inch long with bluish backs and reddish legs, are found across most of North America. One reason for their success may be a remarkable chemical defense system that would seem more at home on a tank than an insect.

The beetle's weapon is a pair of glands, each equipped with a chemical-filled reservoir and a smaller, heavily reinforced reaction chamber. When the bombardier is attacked—say, by a bird grabbing its leg or a toad about to snap it up with its sticky tongue—muscles squeeze the large reservoirs. This forces hydrogen peroxide and a chemical known as hydroquinone into the adjacent reaction chambers, where they mix with enzymes stored there. It's a volatile combination. The liquid instantly reaches its boiling point, and with an audible pop it belches out of tiny nozzles at the tip of the beetle's abdomen. Scientists have discovered that this defensive spritz consists of up to 12 separate explosions, each just two-thousandths of a second long.

What's more, the bombardier beetle can pivot its nozzles as a tank does its gun turret, precisely aiming the scalding spray into the face of a would-be predator. Few linger for a second dose.

Are some animals resistant to snake venom?

In the shuffle of evolution, snakes lost their limbs, but many gained an advantage that made claws or hooves unnecessary: a venomous bite. Whether prowling a steamy bayou, a shady pine forest floor, or a rocky desert flat, these snakes possess glands in the roof of their mouths that dispense toxins and enzymes capable of paralyzing, killing, or even digesting prey—all while the snake lounges about.

The snakes' deadly bite, however, is not foolproof. A few animals (notably, opossums, raccoons, king snakes, and woodchucks) have evolved a chemical defense that renders snake venom harmless, allowing them to tangle fearlessly with these slithering foes. Rice, roof, and hispid cotton rats are also resistant.

Just how these wily animals can survive a snakebite that would fell a full-grown man remains a mystery. Doctors have long tried to unlock this chemical secret in hopes of developing a more effective venom antidote for humans. Current antivenins (the serums used to counter venoms) are produced by injecting horses with venom and extracting the antibodies that form in their immune systems. Humans, however, tend to reject equine proteins, sometimes making the cure worse than the illness.

Equine antivenins also suffer from a narrow range of effectiveness; since each is tailored to a specific snake, bite victims are out of luck if they don't know the species of their attacker. Researchers are hoping that broad-spectrum resistors like the opossum will lead them to an antivenin that works for any bite—even when the snake doesn't stick around for introductions.

Do scorpions really live up to their bad reputation?

Few creatures convey a sense of latent menace quite as effectively as a scorpion. With a tapered abdomen arched high above its body and a curved stinger poised for action, the scorpion has long been regarded as lethal—but appearances can be deceiving. Most of the roughly 70 species in the United States possess a sting no more dangerous or painful than that of a bee.

One species, however, lives up to its lethal looks: the sculptured centruroides. Found in the deserts of southeast California, Arizona, and southwest New Mexico, this brownish, two-inch-long bark scorpion defends itself with a potent venom that attacks the human nervous system and can be fatal to small children and those in poor health. Also known as the Arizona scorpion, the centruroides stings only when provoked, but unfortunately, all it takes is for some unsuspecting person to jostle firewood, overturn rocks, or place probing fingers into a cranny where these nocturnal animals lurk during the heat of the day. Thankfully, an antivenin to counteract its sting was developed in the 1950s, and despite their fearsome looks and deadly reputation, scorpions have caused no documented deaths in the United States in more than 30 years.

The Virginia opossum enjoys a natural immunity to the venomous bite of pit vipers, allowing this wily hunter to feed freely on such deadly reptiles as water moccasins, copperheads, and rattlesnakes.

Between 1929 and 1948 the deadly sculptured centruroides, also known as the Arizona scorpion, killed 64 people in its home state—more than four times the number of humans killed by venomous snakes in the same period.

🐟 *This barracuda poses a greater danger to diners than to swimmers due to toxins in its flesh. Virtually undetectable and impervious to temperature, no amount of cleaning or cooking will diminish the poison's potency.*

🐍 *Contrary to popular belief, rattlesnakes do not always give a warning rattle before they strike. Here a western diamondback prepares to deliver its deadly venom, a complex mixture of up to 90 different proteins.*

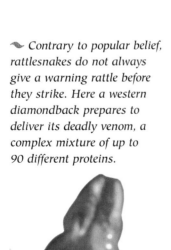

Are barracudas dangerous?

Yes, especially big barracudas, but not because of all those nasty teeth. Despite their belligerent looks, barracudas seldom bite people without provocation. These menacing-looking fish become truly dangerous to humans when they're bitten into.

The barracuda is the primary cause of ciguatera, a foodborne disease produced by poisons called ciguatoxins that accumulate in this predator's flesh as it consumes smaller fish. Symptoms of ciguatera appear within a few hours of eating a toxic fish and include nausea, gastric distress, and diarrhea. These are followed by intense itching; numbness and tingling in fingers, toes, and lips; joint and muscle pain; and a reversal of hot and cold sensations (an ice cube feels hot on the lips and tongue). The illness, for which there is no known cure, may last a few days or linger for several months, even recurring for years.

Ciguatera begins with reef-dwelling dinoflagellates, microscopic, one-celled organisms that produce ciguatoxin. These tiny creatures attach themselves to algae, which is consumed by herbivorous fish, who are in turn eaten by predators. The toxin accumulates on its way up the food chain, reaching dangerous levels of concentration in top hunters like the barracuda.

The barracuda, however, is not solely to blame; roughly 450 species of reef fishes from the Caribbean, South Pacific, and Indian Ocean can cause ciguatera. In the United States the disease was formerly limited to travelers in or returning from south Florida, Puerto Rico, the Virgin Islands, Hawaii, and other tropical edens. But the growing culinary popularity of tropical reef dwellers such as snappers, amberjack, and king mackerel has spread the hazard far beyond their watery realm, affecting as many as 27,000 Americans each year.

Do all snake venoms kill in the same way?

Lashing out at eyeblink speed, a rattlesnake strikes a passing mouse, injecting it with a massive dose of venom. Within minutes the rodent is dead, and the snake is ready to eat.

All of North America's venomous snakes use their deadly bite primarily as a way of capturing prey. Some, like the coral snake, use a venom that kills by attacking the nervous system, interfering with respiration and heartbeat. The toxin causes little pain or discomfort, and the bitten animal may seem relatively normal, even as its vital organs are paralyzed.

The venom of pit vipers, such as rattlers, copperheads, and cottonmouths, in contrast, violently disassembles the tissues it meets. A great deal of pain and swelling accompany the venom as it moves through the circulatory system, literally dissolving blood vessels and muscle, and eventually causing fatal internal hemorrhaging. In a sense the venom begins the task of digestion even before the snake swallows its prey.

Within these broad categories of neurotoxic (nerve-attacking) and cytolytic (cell-destroying) venoms, there are many variations between species and even between individuals. Venom is a regular witch's brew of complex biochemicals that may reduce or increase blood clotting, speed the spread of enzymes, or attack blood cells. Surprisingly, these chemicals may actually prove beneficial to humans, particularly in the world of medicine. Already, one powerful drug that fights hypertension and congestive heart failure was discovered in the lethal venom of a Brazilian pit viper.

⬱ *Unlike a snake, which injects its venom in a flash, the Gila monster holds a victim tight with its powerful jaws while its poison oozes into the bite. The Gila's venom not only immobilizes its prey but actually dissolves some of the victim's tissues, aiding digestion.*

Is the Gila monster's bite usually fatal?

One of two venomous lizards in the world (the other is the closely related beaded lizard of Mexico), the Gila monster of the arid Southwest has a powerfully toxic bite, but fortunately, attacks in the wild are virtually unknown. These rare, reclusive animals are largely nocturnal, preying on birds' eggs and chicks, small rodents, and the young of larger mammals like rabbits. As with snakes, their venom is used primarily for hunting, and only the most careless human behavior will provoke a snapping, defensive bite.

Still, anyone unlucky enough to be bitten by a Gila monster is in for an unforgettably harrowing experience. The lizard clamps its viselike jaws onto its victim with steel-trap tenacity, all the while chewing and chomping. The venom, secreted by glands in the lower jaw, seeps into the wound along the animal's grooved teeth, causing searing pain, as well as swelling, nausea, and fainting. Although Gila venom attacks the nervous system in much the same way as coral snake venom, it is chemically quite different, and no antivenin exists to combat its effects.

While human fatalities have occurred from Gila monster bites, they are, happily, quite rare and, given the lizard's live-and-let-live personality, completely preventable.

Are any mammals venomous?

If North America's only venomous mammal were the size of a lion, or even a house cat, we might hesitate before venturing outdoors. But despite its unimpressive stature ($3\frac{3}{4}$ to 5 inches in length, $\frac{1}{2}$ ounce in weight), the short-tailed shrew is a fearsome predator, sometimes tackling frogs and mice several times its size.

What allows this miniature predator to take on prey larger than itself is its unique, poison-laden saliva, a glandful of which is potent enough to kill 300 mice. When a shrew bites its prey, venomous saliva flows along concave grooves in its lower teeth into the wound. The toxin affects the victim's brain cells and nerves, incapacitating, though not immediately killing, the prey—which is sometimes cached for later feeding. Snacks are rarely kept for long, however; a shrew's metabolism is a fire that must be constantly fed, and within three hours of a meal, the shrew's gut is growling and ready to be filled again.

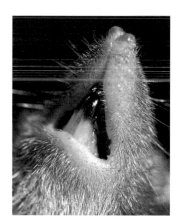

⬱ *The short-tailed shrew poses a dual chemical threat to predators. In addition to its poisonous bite, the shrew exudes a rank, garlicky odor, prompting cats, foxes, or coyotes that catch this tiny hunter to spit it right out.*

Curious Creatures *A sampler of nature's oddities*

How does a sidewinder go forward by moving sideways?

Across the deserts of California, Utah, Nevada, and Arizona, a series of parallel, J-shaped tracks in the sand mark the passage of a sidewinder, a rattlesnake named for its distinctive looping locomotion. While anchoring itself at two points, it skims the rest of its body just barely above the sand. Almost every inch of its length touches down at some point, but never does the entire body lie flat on the ground.

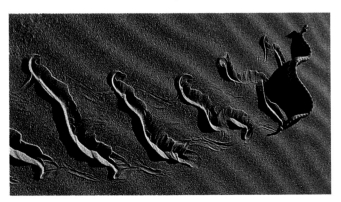

➤ *Sidewinders whip across the ground with a strange, beautiful style all their own. Their peculiar method of travel enables them to grip soft, loose sand while minimizing contact with the hot desert floor.*

To take its first "step," the sidewinder throws its head and neck forward while its middle section remains in contact with the sand. Briefly, it presses its neck against the ground and, with head and tail both providing support, lifts its trunk sideways. This portion lifts clear off the sand to curl forward, then continues the track started by the head. Meanwhile, the head begins reaching forward once more, even as the tail end is still taking off from the starting point.

Though it may sound like an awkward, piecemeal process, sidewinding involves fluid motion, with a series of simultaneous liftoffs and touchdowns. As the snake slings itself sideways, motion ripples down its body—obliquely angled toward the direction of its travel—like a wave making its way through a rope. While the mechanics of sidewinding are clearly understood, they are not so easy to appreciate on paper. Slow-motion footage, though, reveals the full subtlety and complexity of this remarkable reptile's unique locomotion and the sinuous grace with which it seems to float across the sand.

Do all oysters produce pearls?

When it comes to making a silk purse out of a sow's ear, the pearl-oyster has few rivals. The miracle begins in a most unlikely manner. If a grain of sand or a parasite gets into the soft flesh of an oyster, the animal responds by surrounding the invader with a secretion known as nacre, or mother of pearl (the same material that lines the inside of its shell). Over several years layers of this substance build up around the irritant, transforming it into something precious: a smooth, lustrous pearl.

A finished pearl is like a crystalline onion, with each concentric layer composed of hundreds of ultrathin hexagonal platelets. Each platelet is a crystal of calcium carbonate (better known as chalk) deposited by the oyster and glued into place with secretions.

Not every pearl, however, is a "ripe" one. Of the 128,000 species of pearl-forming mollusks, only saltwater pearl-oysters and freshwater pearl-mussels produce pearls lustrous enough to have value. Among these species only a small fraction of individuals contains a buried treasure. To improve the odds, a Japanese man named Kokichi Mikimoto patented a process by which "seeds" of freshwater mother-of-pearl are inserted into saltwater oysters. Today, half of all implanted oysters successfully yield pearls; of these, some 40 percent are commercially viable, and one in eight is of gem quality. Even the best cultured pearl, however, can't compete with a natural one for beauty or value. One perfectly round specimen can fetch as much as $100,000.

Do cougars purr?

Just like a house cat curled up beneath a shaft of sunlight, a cougar purrs—and often for the same reasons: relaxation and contentment. But there's one big difference: due to the animal's 150-pound body, the sound is greatly magnified to what can perhaps best be described as a majestic rumble. Though often called mountain lions, cougars can't roar like their African cousins. Like most smaller wild felines, including the bobcat, lynx, and ocelot, the cougar has a solid hyoid (the U-shaped bone at the base of the tongue). The largest cats—African lions, tigers, and leopards—possess a hyoid with an elastic band of cartilage that enables them to roar, but unlike a cougar or a domestic cat, which can purr continuously, these animals purr only when they exhale.

Roars notwithstanding, cougars are highly vocal. Perhaps their most infamous call is a "scream" guaranteed to raise gooseflesh on even the most woods-wise listener. Early explorers compared the sound to that made by a hysteri-

cal woman wailing inconsolably. Another description, offered by a biologist in Louisiana at the turn of the century, characterized it as "a long-drawn-out, shrill trill, weird and startling." An angry cougar may growl or hiss, and cougar kits mew (a sound recognizable to any tabby owner), but cougars scream so rarely that skeptics long dismissed these accounts. Modern experts have determined that these creatures do indeed yowl, though the reason, they concede, remains a mystery.

Among the varied vocalizations of cougars are birdlike whistles—sometimes whisper soft, other times ear-splittingly loud—that are used by mothers to keep in touch with their offspring.

How do rattlesnakes make their distinctive sound?

Snakes are the Houdinis of the animal world. As they grow in size, they must periodically shed their old skins—as often as two to four times per season if they are well fed. Escaping from their sausagelike casings, these creatures leave behind an inside-out, lips-to-tail body suit. If you pick up this suit of dry scales, you'll find a translucent shell of the snake's former self. What you won't find on a discarded rattlesnake skin, though, is the tip of its tail, or rattle, because the animal holds on to this part and makes clever use of it.

Every time a rattlesnake dons a fresh outer skin, it grows at the tail end of its body a new hat-shaped lobe made of keratin, the protein found in your fingernails. The lobes are hollow and stacked atop one another, the brim of one loosely coupled to the crown of the one below. Only the newest hat (the one nearest the end of the skin) is tightly connected. With each shedding the old lobes are pushed farther to the rear, and the rattle grows longer. Like the baby toy whose name it inspired, a rattle makes an unmistakable noise. When the snake wants to warn a predator or would-be trampler, it holds the tip of its tail erect and vibrates it. As the hats clack against each other at a rate of about 50 times per second, they sound an alarm that is among the most menacing in the natural world.

Why do worms come to the surface when it rains?

For a creature with wet, unprotected skin, the open air is hostile territory. An earthworm caught above ground, exposed to the twin terrors of scorching sun and withering wind, can die within minutes. So worms leave their damp domiciles only when conditions are more favorable—after darkness provides a shield and a twilight dew drenches the grass. Then the earth-

~ *Ironically, a rattler can't hear its own high-frequency alarm. Born without external ears, snakes can sense only low-frequency vibrations (like the footfalls of people), which they channel up from the ground through their jawbones.*

worms stretch out in the cool, humid air, their tails still firmly anchored in their holes, ready for a lightning-fast retreat. Of course, even worms can have too much of a good thing. A gentle summer shower is one thing, but a torrential rain will flood their burrows, forcing them out regardless of the time of day. This is especially common in spring, when the earth is often saturated with moisture. Prolonged rain sends the worms crowding to the surface for air, exposing them to a host of predatory hazards, including birds, shrews, raccoons, skunks, turtles, salamanders, snakes, and frogs.

Does the water shrew really walk on water?

The notion of water nymphs and wood fairies is not so outlandish to anyone who has spied the water shrew in its haunts—usually wet, boggy areas near free-flowing streams in dense forests. This nearly blind, mouselike creature runs like quicksilver along the banks, sometimes diving into the current. Once in the water, its fur coat, which traps tiny bubbles of air, becomes something of a mixed blessing. On the one hand it gives the shrew buoyancy, enabling it to bob up easily and ride high like a duck. On the other it creates drag, forcing the animal to paddle frantically with its tiny, webless feet.

Given the disadvantages of swimming, this remarkably agile creature often opts for another solution: it simply walks—or to be more precise, runs—across the surface of the water. Aided by stiff fringes of hair on the edges of its paws that act like pontoons, the animal keeps itself suspended by striding along the balloon skin of surface tension on the water. In one instance a water shrew was seen sprinting for five feet across a pond without once dipping into the water.

Though it usually prefers to be on the water rather than in it, this creature doesn't hesitate to plunge in when it spots its favorite food: mayfly and stonefly nymphs. Holding its breath like a pearl diver, it paddles in pursuit of its larval prey. As it emerges with its prize, it flings water from its coat and begins taking several hundred breaths per minute while its heart beats some 800 times per minute (nearly 10 times as fast as a human's). To stoke this maniacal metabolism, a water shrew must eat up to three times its own body weight each day.

Big Wheels in Small Packages

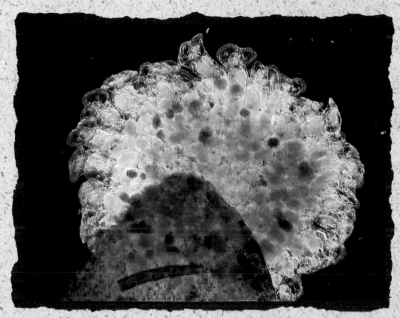

Go for a dip in any lake or pond and you'll be accompanied by hundreds of thousands, perhaps millions, of swimming partners. They are called rotifers (Latin for "wheel-bearer"), and though you'll never see these microscopic organisms, you can be sure they're there. Many types of similar animals can be found in such places, but few are as fascinating as rotifers. In many freshwater habitats these curious creatures comprise nearly half the population of animal plankton—the primary source of food for aquatic life.

Some 2,000 species of rotifers can be found in North America. Among the most common varieties are transparent globular or tubular organisms that float along with the currents or cling to plants by using a trunklike foot. In some species as many as 100 or so rotifers form colonies that may be free-floating or attached to a plant (like the one above). In others individuals are strictly solitary. What they all have in common, however, is that they are equipped with "wheels" of rapidly moving hairlike cilia, which they use to sweep food into their mouths and propel themselves through water.

In most cases eggs can mature without being fertilized, so male rotifers often play no role in reproduction. Males are not totally useless, though. The eggs they do fertilize have tough outer shells, which increase their odds for survival. These sturdy eggs may remain dormant for years, springing to life only when conditions become more favorable.

Why do remoras hitch rides on sharks?

The advantages of hitch-hiking on a shark are so obvious—free rides, free meals on leftovers, protection from predators—that it's a wonder other fishes don't jump on the bandwagon as well. Not that remoras need to depend entirely on the kindness of strangers. These slender, dark gray fish actually swim better and faster than a lot of their hosts. Moreover, the fact that their remains are so seldom found in the bellies of sharks tells us that they are agile enough to stay out of harm's way most of the time.

Whatever the reason, remoras clearly enjoy the lifestyle of a rail-riding hobo. The suction disc atop their "shoulders" is actually a modified dorsal fin. Their dorsal spines are bent outward in opposite directions, forming transverse plates like the slats in a venetian blind. To attach itself to another fish, a remora swims up to it and holds on briefly with tiny barbs until its raised plates have created a vacuum chamber. To slip free, the remora simply swims forward. When tugged by the tail, however, the remora bonds to its host even more securely—so firmly, in fact, that if the animal were pulled hard enough, the suction disc would be torn from its body.

In tropical and warm temperate seas the world over, native fishermen use remoras to catch fish, turtles, and porpoises, as Christopher Columbus witnessed during his second voyage to the New World in 1494. Attaching a line to a remora's tail, fishermen slip it into the water when they spot their quarry. (Some will rub the remora's hide with sand to remove the protective slime and agitate the fish, making it more likely to feel the need to hold on to the nearest security blanket.) Some remoras are finicky about their attachments, as their common names suggest: sharksucker, whalesucker, swordfish remora, spearfish remora. Most, however, are fickle opportunists that will attach themselves to almost anything that swims and to some things that don't, such as ship hulls. More than one person

has waded along the shore only to find that remoras have glommed onto his or her ankles.

Most remoras hang onto the hides of their hosts, but a few are more daring. Some smaller species attach themselves inside the gill cavities of tunas, ocean sunfish, sharks, and other marine heavyweights, and a few are even found deep inside the mouths of sharks and mantas. Such large predators are believed to have a high tolerance for these hangers-on because remoras occasionally eat copepods and other parasites that feed on the flesh of their hosts.

Where do ice worms live?

A glacier seems an unlikely place for life to flourish. The deep gaps that split its surface, and the thin sheets of ice and snow that conceal caves and streams make a glacier treacherous terrain for most animals. Since plants can't colonize a river of ice flowing across the land, there is little to entice hungry creatures to dwell there. Yet this frozen, forbidding realm is home, sweet home, to the ice worm, an invertebrate so well adapted to life at the freezing point that if placed on the palm of a human hand, it would die and even disintegrate within minutes.

Ice worms, or snow worms, live in coastal glaciers from northern Alaska south to Mount Rainier in Washington. These one-inch-long, reddish brown worms thrive at 32°F, their tissues protected by a natural antifreeze that prevents cells from freezing. Like lemmings and other weather-wise animals, ice worms take full advantage of the snow's insulating properties. By burrowing below the surface of the powder-topped ice, they avoid extreme winter temperatures. Though sunlight and bright moonlight also drive them away from the surface, a dimly moonlit night actually lures them out in droves. Wriggling through minute channels in the ice, they dine on algae, fern spores, bits of pollen, and other microscopic fare in the surface snow. Often they themselves become food for ravens and other birds.

Other small animals also flourish in ice and snow. Ice insects, dark crawlers that look like a cross between a cricket and a cockroach, spend much of the year on ice-covered mountains in California, the Pacific Northwest, and northwestern Canada. Crane flies tiptoe across snow in freezing weather, and snow fleas pepper the whiteness of the Arctic and the northeastern United States.

Riding piggyback style, an upside-down remora freeloads on a nurse shark. While they certainly savor the leftovers of larger fish, remoras frequently abandon their hosts to feed on sardines or herrings, then leisurely digest their meal as they wait for the next ride to come along.

In a world dominated by whiteness, the dark red ice worm provides welcome visual variety. The worm gets its color from hemoglobin, the same substance that gives human blood its rich red hue.

Why do horses sleep standing up?

On the ancient plains where horses evolved, sleep was a high-stakes gamble. Animals slept out in the open so that nothing could sneak up on them, and they made sure a sentinel was posted. Even then, they only dozed, standing with their back legs locked, their eyes half-open, and their ears swiveling like radar dishes. Today's horses still remain on their feet when nodding off. Only occasionally (when a lead horse is standing guard) do they allow themselves the luxury of lying down to sleep.

However a horse chooses to sleep, this much is certain: it can't dream while it's standing up. For dreaming to occur, the horse (just like a human) must have entered a stage of sleep known as REM (the acronym for "rapid eye movement"). In this state of deep relaxation, the muscles are arrested in what's called flaccid paralysis. The brain continues to transmit signals for the muscles to move, but the messages never reach their destinations. The only motion possible during this phase of sleep would be roaming eyes, rhythmic breathing, and perhaps an occasional twitch. In short, if a horse were to go into REM sleep while standing up, it would fall down.

How do loons stay underwater so long?

Goose-size, low-riding birds with stark black-and-white plumage and daggerlike bills, loons have been favored with several adaptations for the pursuit of fish and other aquatic prey. An accomplished diver, the bird can disappear underwater so quickly that it seems to vanish in thin air. While a loon may dive in a sudden, dramatic plunge, neck arched and bill thrust downward, more often than not it simply sinks out of sight in the blink of an eye.

To manage this remarkable feat, the bird first expels air from sacs connected to its lungs and squeezes out air bubbles trapped in the vanes of its waterproof feathers. While most birds have lightweight bones full of air spaces that make flying easier, diving birds such as loons have little air space in their bones, thus reducing buoyancy. The loon is also able to store enough oxygen in its blood and muscles to meet the reduced needs of its vital organs during dives, which typically take less than a minute but may last as long as eight minutes. (Often its dives only seem long, for the bird has a way of quietly resurfacing in another place.)

How deep loons can dive, propelled by the synchronized kicks of their huge, webbed feet, remains a question mark. Loons often feed in shallow areas where fish abound, both on the freshwater northern lakes where they nest and on

➤ Despite its size the common loon swims and dives with consummate grace, disappearing beneath the surface with hardly a ripple. Echoing across the northern lakes, its haunting cry—which many liken to hysterical human laughter—gave rise to the expression "crazy as a loon."

the coastal waters where they spend the winter. Although scientists believe that these birds can easily dive up to 100 feet, they are skeptical about stories told by commercial fishermen on Lake Superior, who claim to have found loons trapped in nets set 240 feet below the surface.

Lasting Impressions What fossils tell us

What animal fossils are you most likely to find?

Fossils are snapshots in nature's family album of animals and plants that lived thousands or millions of years before recorded history. Some relatively recent fossils of Ice Age mammoths have been discovered in Siberian and Alaskan permafrost. One frozen pachyderm still had a mouthful of unchewed grass. Occasionally animals crept into caves of the Southwest and died, and their remains were mummified. Sometimes hard objects, such as bones, shells, and teeth, are dredged up from Midwestern gravel pits or the Atlantic sea floor little changed from the time they were deposited eons ago. Fossils are also pulled out of California tar pits and New England peat bogs; tar and the acid in peat preserve the bones and often pickle the flesh.

The fossils that you are most likely to find, however, will not be frozen, desiccated, or pickled. They will be petrified—that is, turned to stone either by minerals deposited in pores or cavities or by minerals completely replacing all tissues, bones, and shells. Among the most common petrified fossils are brachiopods, marine creatures with two hinged, grooved shells. Thousands of brachiopod species fed on ocean bottoms for over half a billion years; they ranged in size from microscopic to a few inches across. You can dig them up wherever shallow seas once covered the land and sedimentary rocks lie near the surface. A few brachiopod species are still alive today.

Trilobites are extinct but, like brachiopods, swam and burrowed in the sea as early as 500 million years ago. Their skeletons are often very well preserved. Many look like oval millipedes with wide helmets, distinct body segments, and pinched tails. Most are no bigger than a bar of soap, but some species grew longer than a foot. Crinoids, or sea lilies, were abundant marine animals, often equipped with stems and food-gathering arms. (Some stemless forms are still alive today.) In places, limestone strata are packed with their sinuous forms—beautiful friezes of undulating life stopped in stone.

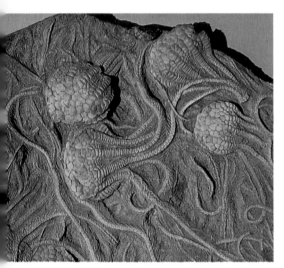

~ Over 100 million years ago, stemless crinoids, relatives of sea stars, thrived in shallow seas covering what is now the state of Kansas. Unlike their stemmed relatives, which lived attached to the ocean floor, stemless crinoids could move from place to place. They used their foot-long arms for filtering tiny plants and animals from the water. These organisms were passed along grooves in the arms to a central mouth.

Which large mammals once lived here?

A sloth as large as an elephant and a cat the size of a riding pony, for starters! There were far more large mammals in North America during prehistoric times than there are today. Many of them match up with their modern relatives as an offensive tackle does with a place-kicker. The giant sloth, for example, was 20 feet long, while its relatives remaining in the American tropics today are a tenth of that length. The giant lion stood head and shoulders above any living lion or tiger and may have been the largest cat ever. The bison of the time could look down its nose at the animal that made Buffalo Bill famous. The short-faced bear had an advantage in height, weight, and reach over the largest Kodiak now alive, and the imperial mammoth could call an African elephant Shorty.

Fossils of these creatures and many other big prehistoric mammals have been found in the La Brea tar pits, natural cauldrons of asphalt in

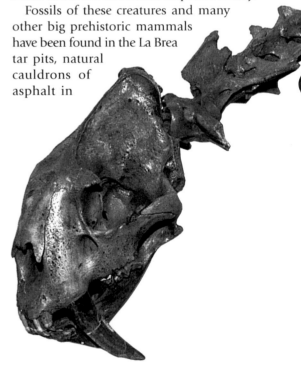

what is now downtown Los Angeles. Animals drinking rainwater that pooled in the pits often became trapped in the sticky goo. Among these were mastodons, low-slung relatives of elephants. As they struggled and sank into tarry oblivion, trumpeting their fear, a feline terror, with fangs as long as butcher knives, was fatally drawn to the prospect of an easy meal. Few, if any, sites in the world today have as many fossils of saber-tooth cats as La Brea.

By today's standards mastodons and saber-tooth cats are bizarre creatures, but some of the large animals inhabiting prehistoric North America were almost identical to creatures living here today. Fossils found at La Brea include those of cougars, jaguars, and deer that were very similar to modern mule deer and white-tailed deer. Camels also abounded at La Brea, as they did throughout the continent. In fact, the camel family first developed in North America; then as sea levels lowered and land bridges were created, some members wandered into South America and Eurasia—lucky for them because they eventually vanished from their place of origin.

➤ Common in North America during the Ice Age, the saber-tooth cat had a formidable pair of backward-curved upper canine teeth. Equipped with serrated rear edges, they were ideally suited for cutting through skin and tearing into flesh. This ferocious feline, the size of a lion, probably first punctured its victims' throats to kill them, then sliced and diced them at its leisure.

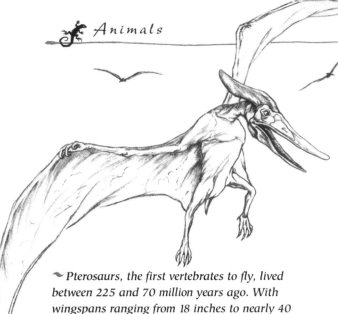

◥ *Pterosaurs, the first vertebrates to fly, lived between 225 and 70 million years ago. With wingspans ranging from 18 inches to nearly 40 feet, some of these winged dinosaurs were the largest animals ever to have taken to the air.*

What was the largest flying reptile?

It's a bird. It's a plane. . . . Well, to be precise, it's neither—but the largest known flying reptile flew just about as well as any bird and had a wingspan larger than those of many aircraft. *Quetzalcoatlus*—it was named after the legendary flying serpent worshiped by peoples of ancient Mexico—seems to have had wings that measured 40 feet from tip to leathery tip, outreaching that of the typical World War II fighter plane and the revered C-47 twin-engine transport. Besides being the largest of the flying reptiles, or pterosaurs, it was among the last, for it cruised the skies at the end of the Age of Reptiles. With its huge head and beak, long neck, clawed digits, and scaly tail, this flying monster was in every respect a real-life dragon, lacking only the ability to spit fire.

Quetzalcoatlus, identified from fossil remains found in Texas during the 1970s, is a relatively recent discovery. The first pterosaur fossils were found in Europe about a century ago, and many have since turned up virtually around the globe. Remains found in the fossils' chest cavities lead scientists to believe that many of these reptiles fed on fish and squid, which they snatched from the water with their long, toothed beaks. Differences in bill shapes among pterosaurs, however, hint at widely varying feeding habits. Some of these flying reptiles may have plucked worms from the mud or filtered shrimp and plankton out of shallow water or pried open shellfish. Undoubtedly, too, some fed on their smaller brethren, caught on the wing.

Where in America are most dinosaur fossils found?

While evidence of dinosaurs has been found throughout the continental United States, the richest deposit of fossilized bones is contained in a layer of sediment laid down during the Jurassic Period, about 150 million years ago. Called the Morrison Formation, it covers much of Utah, Colorado, and Wyoming. Large outcroppings have been pushed to the surface, and it is in these that fossil hunters have found the most dinosaur bones.

Fossils are the result of time and mineralization. For a dinosaur's bones to be preserved, they had to be covered by sand and mud shortly after death. This usually happened on an ancient lake bed, river bottom, or ocean floor. Once the bones were buried, water percolated down, carrying minerals with it. These penetrated the bones, transforming them into fossils.

One of the Morrison Formation's richest bone piles can be found at Dinosaur National Monument near Dinosaur, Colorado. Here, carcasses and stray bones of dinosaurs were concentrated along a riverbank during floods. Over time they were buried by layer upon layer of sedimentary rock, but then a subterranean upheaval pushed their rocky sarcophagus to the surface. Fossil hunters excavating one outcropping uncovered a 200-foot-high cross section where more than 1,600 fossilized dinosaur bones are imbedded like chocolate chips in a cookie. Other fossil-rich areas in Colorado include a ridge near the town of Morrison. A track of ancient footprints left by dinosaurs lines the east side of the ridge, giving rise to the trail's nickname, Dinosaur Freeway. During the late 1800s, 17 new dinosaur species were identified through their fossilized remains at a site near Canon City now called Garden Park Fossil Area. Important finds continue to be made at this location, including the 1992 discovery of a *Stegosaurus* with its back plates still completely intact.

A fossil bonanza can also be found near Price, Utah, at the Cleveland-Lloyd Dinosaur Quarry. Nicknamed the Dinosaur Department Store, this dig site has supplied bones and fossils to museums and universities around the world, including entire skeletons of *Allosaurus*, a fearsome predator similar to *Tyrannosaurus rex*. Another fossil-rich patch of the Morrison Formation has been exposed near Medicine Bow,

◥ *A visitor to Dinosaur National Monument views fossilized sauropod bones partially excavated from sedimentary rock deposited 150 million years ago. The largest sauropods—long-necked plant eaters more than 80 feet from head to tail and weighing up to 100 tons— were the most massive land animals that ever lived.*

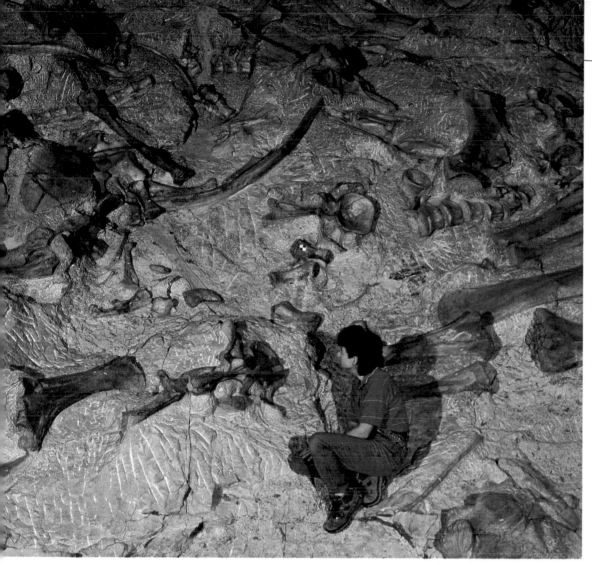

Did mother dinosaurs eat their young?

You wouldn't expect these mighty creatures to be particularly caring parents, but some dinosaur mothers may have been. Consider this family portrait preserved at a Mongolian fossil site: an ostrichlike *Oviraptor* squats on a clutch of eggs neatly arranged in a circular pattern with her arms spread protectively over the eggs.

Some dinosaurs, however, like many modern reptiles, probably had more of a lay-them-and-leave-them philosophy of child care. A few may actually have been cannibals, returning to their nests on occasion to eat remaining hatchlings.

The evidence for such behavior comes from a 225-million-year-old "bone bed" of small bipedal, meat-eating dinosaurs known as *Coelophysis* found in New Mexico. One *Coelophysis* in the deposit appears to have the remains of a smaller one in its rib cage. Why would dinosaurs eat some of their young? Survival of the fittest dictates that the fastest young would succeed and produce fast-running young in the next generation. Another theory suggests that the death may have been accidental. Crocodiles and alligators instinctively snap at small animals around them, occasionally killing and eating their own young inadvertently. Maybe *Coelophysis* and some other contemporary carnivorous dinosaurs had similar instincts.

Wyoming. Called Como Bluff Dinosaur Quarry, it is the scene of a famous rivalry waged by a pair of colorful fossil hunters from the 19th century, Edward Cope and Othniel Marsh. Dinosaur bones are so plentiful in the area that a local shepherd had even built a cabin out of them. The site remains popular with fossil hunters, and new discoveries are regularly made there.

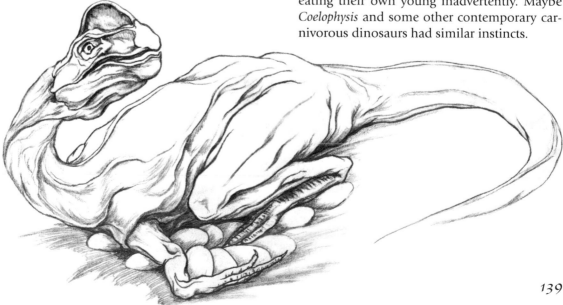

About 80 million years ago, an Oviraptor *apparently brooding eggs was caught in a sandstorm on what is now Mongolia's Gobi Desert, and its remains were subsequently fossilized. Proponents of the theory that birds are directly descended from dinosaurs used this 1995 discovery to bolster their position, arguing that brooding behavior first developed among dinosaurs long before birds evolved.*

Are there any living fossils in North America today?

A Florida crocodile looks incredibly ancient as it happily suns itself in the Everglades, and it's easy to imagine that crocodiles and alligators, or some snaggletoothed cousins of theirs, splashed around in swamps with *Tyrannosaurus rex* millions of years ago. In fact, crocodiles and alligators are almost identical to their Mesozoic relatives of 80 or 100 million years ago, and many other "living fossils" will also surprise you by their similarity to their fossilized ancestors.

Common horseshoe crabs look almost exactly like fossils of *Mesolimulus*, a sea creature that scuttled across seabeds 150 million years ago. The same is true for some starfish. Dragonflies flitting about on papery wings seem fragile, but they might have posed for fossils 100 million years old. Also skittering around in Carboniferous times were cockroaches indistinguishable from today's. Rare millipede fossils suggest, amazingly, that our garden dwellers differ only marginally from some of the first creatures to crawl on land 400 million years ago.

The mammalian Methuselah of the Western Hemisphere is the opossum: its shy, retiring habits and almost-anything-goes diet have served it well for 64 million years.

◆ Flipped on its back by the surf as it came ashore to mate, a horseshoe crab waves its spikelike tail, or telson, back and forth, seeking something to push against. When the tip touches the sand, the creature will arch its abdomen and roll right side up. Crab is really a misnomer. This distinctive living fossil is more closely related to spiders than to crustaceans. Its look-alike ancestors scurried on shallow sea bottoms when the dinosaurs ruled the earth.

What happened to the dinosaurs?

The disappearance of dinosaurs 65 million years ago is one of science's greatest mysteries. Figuring out this whodunit is akin to solving a crime without benefit of an eyewitness, confession, or smoking gun.

Changing climate, starvation, cosmic radiation, parasites, disease, erupting volcanoes, and competition from new species are just a few of the causes cited for the dinosaurs' sudden departure. One theory fingers flowers, suggesting that dinosaurs were poisoned by eating new kinds of plants. Another hypothesizes that butterflies and moths are at fault: when these plant-munching insects first appeared, they had no natural preda-

tors keeping their numbers in check and ate so much plant food that none remained for dinosaurs. Still another theory charges shrew-like mammals with feasting on dinosaur eggs and thus preventing the giant beasts from reproducing in sufficient numbers.

The problem with most theories is they can't explain the fact that prehistoric creatures living on land vanished at the same time as those living in the sea. A more likely cause for the dinosaurs' demise is a comet or a planetesimal—a chunk of a planet—that struck near Mexico's Yucatan Peninsula some 65 million years ago. Scientists have discovered unusual amounts of iridium in ocean sediments dating from the end of the Cretaceous Period, when the dinosaurs disappeared. Iridium is present in comets and meteorites. Scientists figure the force that created the enormous crater in Mexico triggered forest fires and a massive dust cloud that obstructed sunlight for months. If true, many plants and plant-eating dinosaurs would have died.

A comet or planetesimal also helps explain the nagging question of why all living species didn't disappear when the dinosaurs did. Cold-blooded creatures such as crocodiles, turtles, and lizards could have retreated into burrows, relying on lowered metabolism to get them through. Small omnivorous animals could have lived off dead carcasses. Seeds could have become dormant.

Not all scientists believe a comet is the sole culprit, however. They even dispute that all dinosaurs died over a short period of time and point to fossils showing that extinctions occurred over thousands, even millions, of years. Dinosaurs became extinct, they theorize, because their ecosystems collapsed. By the end of the Cretaceous Period, the argument goes, warm, shallow seas that had once covered huge areas drained off. The climate cooled; seasonal land temperatures became more extreme; and many parts of the world became unsuitable for large creatures lacking fur or feathers to keep them warm.

What fossils contain other fossils?

Forever Amber. With a touch of literary license, the title of this famed historical novel could describe how long the remains of small prehistoric plants and animals have been preserved in a fossilized sap called amber. "Forever" may be stretching the point, perhaps, but some of the fos-

Relatively recent arrivals in terms of the geologic time scale, opossums emigrated from South America to North America during the ice ages, when glaciers blanketed northern sections of the continent. By the time the Europeans arrived in America, opossums had ventured as far north as Ohio and West Virginia. Now they are found in Wisconsin, Ontario, and New England.

sils found in amber date back more than 90 million years. Translucent and usually orange, yellow, or red, amber imprisons insects, amphibians, and reptiles as well as plant parts as if they were frozen in time. Amber from New Jersey contains the oldest-known preserved flowers, from an oak that grew in the days of the dinosaurs, and also fossils of a mosquito and a black fly with a biting proboscis so formidable it may have hassled even *Tyrannosaurus rex.* Living things fixed in amber are not like ordinary fossils, in which organic matter has been replaced by minerals. Amber embalmed living things trapped in its sticky grasp by removing moisture and preserving cells, even genetic material, more or less intact.

The trees that produced amber were conifers, related to modern firs and pines. Scientists believe amber turned into its fossil form underground, and indeed, it is often found in bogs today. Exactly how the sap fossilized is a mystery, which is a bit of an irony since amber is helping scientists unlock so many other secrets of the past.

Why are opossums native to North America while most of their relatives live in Australia?

Opossums belong to an odd group of mammals called marsupials, which give birth to tiny young, barely more than embryos, and suckle them in external pouches. When we think of marsupials, Australia, home of the kangaroo, comes to mind, but a third of the world's marsupials live in the Americas.

Millions of years ago marsupials were distributed all over a great supercontinent that existed before the earth's tectonic plates shifted, giving birth to today's continents. In Australia and South America—itself an island continent for 25 million years—marsupials escaped domination by more advanced species. Five million years ago, however, sea levels fell, creating a bridge between North and South America. The opossum was the single marsupial to venture north of this bridge. Now a bona fide Yankee, it is working on Canadian citizenship.

More than 90 million years ago some ants and a praying mantis became mired in resinous sap on the trunk of a tree. The tree eventually died, and the congealed hunk of sap fell to the ground. Impervious to soil bacteria that decompose most organic matter, the sap was buried in acidic soil and fossilized over millennia. When humans found this rough piece of amber, they polished it, revealing its ancient but perfectly preserved inhabitants (left).

The Human Connection *How we touch the lives of animals*

What impact have humans had on the bears in Yosemite National Park?

For thousands of years humans and bears have coexisted—though perhaps uneasily at times—in the cliff-hung cathedral valley of Yosemite. The Miwok Indians shared the lush, oak-studded lowlands and alpine meadows of the northern Sierra Nevadas with grizzlies and black bears, but pioneering Europeans took a dimmer view of the bruins. Considered a menace to both man and livestock, these short-tempered creatures were either shot on sight or captured alive for bloody but popular bull-and-bear fights. In Yosemite Valley shepherds in the late 1800s used poison and traps to kill both grizzlies and black bears, and professional hunters exacted an even higher toll.

By the turn of the century, grizzly bears had been driven to the edge of extinction in California, but the smaller, less aggressive black bears remained. Without competition from grizzlies, their numbers steadily increased. In the 1920s there were so many black bears that the park began to feed them for public amusement. In 1937 at least 60 bears spent the summer in Yosemite Valley, many of them drawn from the high country by an annual feast of more than 120,000 pounds of food.

While popular with visitors, the feeding program created several problems. Conditioned to human food, the bears began panhandling more and more aggressively in campgrounds and parking lots. Some visitors would even feed the animals by hand or tease them with treats. As a result more and more vacationers were injured, and the park was eventually forced to kill nearly 100 bears that were especially troublesome. In the 1940s and 1950s, Yosemite tried to cancel the free lunch program by closing the feeding areas, but many bears simply switched to open garbage dumps. In time tourists flocked to these sites as well.

In an attempt to make black bears return to the ways of the wild, park managers closed the dumps in the 1970s, cutting off the bears' supply of human food. Visitors today are required to keep their supplies in bearproof lockers, and ordinary trash cans have been replaced by slotted, mailboxlike garbage receptacles. The effort has been at least partially successful, but these resourceful creatures are not easily thwarted. Some bears have learned to hang head-down in the slots of the garbage receptacles with their hind feet hooked on the outside. Others have resorted to petty larceny, smashing their way into cars to pilfer food locked inside.

Can animals help solve crimes?

It's a rare witness that can sling slobber 20 feet with a shake of its head and still have its testimony accepted in a court of law. With their baggy skin, pendulous lips, and poor manners, bloodhounds may be messy creatures, but they have an unerring nose for truth. A bloodhound (so named because it was the first breed of dog whose blood, or lineage, was ever recorded)

When the landscape teems with tourists, raiding the icebox becomes a popular pastime for black bears. These less-than-finicky omnivores have voracious appetites and sometimes swallow such inedible items as aluminum foil. Fortunately for them they seem to be protected by remarkably hardy digestive systems.

can sniff the scent left in a room by someone, then successfully follow the person's trail up to several days later—even over uneven terrain on a stormy night.

This astounding feat of detective work is possible because the dog's sense of smell is so acute—up to 3 million times more powerful than a human's and far stronger than the average dog's—that it can recognize even a small number of the 50,000 or so odor-bearing flakes of skin that we shed daily. As the animal puts its nose to the ground and sets out to track down a fugitive, its long, velvety ears sweep up molecules from the person's dead skin cells, and the floppy flesh of the dog's face cups the scent. Even the faintest odor will be captured by the bloodhound's long, convoluted corridor of a snout. Lined with some 23 square inches of olfactory membrane (a surface area 50 times greater than that of its counterpart in a human nose), the dog's snout is a veritable flypaper for smells. Although bloodhounds have deservedly earned a reputation as super sleuths, German shepherds, beagles, golden retrievers, Labrador retrievers, and even truffle-hunting pigs are also used by police to locate missing people, illicit drugs, stolen money, bombs, and illegally imported produce.

Why do wildlife managers sometimes reduce animal herds?

When pondering the "balance of nature," think not of the tempered scales of justice, but of a seesaw during a grammar school recess. Wildlife populations are seldom stable; they wax and wane as animals, plants, habitats, weather, and the other forces of nature interact. Add humans to the equation, and things can get seriously out of kilter. Herd animals, such as deer, elks, bisons, moose, and caribous, are both food for large predators and heavy consumers of forage plants. When the number of predators fluctuates, prey populations tend to go through wild boom-and-bust swings, prompting some conservationists to restore, maintain, or improve the natural balance. In such cases wildlife managers manipulate the sizes of herds by adjusting the length of the hunting season and the bag limits—because either there aren't enough predators to keep the prey population in check, the habitat has become too small, or both. In some countries professional hunters are used to control animal populations. In America, however, regulated sport hunting is preferred.

➤ *Elks roam Wyoming in such large numbers that they would endanger the survival of cattle, bighorn sheep, and other grazing animals if their population were not controlled. Since elks spend most of their time feeding, a herd needs at least seven members to ensure that at least one adult will be on the lookout for danger.*

Which endangered species are making a comeback?

In the deep hollows of the Great Smoky Mountains, red wolves once more move like ghostly shadows through the cool, green shade. In the Southeast, where egrets and ibises fleck the sky like tufts of cotton, the inky waters of swamps and marshes teem again with American alligators. Condors have been returned to the skies of California, gray wolves to Yellowstone National Park, and black-footed ferrets to the prairie dog towns of the High Plains.

These creatures, and many more, owe their existence to laws designed to protect rare plants and animals, especially the U.S. Endangered Species Act (ESA), passed by Congress in 1973. In all some 320 species of North American animals and 434 kinds of plants are officially listed as "endangered," meaning that they are at risk of extinction in all or much of their range. In addition, another 114 animals and 92 plants are considered "threatened"—that is, likely to become endangered in the near future. While some species are on the list because they were killed in great numbers (like the alligators once targeted by poachers), most have dwindled in number because they've suffered from habitat loss. Many are found in such ecosystems as wetlands, native Hawaiian forests, and California coastal scrub that have been reduced by development to fractions of their original size.

Since the Endangered Species Act was passed, seven animals (including the gray whale, eastern brown pelican, and arctic peregrine falcon) have recovered well enough to be removed from the list. More than a third of those still labeled endangered have either stabilized or are increasing in number, thanks largely to habitat protection afforded by law. Not every creature has fared as well, however, and seven species have been declared extinct. They include the dusky seaside sparrow of Florida and the blue pike of Lake Erie—a fish so rare that it may have been doomed even before it was granted protection.

➤ *In a scene that seems to reflect both the majesty and melancholy of our natural world, adult bald eagles perch beside Kachemak Bay in Alaska. Though still threatened, their species is no longer endangered, having rebounded from 417 breeding pairs in 1963 to some 4,000 today.*

Which bird was once so plentiful that no one thought it could ever become extinct?

Once the most abundant land birds in the world, passenger pigeons surged across central North America like a living tide—in numbers that stagger the imagination. One flock of perhaps 4 billion traveled over Ontario in 1866. Measuring one mile wide and 300 miles long, it passed overhead for 14 hours. The passenger pigeon, which at 15 to 17 inches long resembled a larger, blue-hued version of the mourning dove, also nested in huge aggregations, such as the 136 million birds that blanketed 850 square miles of Wisconsin forest in the 1870s.

Like the vast herds of bison that once populated the Great Plains, passenger pigeons were thought to be inexhaustible. Wherever they flew, they were greeted with slaughter. Although many people warned that the pigeons were decreasing in number, and some states passed laws granting them limited protection, the commercialized killing continued unabated throughout the 19th century. In 1878 some 10 million passenger pigeons were shipped to market from one nesting colony alone. Over time the great forests of beech, oak, and hickory that sustained these flocks were replaced by farmland and towns. Pigeon populations were sent into a fatal tailspin. The last known passenger pigeon in the wild was shot in Pennsylvania in 1902, and the very last of the species died in the Cincinnati Zoo in 1914.

➤ *Passenger pigeons, whose massive flocks darkened the skies of North America throughout the 19th century, did everything on a spectacular scale, including eating. Naturalist John James Audubon once calculated that a typical flock (about 1 billion birds) consumed 8.7 million bushels of acorns and beechnuts in just one day.*

How did the house sparrow make America its home?

North America is home to nearly 700 species of native birds—from gemlike hummingbirds to dazzling warblers—but some people are never satisfied. In the late 1800s a craze known as acclimatization swept the continent, fueled not only by the nostalgia of immigrants for the birds of their youth, but also by the desire to find a natural weapon against insect pests. Dozens of varieties of Old World birds (including skylarks, nightingales, and mistle thrushes) were set free in cities from Philadelphia to San Francisco. In such unfamiliar territory most died, but not the house sparrow. This scrappy survivor found the New World much to its liking.

First released in New York City in the 1850s and bolstered by thousands of additional birds shipped in from Europe in the years that followed, house sparrows (also known as English sparrows) took North America by storm. Before long they needed no help from humans; in 1886 alone the species added more than half a million

square miles to its range. In the 1930s one disgusted ornithologist wrote: "Its harsh, insistent chirp became the dominant bird-voice about our homes, where it seemed as though we might never again hope to hear a chorus of native bird-music unmarred by the discordant chatter of this alien."

As automobiles and tractors replaced horses and the ready supply of undigested seeds in manure disappeared, the number of house sparrows declined sharply. Yet they remain one of the most common birds found in cities and can be seen from coast to coast and border to border. Ironically, these unwelcome immigrants have been elbowed out of some urban areas by house finches, small songbirds native to the Western states. Illegally imported to the East as cage birds, house finches were released by pet dealers in New York City in 1940—in an attempt to avoid arrest. These birds now number in the millions, ranging over most of the United States.

Hundreds of species of exotic animals have been introduced to North America, sometimes intentionally but often not. A few, such as Asian ring-necked pheasants, have had little impact on the environment, but others have been unmitigated disasters. Black rats, once the carrier of Europe's infamous Black Death, stowed away with the earliest sailing ships to the New World. The same route was taken by another persistent household pest, the house mouse. European carp, which roil bottom sediments and uproot aquatic plants, have rendered untold lakes and rivers unfit for native species.

With today's burgeoning international trade and travel, the arrival of exotic species is on the rise and the threat to local wildlife continues. Tropical fish from the Amazon, parakeets from Africa, and toxic walking catfish from Asia are just a few of the refugees that have established themselves in Florida, while many of Hawaii's native animals have been pushed to isolated mountain retreats by a besieging army of invaders.

☙ *The European starling was brought to New York City in 1890 by misguided literary buffs intent on importing every bird mentioned in the works of Shakespeare. It has since overspread the continent, usurping scarce nesting holes and devastating the populations of such native birds as flickers and bluebirds.*

Who Goes There? *Tracks, trails, and other telltale signs*

What are some of the telltale signs animals leave behind?

Scratch marks, runways, tooth marks, nests, neatly pecked rows of holes—animal signs are like hieroglyphics, spelling out intriguing stories if you know how to read them. When a bear climbs a beech or an aspen to survey its domain, its claw marks will endure for the life of the tree. A grizzly loves nothing better than a good back or belly rub, and it will have favorite rubbing trees along well-traveled trails, usually rough-barked spruces or pines with scratch marks and bits of fur clinging to the sticky, oozing pitch.

➤ *Found under a tree, a three-inch regurgitated pellet consisting of a rodent skull, other bones, and fur suggests that owls are regularly roosting or nesting overhead. Besides ridding raptors of indigestible matter, these pellets contribute to health by scouring the birds' throats and gullets.*

Buck deer and bull elks prepare for fall's mating rituals by polishing their antlers in mock fights with saplings left shredded and girdled. The antlers are shed in early winter, once the rutting season is over, and they soon disappear, reduced to nubs by chisel-toothed mice and voles craving calcium and phosphorus.

Gnawed antlers are just one sign of the variety of small rodents that inhabit our woodlands, fields, prairies, and deserts by the unseen thousands. Meadow voles cut miniature highway networks through the grass. White-footed mice build thatch roofs over old bird nests for their homes. Harvest mice weave baseball-size grass nests in sagebrush. The red tree mouse of Oregon rain forests lives high in hemlocks in a comfortable nest of needles that can measure two feet or more in diameter.

A beaver's work is easy to spot—a stump or the end of a log that has been gnawed to a point. The telltale tooth marks are one-eighth to a quarter inch wide, and there will be a pile of chips not unlike those left by a woodman's ax.

Predatory birds regurgitate pellets consisting entirely of fur, feathers, and bones. Biologists collect these roughly oblong castings, which range up to four or five inches long for a bald eagle or great horned owl, from beneath nests to find out what the birds have been eating.

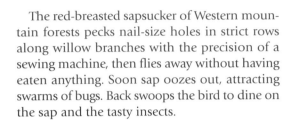

The red-breasted sapsucker of Western mountain forests pecks nail-size holes in strict rows along willow branches with the precision of a sewing machine, then flies away without having eaten anything. Soon sap oozes out, attracting swarms of bugs. Back swoops the bird to dine on the sap and the tasty insects.

Which clues are animals constantly depositing?

Wild animals report on their behavior by dropping hints—literally. If you take the time to consider them, droppings, or scat, provide clues about which animals are doing what. Still, it's easy to be fooled: droppings on open ground are subject to the depredations of weather and foraging insects. Scat from a young coyote may look just like that of a full-grown fox, and deer and elk pellets can be the same size.

Nevertheless, a little time spent looking at scat in the field can be revealing. A spatter of whitewash down a tree trunk may indicate the roosting spot of a large bird such as an owl. Telltale owl's pellets could be lying on the ground beneath. Intact animal parts such as a mouse skull hint at carnivores with shearing teeth that bolt down whole chunks of food. Sharp-edged bones wrapped in fur suggest an animal like a coyote, whose intestines need protection against puncture wounds. Scat loaded with wood particles indicates that a bear was feasting on ants living in a crumbling log.

Soft droppings of mammals generally mean they have been eating green or succulent foods. During the summer, for example, elks gorge on lush grass, but sometimes they overdo it. If so, their droppings are gloppy, formless as pancake batter before it congeals. Dried flat droppings mean that elks have used a place during the summer; pellets pinpoint spots they frequent in winter. Elk droppings full of clay may tell you how far a herd has trudged from a clay lick.

Back in the lab microscopic studies of prairie dog droppings may indicate their plant preferences and the size of their browsing range. Cortisol hormone levels in deer scat can gauge their stress levels, and pellet counts of big game animals can be used as indirect census indicators.

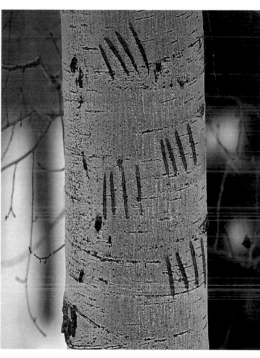

~ Animals leave distinctive calling cards for anyone willing to look and ponder (reading clockwise from bottom center): a silver maple tree about to be felled by beavers; a lodgepole pine trunk partially stripped by a hungry porcupine; an aspen trunk chewed by wintering elks seeking the sap-conducting cambium; an English walnut trunk pecked by red-breasted sapsuckers; an aspen trunk scored by a bear's claws.

⟶ Tracks of a lone Alaskan brown bear bisect the desolate Valley of Ten Thousand Smokes in Alaska's Katmai National Park. The giant bear shambled by shortly after rain had softened the volcanic ash that has covered the valley's floor since a gigantic eruption in 1912. Although these tracks are a day or two old, they still look fresh, with each claw mark clearly etched in the drying ash. Why a bear would choose to traverse this forbidding valley it is impossible to say, but it may have been heading for lakes filled with spawning salmon, located beyond the distant mountains on the horizon.

Where are the best places to see animal tracks?

The outdoors is a dangerous place, filled with stalking, soaring, and slithering predators. So it's no surprise that most mammals are furtive, silent, and out and about only at night. While we see squirrels every day, and white-tailed deer routinely wander into suburban yards, we might never be aware of many of our other wild neighbors if it weren't for their tracks.

Muddy places such as marshes and stream banks are the best spots to find animal tracks most of the year, and shortly after a rain is often a good time to look. Raccoons make delicate prints that look like tiny human hands and feet with bulbous fingers and toes. Muskrats leave thin, undulating tail-drag marks. Beavers' webbed hind footprints and toes-in front prints are often partially obliterated by their broad, trailing tails. Sandpipers patter along sandy beaches, but their delicate footwork will be erased by the next wave. The traceries of beetles and lizards scurrying over windblown dunes are likewise evanescent.

A snowy landscape, however, is a book waiting to be read and interpreted. You can inventory the inhabitants of forest and field after a fresh snowfall, and by assessing the distance between sets of paw prints and their patterns, you can tell if an animal was walking or running. Pairs of paw prints may indicate a trot, but single prints farther apart in a straight line could indicate a high-speed gallop. Chances are the tracks will lead straight to a den, nest, or food cache.

Stories of life and death are told in the snow. The dainty paw prints of a meadow vole and the side-by-side trotting prints of a red fox converge in an open field; there is a drop of two of blood, and only the fox's prints meander on. The frantic, two-foot bounds of a cottontail end in clumps of fur and the broad wing prints of a great horned owl. It's a scary world out there.

Wildlife Viewing Tips

The trick to wildlife watching is to time your visits, keep a low profile, and behave in ways that creatures consider safe. By following the tips below, you'll do more than glimpse animals: you'll experience a part of their lives.

• Busiest feeding times: dusk and dawn; full moon nights; after rains, when animals feast on prey washed out of homes.

• Popular animal hangouts: habitat borders, trail intersections, ledges overlooking open areas, and drinking sites.

• Walk into the wind so your scent trails behind. Keep the sun at your back so animals must squint to see you. Move like molasses and freeze often.

• Make "mule ears": cup your hands behind your ears to amplify sounds. Sudden silence may mean a predator is near.

• Keep pets at home or at your side. You'll see more wildlife without a disrupting chase.

• Kiss the back of your hand (rodent squeal) or say "pish" with clenched teeth (bird call). Brings the curious every time.

• Trust your instincts. Hair standing on the back of your neck could mean a predator is drawing near.

• To zero in on an animal quickly with binoculars or a camera, sight with your eyes while bringing the eyepiece up.

• Steer clear of nests. If parents flee, eggs may chill, young may go hungry, and predators may follow your scent to the nest.

• Don't share your food. Human fare often hurts wild digestive systems and makes animals too trusting.

• Be a crocodile. Animals won't expect to see you gliding toward shore with just your eyes above water.

• Don't unnecessarily disturb wild animals. Retreat at the first signs of ear flicking, pawing, panting, or alarm calling.

OUR BOUNTIFUL PLANTS

Plant Champions *America's record breakers*

Which desert plant has the largest flower cluster?

An *Agave americana* is a giant porcupine of a plant, a huge gray-blue rosette of six-foot-long leaves edged with hooks and tipped with spines. Well adapted to arid conditions, this member of the amaryllis family is at home in Southwestern deserts. Its thick leaves, protected by a waxy coating that reduces moisture loss, act as water storage tanks and shade one another when the sun is overhead and hottest.

A decade or more may pass before the spiky plant shoots out the only flower stalk it ever grows—a last gasp for the agave, which pours all its resources into the display. This stalk towers up to 30 feet high and hoists about two dozen branches, each one a candelabra aflame with yellow flowers three inches or more in length.

Historically, bats were the pollinators who plunged their heads and long tongues into the tubelike blossoms to indulge greedily in the plant's bounty of nectar. With the bat population in decline, however, an agave's sole blooming may be visited only by intrepid bees or the occasional hummingbird.

Popularly thought to take 100 years to flower, agaves, or century plants, do need from 10 to 50 years to produce their tall flowering stems. Once the fruits ripen, the stems topple, and the spiny-leafed plants die. Some 16 species of agave grow in the hot, dry parts of the American Southwest.

What are the biggest and smallest seeds?

The huge, 10-inch-long seeds of the coconut palm bob in the waves like beach balls thanks to their lightweight, watertight husks, which have enabled this plant to colonize tropical islands around the globe by traveling the world's oceans. Nourished by an internal pool of rich, milky liquid and a store of white meat, these seed behemoths sprout after fetching up on shores in favorable climes.

Unlike the giant, well-fortified palm seed, a tiny orchid seed is cast into the world with virtually no nutritional reserves, and it is so small as to be nearly invisible. A pile of orchid seeds is a miniature drift of powder. If orchids held theories about reproduction, their opinion would be that quantity, not quality, is paramount: a single orchid may produce hundreds of thousands of seeds, all of which are entrusted to the wind for dispersal. When they land, the seeds must be infected by certain fungi species that will provide them with the nutrition necessary for early growth. Without this help a sprouted seed soon dies.

Although orchids usually bring to mind tropical rain forests festooned with myriad exotic flowers, some species actually thrive on the tundra above the Arctic Circle. North America is home to about 200 species of orchids. One of the loveliest is the showy lady's slipper, a white flower with a blushing lip that grows in damp woods, stream margins, and bogs. It has the honor of being Minnesota's official state flower as well as the floral emblem of Canada's Prince Edward Island. Its cousin the pink lady's slipper, or moccasin flower, dangles its pouched magenta or white lip above woodland floors on both sides of the border as well.

The moccasin flower (above) uses a sweet scent to lure bees into its pink, slipper-shaped pouch. There the insects find no nectar but are dusted with pollen as they depart.

Some giant sequoias in Yosemite Valley are over 2,500 years old and bear branches larger than any trees east of the Mississippi.

Of all American trees, which are the tallest?

The loftiest tree in the world seems to touch the sky, its trunk reaching higher than the Statue of Liberty. This forest monarch, a coastal redwood in Humboldt Redwoods State Park in northern California, stands about 368 feet tall. A height of up to 325 feet is typical for redwoods over five centuries old.

Not as tall but far more massive is the giant sequoia, a mighty conifer that can measure 100 feet in circumference at its base and weigh over 1,000 tons. Sequoias tower up to 250 feet high, with some behemoths reaching 275 feet. These colossal trees grow only in a few groves on the western slopes of the Sierra Nevada. Far more widespread is the Douglas fir, a tree that grows straight as an arrow to a height of 250 to 300 feet in evergreen forests west of the Rockies.

Champions of Their Kinds

Redwood
Douglas Fir
Giant Sequoia
Grand Fir
Western Hemlock

The towering giants of the American forest are all found along the central and northern Pacific coast, where moisture-laden winds blowing in from the ocean produce abundant rainfall and moderate temperatures. No other region of the world boasts trees as tall or as massive.

155

winds and harsh winters. Gnarled and twisted, with portions of their trunks often shorn of bark, these trees dramatize the impact of countless storms. Some writhe along the ground while others stab jagged spears into the sky. Yet, even trees with half-dead trunks still hold out branches thick with dark green needles.

Methuselah shares its unforgiving habitat with other bristlecones boasting 4,000 or more birthdays. The Great Basin bristlecones also grow in parts of Utah and Nevada. Their kin, the Rocky Mountain bristlecone pines, mark the passage of time at high altitudes in Colorado, New Mexico, and Arizona—though the clock runs out for them after a mere 2,000 years.

How big can pine cones get?

Cones as big as eggplants dangle from the branches of the Coulter pine, a native of rocky California mountainsides. Each yellow-brown cone weighs from 1½ to 5 pounds and measures up to 14 inches in length, earning the tree its alternate name of big-cone pine. Not a fruit to be standing under when it falls, the heavy cone bristles with sharp spines that curve from each scale like a cat's claws.

Longer but lighter is the cone of the sugar pine, a native of California and Oregon that favors cool mountainsides. This pine's fruit measures from 18 to 26 inches. The tree more than doubles the big-cone's height: it reaches a lofty 200 feet, making it North America's tallest pine.

This bristlecone pine may carry on for centuries with only its still-green lower boughs. Its upper branches are dead from centuries of harsh weather. Bristlecones can take 4,000 years to grow from 10 to 30 feet tall.

What are the oldest living trees?

The Great Pyramid's first stone was yet to be laid when the world's oldest living tree sprouted. Known as Methuselah, this 4,600-year-old survivor is a Great Basin bristlecone pine clinging to rocky soil 10,000 feet up in the White Mountains of California. Barely 10 inches of rain a year dampen Methuselah and its tough companions, which grow in defiance of wicked

A California sea lion swims among undulating strands of giant kelp off the California coast. The world's largest marine plant, giant kelp can grow almost 100 feet in a year and reach more than double that length in a seven-year life span.

What plant grows the fastest?

The fastest-growing plant isn't found in a rain forest. In fact, it never gets a drop of rain. It lives in a treeless forest that laps the western shores of North America—a forest of kelp, rippling with the ebb and flow of the ocean. The titan of this forest, giant kelp, forms strands stretching 200 feet long. Capable of growing an incredible two feet in one day, this golden brown seaweed prospers in cool, nutrient-rich waters up to 80 feet deep.

Giant kelp belongs to a group of plants called algae, which are simpler in structure than flowering plants. Instead of roots, kelps have tendril-like structures that anchor the plants to the bottom but don't suck up nutrients. Kelp stipes, structures resembling leaves, lack veins and capillaries. A kelp plant uses all its surfaces to absorb the carbon dioxide, minerals, and water it needs. Like trees on land but unlike smaller algae plants, giant kelp has a transport system to bring sugars produced in the upper portions of its body receiving direct sunlight to lower, shaded areas. By moving sugars around, it is able to grow faster and larger than any of its relatives.

Which pine trees have the longest needles?

The bearers of North America's longest needles are a Mutt and Jeff duo of pines—the tall, dignified longleaf pine of the Southeast and the shorter, untidy-looking digger pine of California. Both grow thin needles in bundles of three. Those of the longleaf pine are deep green in color, measure from 8 to 18 inches, and droop from branches high on the 100-foot-tall trunk. The digger pine, which grows to 60 feet, is sparingly furnished with tufts of gray-green needles up to 17 inches long on the ends of its branches.

The longleaf pine is a timber tree, providing sturdy wood for flooring and construction and yielding turpentine; the brittle, weak wood of the digger pine is suitable only for burning. Straight as a telephone pole, the longleaf is a model of good posture compared to the digger, which often forks near its base and leans sideways as it grows on the slopes of the Sierra Nevada. Both pines are important wildlife food sources. Southern squirrels, quail, and turkeys devour seeds of the longleaf pine's slender cones; West Coast deer, birds, and rodents dine with equal relish on the large seeds of the digger's chunky cones.

157

This grove of aspens is actually a single, gigantic plant. The seemingly separate trees sprang up when fire created an opening. Stunted parent trees, connected by the roots, were unable to reach tree size in the deep shade of dominant spruces but grew rapidly into a stand of clones once the shading trees were destroyed. The aspens, however, will enjoy only a few years in the sun. Spruces, growing under the aspens, will eventually shade them out again.

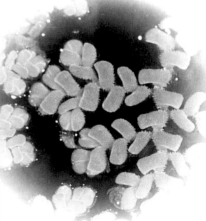

Tiny floating flakes of green, Wolffia are our smallest flowering plants, some varieties measuring just one-sixteenth of an inch across. Wolffia plants have no leaves or stems and produce only very simple flowers. They flourish on the surface film of stagnant water, multiplying there mainly by budding.

158

What is the largest living thing?

Big comes in many packages. Something may be longer, taller, or heavier. For example, redwoods grow tallest, but sequoias grow bigger around. So which is the larger tree? Even the winner of such a dispute does not qualify as the most massive living thing. For that honor we must look beyond redwoods and blue whales.

Throughout the world's forests grows a fungus known as *Armillaria*. It grows mostly underground, sending up spore-bearing bodies that collectors call honey mushrooms. *Armillaria* specimens occupying 40 to 100 acres underground are not uncommon, but a few in western North America top 400 acres. Still, even they are not the largest living things.

The quaking aspen tree can legitimately claim this title because it reproduces by sprouting from its roots. New sprouts emerge as the root system expands each growing season. They eventually form a grove shaped like a circus tent. The mother trees stand tall in the middle, and the generations of shorter, younger trees march outward.

Aspen trunks growing hundreds of yards apart are connected by their roots. Genetically identical, they are part of one enormous organism. Such a grove of clones in Utah, covering 107 acres, included 47,000 trunks. Aspen clones have more bulk than *Armillaria* fungi. Not the tallest or longest or widest, an aspen grove wins honors as the largest living thing by being the bulkiest.

How small is the tiniest flowering plant?

Scooping up a handful of pond water blanketed with minute *Wolffia* plants is like cupping a flower garden in one's palm. Each green speck is a plant measuring barely one-sixteenth of a inch across. About 250 of these aquatic plants could fit easily on a postage stamp.

A *Wolffia* plant lacks stems and leaves and must float on fresh (nonsaline) water to survive. This tiny bead catches our attention only when it masses into sheets of green rather like algae scum. Barely visible *Wolffia* flowers rarely appear because the plants often reproduce simply by shedding buds. Although an overabundance of *Wolffia* can choke a body of still water, the plants are an important food source for snails, insect larvae, fish, and ducks, the last often serving as unwitting couriers by carrying cargoes of *Wolffia* nestled amid their belly feathers to new locations.

Which are the tallest cacti?

Weird and wonderful cacti grow in Arizona, southeastern California, and northern Mexico. Like renegades from a tale by Dr. Seuss, they resemble barrels, pancakes, buttons, organ pipes, antlers, and teddy bears. But it's the giant saguaro reaching for the sky with massive, upraised arms that epitomizes the American desert.

These pleated cacti reach 50 to 60 feet in height, nearly that of the bulkier cardón cacti growing in Baja California. A saguaro takes more than a century to achieve full stature. The seedling grows slowly, measuring just half an inch in its third year. By age 50, the cactus stands as tall as a man and wears a crown of white flowers. Arms bud in its 75th year. A full-grown specimen boasts an impressive complement of 12 to 50 spiny limbs and may survive 200 years or more.

The largest cactus native to our country, a saguaro can grow more than 50 feet tall and weigh 10 tons. Shallow roots radiating from the pleated trunk like spokes in a wheel can absorb half a ton of water from a good rain.

Plants, Plants Everywhere *Even on rocks!*

What kinds of plants grow on solid rock?

While strolling through the woods, you come upon a rushing creek blocking your path. Spotting a promising place to cross, you rock-hop once, twice, and—splash!—you're in the water, having lost your footing on one of nature's most slippery substances: the green "velvet" atop river rocks. This slimy coating is actually a plant, or more accurately, a colony of single photosynthesizing cells called algae. Green algae also grow in a multicellular form that streams like hair from the skulls of submerged rocks.

A different family of algae inhabits the rollicking zone at the ocean's edge, halfway between high and low tide lines. These two- to four-foot-long brown algae, known as bladder wrack, sea wrack, or simply rockweed, grow air-filled bladders that allow their fronds to float atop the tides, close to the light. To keep its footing, rockweed grows clawlike holdfasts that look as if the plant's stem has melted, dripped around the rock, and fused. Rockweed regularly loses parts of its rubbery body to riptides and rogue waves, but as long as the holdfasts grip, the plant survives. The shredded fronds will regenerate in as little as a week. This impressive growth rate allows people to harvest brown algae for mulch, cattle forage, or algin, a versatile polymer used in everything from meringue to cement.

Algae can also dab dry, inland rocks with their living color. The algae become enveloped and anchored by a fungus, which keeps them from drying out. In return the algae provide their captor with a source of sun-forged carbon that it can't manufacture itself. Together, they comprise a composite plant called a lichen, which, like river algae and rockweed, can stubbornly grow where few plants find purchase.

Why does the water in ponds sometimes turn green?

One of nature's most peaceful sights is that of a small turtle climbing from a pristine pond to bask in the summer sun, but in countless areas across our continent, such scenes are vanishing fast. The greening of ponds—a process called eutrophication—is yet another by-product of human progress.

While algae occur harmlessly in many ponds, their growth can be dangerously spurred by rising concentrations of nutrients in the water. Even a slight increase may result in an algal bloom: an explosive growth of blue-green algae that renders a lake or pond unfit for life. A thickening carpet of surface algae robs submerged plants of life-giving sunshine, while decomposing algae below chokes off the pond's oxygen supply, eventually suffocating fish and other aquatic creatures. Extensive algal surface scum is a sure sign of a pond already in trouble.

Although eutrophication can occur naturally as sediments or ground-leeched nutrients accumulate in a body of water, it is increasingly brought on by manmade factors. Industrial dumping and agricultural and urban runoff introduce fertilizers, sewage, and other algal nutrients (particularly nitrogen and phosphorus) to previously pristine waterways.

The process, however, is not irreversible. One of nature's wonders is its astonishing regenerative power, which can halt and even heal the damage of eutrophication if fertilizers and pollutants are removed from a pond's surrounding land. Oxygen and clear water return, and once again, fish, frogs, crayfish, and all the myriad life forms that fill a healthy pond can thrive.

Appearing over 350 million years ago, mosses have remained among the plant kingdom's most primitive and resilient members, taking up residence in caves, on rotting logs, and sometimes on stones.

↜ *Mangroves provide a vital link in the food chain of the marshes they inhabit. Leaves and limbs that drop to the water decompose into a nutrient-rich muck that is consumed by crustaceans and bottom-feeding fish, who in turn nourish birds, turtles, and larger fish.*

What trees can survive in salt water?

What is the reason that the sea nourishes not trees? So pondered the Greek essayist Plutarch more than 2,000 years ago. Seawater, he proposed, "can neither penetrate the roots, because of its grossness, nor ascend, because of its weight." Plutarch was a pretty good naturalist for his day, but he had never seen a seacoast entangled in a web of mangroves—a group of maritime trees that has ways of dealing with the "grossness" of salt water. Some species secrete salt from their leaves and roots, while others store salt in older leaves before they drop off.

Mangroves do not need salt water to survive. In fact, experiments have shown that some species thrive in fresh water. In nature, however, mangroves grow only at the edge of the world's warmer oceans. Most mangroves have roots that reach partially above the waterline, providing air to the root system below the surface or buried in the tidal mudflat. The red mangrove, for example, is found along the Florida coast perched on arching, stiltlike roots that resemble the spindly legs of a spider. These "legs" support a thick trunk that develops several feet above the ground. The root system of the black mangrove, which grows along the coasts of Texas, Louisiana, and Florida, acquires oxygen by sending up hundreds of slender branches, called pneumatophores, which serve as respiratory organs.

Red and black mangroves grow in intermingled stands whose tightly woven roots form vast silt-trapping nets. While sheltering young fish and mollusks, these root systems also prevent coastal erosion and can eventually capture enough silt to fill a marsh and build up new land.

A ghostly gray mane of Spanish moss festoons the branches of this bald cypress tree. Despite its muted hue, Spanish moss actually contains chlorophyll, the green pigment used to convert sunlight into nourishment.

How do some plants survive without roots?

As any gardener knows, victory over weeds cannot be declared until every last root has been yanked out, for broken ends left in the ground will surely sprout new tops in a matter of days. Roots are a plant's lifeline to the earth, serving both as anchors and as links to water and nutrient sources. It's hard to imagine any plant that could survive without this subterranean support system, but many have done just that.

Some very small aquatic plants, such as algae, simply absorb nutrients directly from the water in which they float. A similar strategy is employed by watermeal, which can smother a pond under a blanket of millions of pinhead-size plants with double-lobed leaves.

Other plants, while descended from rooted ancestors, have long since taken up new careers as air plants, parasites, and even predators. Spanish moss, for one, has made its home in treetops, far from the earthy origins of its kind. Despite its name this familiar lacy drapery, which adorns live oak and cypress limbs throughout the South, is neither Spanish nor a true moss, and legend aside, it's not a parasite, either. Actually a rootless relative of the pineapple, this ill-named plant ranges from Texas to Virginia and as far south as Brazil. An epiphyte, or air plant, Spanish moss derives its sustenance entirely from sunlight and particles borne on wind and rain. Its scaly gray leaves not only absorb moisture directly from its humid environment but also collect bits of dead bark (a nutrient-rich food source) swept down by rain from its host's upper branches.

While Spanish moss poses no active threat to the trees on which it rests (although the sheer weight of it can sometimes snap a limb), not all rootless flora are so benign. Parasites like mistletoe and dodder attach themselves to a host with rootlike structures called haustoria, which they use to siphon off vital nutrients, sometimes killing their victims in the process. Still other rootless plants have turned to the animal kingdom for nourishment. The aquatic bladderwort, for example, feeds on tiny swimming animals sucked into the hundreds of traps that adorn its submerged stems.

Can flowering plants bloom underwater?

Comedian W. C. Fields once quipped that he never drank water because fish mate in it. They're not alone, either: a few plants also conduct their private affairs below the surface.

Water is a difficult reproductive medium for flowering plants, which originally developed on dry land. The pollen that carries the male flower's genetic material tends to rot when wet, and ordinarily encounters moisture only in the female ovary. Consequently, most aquatic flowering plants—waterlilies, for example—still raise their blooms above the water to propagate.

In shallow, briny bays along our continent's northern seacoasts, however, grow dense beds of greenery that seem to defy the odds. Dulled by silt and lying limply on the bottom at low tide, these grassy stands brighten and sway gracefully with the swell of incoming waters. The plant is eelgrass, and it is North America's only flowering plant that blooms—and in fact conducts its entire reproductive cycle—underwater. Unlike many land plants, eelgrass offers no big, bold blossoms to enchant us, but close examination reveals small flowers half hidden among its ribbonlike leaves. The male flowers produce a stringy, sticky pollen well-suited to their undersea environs. Swept by currents to awaiting females, the pollen clings to them with a waterproof adhesive that holds fast against rushing tides.

While other North American plants produce submerged flowers, none actually bloom underwater. Water starworts, for example, produce open flowers above the surface, and closed, self-pollinating flowers below. But the Rube Goldberg prize for aquatic pollination must go to water-celery, found in freshwater marshes throughout the East. Packets bearing male flowers break away from submerged stems and pop to the surface, where they split open. These pollen-laden "pontoon boats" then drift until they contact and fertilize the female flowers, which dangle from long stalks at the water line. Once fertilized, the female flowers slip below the surface on coiled stalks, and the seeds ripen underwater.

Rippling tresses of eelgrass were once a common sight along the Atlantic coast, but in the 1930s the plant was nearly wiped out by an unknown disease or parasite. Only recently has it made a comeback off Eastern shores.

Creative Lifestyles *The art of adaptation*

When do most woodland wildflowers bloom?

"Sweet April showers do spring May flowers." This enduring but often misquoted aphorism, penned by a 16th-century English poet, may ring true for more northerly latitudes. In the Pacific Northwest, though, wildflowers may start blooming as early as April and fade in August. In the deciduous woodlands of eastern North America, the parade of spring blossoms begins even earlier (in March) and winds down by May Day. Such beloved wildflowers as candy-striped spring beauties, white mountain lilies, blue hepatica, and orange columbines certainly benefit from early rains, but what they need most of all is plenty of unfiltered sunlight. So these spring ephemerals, as botanists call them, rush to bloom before the leaves of beech, maple, oak, and birch trees unfold.

By mid-May, when the foliage of canopy trees and understory shrubs has fully expanded, the amount of sunlight reaching the forest floor will have decreased by 87 percent. Yet a few of our perennials, such as the triple-leaved, white-flowered American ginseng, manage to thrive in this shadowy province due to increased photosynthetic efficiency and their ability to store carbohydrates in their roots.

Are wildflowers as short-lived as they seem?

From Newfoundland to Georgia, from Manitoba to Arkansas, early spring is a time when the forest floor becomes a veritable magic carpet of burgeoning blossoms. Sometimes called Appalachian wildflowers for their extraordinary abundance in that mountainous region, these delicate delights often have names that are as vivid as their colors: wakerobin (deep maroon), trout-lily (lemon yellow), Dutchman's-breeches (creamy white), and jack-in-the-pulpit (green-and-white pinstripes).

To us they are among the most fleeting features of the landscape, blooming one day and gone the next—sometimes literally. Just below ground, however, are the long-lived bulbs, tubers, and rhizomes from which these fragile

➤ *Shy and slight, spring beauties are among the most fragile wildflowers, wilting at once if they are picked. Yet, ironically, to reach the forest floor, they must push up past rocks and roots through 10 or 12 inches of cold soil.*

flowers grow—unseen segments that may outlast their visible counterparts by decades.

Among our most durable wildflowers are native orchids, found in moist habitats throughout North America. Some may go for years without blooming or even producing leaves above ground. The most notorious no-shows among them are the pogonias. These Rip Van Winkles of the plant world may "sleep" for over a decade before popping up again, but they can live as long as a human.

In places where wildflowers have remained undisturbed, we find the real veterans of the plant kingdom. Heartleaf plantain, a giant cousin of the plantain found in weedy lawns, grows along wet shores on the Atlantic and Gulf coasts to the Mississippi River. One stand on the Hudson River tidal shore is known to be at least 110 years old. That's how long botanists have been observing this group of plants, which in all that time has numbered exactly 36 individuals.

➤ *Blooming in April or May, the jack-in-the-pulpit (a relative of skunk cabbage) is named for its distinctive hooded flower spike.*

How do delicate poppies manage to survive in deserts?

By means subtle or blatant, desert plants have no choice but to cope with the rigors of their hot, dry environment. Some sport silvery leaves that reflect harsh sunlight, while others are clothed in furry hairs to reduce evaporation. Cacti have adapted by dispensing with leaves and hoarding water within thick, engorged stems. Some annual wildflowers, though—like the Mexican gold and California poppies, which can cloak the desert with sunny expanses of yellow or orange—have few such safeguards. Instead, they gamble on the weather, managing to sidestep the worst of the heat and drought.

Wrapped in its watertight shell, the seed of a Mexican gold poppy rests in a kind of suspended animation through the long, brutal summer. Only with the arrival of autumn, which brings cooler days and more frequent rains to the Sonoran Desert of Arizona and neighboring states, does the embryo nestled inside come to life. The seeds sprout by November, but the chill of December and January halts their development for a time. Yet if the winter rains come on time and in due measure, and if it's neither too cold nor too hot, by February the poppies grow with abandon, raising their spectacular flowers in stands so thick that they transform the desert into a garden. Within weeks they have set their seeds and died, completing their life cycle before the driest season begins. Not every year is so generous, however. Sometimes the damp promise of autumn withers into drought or unseasonable heat, and most of the seedlings perish.

➤ *Despite its name the California poppy ranges well beyond the Golden State into Utah, carpeting grassy hills and arid slopes with its golden blossoms. Even in a good year, not all of its seeds will sprout—a policy that ensures a supply of seeds whatever the whims of the weather.*

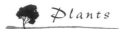

━ *Beach grass flourishes in sand a few feet above the high tide mark. Its root network holds the sand in place, making it the most important grass species in the sand dunes from Virginia to Maine. Even when completely buried by windblown sand, beach grass can send new shoots up to the surface.*

How have plants adapted to life in ponds and along the seashore?

As every gardener knows, too much water can be just as harmful to many plants as too little, and too much salty water is even worse. But some plants have adaptations that help them overcome the trials and tribulations of a watery lifestyle. Take the duckweeds, tiny flowering plants that float on the surface of ponds, for example. Some have neither stems nor leaves, but many species do have threadlike roots. Hanging down from the underside of each green speck of duckweed, they never reach the rich muck on the bottom, yet they can absorb all the nutrients they need directly from the water.

By contrast, beach grass lives in the relative dryness of coastal sand dunes. Its roots form elaborate networks reaching deep and spreading wide to capture water from the parched sand. Beach grass ends where high tide begins because its roots will not tolerate a twice-daily bath of salt water. Between these extremes is salt marsh cordgrass. Marching from land into the sea's intertidal zone, where the salty sea rises over it, this plant is the vanguard of salt marsh vegetation. It too has strong roots that anchor it against the unrelenting assault of wind and waves, but it would not be able to survive in such salty (and potentially lethal) surroundings were it not for a secret weapon: special glands that collect absorbed salt and excrete it through the leaves.

Do tall trees have any trouble drawing water to their leaves?

To send water to the upper floors of a sky-scraper, engineers rely on powerful pumps. Trees enjoy no such mechanical advantage, yet even a towering sequoia can transport hundreds of gallons of water from the ground to its leaves each day—with no moving parts.

The secret lies in a tree's internal plumbing. A cross-section of red oak may seem solid, but it's really quite porous (especially the new wood toward the outer rim of the trunk, which is jammed with fine, vertical tubes that are closely packed beneath the living layer of bark). As water molecules evaporate through minute openings in the leaves, they draw replacements up through the trunk's intricate network of vessels, a chain reaction of suction that pulls great quantities of water skyward. So much pressure is exerted, however, that the tree might face the same problem one encounters when trying to drink a thick milkshake through a collapsing straw. Fortunately for the tree, the rigidly reinforced walls of its vessels ensure smooth passage.

On a dry, sunny day when its leaves are rippling with photosynthetic action, a large hardwood tree such as a cottonwood may move nearly 70 gallons of water per hour through its plumbing—and it does so with considerable speed. Water rising through the vessels of an oak may zoom upward at 200 inches per hour. Pines, larches, and other conifers (which lose less water through their thin, waxy needles) move liquid at a more sedate pace and lack the relatively wider vessels of hardwoods. Instead, their trunk is made up of overlapping cells pitted with holes through which the water flows.

How do vines climb?

Except for dodders and a few other varieties, vines are not really parasites, but they are freeloaders. By using trees, shrubs, and sturdy herbs (even inanimate objects such as buildings, cliffs, and the ground), vines elevate themselves toward the sun. In doing so, they dispense with stiff, bulky trunks and limbs and remain lean and fast-spreading.

Many vines, including bittersweet, wisteria, and bindweed, simply twine around other plants as they and their supporters grow. Over time they become so large that they strangle their host with boa constrictor–like coils or pull the host down with their enormous weight. Grapes use specialized structures called tendrils. Tender and pliant when young, tendrils spiral around stems and shrink to a choke hold as they toughen in maturity. When a grape tendril finds nothing to embrace, it grabs air. This happens often, resulting in marvelous curlicues of infinite variety.

Why do plants form partnerships with fungi?

The real powerhouses behind the world's forests are so small that you would need a magnifying glass to see them. Beginning life as microscopic spores, so-called mycorrhizal fungi grow into a cobwebby mass of underground filaments, each more than one thousand times finer than a human hair. What makes these threads vital is their relationship with the roots of redwoods, pines, beeches, and just about every other tree, shrub, and herb.

When a helper fungus comes in contact with the root of a redwood seedling, for example, it envelops it like a sleeve and sinks tiny threads into the outer layers of the root. As the seedling struggles to make a name for itself above ground, the root rider plays nanny, delivering water and minerals from the soil to the plant.

Besides being a conduit for nourishment, soil fungi also act as guards. They protect roots from harmful microbes and parasites either physically or by secreting antibiotics into the soil. Other species of protective fungi are known to consort with plants above the ground. The surface of a leaf may harbor dozens of different fungi species, all producing noxious chemicals that help ward off diseases and insect pests. The fungi that grow on tall fescue grass, for instance, protect your lawn, while those found on the Pacific yew tree produce a substance that, besides protecting the tree, has also proven deadly against human ovarian cancer cells.

Fungi perform such good deeds because of their inability to photosynthesize. Neither producers nor decomposers, mycorrhizal fungi need their chlorophyll-laden hosts. In return for the protection and the minerals and water they supply, they derive energy-rich sugars from the plants they inhabit.

➤ *The most specialized attachments for climbing belong to the Virginia creeper, which (like the English ivy of Ivy League fame) produces short branches with adhesive discs that resemble the toes of a tree frog. So strong and secure is their grip that they can ascend even a smooth pane of glass.*

Secrets of Survival *How plants triumph over adversity*

Which plants could not exist without forest fires?

A marvelous invention, the pine cone consists of a spiral staircase of scales arranged in such a way that no two overlap. At the base of each scale lie two seeds, and while they ripen, the cone remains tightly sealed with resin. As the seeds mature, the scales dry out, swing open, and spill their bounty—much to the delight of squirrels, chickadees, and other critters.

However, the cones of a few species, such as the lodgepole pine of Western mountain slopes and the pitch pine of New Jersey's southern barrens, open only after exposure to the intense heat of a forest fire (though a 110° F day may also cause some of their seeds to spill). When a wildfire sweeps through an area, eliminating competitive trees and enriching the poor soil with ash, it prompts remaining pines to release their seeds, creating nearly pure stands of same-age trees.

One example of this strategy is the knobcone pine of arid coastal mountains in Oregon and California. Its cones, as hard and heavy as granite, remain fixed to the trunk or large branches for decades until they become imbedded in or swallowed by the expanding wood. The cones remain viable even if the tree dies. When fire eventually races through the valleys, they explode like popcorn, planting a new knobcone forest.

⬥ As a knobcone pine matures, it sets new crops of cones on its upper branches. The old cones remain on the tree (or in it, if they've been grown over) for the remainder of its life. Clustered in threes, they bend downward at steep angles in the shape of a comma. In the aftermath of a fire, lodgepole pines in a Montana forest (below) rise like phoenixes from the ashes.

How long can coastal redwoods live?

Coastal redwoods are not only the world's loftiest trees (many of them taller than a football field is long) but also among the oldest. These giants often live from 500 to 700 years and can easily stand in their cool, fog-shrouded groves for a dozen centuries. In 1934 loggers sawed down one specimen that was 2,200 years old—the most ancient redwood on record.

Despite their imposing size (the current champion tops out at 368 feet), most redwoods start small, with a seed no larger than a tomato's and a cone the size of a grape. Other redwoods don't need seeds at all, simply rising from sprouts in fallen or damaged trees. Either way, saplings have to fight hard for the scarce light that filters down to the forest floor. Once they're established, though, there's almost no stopping them. Their bark (often a foot thick) grows quickly and contains few flammable resins, deflecting most wildfires.

Can plants grow atop volcanoes?

The crater formed by Haleakala, the biggest volcano on the Hawaiian island of Maui, is about the last place you would expect to find vegetation. Yet this land of lava rock and cinder cones is home to a magnificent blooming beauty—the silversword. Clinging tenaciously to the gritty soil 10,000 feet above sea level, where it braves blistering heat and occasional snow, this hardy plant has a gelatin-like substance within its leaves that allows it to store water efficiently. Moisture loss is further reduced by the silversword's lancelike leaves, each densely cloaked with a soft, silvery fuzz that reflects sunlight and protects it from harmful ultraviolet rays.

The silversword blooms but once, and for just a few weeks, yet it goes out in a blaze of glory, brightening the barren landscape with a brilliant array of blossoms. Years of uncontrolled goat grazing nearly drove these plants to extinction. Now legally protected, some 44,000 of them literally rise from the ashes of Haleakala.

Looking like a giant, frosted sea urchin, a full-grown silversword sprouts from Haleakala's crater—the only place on earth where this species can be found. It may take 20 years for the plant to mature, but when it finally does, it erects a shimmering flower stalk up to eight feet high with hundreds of reddish purple blossoms.

How do cacti conserve moisture?

The emptiness of a desert expanse broken only by a stately saguaro or a craggy rock outcropping belies a very different world just beneath the surface. There the shallow, thirsty roots of cacti branch out like an intricate road map. Covering an area sometimes as large as a tennis court, they drink moisture from the lightest rainfall, even from morning dew. The roots of some cacti are also succulent. Beneath the delicate night-blooming cereus, for example, lies a root weighing up to 50 pounds. Some small cacti have a central root that actually enables them to hide in periods of drought. As the root retracts, it pulls the stem downward so that wind-blown soil partially covers and shades it.

In all their splendid variety—from the rainbow cactus with its butter-colored blooms to the jumping cholla, whose spines can puncture a tire—desert-dwelling cacti look the way they do in order to survive. The waxy exterior of the stem (the part above ground) shields the plant from winds and protects its cargo of moisture from the sun. Many species have thick, pleated stems designed to hoard water and allow the cactus to expand and contract without splitting.

The cactus's lack of leaves offers another clue to its conservation skills. Leaves permit tremendous water loss through their stomata, or pores. Although the ancestors of cacti in Central America probably had leaves, these shrank dramatically or disappeared entirely as the cacti evolved to survive in increasingly arid regions. The stomata began to appear on the stem, tucked and recessed beneath spines that screen the sun's rays.

Even the timing by which the stomata open and close is linked to the plant's need to save water. As protection against the desiccating rays of the sun, the stomata close by day. In the cooler evenings, however, they open to admit carbon dioxide, which is stored all night in the form of an acid. At dawn the stomata close, and chlorophyll begins to convert the acid into sugar and starch. Although this system is economical for the cactus (a 12-foot saguaro may lose only one tablespoon of water all day, while an oak might shed 150 gallons), it creates a problem for some animals. Cattle crunching cacti in the early morning, for example, often get acid indigestion.

Which plant has survived for nearly 12,000 years?

Despite its wispy look, the creosote bush is one tough shrub. Standing 10 feet tall, it dominates the deserts of the Southwest, superbly adapted to its harsh climate. This scrappy survivor has a number of defenses that help it fend off the elements. Its tiny resin-coated leaves lose little water to the parching air, and animals avoid eat-

A Master of Mimicry

In nature, as in life, things are not always what they appear to be. Just ask the Helconius butterfly. This native of the Gulf states (look for bright colors and elongated forewings) has a particular passion for some species of passionflowers, which it not only feeds on but uses to raise its offspring.

Because its larvae are cannibalistic, the Helconius lays individual eggs—each one no larger than a grain of rice—in isolated parts of the plant, well away from any potential predators. In most cases the butterfly glues its eggs to tendrils, stipules, or leaf tips.

Several days later a caterpillar starts eating its way out—the first step toward its transformation into a butterfly.

To ward off such freeloaders, some passionflowers turn to their bag of tricks. These clever copycats have developed yellow budlike protrusions that so closely resemble the eggs of the Helconius that the butterfly looks elsewhere. As if that ruse weren't ingenious enough, the leaves of some passionflowers secrete a sugary solution that's irresistible to ants and wasps—which just happen to eat Helconius larvae.

The creosote bush, like this solitary specimen in Death Valley, California, keeps its distance from neighbors to conserve moisture. Animals, in turn, stay away from the plant because it never fails to live up to its nickname: stinkweed.

ing it because the resin disrupts their digestion. To protect its meager water supply, the plant releases a chemical into the soil that stops seeds from sprouting and competing for moisture. A network of shallow roots stakes its claim, extending outward up to 13 feet to quickly soak up any moisture that falls. A vertical root may also reach down to tap deep, hidden pockets of water.

When conditions go from bad to worse, though, the creosote bush relies on other unique characteristics. While many plants shrink from the full onslaught of the desert summer by escaping into dormancy, the creosote faces it head-on. The leaves of most plants would shrivel up and die if they lost 25 to 50 percent of their water content, but those of the creosote bush hang on until they're down 70 percent. This plucky plant has even been known to cheat death. The creosote can actually clone itself. If a branch gets buried or the root crown splits, new roots sprout and produce an independent individual. Clones make clones, creating a ring or clump of shrubs, all identical to the original, which may have perished years before. One such clump in the Mojave Desert is believed to be 11,700 years old.

Why do fruits change color as they ripen?

The sound of a brown apple falling to the ground—a soft, mealy plop—is the sound of failure. Overripe, the apple will rot and its seeds will sprout in a shady place. The secret to a fruit's success is for the seed to be swallowed in its prime, carried to a sunny spot, and planted with a dollop of fertilizer. To make sure this happens, plants grow luscious "wrappers" for their seeds, offering animals an irresistible treat.

As is so often the case in nature, timing is everything. A plant doesn't want to give its fruit away before its seeds are ripe, nor does it want insects to find it. Hence, some plants (including blackberries, blueberries, mulberries, and black cherries) wage clever advertising campaigns. A few days before ripening to blue or black, their berries blush red, telling local birds what's in store for them. Migrating birds, however, don't have the luxury of advance notice. To alert them to what's available, fall-ripening plants such as dogwood and spicebush change into their autumn colors while other plants are still green. These bright foliage flags are nature's billboards, erected neither a moment too soon nor too late.

To avoid being picked or preyed upon prematurely, plants like the persimmon grow hard fruits, lace them with bitter, astringent chemicals, and camouflage them with leaves. When their seeds finally ripen, the fruits soften, become sweeter, and change their hue from green to red, orange, or yellow.

As the maple behind it goes out in a blaze of glory, this apple tree in the Hudson Valley stands bare and leafless, having already shed its fall finery. Despite its appearance the tree is packed with energy in the form of carbohydrates, put into storage the summer before and ready to be activated come spring.

Why do trees lose their leaves?

By the time autumn is through casting its magical spell, a mature red maple will drop about 200,000 leaves, and the forest it calls home will be carpeted with some 10 million leaves per acre. Most are of the broadleaf variety, though deciduous conifers such as tamaracks can get into the act as well, raining countless golden needles on the forest floor. It all happens in response to the earth tilting away from the sun, bringing cooler temperatures and shorter days to the temperate forests. Plants can't migrate south the way birds and butterflies can. Nor can they risk business-as-usual during a season when water, frozen in the ground, is unavailable to roots. In the throes of a winter thirst, a canopy of maple leaves, which on a summer day would be able to transpire as much as 900 gallons of water, becomes a liability.

To turn off this leaky valve, trees produce a chemical that causes a corky ring to form at the base of the leaf's stem. As days go by, the noose thickens, choking off the flow of precious water

How do rhododendrons keep warm in chilly weather?

During June and July the spicy fragrance and pastel palette of rhododendron blossoms grace yards and gardens across America, while their wild counterparts bloom in swamps and mountains of the Eastern states. In the warm, moist summer air, the evergreen leaves of this popular shrub spread in whorls to capture sunlight's energy, but in the chill of winter, they droop down and roll up into tight tubes to conserve moisture, a reaction triggered by cold air.

Deciduous plants reduce moisture loss in the cold months by dropping their leaves before the onset of winter, but lacking this option, evergreens conserve moisture in other ways. Most evergreen leaves have a waxy, waterproof coating. The leaves of pines and spruces are "needles" whose small surface area reduces evaporation. The rhododendron's droop-and-roll strategy makes the leaves narrower and needlelike, reducing direct exposure to desiccating sunlight.

Which tree is famous because it "came back from the grave"?

If trees could speak, in 1975 Ashe's birch might have echoed Mark Twain's quip that "reports of my death have been greatly exaggerated." Native to the mountains of Virginia, this slender birch with blackish brown aromatic bark was discovered in 1914 by forester William Ashe along a stream he identified as Dickey Creek. That same year, a man named Horace Ayers came across a stand of these trees along nearby Cressy Creek. Leaves collected by both men were sent to Harvard University and stored in its archives.

For reasons unknown, botanists forgot about the Cressy Creek birches and, although they combed the woods, could not relocate those at Dickey Creek. By the 1950s the birch was believed to have vanished. In 1973, however, a botanist noticed that some of the leaves stored at Harvard were labeled "Cressy Creek." Armed with this information, two scientists began to independently scour the area near Cressy Creek in search of the elusive birch. In the summer of 1975, both of them found a grove of about a dozen trees by the stream bank. What ever happened to the Dickey Creek birches? Either they died out, or Ashe had actually found the same birches as Ayers, but simply confused his creeks.

➤ *Like underdressed people who try to keep warm by hunching their shoulders and hugging themselves, rhododendron leaves (which can measure up to 10 inches long) curl up into cylinders to shield themselves from winter's cold air and drying wind.*

and minerals to the leaf. Dried, yet flaming with color, it finally flutters to the ground along with countless companions, becoming a mulch that nourishes a whole new flush of leaves.

In the desert, leaf dropping takes a different tack. Palo verdes, ocotillos, and other plants may abort their leaves just after spring, thereby avoiding the wicking effect of sunshine. Their stems and twigs take over the task of food production. When things cool down, or rain falls, some plants unfurl a second set of leaves, which assume the job of making sugar from the sun.

Poisonous Plants Dreadful, dangerous, and sometimes deadly

Can some plants sting?

According to legend, when Julius Caesar's tunic-clad soldiers invaded the colder climes of Britain in 54 B.C., they kept themselves warm by rubbing their bare legs with the leaves of stinging nettle (*Urtica dioica*). The story may be apocryphal, but this pernicious plant, which thrives in open weedy places throughout eastern North America, certainly generates heat. The underside of the nettle leaf is covered with hollow, bristly hairs. Like tiny hypodermic needles, these hairs can puncture the skin, injecting formic acid (the same burning chemical found in bee stingers). The good news is that the discomfort usually fades in an hour or so.

Stinging nettle is not the only plant that should be handled with kid gloves and long pants. Tread-softly, found on sandy soil from Virginia to Texas, has white trumpet-shaped flowers and a name whose warning should be heeded. Another plant, stinging lupine, has reddish flowers that serve as a warning not to touch this pretty but perilous native of southern California. Both plants inject an irritant into the skin of those who brush up against them. If you become a victim, treat the wound as you would a bee sting—and avoid scratching (it only makes things worse).

Why is poison ivy so poisonous?

More than 60 species of animals and innumerable insects feed on the ivory berries and glossy leaves of poison ivy (*Toxicondendron radicans*), but most humans are so highly allergic to this plant that we will surely never join their ranks. A relative of the cashew, this immobile prey employs a chemical called urushiol to teach its attackers a lesson they'll never forget.

Urushiol is an oily resin found in the leaves, flowers, berries, bark, and roots of poison ivy, poison oak, and poison sumac. Plant eaters that can't detoxify this poison—a category including no known animals but 85 percent of all Americans—soon learn to keep their dis-

Of all the toxic plants in North America, perhaps the most infamous—and ubiquitous—is poison ivy. The plant is particularly deceptive when it grows up a trunk, for its leaves can easily be mistaken for those of the tree.

To be injured by stinging nettle, one need only brush up against it. Even the slightest touch is enough to pierce an intruder's skin with stiff hairs and introduce an irksome poison into the wound.

tance. If you're like most people, your first brush with poison ivy is unlikely to cause a reaction. Urushiol seeps into your skin and joins with a protein, only then becoming tagged as an invader. White blood cells, now carrying a memory of urushiol, fan into your bloodstream to await the next attack. After a few more encounters, the growing phalanx of bodyguards closes rank, and you become allergic. Urushiol can hitchhike on clothes, dog's hair, and garden tools. Even a touch can cause up to two weeks of itchy, weeping blisters. Because the particles can remain potent for a year, your best defense is to scrub tainted items with brown soap and water. Your best offense is to remember that urushiol, and the misery it brings, is the plant's way of saying "Leaves of three, let them be."

What is locoweed?

In old Westerns bad guys wear black hats, the cavalry arrives just in the nick of time, and horses that eat locoweed buck their riders into the nearest cactus patch. Well, Hollywood got it partly right. *Locoweed (Oxytropis* and *Astragalus)* is the common name for certain members of the legume family of plants. Found throughout the western United States and Canada, these perennial herbs take up selenium, barium, molybdenum, arsenic, tin, and other toxic elements from the soil in which they grow. When grazing animals, such as sheep, cattle, and horses, eat large amounts of locoweed, they develop locoism, a disease that gets its name from the Spanish word *loco,* meaning "crazy."

While that's a fair description of the symptoms, the early stages of locoism are more apt to cause horses and cattle to drag their feet rather than buck. As the disease progresses, its victims become standoffish, stop eating, and eventually die.

Locoweed comes in a variety of species. Two-grooved milk vetch grows from Manitoba to New Mexico. Spotted loco thrives from eastern Washington to California. Red-stemmed pea vine is found in western Texas. Animals raised in locoweed territory usually won't eat it as readily as imported livestock will. Once they get a taste for it, however, they develop an often fatal craving. As crazy as it sounds, the cure for locoweed poisoning is a dose of arsenic or strychnine.

➤ *For landscape lovers the purple and white clusters in this field of locoweed make for dazzling scenery. For grazing animals, however, they spell disaster. The slow-acting poison within often leads to a violent death.*

~ *The highly tempting berries of bittersweet nightshade (Solanum dulcamara) (right) account for most of its poisonings, but the entire plant is considered toxic. The deathcap mushroom (below), which grows in woods and along their borders, is thought to be responsible for as many as 90 percent of all fatal mushroom poisonings, perhaps because its victims fail to seek medical help in time. Someone who eats a deathcap will feel better after the initial symptoms fade, only to slip into a coma several hours later.*

~ *One of two species of poison oak that afflict an estimated 2 million Americans annually, this West Coast variety (Toxicondendron diversiloba) has been dubbed "the pariah of the Pacific."*

Which plants are the most poisonous ones?

We conduct our daily lives oblivious to the garden of death that surrounds us. Poisonous plants grow almost everywhere: in our fields, our gardens, even in our homes—often profusely. Some 700 species of poisonous plants are native to North America, and at least as many have been imported from abroad. Though many resemble harmless, edible plants, they can be more deadly than the most venomous snakes.

Among poisonous plants, the most toxic of all is the water hemlock *(Cicuta maculata)*. Standing two to eight feet tall, it grows in low, wet pastures and along stream banks throughout North America. Just one bite of its long, fingerlike, clustered roots (which look and taste like parsnips) is all it takes to kill. Its lance-shaped leaflets, which are also toxic, and clusters of white flowers resemble those of dill, coriander, and other plants in the parsley family. The only feature that visibly distinguishes the water hemlock from other plants in this family, however, is the way the veins on its leaves end in the notches between the teeth on the leaf's edge rather than at the points of the teeth. One-third of all water hemlock poisonings are fatal. Such virulence made one of its relatives, poison hemlock, the suicide potion of choice among ancient Greeks. It was, in fact, the one Socrates used to kill himself.

Some mushrooms are also poisonous. The name of one highly toxic species says it all: deathcap *(Amanita phalloides)*. Widely distributed in North America, it has a dingy yellow-green color with white gills underneath the cap. It is fatal if eaten raw or cooked. When sliced up, it emits an odor akin to smelly sneakers.

Another lethal plant is deadly nightshade *(Atropa belladonna)*. Growing up to five feet tall, this untidy shrub has long, dark, woody stems arching outward, and long, pointed, dull green leaves that resemble the lilac's. The plant's most obvious feature, though, is its crop of large, shiny black berries, each about the size of a cherry but flattened a bit and dimpled.

Among the hundreds of plant poisons known, one of the most potent varieties is alkaloids, odorless but bitter organic compounds found in about 10 percent of all flowering plants, including jimsonweed, thorn apple, and black nightshade. Because flowering plants began to multiply just as the number of dinosaurs began to decline, some scientists speculate that poisonous plants may actually have led to their demise.

Do some plants wage chemical warfare on others?

The notion that one plant would be able to poison another is not as strange as it sounds. Plants grow thorns, leathery leaves, scaly bark, and foul-tasting leaves to thwart hungry predators, so why not also discourage other plants? In the quest for limited sunlight, water, and minerals, elbowing with roots and branches is only one way to draw boundaries. A chemical "fence" is a far more elegant strategy.

A case in point is the relationship between purple sage *(Salvia leucophylla)* and grasses in the California chaparral. A flyover shows a simple pattern of vegetation-free zones around every clump of sages, as if a fastidious gardener had been hard at work cutting borders. The culprits are the same chemicals that give the chaparral its spicy smell. Toxins, such as camphor and cineole, burst from the leaves and settle like mist to the ground, adhering to dry soil particles. An occasional rain washes a barrage of these poisons from the leaves, stonewalling any incursions by other plants.

The more closely scientists look, the more of these suppressive plants they find—evidence that chemicals may be more pivotal than once thought in determining who grows next to whom and how natural succession proceeds. Many of the players in old-field succession may be engaged in outright plant-to-plant combat. Using certain toxins, asters and goldenrod inhibit sugar maple and black cherry; sumacs, rhododendrons, elderberries, and bracken ferns keep the lid on Douglas fir; oaks inhibit herbs and grasses; and sugar maples keep yellow birch at bay.

The more than 120 species of Amanita fungi found in North America include some of the most lovely, and deadly, mushrooms in the world. This yellow variety is named mus-caria (Latin for "fly") because it was tradi-tionally used to poison houseflies. In the East-ern states it is often found under pine trees.

Green Magic *Making food from air, water, and sunlight*

A whorl of magnolia leaves catches the sun. Each leaf is positioned to shade its neighbors as little as possible. Leaves of a mature forest canopy fit together like the pieces of a jigsaw puzzle, allowing little sunlight to fall directly to the floor.

Why do plants need leaves?

Leaves are nature's alchemists, conjuring up substances more valuable than gold. Whether they are lily pads undulating in the ripples of a pond or aspen leaves fluttering in a gentle mountain breeze, they are constantly converting sunlight, air, and water into food while generating oxygen. We and all other land animals ultimately depend on the miraculous work of leaves for our very existence.

Leaves by the trillions clothe our planet, each one reaching for its place in the sun and situated to cast as little shade as possible on other leaves of the same plant. The broad, oval leaves of a common milkweed grow in opposite pairs, each positioned at right angles to the set below, so as not to shadow them. Many other plants arrange their leaves in long, ascending spirals around their stems, so few leaves are situated directly above one another, minimizing loss of light at lower levels. Leaves greatly increase the surface area of a plant. The 700,000 leaves of a mature maple tree, for example, expose about half an acre of surface to the sun.

Leaves are designed so that every cell can get the air, water, and sunlight that it needs. Most leaves are thin, allowing sunlight to shine right through to their undersides. Each leaf is laced by a network of veins and capillaries that circulates water from the plant's roots and adds rigidity to keep the leaf's surface fully extended in the sunlight. Thousands of microscopic pores called stomata, located mostly on the underside, admit air to the leaf's interior.

Suspended in every leaf cell but concentrated in those of the upper surfaces are tiny green particles in which the vital process of photosynthesis takes place, driven by the energy of sunlight. In a series of complex chemical reactions, water is broken down into atoms of oxygen and hydrogen. The oxygen atoms are exhaled through leaf pores, and the hydrogen atoms combine with the carbon atoms of carbon dioxide from the air, forming sugars, starches, and other carbohydrates. Green plants use these foods to create their tissues, storing any excess in branches, trunks, and roots for future consumption.

Animals, in turn, breathe the oxygen continually produced by photosynthesizing plants and obtain all of their food by feeding directly on plant tissues or on other animals that prey on plant eaters. The absolute dependency of animals on the work of leaves is summed up vividly and succinctly in the Bible, which reminds us that "All flesh is grass."

What makes grass green?

O f all green things," wrote naturalist Joseph Wood Krutch, "grass is one of the humblest . . . and the most stupidly taken for granted." Grass for most of us means just the dozen or so varieties growing in our yards, meadows, parks, and playing fields. There are, however, some 7,500 species of grass growing around the world, and among them are three of the most widely cultivated and indispensable of all our farm crops: wheat, rice, and corn.

Grasses share their green color with other members of the plant kingdom—a kingdom with approximately three-quarters of a million subjects. The stuff that makes plants green, chlorophyll, resides in leaf cells, and grass plants are almost all leaf.

Chlorophyll is not spread evenly throughout leaf cells but is concentrated in chloroplasts, microscopic bodies floating in the cellular fluids. Chloroplasts are so small that nearly half a million could fit in an area no bigger than the period at the end of this sentence. In these tiny specks photosynthesis, the most important series of chemical reactions in the living world, takes place. Here leaves manufacture food from air and water, powered by the energy of sunlight. Ironically, green wavelengths are the rejects of the photosynthetic process. The chlorophyll in chloroplasts reflects them, while absorbing most of the red and blue-violet ends of the spectrum. That's why grass looks green—our eyes see only the wavelengths not involved in photosynthesis.

Tolerant of salt water, hardy Spartina *grass grows along protected beaches and at the edges of mud flats. Once it is established, its roots form dense mats, which help to stabilize shifting sands and reduce shoreline erosion.*

How do plants breathe?

While plants don't actively inhale and exhale the way animals do, they must exchange gases with the atmosphere to survive. The surfaces of most leaves, however, are covered with a waxy coating known as the cuticle, which is especially thick on top, where sunlight strikes the leaf. While the cuticle reduces water evaporation, it also cuts off most of the flow of gases.

The leaves' only portals to the outer world are their stomata. Invisible to the naked eye, each stoma (from the Greek word for "mouth") is a minute hole that allows air to pass through the cuticle to interior cells. Framing the hole are two banana-shaped guard cells. When full of water, they curve away from each other, opening the stoma; when low on water, they collapse, sealing the stoma. The stomata also close at night, when photosynthesis ends (except those on cacti, which open at sunset as the air cools).

Stomata are packed together in astounding numbers—up to half a million per square inch on some leaves, with the majority on the sheltered undersides, except on floating leaves. The leaves of waterlilies have their stomata on the dry upper surfaces, and sinuous, air-filled chambers stretch down long stems to the submerged roots.

New leaves apparently act as air intakes, drawing fresh air down into the system, while the tubes in older, larger leaves expel depleted air to the surface.

Can plants get by without chlorophyll?

Some plants lead a parasitic existence, filching nourishment from green plants that photosynthesize their own food. Common dodder, also called love vine, twines around its neighbors, but there is nothing affectionate about its intentions. The dodder's tangle of leafless, orangy stems embrace the host plant with flattened suckers, penetrating tissues and siphoning off nutrients. Other flowering plants follow this larcenous lifestyle. Squawroot, resembling a slim, yellowish pine cone more than a flower, is a parasite on the roots of oak trees, while beechdrops depend on beech roots.

The oddest group of plants to forgo chlorophyll, though, are the monotropoids, including the Indian pipe, or corpse plant. Its translucent flowers can be found rising on eight-inch stalks in forests across southern Canada, the Pacific Northwest, and the eastern United States. The stony root mass of Indian pipe is encased in a layer of fungi called mycorrhiza, which also coats roots of nearby oaks and conifers, helping them absorb minerals from the soil in return for sugars. Indian pipe appears to be a harmless parasite on the fungi and, ultimately, the trees, draining off a tiny portion of nutrients without providing any compensation.

Ghostly white Indian pipe sprouts from leaf litter amid the shadows of forest floors from Maine to California. A flowering plant that is completely lacking chlorophyll, Indian pipe has only a few vestigial, scalelike leaves. Each three- to eight-inch stem, topped in summer by a downturned, cup-shaped flower, does indeed resemble a small clay pipe.

A yellow tangle of dodder blankets tall grasses, milkweeds, and other plants in an overgrown corner of a pasture. A finicky parasite, dodder doesn't latch on to its victims at random but somehow senses their health. Only those that are rich in nutrients are attacked by the vine's invasive suckers.

➤ *With autumn's onset maple leaves flaunt their orange carotenoid pigments as chlorophyll breaks down. If nights are chilly but frost free and days are relatively warm and sunny, sugars build up, stimulating leaves to blush crimson with anthocyanin pigments. If weather is rainy, the oranges predominate.*

Why do leaves change color?

With the arrival of autumn, a deciduous tree faces a crisis: the coming dry winter air would quickly rob its leaves of moisture at a time when freezing soil would make replacing it difficult. So the tree cuts its losses. As the temperature falls and days shorten, a corky layer of cells forms at the joint between each leaf stem and twig, cutting off the flow of sap and weakening the bond that holds the leaf in place. The leaves' chlorophyll decomposes, while other pigments remain. The amounts of these pigments and their specific combinations determine which stunning colors will paint the landscape.

Chlorophyll's departure unveils a palette masked all summer long. Tulip trees shimmer with gold from the yellow pigment xanthophyll. Oaks wrap themselves in the mellow orange and rust tones of carotenoid pigments. Maples blaze with vivid scarlets as sugars marooned in their leaves decompose into anthocyanin. Of course, not every leaf loses its green. Most conifers retain their needles, which are protected by waxy coatings, as are the broader leaves of holly and mountain laurel. Sheltered from cold, desiccating winds by snow, plants such as wild mustard keep their photosynthetic engines humming with any light that manages to reach the ground.

Freeloaders and Flycatchers *Ingenious parasites, ruthless predators*

Which plant uses a light show to lure its prey?

In a nutrient-starved bog or rain-leached hillside, there's usually more nitrogen flying by in the bodies of insects than there is in the soil. In these forbidding locales, some plants find that it pays to use their leaves to capture not only solar energy but also the occasional insect.

Such a plant is the sundew. Ranging from chilly Alaskan bogs to steamy Southern wetlands, this insectivore dazzles its prey with a sparkling display of light. Dozens of globes of glue, perched like crystal balls upon tiny stalks, refract and reflect sunlight off its rosette of leaves. As soon as a curious insect touches down, its feet, wingtips, and antennae become mired in the glue, called muscilage, which is produced by glands atop each stalk. The commotion triggers a growth response on one side of the stalks, causing them to bend toward the center of the leaf, conveying the insect to the digestion zone.

With the prey secured, the glands that first produced glue now pump out a stream of digestive juices that break down the insect's body tissues, leaving only its hard shell behind. The digestive glands then reverse the flow, and the cocktail of nutrients is sucked into the leaves. When it's time for another meal, the glands once again squeeze out their alluring crystal balls, a deadly bait for bedazzled eyes.

Do plants ever kill each other?

A bird relieves itself on the branch of a Florida oak, inadvertently delivering a deadly visitor: the seed of a strangler fig. The invader soon sprouts and spirals its roots, which may grow to 120 feet in length, around the trunk of its host. On the way down, it sinks fingerling roots beneath the bark to siphon out nourishment.

The fig's roots eventually reach the soil, enabling it to garner its own water and minerals. Fortified by this new food source, the lattice of fig roots expands in girth and complexity, slowly putting the squeeze on its host. Meanwhile, fig branches multiply above, shading the leaves of the oak and cutting off its source of energy. Slowly starved and strangled, the tree dies and rots away in the fig's vigorous embrace. It can be unsettling to come upon the remains of the struggle: a living, tubular cage looming 60 feet in the air, hollow where a mighty oak once stood.

Another conspicuous plant killer is kudzu, a vine brought to America from Japan a century ago. Kudzu was first used as a shade plant and later as a ground cover to help control erosion along Southern highways. But the kudzu wouldn't stay put. The incredibly fast-growing vine, which can increase in length by up to 100 feet in a single season, began spreading over large sections of the Southern countryside, creeping over railroad tracks, twining around telephone poles, crawling up buildings, and smothering hundreds of acres of fields, shrubs, and trees. Once enveloped in kudzu's leafy embrace, native trees and shrubs usually die from lack of sunlight.

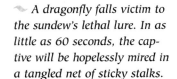

A dragonfly falls victim to the sundew's lethal lure. In as little as 60 seconds, the captive will be hopelessly mired in a tangled net of sticky stalks.

How does a bladderwort trap its victims?

Next time you find an aquatic plant washed to the edge of a pond, take a close look. Instead of roots you may find a tangle of tube-like leaves studded with hundreds of bladders one-tenth of an inch long: tiny traps used by the bladderwort to snare mosquito larvae and other small aquatic prey. When the bladders are full, they resemble bloated wineskins, dark with the partially digested remains of their prey. When set to capture a new meal, they are translucent, green, and suctioned nearly flat.

A one-way swinging door vacuum-seals the bladder until an unwitting victim trips the sensitive bristles around the threshold. These lever the door ajar, breaking the seal and letting water rush in to fill the vacuum. The prey tumbles in

with the tide, and in as little as one-thirtieth of a second, the trap door swings shut, sealing the victim's doom.

Cued by the capture, glands in the bladder walls pump out digestive juices, turning the bladder into a miniature stomach. The prey dissolves, and other glands absorb the liquefied nutrients. As the last slurp disappears into the walls, the trap flattens and is set once again for the next unlucky visitor.

This ingenious suction feeding system allows bladderworts to get nutrients without having to grow roots. Although bladderworts thrive in all kinds of wetlands, these self-sufficient carnivores are especially suited to stagnant pools and bogs where nitrogen is in short supply and an aggressive survival strategy is a necessity.

A stand of bladderworts blooms in the shadow of towering cypress trees. Despite their delicate appearance (different species sprout white, blue, purple, or yellow flowers), bladderworts are killers. Below the surface a single plant sports hundreds of traps on a branch system (inset) that may reach 10 feet across.

What is the pitcher plant's secret to survival?

The man-eating plants of old Tarzan movies may have been a Hollywood invention, but a few species, such as the northern pitcher plant, prey on animals in ways as strange as any fiction. This trademark wildflower of sphagnum bogs grows green-and-purple leaves that form in the shape of a tall vase or pitcher. Within collects a deadly soup of rainwater and digestive enzymes secreted by the plant. A trail of sweet nectar on the outer wall of the pitcher lures ants, beetles, and other insects to its slippery rim, where they slide or crawl down the chute in search of more honey. Once inside, the insects are trapped by stiff, downward-pointing hairs. Exhausted by their struggle to escape, they eventually drown in the digestive mixture, which dissolves them for consumption.

Although pitcher plants grow only in boggy habitats in the eastern United States and Canada, a similar species is found in the West: the cobra lily. A bulbous hood over the mouth of its pitcher and lobes resembling a snake's forked tongue give this sinister-looking plant its name. Translucent spots let sunlight into its pitcher so insects are not discouraged from entering. Once inside, they attempt to escape through these false exits, only to tire from the effort and tumble to the digestive pool below.

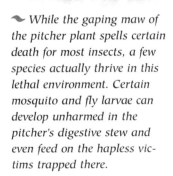

➤ *While the gaping maw of the pitcher plant spells certain death for most insects, a few species actually thrive in this lethal environment. Certain mosquito and fly larvae can develop unharmed in the pitcher's digestive stew and even feed on the hapless victims trapped there.*

Where does mistletoe grow?

When holiday revelers smooch under the mistletoe, they probably give little thought to where that sprig of greenery came from. Mistletoe grows on trees, but not as apples or leaves do. While a tree's fruit and leaves are its own, mistletoe on a living tree branch is a parasitic invader. Its seeds may be sown on branches through the drizzly excrement of perching birds that have eaten the mistletoe's berries. As the mistletoe seedlings grow, they send feeders into the wood, extracting nutrients from the tree. Mature plants look like tangled tumbleweeds blooming from tree limbs and branches.

While mistletoe is often associated with winter, most of its 2,000 species are tropical. Of these, only two species grow in North America, where they have met with varying degrees of success. In New York, American Christmas mistletoe disappeared before 1880, possibly due to overzealous yuletide pickers, but in Oklahoma the plant was immortalized as the state flower.

To find wild mistletoe, look on maple, tupelo, or hackberry trees in the South, on spruce in the North, and on juniper or oak in the West. But beware: despite mistletoe's festive reputation, its berries are poisonous to humans.

How does the Venus flytrap snare its food?

Although it may be the world's most easily recognizable carnivorous plant, the Venus flytrap resides only in a tiny area of coastal North and South Carolina where the sandy soil holds few nutrients. The flytrap is quick to supplement its paltry diet, snapping up bugs in a flash with its fringed clamshell of specialized leaves.

The plant moves with remarkable speed, but the mechanism that works the trap is even more astonishing. The inch-long lobes, which sit at the end of arching, flattened stems, are hydraulically powered. The plant pumps fluid into special motor cells along the midrib that hold the paired leaves open with hydraulic pressure. At the same time, nectar glands on the inside surface secrete a sweet liquid, which, along with the lobes' reddish color, attracts insects—sometimes flies, but more often ants, beetles, and other crawling species. When a bug steps into the trap, it encounters several prickly trigger hairs jutting into its path. If the insect bumps one of the hairs twice within 20 seconds or hits two different hairs within the same time span (insurance against a false alarm), the trap springs into action. The hairs send an electrical impulse to the motor cells, which instantly dump their load of fluid. The sudden loss of pressure causes the trap to close in about one-thirteenth of a second, the teeth meshing together like jail bars. Over the next few hours, the leaves compress tightly, sealing the insect in an enzyme bath that reduces it to digestible liquid.

The leafy jaws of a Venus flytrap claim another victim. A mature flytrap may sport a ring of more than a dozen disposable traps. Each is used to capture three or four insects before it withers and is replaced.

Seeds, Spores, and Clones *How plants produce their progeny*

What happens when you disobey a touch-me-not?

Growing from two to five feet tall, touch-me-nots have no sharp thorns, stinging hairs, or poisonous sap to warrant such a strong warning for a name. So what is it that we should not touch? The succulent green stems do not respond to our fingers, nor do the thin, oval leaves. Even the dangling yellow flowers ignore pokes and squeezes. But beware the swollen, cigar-shaped seed pods—if touched, they explode!

This startling reaction is caused by a release of the tension that builds up in the outer casing of the pods as they mature and expand. If you pinch the bottom tip of a ripened pod, the outer case bursts into five stringy sections, instantaneously hurling the plant's tiny seeds up to a distance of six feet.

But an explosive surprise is not all that this ominously named plant has to offer. When rubbed on the skin, the fresh juice from its crushed leaves and stem is said to relieve itching and prevent poison ivy rash. So if a mosquito gives you an annoying bite or you brush against some poison ivy, head for the nearest touch-me-not. Relief may be only a touch away.

Can plants reproduce without seeds?

Although seed-based reproduction may be the most familiar, many plants have found other means of propagating their species. For those of us with but a single means of reproduction at our disposal, the diverse methods of plant propagation can seem like magic.

Given the proper conditions, some plants need no more than a piece of leaf or a broken branch to produce an offspring identical in every way to its parent. In mosses, for example, small fragments of the stems or even single cells from the leaves can develop into whole new plants. Meanwhile, ferns and fungi need only microscopic windborne spores to spread their species.

Other plants have developed specially modified stems, leaves, or roots to serve as reproductive organs. Some, including many grasses, have slender horizontal stems, called runners, that snake over the ground. Every few feet they sink roots, from which new plants sprout.

Potatoes, day lilies, dahlias, and irises are more discreet in their reproductive processes, employing subterranean roots and stems specially adapted for propagation and food storage. The potato itself is such a storage stem, called a tuber. Roots and shoots sprout from its "eyes," or growth buds, producing new plants, which are nourished by the nutrient-rich tuber until their leaf and root systems are established.

Like tubers, lily and onion bulbs also grow underground. Bulbs consist mostly of leaf tissue (the layers of an onion are actually tightly packed leaves) around a central bud. They reproduce by forming smaller bulbs, each capable of developing into a separate plant. Bulbs also provide food for the new plants, allowing them to get a well-nourished start in life.

Similar to the bulb is the corm, but instead of leaves, the corm is comprised of stem. Corms sprout cormlets, which eventually break away and grow into full-size plants. Crocuses and gladioli both grow from fleshy, underground corms, which store nutrients to tide the plants over dormant periods.

Among trees kudos for creative reproductive practices must go to willows and poplars, which can literally produce offspring at the drop of a branch. Both species are notorious for the way their limbs, however broken they may be, can take root. Many an unwitting farmer has used fresh willow poles for fence posts only to discover, much to his amazement, that he has produced not a fence but a blooming hedge.

➤ *The fast-growing runners of a strawberry plant, called stolons, skip across the soil, developing roots where they touch ground. Each leafy shoot will mature into a new plant, which can also reproduce via seed-studded berries.*

Is there anything dandy about dandelions?

Not a thing, if you like your lawn as manicured as a golf green. If, however, you look to the dandelion's means of rapid-fire reproduction, you'll find something special indeed.

Unlike most flowering plants, dandelions (and a handful of others, including hawkweed) can produce seeds in two ways: with or without sex. The seeds of typical flowering plants begin to grow when eggs in capsules called ovules are fertilized by sperm from pollen. Dandelions routinely create seeds in this manner, but sometimes their seeds form without pollination, giving dandelions an advantage in the race to reproduce.

Frequently, a cell in the dandelion's ovule begins dividing into new cells even though it has not been fertilized. Sometimes this self-starter is an egg cell; other times a cell buds off the ovule's interior wall. Either way, the process results in a seed.

The mature seeds are too large to be scattered by the wind, but the ever crafty dandelion has found a solution. Each seed is tethered to a tuft of whitish hairs that can keep it aloft in a breeze. When the wind ceases, the seeds settle to the ground, soon to sprout those familiar weeds with lion-toothed leaves and tenacious taproots that grip the soil like fingers of steel.

Once established, dandelions can play havoc with well-groomed lawns, regenerating from roots alone if the plant itself is pulled out. Even so, some epicurean souls welcome these bright yellow interlopers because their leaves make a salad that tastes downright dandy.

➤ *A field of seed-laden dandelions stands dormant in the still spring air. Each stalk supports a spherical head of as many as 200 tufted seeds, which can remain aloft for hours if swept up in a dry breeze. In high humidity, however, the seeds will sink to earth, heavy with moisture.*

Scientists estimate that if the roughly 7 trillion spores contained within a single puffball were lined end to end, they would stretch around the globe.

What is the powder in a puffball?

Walk on a woodland trail, lawn, or field, and you may unwittingly tread atop a vast network of underground fungi. Their threadlike tissues criss-cross the soil in massive living webs that can extend for miles. Every now and then the threads form a reproductive body that pokes its head above the ground: a mushroom.

Puffballs are spherical mushrooms, ranging in size from golf balls to 24-inch beach balls. Their flesh is white and supple at first but quickly seasons into a solid shell filled with dark "dust." The dust actually consists of spores, the microscopic fungal equivalent of seeds. A raindrop reverberating on the puffball's woody shell is all it takes to send a powdery plume of these tiny reproductive cells through the "blowhole" at its top. As the ball decays, the roof caves in, giving the wind full purchase on the spores, which stream like smoke from the collapsed shell.

Although a puffball may release millions of spores in a single spurt, very few will ever come to fruition. Unlike seeds, which have a built-in food supply and a protective shell, single-celled spores consist of little more than genetic material and cannot survive unless they land in conditions perfectly suited to their growth. A lucky few, however, do make it, ensuring a fresh supply of these powder-puffing curiosities.

How do plants "travel"?

One meaning of the word *plant* is to fix firmly in place, and plants are viewed in just this way. In at least some stages of life, however, plants can be as freewheeling as bugs, birds, beasts, and people.

Generally, seeds are the most mobile of a plant's life stages. The bristles of burdock tangled in a dog's coat or milkweed parachutes sailing on the wind can travel quite a distance. Sycamore and willow seeds float down streams. Birds that eat wild cherries later disperse the undigested seeds in their droppings. Insects feed on the oily coatings of violet and trillium seeds, carrying them into burrows, where they sprout.

A more explosive way to move seeds is employed by the wild cucumber, an annual vine found in moist thickets from the Southeast to the Dakotas. Also known as squirting cucumber, it fills its spiny pods with gas as they mature; when the seeds are ripe, the pressure ruptures the pod, shooting the seeds up to 20 feet away.

Longer voyages are made by seeds embedded in car and truck tires—like those of purple loosestrife. Introduced from Europe, it extended its range from the Atlantic Coast to the Midwest by hitching rides with humans. Purple loosestrife is only one of hundreds of foreign species brought here either accidentally, as stowaways aboard ships and planes and in the shoes and clothing of travelers, or intentionally, as crops or garden plants. Without their natural enemies to control them, some introduced species, like ragweed, kudzu, and garlic mustard, have become troublesome pests.

Among plants that provide their own transportation, a unique form of locomotion is employed by the elegant walking fern. Its leaves taper to long, threadlike "legs" that arch over to adjacent tufts of moss, where they take root and grow new plants. By "walking" in this way, the fern slowly wends its way across a rock face.

A more adventurous method is used by Appalachian wildflowers such as Dutchman's breeches, jack-in-the-pulpit, and wild ginger. Often growing on unstable slopes where loose soils slide downhill, these plants produce underground bulbs or brittle roots that drift with the dirt of slow avalanches. When the soil settles, the bulbs and root fragments sprout tops, establishing new colonies. Seeds that are carried uphill in bird- and mammal-borne berries keep these tumbling plants from all winding up at the foot of the mountain.

Familiar residents of wetlands throughout North America, cattails are vigorous travelers. They hop from spot to spot by sending out thick underground stems, called rhizomes, which sprout new plants as they worm their way through the muddy marsh floor.

A lone Swainson's thrush stands watch over a king's ransom of spicebush berries, savoring the plump fruits one at a time. When it takes wing, the thrush will spread the undigested seeds of this shrub far and wide, depositing a dollop of bird-made fertilizer along with each seed.

Why are most berries brightly colored?

Luscious and alluring, the vibrant hue of a ripe berry is a natural billboard, advertising a free meal to birds, bears, and squirrels alike. Among these fruit eaters, birds have the best color vision, and they are especially drawn to the red and orange shades of ripe fruit—a great advantage to plants that bear bright berries. Since birds have the ability to spread seeds over a vast range, any plant that can attract them enhances its chances of successful propagation. Berries make for a win-win situation, providing both a healthy fast-food for animals and, when the animals pass the undigested seeds, an efficient means of dispersing offspring for the plants.

When it comes to appearance, berries are on a strict natural timetable and don't don their vivid hues until the seeds within them are ready to be sown. During development they instead sport a green cloak of chlorophyll—a camouflage to fool animals that might otherwise consume them before their seeds are fully mature. Once ripe, the sumptuous shades of berries serve as another sort of disguise: since most insects cannot see the color red, ripe fruits are often hidden from creatures too tiny to disperse their seeds.

But just because a berry is bright does not mean it is fit for consumption. Since the seeds of some plants cannot survive digestion, they use poison to discourage or even eliminate animals interested in eating them. Take, for instance, the seeds of the yew, an evergreen shrub found in Eastern and Western mountains and planted widely as an ornamental. Yew berries look like color-reversed stuffed olives, and while the outer scarlet flesh is edible, beware the green pit—it contains a deadly poison.

How do ferns reproduce without seeds?

Although ferns first appeared hundreds of millions of years ago—long before the age of the dinosaurs—it was not until the early 19th century that humans discovered just how this plant form, one of the earth's oldest and most widespread, could propagate without seeds. While scientists were baffled by the fern's mysterious reproductive abilities, superstitious folk suspected the influence of witches, who were thought to lurk in the damp, secluded woodlands where most ferns are found.

Ultimately the answer to the riddle was found in science, not sorcery. Researchers discovered that the brown patches, or sori, on the undersides of fern fronds in late summer each contain thousands, if not millions, of microscopic spores. When these patches dry out, they split open, freeing their countless spores to waft on the wind. Any spore lucky enough to land in a patch of moist soil soon germinates into a green, heart-shaped disc called a prothallus. This dime-size growth serves as the stage for fern fertilization, producing both male sperm and female eggs, which merge to create new ferns. When the ferns sprout, the prothallus that spawned them withers and dies.

Ferns do not, however, reproduce via spores alone. The fronds of the walking fern end in leglike arches that droop to the earth, take root, and form new plants on the spot. Other ferns send out small shoots, called runners, that snake along the ground. Every now and then the runner sends down roots, and a new plant is born. Using this method of propagation, gardeners cultivate popular seedless plants such as the elegant Boston fern.

➤ *Rows of spore-laden sori, also called sporangia, adorn the ample fronds of a rabbit's foot fern—a leathery, four-foot-high species common to the South and the tropics of South America.*

So while ferns have nothing to do with witches, these seedless wonders are one of the best and oldest examples of nature's wizardry.

Why do some trees produce tiny seeds and others large nuts?

Whether it is the downy blanket of millions of willow seeds quivering in the wind or the sleek brown shell of an acorn poking from a squirrel's mouth, the seeding strategy of a tree is always optimally suited to its environment.

Lightweight seeds travel far on wind or water, and since animals do not eat them, the more seeds produced, the more will sprout and grow.

But tiny seeds provide no food or water for the growing seedling, so only those that land in moist, fertile soil have a chance. Consequently trees with tiny seeds—willows, alders, sycamore, cottonwoods, and sweetgums—tend to live in lowlands, especially in swamps and floodplains.

By contrast, in dry woodlands where oaks, hickories, and walnuts grow, a seed must provide ample food and even some water for the tender seedling to survive. The meat of the nut serves as sustenance for the seedling, and while a few animals also use nuts for food, trees cut their losses in the timing of nutfall. Whereas willows and cottonwoods seed in summer, hickories and walnuts seed in autumn, just when squirrels are stocking up for winter. In the end, no squirrel remembers the location of every nut it buries, so in effect the animals plant the seeds they don't eat.

How do seeds use parachutes to get around?

There are sunny days when the wind literally shimmers with its cargo of trillions of airborne seeds. Dandelions in spring, goat's beard in summer, and milkweeds in autumn are just a few of the wildflowers whose small and almost weightless seeds are carried aloft on gleaming "parachutes" of long, silky or feathery bristles. Parachutes are one of nature's most effective means of distributing seeds, and depending on the whim of the wind, the seeds will settle and germinate on waysides and fields that may lie across the road, over the hill, or in the next county. Because these plants, which most people think of as weeds, are prolific seed producers, they quickly overwhelm abandoned fields or any ground that has been disturbed by bulldozer or plow.

Among the most successful of airborne seeders is the misnamed Canada thistle. Actually brought to North America by early European settlers, the Canada thistle has proved such an aggressive invader that in many states it is illegal to let it grow on one's property. Each thistle flower produces roughly 45 seeds whose cottony parachutes can carry them hundreds of feet or more. Once settled, the seeds germinate into prickly pests that infest croplands, compete with native plants, and render fields and meadows impassable with their tough, spiny leaves.

➤ *The Canada thistle doesn't rely solely on its windborne seeds for propagation. It can also reproduce via rapidly growing roots that sprout new plant tops as they bore through the top layers of soil.*

Private Life of Flowers *Birds, bees, and other pollinators*

Why do some flowers close at night and others open?

Nectar, the sweet bribe that flowers offer to pollinators, is expensive to produce. Plants give it away only to just the right bird, bat, insect, or lizard—the one best adapted for picking up the pollen and delivering it to a blossom of the same species. When day-active pollinators stop shopping for the night, flowers such as brilliantly orange poppies may shutter their window displays until the next business day, preventing the precious nectar from evaporating in the wind or being diluted by rain.

While some plants are closing up, however, others are just opening. In desert regions, where oven-hot days stifle activity, organ-pipe cacti, saguaros, and agaves open at night to troll for nectar-feeding bats. Bat-pollinated flowers are usually wide mouthed, robust, and light in color so they stand out in the dark, and their fragrance, resembling a cross between cabbage and urine, is something only a bat could love.

Plants of cooler climes also pitch their wares to nighttime pollinators. The yellow evening primrose unfurls its three- to four-inch blossom at dusk, moving as deliberately as an animal. Its pale blossoms glow in the moonlight, along with jimsonweed, honeysuckle, and other night bloomers. Their cloyingly sweet smell is an olfactory beacon to hovering hawkmoths.

What causes wind-pollinated plants to grow in dense stands?

The lone pine on a mountain may be picturesque, but it's not prolific. An isolated plant picks up almost no pollen from distant neighbors, and most of its own pollen falls short of them. In contrast, closely packed plants are bound to be fertilized; pines and other wind-pollinated plants become well established when numerous seeds sprout in the same location. Compared to the special delivery service of birds and bees, wind is a hit-or-miss pollen courier, most effective at close range.

It isn't surprising, then, that the seeds of many wind-pollinated plants—the heavy nuts of hickories, oaks, and beeches and the propeller seeds of pines and maples, which twirl relatively short distances—fall close to their parents.

The wind works for trees and shrubs because they are relatively tall, but it also works for grasses, which evolved from insect-pollinated ancestors about 75 million years ago, when many parts of the world became cooler and drier. On the Plains, the grazing of large herbivores favored these plants, whose growing tips lay close to the ground, out of reach of chomping teeth. Winds blowing across prehistoric prairies inhibited flying insects, so grasses turned to the breeze for pollination, their flowers losing the colorful flags that once lured bees and beetles.

➤ *Highlights in the short life of a single jimsonweed blossom at Joshua Tree National Monument in California are captured in these three photographs. From left to right, the first one reveals the flower furled at dusk; the second, snapped a scant eight minutes later, shows the flower fully opened; the third, taken after a few more minutes have passed, catches a hawkmoth sipping nectar.*

Which plant in the high Arctic is pollinated by mosquitoes?

Windswept, treeless, and underlain by permafrost, the Arctic tundra is a hostile place for insects such as bees, wasps, and butterflies, on which most plants depend for pollen transfer. Mosquitoes, however, swarm by the billions during the brief northern summer. Although we regard them as little vampires, mosquitoes like sweets, especially nectar, in addition to blood.

Several orchids of the northern states and Canada—twayblades, frog-orchid, and adder's-mouth, for example—include our whining, biting nemeses among their various insect pollinators. For the most northerly species, the woodrein and blunt-leaf orchids, female mosquitoes are the main pollen carriers. Both of these hardy orchids bloom at the height of the mosquito season, from late June to September.

To reach the nectar ensconced deep in the spurs of the orchid's tiny, pale green blossom, the insect must pull itself completely into the flower, where waxy blobs of pollen get stuck to its head, often on an eye. Because its legs can't reach its head, the mosquito must wait to rub the troublesome stuff off on the pistil of the next flower, fertilizing it in the process.

How do honeybees pollinate plants?

Attractive flower, newly opened, seeks hardworking pollinator for brief, but mutually rewarding, relationship.

If you think people have a hard time finding a mate, imagine what it's like for flowers. Permanently rooted in one spot, they can't go looking for partners. They must rely on matchmakers, known in botanical circles as pollinators.

For most of the thousands of plant species that inhabit the earth, these matchmakers are bees—although birds, bats, butterflies, and beetles also moonlight as "pollen couriers." Their sole function, as far as the plant is concerned, is to pick up pollen from the male part of one flower and deliver it to the female part of another.

To attract pollinators, plants use several different strategies. They produce flamboyant flowers in the colors bees like most: yellow, blue, and violet. They wear seductive perfumes. Some even use nectar guides, "arrows" pointing to the syrup hidden inside their flowers.

What's in it for pollinators? Fortunately for plants, bees need flowers as much as flowers need bees. The pollen and nectar that flowers offer are necessary for bees' survival. Young bees eat only pollen, while adults eat mostly honey, which they make from nectar.

Buzzing across a meadow in search of a good meal, a foraging honeybee enters a dazzling bazaar of colors and scents. Flowers of every conceivable hue, some with ultraviolet markings, nod their perfumed heads as they vie for the bee's attention. Lured by a distinctive combination of color, shape, and aroma, the bee comes in for a landing. As it loads up on pollen and probes the flower for nectar, thousands of tiny pollen grains cling to its fuzzy body. Nestled among the hairs, the pollen hitches a ride to the next flower the bee visits. Since bees are notoriously single-minded, the next flower is almost certain to be the same species as the first. There, the pollen literally "jumps" off the bee and onto the female stigma, thanks to static electricity the bee builds up while flying. On the sticky stigma the pollen germinates, fertilization occurs, and seeds develop to produce the next generation of plants.

A bee (above) with pollen packets on its legs probes for nectar among dozens of tiny flowers on a sunflower's head. Lured by veinlike nectar guides on an iris's showy sepals (below), a bee crawls under a pistil and capsule shaped anther and gets a pollen dusting while seeking nectar near the flower's center.

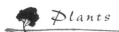

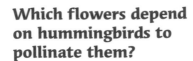

➤ *Wild columbine flowers dancing seductively in a breeze are bound to be visited by a hummingbird sooner or later. The tip of each red floral spur contains a drop of nectar, a bird's sweet reward for probing with its beak and tongue while being dusted by pollen from the flower's protruding yellow stamens.*

➤ *A typical flower (below) has four major structures: sepals, petals, pistil, and stamens. Sepals protect the growing flower; petals act as pollinator attractors; the pistil, with its sticky stigma to catch pollen, is the female organ; stamens, the male organs, are topped with pollen-producing anthers.*

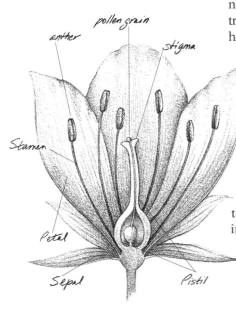

Which flowers depend on hummingbirds to pollinate them?

In marshy forest glades and meadows, two closely related wildflowers take completely different approaches to pollination. Great blue lobelia, which carries a spike of short cobalt flowers, keeps its reproductive organs tucked down inside blossoms, where bumblebees probing for nectar are sure to brush up against them. The stunning lobelia known as the cardinal flower, on the other hand, mounts its pollen front and center. Its brilliant red flowers have long, tubular necks that thwart bees but neatly match the slender beak of a hungry hummingbird. When the tiny bird pushes forward for a drink, its forehead brushes against the flower's pollen-bearing stamens, which project up and out from the opening. At the next flower the pollen rubs off on that plant's pistil, or female organ, and another generation of cardinal flower seed is on the way.

Other plants also produce flowers that hummingbirds visit. Most, such as the cardinal flower, hummingbird trumpet, bee balm, and Eastern columbine, are red or deep orange, colors rarely found in insect-pollinated plants and especially attractive to hummingbirds. Dangling on arching stems, the blossoms—with their long, narrow corollas, or necks of fused petals, and protruding stamens and pistils—set a perfect table for hovering hummingbirds.

Do all flowers have petals?

"He loves me, he loves me not," repeated with each plucking of a daisy petal, is supposed to divine a suitor's true feelings, but is the love-struck lady really pulling petals? In the daisy's case, yes, but when the last, telling petal is plucked, what is cast aside is not just a single flower. A daisy's yellow center is composed of hundreds of flowers, the inner ones without petals, the outer ones each with a single petal, or ray.

Most of our favorite flowers have prominent and colorful petals to attract pollina-

tors. Different plants have developed these petals from different flower parts. Some flowers, such as roses and pansies, derived their petals from stamens that lost their pollen-producing anthers. White water lilies, on the other hand, evolved their petals from sepals, the protective leaflike structures that cover buds.

Petals are not, however, always big and showy, and big, showy flower parts are not always petals. The petals of anemones and common yellow pond lilies are tiny and drab, and the sepals serve as the colorful flags. Flowering dogwood's four big white "petals" are actually modified leaves (bracts, in botanical parlance), which have lost their chlorophyll and serve only as bug lures.

Some flowers have no petals at all. For example, the blossoms of stinging nettles, which look like dangling strings of green beads, have sepals but no petals. Another floral oddity forms dense stands in open shallows along streams in the Eastern states. This knee-high herb sports a tapered spike bearing hundreds of tiny white flowers with neither petals nor sepals, inspiring its name, lizard's tail.

Can a plant be male or female?

Linnaeus, the 18th-century scientist who named in Latin every plant he could find, distinguished plants by their sexual "living arrangements." His racy descriptions, such as "the wife in bed with twelve husbands," shocked some people, but he was referring only to combinations of male and female organs in flowers.

A plant's sexual identity resides in its flowers' parts. Stamens, the male organs, bear pollen on stalked anthers, while the female pistils receive it. The basic configurations are three: flowers with both stamens and pistils, as in most showy flowers; separate male and female flowers, as in pines and willows; and flowers of opposite sexes on separate plants, as in sassafras.

This variety balances the need to reduce inbreeding with the need to have offspring. Plants avoid inbreeding by bearing male and female organs on separate flowers or by staggering timing of pollen release and pistil receptivity, but both strategies are risky. If pollinators are scarce, flowers may not be pollinated. Some plants, such as dandelions, don't have this problem: in a pinch they can pollinate themselves.

How is the water lily pollinated?

The Nymphaea odorata . . . sweet water-lily, how . . . wholesome its fragrance. How pure its white petals, though its root is in the mud!" So wrote Thoreau in 1852, and today one still marvels at this brilliant, many-petaled flower rocking gently on quiet ponds and lakes.

The water lily blooms for only four or five days at most. On the first day of flowering, the pistil, or female part, is open and ready to be fertilized. Not until the second day do the anthers on the golden stamens explode, releasing their stores of pollen, but by then the pistil is infertile.

This lack of synchronization between male and female parts helps the plant's long-term survival, ensuring that self-fertilization cannot occur. Repeated self-fertilization might leave a species unable to adapt to changing conditions. For cross-fertilization to occur in the water lily, pollen must travel from an older to a younger flower. Bumblebees and honeybees drawn by the lily's fragrance zigzag from flower to flower, feeding on nectar. Sticky pollen clings to their bodies. After visiting older flowers, they may alight upon a fertile, day-old bloom and leave pollen behind.

Resplendent in the late morning sun, water lilies float upon the dark, still waters of Georgia's Okefenokee Swamp. Boat-shaped white sepals, which look like petals, ring the flowers' bases. Air sacs in both sepals and petals give them their brilliant white hue while providing buoyancy. Once pollinated, the flowers are pulled below the water's surface by their coiling stems.

Although calypso orchids lure woodland bumblebees with showy flowers and sweet scents, the visiting insects find neither nectar nor pollen to eat, but they do unwittingly serve their hoodwinking hosts. Pollen grains from dispensers on the petals' upper surfaces stick to the bees' backs and are carried to the next orchids they visit.

Like its Eastern counterpart, the Western skunk cabbage grows in wet places, blooms in early spring, and emits a foul odor like rotting meat that brings in the first flies of the season.

What clever come-ons do some flowers use to attract pollinators?

Why should a bee or butterfly bother to pick up and carry a cargo of pollen from one flower to another? The payoff most often is food, either protein-rich pollen or sweet nectar. Potential consumers need to know the food is available, so flowers advertise, and their gimmicks are remarkably like our own: eye-catching signs, games and prizes, complimentary drinks and samples, even child care.

All nectar is sweet, but flowers of the arum family, such as the white wild calla of cold swamps and the arrow arum of streams and lakeshores, spike theirs with a narcotic so intoxicating to bees that they seek out more arum flowers. On the northern Canadian tundra, the flowers of mountain avens and arctic poppy generate heat, a welcome energy boost for cold-blooded beetles, flies, and mosquitoes, who stop by to warm up and leave with a dusting of pollen. Even more generous is the yucca, which offers a few of its ovaries as nurseries for its pollinators, small white yucca moths. This sacrifice assures a troop of pollinators the next time the yucca blooms.

Deceptive advertising is practiced by the small pink adder's-mouth and calypso orchids of the Northeast, whose false stamens and nectaries (showier than the real ones) promise food rewards for bees but deliver nothing. The insects poke around in vain looking for nectar and pollen, visiting and pollinating flower after flower. The fact that the calypso orchids' patterning, colors, and scents can vary from one clump to the next makes it even harder for the bumblebees to learn their lesson and resist the flowers' fraudulent charms.

Why are there so many different flower fragrances?

Plants began making scents around 80 million years ago to entice insects into pollinating their flowers. With that first whiff of perfume, a thriving economy was born. Fragrance is the perfect come-on, traveling through the air like a radio commercial, and it wasn't long before flowers started targeting their markets, manufacturing distinctive scents to lure a select clientele. For example, our two skunk cabbages (both the Eastern and Western species) smell like dead animals and attract early spring carrion flies. Bouncing bet's heady fragrance and white flowers appeal to night-flying moths, while Deptford pink's sweeter scent and magenta blossoms lure day-flying butterflies.

The long interaction of flowers and insects has resulted in aromatic combinations numbering in the thousands. Human perfumers have taken advantage of this profusion to create countless exotic blends of elemental scents, many from flowers such as rose, jasmine, bergamot, and lily. It is said that 500 aromatic compounds are needed to make a good rose perfume, and one expensive brand is a blend of over 800 essential "notes."

Why are spring flowers often blue, white, or yellow?

Trying to understand how insects see the world, scientists have performed experiments that explain why flowers such as glacier lilies and spring beauties have adopted their pastel color schemes. Using colored paper and watch glasses full of sugar water, these investigators found that bees prefer yellow, blue, and white, the commonest springtime colors. Bees and insects with similar vision are the most numerous spring pollinators, and flowers such as yellow marsh marigolds, blue Virginia bluebells, and white mayapples clearly cater to their color tastes.

Achieving these insect-attracting hues is a chemical art. Petals are composed of water-filled cells floating with pigment molecules, sugars, acids, salts, and other compounds. The interaction of these chemicals, like the mixing of paints on an artist's palette, causes hues to change. A flower filled with anthocyanin pigment will be as blue as a bluet, for instance, but only if the cell sap is alkaline. Differing mixtures of pigments called anthoxanthins lead to colors ranging from the pale ivory of grass of Parnassus to the deep yellow of butter and eggs. The white in Dutchman's breeches, however, is not created with pigments. Instead, thousands of tiny pockets of air in the transparent petals reflect light in all directions—the same phenomenon that whitens a pile of snow crystals.

What flowers change color day by day?

In the early days of spring, when Eastern woodlands have little more color than an overcast winter sky, Virginia bluebells push their leaves up into chilly daylight. Arched stems soon rise, carrying tiny pink buds that grow into trumpet-shaped flowers. As the blossoms swell and open, though, they change color, shifting to a rosy purple and finally to a clear, delicate blue.

Many wildflowers change color, either as they grow from bud to bloom, or as the blossom ages. The shoe-shaped flower of the pink lady's slipper changes from pale green to a rich pink in a matter of days as its reaches full size. The tall, daisylike blooms of purple coneflowers, which spangle grasslands, start out rose-purple, but sun, rain, and the nibbling jaws of insects reduce them to a faded echo of their original color

within a week or two. Eventually they may blanch almost white before the petals drop off entirely. The group of native wildflowers best known for changing color are the trilliums, whose two dozen species, including tiny dwarf trillium and the famous large-flowered trillium, grow in moist, shady woodlands. The flower of the coast trillium (still known by its folk name, wakerobin, for its early spring bloom) starts life with three unsullied white petals. As they age, though, the petals become tinged with pink, which deepens to rose by the end of about two weeks—a lovely prelude to the flower's brown, withered end.

➤ *Dubbed marsh marigolds, these water-loving plants in fact belong to the buttercup family. Early spring bloomers in wetlands, they attract bees, gnats, and flies to pollinate their waxy yellow flowers.*

Marvels of Form and Function *Lovely designs, brilliant devices*

Do plants have "fingerprints"?

There are no loops and swirls, it's true, but the continuously branching veins of plants' leaves seem to vary slightly from one specimen to another. One might wonder if a "leafprint" is the equivalent of a human fingerprint or palmprint. The five-pointed leaf of the maple, for example, looks quite handlike, but scientists haven't bothered to study its vein variations. However, botanists use leaf-vein patterns to distinguish the two types of flowering plants: dicots and monocots.

The veins of dicots, or flowering plants with two seed leaves in their embryo, form a netlike pattern. The American beech, for example, has a single strong vein, with numerous side branches, running the entire length of its sawtooth-edged leaf. The long, compound leaf of the honey locust tree also has a prominent central vein. But other dicots, like maples, geraniums, and sunflowers, have a number of veins radiating from the leaf stem in a handlike pattern.

The other major group of flowering plants, the monocots, have but one seed leaf in their embryo, and their leaf veins run roughly parallel to one another. The long leaves of corn have these closely spaced parallel veins, as do the daintier leaves of irises. Only a few treelike plants, such as palms and bamboos, have leaves with parallel veins.

Another way of telling the difference between the two types of flowering plants is by the flower parts. Dicots have parts in multiples of four or five, such as four stamens or 10 petals, while monocots have flower parts in threes.

Although plants lack unique prints, there are ways to identify individuals. In plants, as in animals, differences between individuals can be detected through their genetic material, or DNA. With a technique called DNA fingerprinting, it's possible to determine how one plant is genetically different from another. Except for clones, no two plants have exactly the same DNA sequence.

➤ *A pumpkin leaf's veins form a branching, netlike pattern typical of dicots, one of the two main groups of flowering plants. Similar in function and appearance to the blood-carrying veins and arteries of animals, leaf veins channel nutrients and water to all parts of the leaf.*

What trees don't have bark?

The answer is palms. That is, if a plant such as the Florida royal palm, whose leafy crown can be 100 feet above the base of its arrow-straight trunk, fits the description of a tree. Palm trees don't have bark or branches. They grow only straight up, from a bud in the crown. If this bud—the source of delicious hearts of palm—is removed or otherwise destroyed, the tree eventually dies.

A palm trunk is unlike a typical tree trunk, which has several circular layers, including two sets of inner woody ones and the outermost bark. Like a cornstalk, a palm trunk consists of the same fibrous material throughout. Although not true wood, palm logs are strong and, in some parts of the world, are used for houses. The palm trunk's surface hardens as it grows, giving the illusion of bark, but the trunk doesn't thicken by adding a new outer layer every year. It expands continually as new cells form in the core.

Which plants stave off browsers with thorns but offer tasty fruit?

Thorns protect plants in the same way that quills protect porcupines: they persuade hungry animals to seek an easier meal elsewhere. The honeylocust tree of the Midwestern and South-Central states protects its bark and leaves from hungry deer with clusters of pronged thorns that stab out from its trunk and limbs. These spears, which may be several inches long, are modified branches. Just as the porcupine's hair evolved into deadly quills, so too did the honeylocust develop a defense system by turning innocuous limbs to a new purpose.

The black locust, a graceful tree native to the Ozark and Appalachian Mountains, is a relative of the honeylocust. It, too, has modified a part of its anatomy to fend off leaf eaters. The pair of scales covering the base of each leaf has evolved into a set of half-inch spines that snag the tongues of leaf-stripping browsers.

Catbriers of Eastern forests create impassable barriers with their spiked stems, which have inspired alternative names such as hellfetter and tramps' troubles. Wicked prickles also cover the stems of blackberry bushes, leaving the plump berries unprotected and available for the picking. This is nature's way of discouraging browsers from munching on the bush's leaves and gnawing on its bark, steering them instead to the colorful, tasty fruits embedded with seeds, which the animals unwittingly scatter in their scat.

Honeylocust and black locust fruits lure animals too. The trees' seeds are eagerly ingested by deer, rabbits, squirrels, and a variety of birds. The seedpods of the honeylocust offer an inducement—a thick, sweet pulp—as if to make up for its grudge against deer and cattle.

Why are the tiny flowers of a daisy crowded together in a disc?

It is obvious that a company employing a couple of hundred workers can far outproduce a single person working alone. That's why a daisy can generate scads more offspring than, for instance, a cherry blossom. What we commonly call a daisy flower is a composite of hundreds of closely packed flowers, while a cherry blossom is just one flower producing one fruit with one seed. Each minuscule flower in the daisy's central disc contains its own reproductive apparatus, including pollen receptors and pollen producers. A single visit from a pollen-laden bee can fertilize several flowers. The buzzing insect also collects a fresh load of pollen, which it carries to other daisies.

Each daisy flower has its own ovary, where its fruit forms, producing seed. The fruits of these composite flowers are obvious in the autumn, when the smallest daisy's head bursts with seeds. It is even easier to see the seeds of a sunflower, a relative of the daisy.

In addition to the hundreds of tiny flowers on its disc, a daisy has others as well, fewer in number but far more conspicuous. Each of the "petals" surrounding the disc is a flower unto itself, with an enlarged corolla, or set of fused petals. The tiny flowers lack reproductive organs but nevertheless play a big part in making more daisies. Their corollas attract pollinators and provide landing decks and places to perch.

Closely related to daisies, sunflowers have the largest flower heads among composite flowers, a floral group that first developed in Mexico millions of years ago. Each head may consist of up to 2,000 tiny individual flowers. Farmers frequently keep beehives near their sunflower fields to improve pollination.

As a sugar maple unfurls its leaves in spring, it initially uses sugars stored over the winter in its limbs, trunk, and roots to sustain this explosive burst of new growth. Once the leaves are fully opened and producing food on their own through photosynthesis, they will send sugars back through their stems to be stored for the next year's crop of leaves.

When does the sap begin to rise in sugar maples?

History doesn't record the name of the first New England colonist to pour rich maple syrup over a stack of pancakes. But when Indians taught settlers to boil down the "sweetwater," or sap, that drips from wounds in the bark of sugar maples in late winter and early spring, it not only revolutionized breakfast but launched a thriving cottage industry.

Every tree manufactures sap—a solution of water, nitrates, phosphates, sugars, and proteins—which circulates through its tissues and, like human blood, is essential for life. Maple sap, however, has an especially high sugar content, as much as 10 percent.

Farmers know that sap will run in a sugarbush, a woodlot dominated by mature maple trees, during periods of freezing nights and thaws during the day. Sap flows most profusely in spring in order to nourish new buds, but no one knows exactly how sap in a leafless tree defies the laws of gravity by ascending to the treetops at a rate of up to four feet per hour.

Despite its high sugar content, maple sap is thin and rather tasteless and needs to be reduced to a point of 66.5 percent sugar to make syrup. Between 30 and 50 gallons of sap are needed for 1 gallon of syrup. That's the average yield of four large maple trees. One gallon of syrup, reduced further, will produce eight pounds of maple sugar—the ultimate treat for anyone with a sweet tooth.

What causes younger leaves to differ in color from older ones?

As buds unfold in early spring, a wash of pale green begins to cloak the sharp tracery of branches and twigs. These first delicate leaves, soft as a mouse's ear, are the early promise of lush treetops to come. Released from their protective coverings, these bits of foliage deepen and darken in color as they grow to become food factories.

This change takes place when sunlight stimulates leaves to increase their production of chlorophyll, the green pigment that captures the sun's energy and makes it possible for plants to create food from water and air. The green usually blots out carotenoid pigments, which daub leaves with yellow, orange, and red hues in autumn. Although unseen, these colors also play an important role in photosynthesis: they absorb some of the green wavelengths in sunlight, which chlorophyll does not, and pass its energy on to the vital green pigment. When autumn eventually stops leaves from renewing their chlorophyll, the carotenoids become visible again in a burst of gold and orange. Then if bright days and cold nights conspire to transform sugars in leaves into red and purple pigments called anthocyanins, autumn colors reach a flamboyant climax.

Why are some leaves fuzzy?

Often when a leaf looks white, it is sporting what botanists call pubescence, evocative of the peach fuzz on a male preteen's face. For a leaf a covering of silky hair is a survival tactic in a habitat of intense sun and aridity. It is not by chance that many hairy-leafed plants grow on mountain slopes, deserts, and prairies.

Besides shading leaves exposed to intense and prolonged sunlight, leaf hairs reduce moisture loss and discourage hungry insects.

Hairs alter the energy balance of a leaf in the same way that putting on white clothes does for us. By reflecting light away, the hairs keep the leaves cool, shielding them from water-robbing heat. Each hair, an outgrowth of the leaf's epidermis, has a shape that is unique to the species. Under a powerful microscope, hairs may look like stars, umbrellas, or the letter *T*. Sages and mints have dendritic hairs, branched like little trees, while common weeds such as pigweed and salt-bush have bulbous hairs, like tiny balloons on a stalk. Cotton and sunflower hairs are linear and densely interwoven, working like a sun umbrella against the elements.

In more temperate climes hairy leaves sometimes have a different agenda. Sundews and other plants have oozing glandular hairs that help them attract insects for pollination, repel defoliating insects, or trap insects with glue. The leaf hairs of bromeliads (air plants) are like sponges, soaking up rainwater that collects in the cups formed by the bases of their leaves. The hairs on beans do just the opposite; they act as safety valves, running with tears when the plant is waterlogged.

What is the purpose of a bald cypress's knees?

Paddle a canoe through a Southern swamp, and everywhere you look you will find bald cypresses—tall, graceful trees with fluted bases and delicate needlelike leaves. Around each tree strange, knobby protuberances rise from the water. Some resemble ladies in flowing skirts; others, soldiers standing at attention. If the sun is shining and the air is warm, several may serve as basking places for alligators or snakes.

The function of these odd structures, called knees, has been much debated by botanists. One theory contends that the knees, which grow from the roots, store starch rather like potatoes. Another suggests that they buttress the tree, helping to give it stability on a muddy bottom. A third theory asserts that they absorb air for the roots, which spread in soil that has little dissolved oxygen. Some scientists favoring this idea believe cypress roots may not branch without oxygen from the knees. The cypress's root system serves as an incredibly stable base for one of the few life forms to have survived Hurricane Hugo in an upright position.

Most mature bald cypress trees growing in water are surrounded by a retinue of knees—hollow, bark-covered cones extending from the shallow roots. Bald cypress knees may provide oxygen needed for the trees' roots.

What do the rings in the trunks of trees tell us?

The stump of a felled tree or the cut end of a log shows a pattern of concentric circles just like the ripples made on a pond by a tossed stone. Though a tree can't speak, its sequence of rings tells a most eloquent story—and many other unexpected tales, including those of storms, earthquakes, plagues, and pollution.

The rings reflect a tree's growth, which is highly influenced by weather. In temperate climates growth is fast in spring, resulting in a wide, light band, and slow in summer, making a narrow, dark band; the two bands together form a ring. Where seasons are regular, each ring outward represents another year, and a ring count gives the tree's age. A three-foot-wide white oak may have several hundred rings, and the largest giant sequoias (30 to 40 feet in diameter) could have up to 3,500 rings. In desert areas trees may add more or less than one growth ring per year—one for each rainy spell.

The size and shape of the rings reveal a tree's personal trials and tribulations. A series of very narrow rings indicates a period of stress, perhaps from drought or attacks by leaf-eating insects. Squeezed rings on only one side usually mean an injury; dark stains, an immune reaction to fungus or bacteria. Chemical changes in the wood are evidence of environmental factors: air and water pollutants, ash from volcanic erup-tions, varying concentrations of soil nutrients.

Tree rings may even help scientists predict nat-ural disasters. Trees buried in the volcanic ash of the Pacific Coast's Cascade Mountains, for exam-ple, are being studied to find patterns of vol-canic activity and possibly to anticipate impending eruptions like that of Mount St. Helens in 1980. With the help of tree rings, researchers in Texas are correlating droughts of the past three centuries with known weather patterns in an attempt to forecast future dry spells similar to the dust bowl of the 1930s.

Is there a logic to the way leaves are arranged on trees?

As you stare up through the boughs of a red maple, it's hard to imagine that such a peaceful scene was shaped by so much strife. A tree's canopy is the front line in the battle for sun-light, and its leaves—nature's solar panels—are strategically placed to capture every incoming photon of light energy.

On first consideration the vertical tiering of tree branches might seem inefficient. Several leaky umbrellas piled on top of one another would appear to be less effective than one wide, unin-terrupted canopy. In fact, however, when light fil-ters down through interstices in a broadleaf tree's first tier of leaves and soaks into the second, enough food is produced through photosyn-thesis to equal the output of one large, continu-ous umbrella. Each lower level of leaves provides an additional bonus. As long as sunlight is abun-dant, a three-dimensional, multitiered leaf array yields more food for the tree than a single, con-tinuous layer would.

Where light is already filtered down to low levels, however, understory trees like dogwood may dispense with the tiering and opt for a sim-ple umbrella. Young evergreens such as the Dou-glas fir or white spruce get sunlight by putting out progressively wider and wider tiers toward the bottom of the tree, assuming a classic Christ-mas tree shape. Young hardwoods like the tulip poplar fight back with a gradient of leaf sizes, growing monstrously outsized leaves on their lower branches.

Besides leaf size and placement, trees can also adjust leaf angles. Deep in their shady ravines, for instance, hemlocks lay their leaves at a flat-out horizontal, poised like tongues to intercept the slimmest ray of light. Come the height of sum-

A tree's autobiography is written in the rings of its trunk. Although the outer por-tion of this log's cross section is oil stained from a chain-saw, all the growth rings are still visible. By studying the size and shape of the annual rings, a careful observer can tell which were good growth years and which were not.

mer's inferno, however, even sun worshipers like aspens will tilt their leaves Venetian blind style to shed excess heat.

When you multiply this miracle tree by tree, you come up with millions of leaves tilting, swiveling, and jockeying for position in the boughs above. The fact that it all looks so peaceful is proof that nature's real talent is to fool the eye with beauty, making the orderly look random, and the intricate, easy.

Why are spruces and firs usually cone-shaped?

The classic Christmas tree shape of a silvery Colorado blue spruce or a Western alpine fir is dictated from the top down by its terminal bud, the nubbin of growth on the tip of the tree's main stem. Plant growth regulators called auxins flow downward from this bud, stimulating the stem to lengthen while repressing the growth of buds along its sides. But as the termi-

nal bud's star rises, its influence wanes. The auxins can dominate only buds close to the tip; distance negates their impact on lower buds. Thus, shoots on the same level—the same distance from the terminal bud—tend to grow uniformly. With each level increasing in length every year, the result is a conical tree.

Many young trees assume a triangular form early in life, but it's largely the conifers that maintain it throughout their lives. Though various pines have a shaggy-dog or rounded form as they grow, spruces and firs continue pointing to the heavens like evergreen steeples. A conical shape serves these trees well in the snowy regions they inhabit. Each flexible limb sags beneath its burden of ice and snow, eventually coming to rest on similarly drooping limbs beneath it. In this way the tree is transformed into the evergreen equivalent of an A-frame ski chalet; limbs are braced and subsequent snowfall tends to slip easily down the sloping sides.

Steeple-shaped subalpine firs cluster on the slopes of Mt. Rainier. Their elongated canopies, which easily shed snow, are well suited to the mountains of the Pacific Northwest, where annual snowfalls often exceed 50 feet.

203

Legend and Lore A potpourri of fascinating facts

Which of today's plants closely resemble their ancient ancestors?

When children with toy dinosaur sets look for appropriate greenery to surround *Triceratops* and *Tyrannosaurus*, they often select mosses, ferns, and—if they can find them—horsetails. Their instincts, of course, are correct, for these are among the plants that have changed least over the millennia. Many groups of plants have thrived and then disappeared, or given rise to new and different forms. The most recent explosion of radically new plant types was that of modern flowering plants some 60 million years ago. So quickly have they evolved that many in existence today are considerably different from their ancestors of only a few million years back.

The earliest and simplest plants (red and blue-green algae) have changed very little since they debuted over 2 billion years ago. Today, both kinds inhabit shallow, tropical ocean bays—the same habitat as their fossil ancestors. The closely related green algae, which turn pond water chartreuse in summer, date from about 600 million years ago, when life began settling the land.

The ferns, club mosses, spike mosses, and horsetails found in moist regions of our continent are actually miniature versions of tree-size progenitors that dominated coastal swamp forests from 375 to 275 million years ago. These plants survived by evolving features that enabled them to live in drier habitats: efficient water storage and the ability to go dormant during a drought. Perhaps the best companion of all for model dinosaurs is the Asian ginkgo tree, which is often planted along city streets in the Northeast. It has remained virtually unchanged since it shaded and fed the earliest dinosaurs 200 million years ago.

➤ *Though it's hard to believe by looking at these horsetails (which rarely exceed two or three feet in height), their prehistoric ancestors grew to the size of trees. Hundreds of millions of years ago, these spore bearers dominated much of the earth, but over time they were eclipsed by seed-producing plants.*

What makes the wood of bald cypress trees so durable?

Often called "the wood eternal," lumber from the bald cypress has long been favored for such items as shingles, caskets, and stadium seating because of its ability to resist rot even when exposed to extreme moisture. It's a quality one might expect of a tree that spends much of its life in a swamp. The secret of the tree's resistance lies in its heartwood, the hard innermost core of the trunk. Composed of aged, inert cells, heartwood serves as a tree's structural support and provides its prime lumber. The older a tree, the larger its heartwood core, and bald cypresses can be old indeed, some dating as far back as 1,000 years. Whatever their age, these trees have proportionately more heartwood than most other types, and all of it is laced with chemicals that combat insects and fungi, both of which can cause decay and disease.

Is Kentucky bluegrass really blue?

Kentucky bluegrass is a myth. First of all, it's not blue at all. It's not even greenish blue; it's pure green. Most biologists feel the misnomer arises from the fact that in May, when the grass flowers, its blossoms are purplish. Still, the flowers of this grass are so tiny that you would need a large stand of Kentucky bluegrass to even notice the purple.

There are a few grasses (including certain tall prairie grasses) that are slightly blue, but Kentucky bluegrass is not one of them. In fact, only Canada bluegrass is slightly blue or, as biologists insist, blue-green. Even then, they say, it needs to be next to something really green—like Kentucky bluegrass—for the blue to be discernible.

The myth doesn't end there, however. Kentucky bluegrass is not originally from Kentucky. Though Kentucky's unofficial nickname is the Bluegrass State, its bluegrass is actually from Eurasia. English settlers brought it over in the early 1600s, and it quickly spread, replacing native stands of cane that were not as tolerant to cattle. The English called it smooth-stalked meadow grass, while one American Indian name for it translates as "white man's foot grass."

Can plants talk to each other?

Not in so many words, but they do seem able to communicate some kinds of information, including alarms that danger is nibbling nearer. For example, there is tantalizing evidence to suggest that trees may be able to warn their neighbors of the presence of leaf-eating animals such as caterpillars. Not all scientists accept this notion, but many now believe that plants under siege may release airborne substances, spurring their neighbors into action.

That action is largely invisible, a marshaling of the plant's chemical armory. Once insects feed on the leaves of an oak, the tree produces phenols (noxious chemicals that are ingested by caterpillars). By interfering with a caterpillar's ability to digest proteins, these chemicals stunt its growth, as well as reduce the size and viability of any eggs the insect will lay as an adult.

Ironically the oaks' defense mechanism may backfire. Under assault from infestations of gypsy moth caterpillars, which may strip leaves from tens of thousands of acres, the trees crank out more phenols. Yet while these chemicals reduce the caterpillars' growth, they also hobble wilt virus, a natural enemy of the gypsy moth and one that can cause mass destruction of the caterpillars. In fact, gypsy moths actually prefer to eat phenol-rich oaks, thanks to an enzyme in their gut that allows them to partially disable the tree's defensive compounds while enjoying protection from the disease.

In the Deep South the live oak is prized as a shade or ornamental tree because of its wide-spreading branches. In the days of sailing ships, it was valued for its timber, which is strong enough to give vessels a life expectancy of 100 years and so odorless that it caused no nausea to sailors confined to the hull.

Joshua trees so dominate the Mojave Desert that they are often used by scientists to mark its boundaries. The oldest specimens, reaching a height of 40 feet or more, date back nearly 800 years. In spring the Joshua tree produces clusters of white flowers at the tips of its arms. After the annual blooming new limbs grow at right angles to old ones, accounting for the plant's often grotesque shape.

How did the Joshua tree get its name?

When Joshua did as the Lord commanded, and stretched out his javelin with arms uplifted before the city of Hai, he earned his way into not only biblical history but natural history as well. His name would become immortalized as the captor of Hai and (many centuries later) as the inspiration for one of America's newest national parks. According to legend, when pioneers in the 1850s first glimpsed the giant yucca plant found in and near the Mojave Desert, its upstretched limbs reminded them of the prophet's raised arms, beckoning them, it seemed, to a promised land. At Joshua Tree National Park, which covers some 800,000 acres of desert in southern California, these picturesque "trees" abound, thriving on the extremes of temperature and hard winter freezes found at elevations of 3,000 to 5,000 feet.

What makes pine trees so fragrant?

Snap a living twig from a coniferous tree, and the thick, gummy sap that wells out to coat the wound is charged with nose-tingling aromas that rekindle fond memories of freshly cut Christmas trees and summer camping trips. On warm days the air beneath a stand of ponderosa pines in the Rockies or loblolly pines on the Atlantic Coast is rich with this intoxicating scent, a combination of oils, resins, and other volatile compounds in the sap of the tree.

Today, "pine-scented" products generally use synthetic chemicals, but for centuries real pine oils played an important role in daily life and commerce. In Colonial days the pitch pine, one of the most resinous species, provided pitch, turpentine, and an excellent axle grease. Pine knots, formed at the base of branches, were commonly used as torches—as long burning as they were aromatic.

What does catnip do to cats?

The leaves of the catnip plant, a mint, brim with pungent chemicals stored in easy-to-rupture glands. The slightest touch releases airborne molecules that can either warn or woo—all depending on who receives them. For leaf-eating insects the odor may be a warning, sending munchers packing, frantically cleaning their antennae as they go. The chemical they abhor is similar to one that prey insects, such as odorous house ants and rove beetles, use to ward off predatory insects like ant lions or tiger beetles. In an evolutionary sleight of hand, the catnip plant has managed to manufacture a convincing facsimile of the repellent as a survival mechanism.

Cats, however, are another story. Instead of fleeing the way leaf-eating insects do, cats of all stripes (from tabbies to lions) can't seem to get enough of nepetalactone, the active ingredient in catnip oil. If there is as little as one part per billion in the air, cats will come to sniff, bite, kick, fondle, and roll on the leaves with abandon. Neurologists find it hard to pin down precisely what "buttons" are being pushed by the aroma, but the effect is not unlike a pinball hitting random bells. For about 15 minutes cats veer from one behavior to another: wild, frisky, amorous, blissful, drunk, and when the roller coaster has finally run its course—exhausted. Human thrill seekers will be disappointed to learn, however, that only felines are susceptible to catnip. The most it can do for us, say herbalists, is soothe indigestion or stave off a cold, bringing relief, perhaps, but certainly not rapture.

What's the magic of witch hazel?

What else could it be but witchcraft? That's what early New Englanders thought when they named this small tree that blossoms only after it—and every other tree—has dropped its leaves in autumn. In addition these early settlers seem to have confused the plant with the hazel tree they knew back in Europe, a tree that was said to have the power to detect witches.

The witch hazel, however, has its reasons for being a late bloomer. By waiting until other plants have become dormant, it has little competition in attracting insects to pollinate its flowers during the last warm days before winter. In fact, it is so well adapted to the unpredictable weather of this season that if the temperature suddenly drops, the flowers will curl up into tight buds and open again when it warms. Seldom growing more that 20 feet tall, the witch hazel is commonly found beneath the larger trees of Eastern woodlands. Look for its spidery, yellowish flowers around Halloween.

Does skunk cabbage smell anything like its namesake?

When Edwin Way Teale, the renowned American naturalist, noted that "spring begins in the swamp," he was referring to skunk cabbage, the earliest harbinger of the season and arguably the oddest of all our common swampland wildflowers. The actual flowers are golden, daisylike dots that pop from buds crowded on a spongy knob called a spadix. The spadix, in turn, is hidden inside a tentlike leaf called a spathe. The whole affair is formed in the marshy ground in the fall. When skunk cabbage begins to grow with a rush in February, it actually generates enough heat to thaw the frozen ground and melt its way through lingering ice and snow without risk of frostbite.

You would have to sprawl in the mud and pry open the flaps of the spathe in order to examine the plant's tiny flowers. While not exactly skunkish, they do suggest the foul aroma of ripe carrion (an impression further enhanced by the brown to purple color of the plant's outer leaves). The fragrance will never be bottled, but it works just fine to attract pollinating flies, which think they're laying their eggs in decaying flesh. The plant's sprawling leaves, which appear after the spathe withers, become even more pungent if they are stepped upon and broken.

➤ *The writer and naturalist Henry David Thoreau wrote of the skunk cabbage that its leaf "makes the best vessel to drink out of at a spring." Despite its offensive odor, he noted, the plant does not flavor the water one bit.*

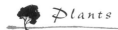

Where do tumbleweeds come from?

When skies turn gray and the screen doors of abandoned farmhouses start flapping, tumbleweeds go cartwheeling across the Great Plains. After breaking off at the stem, these plants roll with the wind, snagging on the wire of neglected fences. Several kinds roam the American West, including tumbling pigweed, tumbling mustard, and Russian thistle. Most flourished only after farming and grazing removed competing native plants and bared the soil to the wind.

Russian thistle stole into South Dakota in 1877 as an impurity in imported flax seed and has since tumbled as far west as California and as far south as Texas. It starts the summer as a densely branched, globe-shaped shrub with small, spiny green leaves. Over time it grows to the size of a softball or even a beach ball. By fall the plant dries out, turning brown or red. On a windy day the stem breaks and the plant goes rambling. It spins and bounces, leaping over gullies and whirling across highways. A steady wind may dribble it up to two miles in one day.

Anchored to the soil before they flower, tumbleweeds wither and snap free from their roots afterward. Their vagabond lifestyle is actually a virtue. Wandering wherever the winds take them, they sow their seeds far and wide.

How did scurvy grass get its name?

In 1633, when Dutch explorers prepared to winter in the Arctic, one of the foods they gathered was a foot-tall biennial herb with small white flowers. Because they happened to store it in an empty, frigid building, they effectively freeze-dried the plant, preserving its high concentration of vitamin C. Though bitter and salty, the plant was most welcome to sailors deprived of adequate food, but its real value, unknown to the Dutch, was the protection it offered against a common and lethal disease known as scurvy.

Throughout most of history scurvy, which causes pain, hemorrhages, and eventual death, ravaged populations from China to America, but its cause—lack of vitamin C—remained a mystery. Astute sea captains noticed, however, that when their crew's diet included fresh fruits and vegetables, the men were free of scurvy, so at every landing the search was on for edible plants. One of these, a member of the mustard family that grows in northern climes along seacoasts, rivers, and salt marshes, proved so effective in thwarting the disease that it came to be called scurvy grass. During the 19th century the U.S. Army planted a close relative, watercress, along the Santa Fe Trail in Kansas to prevent scurvy among westward-bound pioneers.

What are swamp potatoes?

Though not a potato at all, the arrowhead's crunchy "root" tastes a bit like one, earning it the name coined by European settlers. They were, however, hardly the first to appreciate the value of this wetland native. Indians throughout North America harvested the plants, often by wading barefoot into freezing water and digging them out with their toes; once free, the buoyant corms (buried stems that look like roots) bob conveniently to the surface.

Named for its tapered, arrowhead-shaped leaves, the plant is usually easy to recognize, though not all of the several dozen species in North America have the distinctive, back-pointing flanges. In midsummer it produces three-petaled white flowers on slender stalks rising above the leaves, followed by marble-size seed heads. Arrowhead leaves, seeds, and corms are so popular with mallards and canvasbacks that one of its other common nicknames is duck potato.

⤷ *Tennessee's state bloom, the passionflower was used as a natural sedative by early Indians, who also applied its crushed leaves to bruises.*

Which flower has come to symbolize the Crucifixion?

People have always named new things after those they already know, and the Roman Catholic missionaries who came to Latin America were no exception. When these early explorers discovered a long vine crowned with radiant lavender flowers, they saw in it images of the suffering and Crucifixion of Jesus. The plant seemed to them a divine assurance that their efforts to convert the natives to Christianity would be successful. Hence, they named it Flower of the Passion, or passionflower. What is surprising is just how many devotional symbols they found in its blossoms.

In the fringed circle of hairlike rays above the petals they saw the crown of thorns worn by Christ during the Crucifixion. The five petals and five sepals collectively reminded them of the 10 faithful apostles (minus Peter, who denied Jesus, and Judas, who betrayed Him). The ovary represented a hammer, while the three knobbed stigmas resembled the nails that fastened Christ to the cross. The five stamens called to mind the five wounds inflicted upon His body. Other parts of the plant were also symbolic. The deeply cut leaves were said to represent the hands of Christ's prosecutors, while the curling tendrils were reminders of the scourges used to whip Him. Even the pillar of the cross was identified in the column of the ovary.

One variety of passionflower (there are several in North America) grows in thickets and along hedges throughout the Southeastern and South-Central states. In these regions the plant is also known as maypop—a name derived from the fact that the two-inch fruit bursts like a balloon when you squeeze it. This sudden collapse occurs because the fruit is filled inside with air and seeds that are surrounded with a jellylike pulp. According to those who have eaten the pulp, its taste can best be described as heavenly.

Is there a plant that can actually give directions?

Some 200 years ago the midsection of America was covered by a vast grassland, the prairie. Stretching across an area that would one day include seven states, this flat landscape was dominated by tall grasses that in some places reached higher than a man. But if you lost your bearings in this seemingly endless sea of grass, there was a towering, sunflower-like plant that could help you find your way. The early pioneers called it the compass plant.

Rough and bristly, the compass plant may grow up to 12 feet tall. It gets its directional nickname from its leaves, which line up along a north-south axis, providing a rough orientation for travelers. The plant, also known as rosinweed, looks wide when viewed from the east or west and slender when seen from the north or south. This unusual arrangement allows the leaves to avoid the scorching midday sun and puts them in an ideal position for collecting the gentler light of morning and late afternoon.

In some parts of the country, prickly lettuce is also called a compass plant. This tall, rangy plant (an ancestor of all lettuce plants) was introduced from Europe not long after Christopher Columbus's voyages to the New World. Today prickly lettuce has spread across the country, growing along roadsides, in fields—anyplace where the soil has recently been tilled. Like the compass plant of the prairies, it also twists its leaves until their edges line up in a single direction.

⤷ *The compass plant aided not only lost pioneers but their horses as well: when mixed with hay, the perennial prevented heaving. Longfellow immortalized the weed in his poem* Evangeline, *writing that God had planted it* "to direct the traveller's journey."

Plants for People   *From decorating homes to saving lives*

Are any wild plants suitable as houseplants?

A dozen cut roses are beautiful all by themselves, but even more so when dressed in the delicate lacework of maidenhair ferns, favored by many florists as ornamental greens. The fragile elegance of the maidenhair, which puts forth a swirl of leaves from well-drained woodland soil, has also made it a popular houseplant. Despite the plant's delicate appearance, its roots are surprisingly strong, so it can be easily transplanted. (Resist the temptation to dig up maidenhair in the wild, however, since these ferns have been drastically reduced in number by overzealous admirers.) Another wild plant that is grown indoors is the piggyback, a West Coast native that measures two feet high and has greenish white flowers. It is a favorite for the home because the new plants that bud from the base of its leaf stalks can be separated and then repotted.

People who prefer a touch of exotica may opt for the sago cycas, or sago palm, a Japanese plant that has been introduced into warmer parts of the United States. When mature, the sago palm stands more than six feet tall—admittedly large for a houseplant, but it takes more than 50 years to reach such a height.

Why do some Indians prize the saguaro cactus?

In the blistering oven of an Arizona summer day, when waves of heat make the arid landscape dance and shimmer, women of the Tohono O'odham tribe follow a tradition almost as old as the Sonoran Desert. Using long, stiff poles made from the ribs of a dead saguaro cactus, they carefully pry red fruits free from the crown of flowers and pods that top the ends of living saguaro trunks and arms. As the juicy masses break off, companions catch them in a basket. It is a model of skill and teamwork that takes many years to perfect.

Saguaro fruit holds a sacred place in the life of the O'odham (formerly Papago) people, for

➤ In the Southwest the juicy figlike fruit of the prickly pear is made into syrup and jelly, while its pads are peeled and eaten raw as a vegetable.

it ripens in the scorching dry season of summer when other natural foods are scarce. Once the seeds and pulp are strained out, the sweet juice is boiled down to a thick syrup, the foundation for candy and jam. Moreover, the seeds are used for mealcakes, and the juice can be fermented to make a mild wine.

Which plants make the best chewing gum?

Humans seem to have a universal fondness for chewing gum, and cultures the world over have found natural substances that fit the bill—whether or not bubbles could be blown with them. Modern chewing gum originally came from the sap of the tropical chicle tree, but long before that, Indians used a variety of North American plants for the same purpose.

Native hawkweed, a low, scrubby plant with dandelion-like flowers, was chewed by tribes of the Pacific Northwest and Rockies. On the grasslands of the eastern plains, the gum of choice was prairie-dock, a dramatic relative of the sunflower, growing more than 10 feet tall, with huge, arrowhead-shaped leaves. The resinous sap of many coniferous trees, once dried, can also be chewed. Loggers relied on the hardened gum of black spruce—a pungent, jaw-tiring treat that is still sold commercially. The root of chicory, a European import whose pale blue flowers today spangle roadsides, was chewed by colonists, who often roasted the root to create a passable substitute for coffee. Be warned, though, that many plants with gummy, sticky sap, such as milkweeds, can be quite toxic. Never eat any wild plant unless you are absolutely certain of both its identity and safety.

What plant forms a lather with a wide range of uses?

Pennsylvania Dutch pioneers loved their beer with a frothy head of foam. So they spiked their favorite beverage with an additive that they obtained from a common weed known as bouncing bet. The plant is one of several that contain chemicals called saponins, which create a thick lather when mixed with water and shaken. Modern brewers, however, seldom—if ever—employ saponins because they unfortunately give beer a bad taste and, if used improperly, can be toxic.

People have long relied on plants containing saponins for another purpose: to clean things. Because it emulsifies dirt, saponin lather is not only a natural detergent but an all-purpose one, gentle enough to clean delicate fabrics such as lace, yet powerful enough to make pewter sparkle. It was once used extensively by New England textile mills to revitalize fabrics before they were sent to market.

The plant parts that contain saponins vary from species to species. They are found in the leaves and roots of bouncing bet; the orange-brown or yellow fruit of soapberry trees; the bulbs of a white-flowered lily called the soap plant; and the roots of another member of the lily family, whose leaves are responsible for its name, Spanish bayonet. Southwestern Indians found that the Spanish bayonet offered them another bounty as well: a fruit that looks and tastes like a banana. This meant that the same plant offered them both a meal and the means to wash their hands before they sat down to eat it.

Is the plant called "heal-all" really a cure-all?

Though heal-all may not fully live up to the promise of its name, this foot-high plant with purple flowers has long been used to make a tea that successfully treats sore throats. In fact, heal-all attained a certain measure of fame when physicians used it during the 16th century to combat an outbreak of sore throat and fever. (The fact that the victims were troops in Germany's imperial army probably helped catch public attention.) Native to Eurasia but widely naturalized throughout the United States, heal-all is now believed to have little medicinal value. Without careful scientific study, though, it can be difficult to establish a plant's therapeutic agency—or lack thereof.

Consider, for example, the curious case of colic root, a member of the lily family recognizable by a single stalk growing three feet high from a rosette of leaves. This native North American plant was highly regarded by some as a remedy for colic and menstrual problems. In the 1940s, however, it fell out of favor, but

recent studies indicate that it may, in fact, help curb stomach pains and menstrual cramps. Appalachian mountaineers had another use for colic root: they mixed it with whiskey or brandy to relieve the pain of backache.

Although many members of the plant kingdom have well-established healing properties, those who seek natural remedies should exercise extreme caution. Using a plant for its medicinal value without being informed about the possible risks or side effects is no less dangerous than swallowing pills from an unlabeled container.

⬥ Renowned for its ability to help restore human tissue, the juice of aloe vera is used in a host of skin preparations and salves. Cultivated in parts of the country where the temperature stays above 40° F, the plant can also be grown indoors on a sunny windowsill. Many people keep it in the kitchen as a handy treatment for burns.

~ *Acid precipitation and other forms of pollution are suspected in the massive die-offs of red spruces and firs throughout the Black and the Great Smoky Mountains of the southern Appalachians and the Green and the White Mountains of New England. This scene of devastation is from North Carolina's Mt. Mitchell.*

Why is acid rain harmful to trees and other plants?

Wrapping the rugged hills like cotton batting, the mists that give the Great Smoky Mountains their name may actually be killing the forests they shroud. Along the Appalachians—and in many other locations in North America—acid rain, snow, and fog are being blamed for the sickness and death of millions of trees.

Factories and power plants that release sulfur dioxide and nitrogen oxide into the air can create acid precipitation miles downwind. This rain is often hundreds of times more acidic than normal rainfalls, exacting a terrible toll on lakes, streams, and forests—especially stands of red spruces and firs. Lingering fogs immerse the trees in a continuous bath of dilute acid, while each spring's snowmelt soaks the earth with a winter's worth of poison. Acid precipitation erodes the waxy coating that protects a conifer's needles, interferes with the germination of its seeds, and cripples its ability to absorb nutrients. The acid also kills microorganisms in the ground, eventually reducing the fertility of the soil and transforming a lush forest canopy into a haunting, skeletal skyline.

Which wild plants can we eat safely?

Meadows, gardens, and even untended yards can be treasure troves of edible plants. This is not so surprising when we remember that our familiar vegetables have been cultivated from wild ancestors. Since poisonous look-alikes can be mistaken for some edible wild plants, you should be absolutely certain of a plant's identity and safety before eating from the wild. Care must also be taken to ensure that the plant is free of pesticides. Generally, leaves should be picked when young and tender, as they toughen and grow increasingly bitter with age.

Many edible plants have so overrun our gardens and lawns that they are regarded as weeds. One of these, common purslane, is a tasty mild green that grows in all 50 states and is a favorite of wild-plant eaters. Its fleshy, oval leaves have a tart citrus flavor and are a good source of vitamins A and C, while its creeping red stems can be pickled like cucumbers. Tender purslane shoots can be boiled in salted water or eaten raw in salads. Similarly, the young leaves and shoots of lamb's-quarter can be boiled until tender and are often substituted for spinach or chard in recipes.

Great burdock, or edible burdock, is also popular among wild-plant connoisseurs. Common across the continent, almost every part of this one- to five-foot-tall, spiny-flowered weed is edible. The roots can be peeled and boiled, while the core of the flowering stem may be eaten cooked or raw. The leaves make a good potherb, and the leaf stalks can stand in for celery and actually taste better to many palates.

Though despised by groundskeepers, the dandelion is a versatile delight to plant enthusiasts. The dandelion's young leaves impart a sharp, mildly bitter taste to salads. Besides wonderful flavor, the uncooked greens are rich in essential minerals such as iron, calcium, and copper. When boiled in two changes of water, the dandelion's bitterness disappears, making it a marvelous potherb. The white root top can be sliced into salads or cooked as a vegetable. The tap root itself can be boiled to produce a robust coffee substitute, while fermented dandelion flowers produce a delicate wine.

Mustards are edible weeds that grow in hundreds of varieties. While their cultivated relatives include mild vegetables such as broccoli, cauliflower, and cabbage, wild mustards possess coarse, peppery-tasting leaves that can be eaten uncooked when young, or sautéed when older.

Edible wildflowers include the dainty blue blooms of the violet, once savored raw with lettuce and onions. The petals of wild roses add color and fragrance to salads and can also be made into a jelly. The unopened flower buds of the day lily make an excellent snack when boiled in salted water, while opened flowers can be dipped in batter and fried like fritters. Its firm young tubers have a pleasantly nutty flavor when eaten raw, but taste a bit like corn if boiled.

What weed saved the lives of thousands of sailors?

Stroll through a lot strewn with weeds and you just might come across one of World War II's great unsung heroes: the milkweed. At the beginning of the war, U.S. Navy life jackets were stuffed with kapok, a lightweight fiber harvested in Java. But when the kapok supply was cut off by the Japanese invasion of the

Dutch East Indies in 1942, the navy turned to home-grown milkweed seed-pods, which produced a buoyant, water-resistant floss perfect for life preservers. A reward of 20 cents was offered for every gunnysack crammed with ripe seedpods, and children were encouraged to "pick a weed, save a life!" By war's end, more than 1 million "Mae West" life vests were stuffed with milkweed floss, and thousands of Allied sailors owed their lives to the once lowly weed.

➤ *Milkweed's usefulness is not limited to life vest stuffing: Thomas Edison produced natural rubber from its sap, and during the oil shortage of the 1970s, federal agencies looked to its seeds as an alternative fuel source.*

Which plant keeps millions of heart patients alive?

The line between toxin and tonic can be a thin one, as is proved by foxglove, one of the first plants brought to North America by the early colonists. Foxglove leaves contain a deadly poison, yet this same compound, called digitalis, is among mankind's most useful drugs—if administered under the right conditions at the proper dosage. Digitalis strengthens and slows the contractions of disease-weakened heart muscle, and several forms of the drug are widely prescribed for patients with congestive heart failure and other cardiac disorders. Foxglove's medicinal value was recognized early by doctors; one English physician used it to treat dropsy in the late 18th century.

Many, perhaps most, of our medicines originally stem from plants. Oleander, another toxic Old World flower naturalized in many warm regions of the continent, contains chemicals similar to digitalis that are now under study. Willow bark contains methysalicylate, which the human liver converts to salicylic acid—the active ingredient in aspirin. The bark of Pacific yew trees yields taxol, a controversial treatment for cancer. Yet, as scientists point out, only a small percentage of North America's native plants have been tested for pharmaceutical properties despite such promising leads.

➤ *Despite its lovely looks, the foxglove has earned another, more sinister moniker: dead men's bells. Even a nibble of its leaves can be deadly, causing nausea, abdominal cramps, and wild disturbances of the heart.*

LIVING LANDSCAPES OF AMERICA

Habitat Champions *America's record breakers*

What's the longest path ever followed by a tornado?

As a rule, nature's twisty tantrums are terrifying but mercifully short. Tornadoes seldom travel more than 30 miles and rarely last more than an hour. But on May 26, 1917, two giant blue-black cloud masses collided over Mattoon, Illinois, and turned into a monster vortex that, over a period of seven hours and 20 minutes, swept across 293 miles to Charleston, Indiana. It created the longest continuous tornado track measured in the 20th century (though it may have skipped into the air briefly during its early stages). Like most large tornadoes, this one also took its toll in lives and homes, but that's a fact of life for America's central Plains. This area of our country sees more twisters—violent upshots of warring warm and cool air masses—than any other place in the world.

➴ *A photo snapped by a North Dakota farmer in 1978 shows a tornado 11 miles away with a funnel 600 feet wide at its base. Its 20-mile path was about average in length—some 273 miles short of the record.*

How fast is North America's fastest-moving glacier?

Glaciers, the world's slowest-moving rivers, are abundant along Alaska's icy coastline. Prince William Sound, which is nestled in the coastal arc of the rugged Chugach Range, has more than 20 glaciers terminating at sea level. The largest of these huge slabs of frozen landscape is the Columbia Glacier, which slides along at an eye-popping average speed of 65 feet per day—a faster continuous rate than any other glacier monitored by scientists. Despite its rapid forward motion, the Columbia Glacier is receding up its ocean inlet at the rate of half a mile per year as hundreds of gigantic icebergs calve, or break off, and float out to sea.

Which lake is the deepest one in the United States?

What you can clearly see is the deep blue color of its waters. What you can't see is just how profoundly deep it is: 1,932 feet, or more than a third of a mile—some 600 feet deeper than Lake Superior at its deepest. Crater Lake, like a magnificent sapphire embedded in a jagged bracelet, lies on the crest of the Cascade Range in southern Oregon at an elevation of 6,164 feet. The crater itself was created about 6,500 years ago by cataclysmic eruptions of a volcano once 12,000 feet high. Over the millennia rain and melting snow slowly filled in what the collapsed mountain left behind: an immense hole some 26 miles around with no outlet.

❧ *Called Deep Blue Lake by early gold prospectors, Crater Lake in Oregon assumes an incredible deep violet-blue color on cloudless summer days—the result of the extraordinary purity of its water and its great depth. The lake's surface is about 2,000 feet below the rocky rim of a caldera six miles wide and three-quarters of a mile deep.*

Where is our longest cave system?

In central Kentucky there is a subterranean wonderland of labyrinthine passages and underground rivers decorated with sparkling gypsum crystals, stalagmites, and stalactites. Located in Mammoth Cave National Park, this cave system is the world's longest, with a currently mapped length of 348 miles. Acidic groundwater, seeping through cracks in soluble limestone, has carved out the upper passageways over the past several million years, while the flowing waters of underground streams, such as the navigable Echo River, continue to enlarge the lower passages, creating fresh habitats for blind beetles, ghostly spiders, eyeless fish and crayfish, and other living wonders adapted to the dark.

➤ *Groundwater saturated with dissolved calcium carbonate deposits its mineral cargo in a variety of fanciful, sometimes translucent forms in Mammoth Cave's open passageways. Mineral impurities tint them yellow, orange, brown, or even black.*

What river is America's longest?

From its source at Minnesota's Lake Itasca, the Mississippi River snakes southward through 10 states in the heartland of America and forms a crow's foot of three navigable passages as it discharges 350 billion gallons of water per day into the Gulf of Mexico. In the course of dividing the United States into its eastern and western halves, our longest river journeys an astonishing 2,350 miles. Because of the many streams and rivers that flow into it on the stretch between St. Paul and St. Louis, the Algonquian Indians named it *Misi Sipi*—literally "Big Water" but more accurately translated "Father of Waters." Just above St. Louis at the junction of the silt-laden Missouri River, the mighty river immortalized by Mark Twain swells to its full grandeur, becoming the wide, sometimes treacherous, muddy Ol' Miss, flowing south all the way to its delta below New Orleans.

➤ *Below Cairo, Illinois, the Mississippi becomes a muddy, meandering giant, changing course often as it creates new horseshoe bends and cuts across old ones.*

How tall is our highest waterfall?

The late spring waters of Yosemite Creek tumble through a pass in the Sierra Nevada, then fall abruptly—and spectacularly—into the lap of Yosemite Valley and its groves of ancient sequoia trees. From top to bottom, Yosemite Falls measures 2,425 feet, making it one of the world's highest cataracts. But the drop occurs in three sections: Upper Yosemite is 1,430 feet, the middle Cascades are 675 feet long, and Lower Yosemite is 320 feet. Those who argue that the title of highest waterfall belongs to the one with the longest single drop need only travel a few miles to the southwest to Ribbon Falls. At peak flow from May to June, when the snow melts, Ribbon Falls has a drop of 1,612 feet—which is greater, by more than 200 feet, than the height of the Sears Tower in Chicago, the tallest building in the United States.

As high as 13 Niagaras, Yosemite Falls plunges nearly half a mile to the valley floor in two thundering cataracts separated by leaping cascades. The falls is most spectacular in spring, when melting snows swell Yosemite Creek. By fall the flow diminishes to a trickle.

⬿ *Summer temperatures often climb above 120°F in sunbaked Death Valley, California, but rarely exceed 63°F in Barrow, Alaska (inset), America's most northerly city.*

Where are the hottest and coldest places in the country?

Flanked by towering mountains and located 282 feet below sea level, southern California's Death Valley is a natural broiler. It's the only place in the United States where summer nighttime temperatures can reach 100°F or more. Not surprisingly, Death Valley also holds the record for the all-time daylight high. On July 10, 1913, at a place once known as Furnace Creek Ranch, the temperature rose to a scorching 134°F.

On the extreme low end of the thermometer's scale—an almost unimaginable 200° or so less—is the lowest temperature ever recorded in the United States, –79.8°F, on January 23, 1971, at Prospect Creek Camp in central Alaska. But the places with the lowest and highest average annual temperatures are logically also the northernmost and the southernmost places in the United States. At the top of Alaska, Barrow experiences a bone-chilling 9.6°F on average, while at the tip of Florida, Key West scores a balmy average of 77.7°F.

How big is our largest marsh?

The Seminole Indians call it Pa-hay-okee, which means "Grassy Waters." Though an accurate description, the words don't do justice to just how large this marsh lying at the southern end of Florida is. Fed by waters from Lake Okeechobee, the place we call the Everglades encompasses nearly 4,000 square miles, of which 2,135 square miles—an area larger than Delaware—are protected in a national park. The Glades sit atop a limestone shelf sloping imperceptibly toward the Gulf of Mexico. The dominant vegetation is a tall, razor-toothed sedge known as sawgrass. Scattered

➣ *A sea of sawgrass surrounds Shark Valley Observation Tower, located in the northwest sector of Everglades National Park. The 50-foot structure affords visitors an outstanding view of one of the largest sawgrass expanses in this 1½-million-acre wetland park.*

over this huge plain are bodies of water and low islands, or hammocks, thick with cypress trees and tropical hardwoods.

Its mild subtropical climate and 55 inches of rain a year make the Glades a paradise for such wading birds as slender white egrets, curve-billed ibises, and long-legged herons, as well as for panthers and the Everglades' most notorious denizens—the alligators.

What is America's foggiest spot?

On Washington's rugged coast at the mouth of the Columbia River lies a nob of land called Cape Disappointment. The cape was so named by a British captain who, in 1788, searched for and, thanks to fog, failed to find the mouth of the great river said to exist there. No wonder. This cape is covered in nature's own pea soup for about 106 days per year on average—more than

any other place in America. The fog, which is actually a cloud with its base on the ground rather than in the sky, is anchored here at the tip of the Long Beach Peninsula for a simple reason: breezes laden with moisture from surf breaking on offshore sand shoals are forced upward when they smack into the cape's 200-foot cliffs. As the ocean air rises, it cools and produces a bank of stagnant fog.

➣ *North Head Lighthouse stands just a few miles from Cape Disappointment near the Columbia River. For a century it has warned ships of one of the world's most treacherous river-mouth sandbars.*

No other mountain in the world displays such an immense snow-covered face as Alaska's Mt. McKinley. Only its lowest foothills are free of snow in summer, and even those have no trees because timberline here is at 2,700 feet. Located next to a great fault line in the earth, Mt. McKinley and the mountains surrounding it are getting a few fractions of an inch higher every year as the crustal plate underneath them overrides another plate to the north.

What is North America's tallest mountain?

If you want to get on top of it all, there is only one place to go. About 130 miles northwest of Anchorage, Alaska, near the center of the Alaskan Range, lies Mount McKinley. At 20,320 feet above sea level (nearly four miles), the southernmost of Mount McKinley's twin peaks is the highest place in North America. Though only about two-thirds Mount Everest's height, McKinley extends nearly 18,000 feet from base to peak, a greater rise than any other mountain on earth. No wonder native peoples dubbed it Denali, or "High One," and the Russians, who owned Alaska until 1867, called it Bolshaya Gora, or "Great Mountain."

Where can you find the oldest rocks on our continent?

The oldest rocks ever found on the surface of the earth just happen to be in North America. About 150 miles north of the Great Slave Lake in Canada's Northwest Territory, past the dense forests of spruce and aspen, is a largely barren, lake-studded landscape inhabited by wolves, grizzlies, and musk oxen. Near one of these shallow, glacier-scooped lakes, Acasta Lake, lies an outcrop of very old gneiss, a rock formed by great heat and pressure deep inside the earth. The oldest layer of this coarse-grained, striated rock, known as Acasta gneiss, is estimated to be 3.96 billion years old. When this rock formed, the earth was a youngster of a planet—a mere 500 million or so years old.

Which of our active volcanoes is the largest?

The island of Hawaii is host to the most massive active volcano in the world. Mauna Loa, which means "Long Mountain," reaches an elevation of 13,680 feet, though more than three-quarters of its enormous volume lies out of sight below sea level. This broad, gently domed mountain is a prodigious lava producer, with flows reaching as far away as 50 miles and covering as much territory as the entire state of Delaware. Its summit crater alone, Mokuaweoweo, is three times the size of Central Park in New York City and so deep that the Washington Monument could fit inside it. During the past century and a half, the volcano has erupted, on average, once every 4½ years.

Leaping 40 feet into the air, molten lava (upper right corner) boils out of a fissure 9,000 feet up on the flanks of Mauna Loa. Forming a 20-foot-wide river of fire (foreground), the lava sweeps downhill at 35 miles per hour.

Where do the strongest winds blow in the United States?

Chicago springs to mind, but that city isn't even among the 10 windiest. Top honors go to Cheyenne, Wyoming, with an average wind speed of 12.9 miles per hour. The strongest winds in all of North America, however, were recorded on New Hampshire's Mount Washington. Rising just 6,288 feet above sea level—an unimpressive elevation by the standards of our Western mountains—this peak nevertheless endures gales ranking among the most severe on earth, thanks to the convergence of two factors. First, it stands just at the point where cold air sweeping down from the Arctic often collides with warm fronts blowing up from the southeast. Second, it has few surrounding peaks to break the wind. On average, breezes on Mount Washington bluster by at 35 miles per hour, but they can at times run faster than any standard automobile. During a storm on April 12, 1934, for example, winds at the summit raged at up to 231 miles per hour.

➤ Plumes of snow create a frigid haze near the summit of New Hampshire's Mt. Washington. Intrepid winter mountaineers must dress to withstand brutal subzero gales. Even in summer, when mountaintop temperatures are 40° to 50°F, a 50-mile-per-hour breeze will push the chill factor down to a frosty 10°F.

➤ Gigantic basalt cliffs 2,000 feet high rim the Snake River on its 125-mile run through Hell's Canyon at the border of Idaho and Oregon. This awesome gash in the earth bisects a great plain of congealed lava that was extruded from gaping, mile-long fissures in the earth some 3 million years ago.

What is our country's deepest canyon?

The Grand Canyon might seem to be the likeliest candidate. This magnificent cutout of the Colorado River is the largest land gorge in the world, but its greatest depth is no more than 5,500 feet. The distinction of being the deepest belongs to two other canyons in the western United States. The deepest in a high mountain setting is Kings Canyon, which runs through the southern part of California's Sierra Nevada. In the area where the middle and south forks of the Kings River converge, the steep, flaky walls of the canyon tower a spectacular 8,200 feet, or more than a mile and a half. In slightly less mountainous territory, richly colored Hell's Canyon holds the depth record over a distance. At one point this gorge—cut by the Snake River in southwestern Idaho near the Oregon border—reaches 7,900 feet in depth, and on a spectacular 67-mile stretch, the depth of the yellow, red, and orange trench averages 6,600 feet.

Which desert is our biggest?

It's not like other deserts. It's hot, but only in the summer. In the winter, frost and snow are common. There are cacti here, but they're few and far between. Most of the vegetation is big sagebrush, recognizable by its three-toothed leaves and spicy odor. Yes, it's sandy here, but there are also wetlands and salt lakes in this desert. This vast, often empty, little-known place is the Great Basin Desert. Its 200,000 square miles cover most of the state of Nevada and western Utah, reach into California, and stretch north into Oregon and Idaho, making it the largest desert in North America. Because of its more northerly latitude and high elevations, the Great Basin is colder than many people imagine a desert can be. Nevertheless, low precipitation is a desert's defining characteristic, and with only 7 to 12 inches of water annually, the Great Basin easily qualifies as a true desert.

➤ *Snow-covered 14,242-foot White Mountain Peak looms over the Columbus Salt Flats and sagebrush desert near the Nevada–California border. Sagebrush and salt flats are hallmarks of the Great Basin.*

Up, Up and Away! *Sky-high spectacles*

Can air be too clean?

If you're among the 140 million Americans who live in areas with unsafe levels of smog, then you probably doubt that air can ever be too clean. The truth is, however, that it can. While the air we breathe does contain harmful man-made pollutants, many of nature's cast-offs are vital ingredients. Air contains molecules of atmospheric gases, such as argon and nitrogen, whose atoms were thrown out by distant stars billions of years ago. There are also molecules of carbon dioxide, hydrogen, oxygen, sulfur dioxide, and methane—essential elements discharged by plants, animals, and volcanoes.

Some of the most important cast-offs found in the air are tiny particles of dust, smoke, and salt from ocean spray. Though often microscopic, these minuscule bits of matter are the building blocks of clouds that help cool our planet and give us rain. The condensation of water vapor around particulates in the atmosphere produces water droplets. When enough of these droplets collect, they create a cloud that floats in the air. If air were totally pure, clouds and mists would not be able to form.

Air also contains pollen, tiny grains thrown to the wind by tens of thousands of species of trees and grasses to help ensure their survival. Pollen (its Latin root means "dust") is a living cloud of male sex cells, and many plants depend on air to spread their pollen. Without it, we wouldn't have the plants that produce paper, bread, cotton, and beer, not to mention most of the oxygen that sustains us.

Did dinosaurs breathe the same air we have today?

It's quite possible that your next breath will include a molecule of oxygen, carbon dioxide, or nitrogen that passed through the lungs of a *Tyrannosaurus* 80 million years ago. The most common elements of air, water, mineral, veg-

➤ *Unlike the larger, sticky pollen grains distributed by animals, those carried by the wind are tiny, smooth, dry, and powdery—perfect for floating in the air. Buoyed by winds, some of the pollen released from pine cones such as this one may travel thousands of miles.*

etable, and animal matter exist in finite quantity and must therefore be continually recycled. The same carbon atom found today in a lilac bud, for example, may once have resided in the kidney of a mouse.

As to whether dinosaurs breathed the same kind of air we do (that is, the same ratio of gases), there isn't enough evidence to prove any one theory. We do know that by the time dinosaurs appeared on earth, the atmosphere was essentially like that of today—breathable by land animals big and small. Since many dinosaurs were energetic, aerobic animals with large, powerful lungs and hearts, they could never have existed without oxygen-rich air.

Some scientists believe that more oxygen was contained in prehistoric atmospheres than at any other time in the earth's history. They theorize that the giant insects of the predinosaur period—cockroaches the size of hamsters and dragonflies as large as hawks—could have survived only in an environment with a high level of oxygen because an insect's respiratory system brings air directly to each cell through branching tubes. If a dinosaur could somehow be recreated from fossil DNA, would it be able to breathe today's polluted air? We'll probably never know. If we could travel back to the days of the dinosaur, though, we might be amazed at the freshness of the air.

What do trees tell us about sunspots?

As early as 28 B.C. people in China noticed dark blotches on the sun. Given ancient beliefs in the sun's godlike purity, these so-called sunspots seemed puzzling or even alarming. The invention of the telescope, however, revealed them to be not storms, as some scientists had believed, but regions of relative calm in the turbulent solar atmosphere, where winds of 90 miles per second are commonplace.

Around 1920 a researcher studying tree rings found that wider ones coincided with peaks of the sunspot cycle (approximately 11 years long), and concluded that sunspots increase rainfall and thus tree growth. The effect seems strongest in cold climates, where increased sunspot activity appears to warm the atmosphere, melting glaciers and giving trees a longer growing season.

The study of solar cycles through tree rings has been greatly enhanced by the discovery that radioactive carbon, absorbed by trees from the air, always decreases as sunspot activity increases. Though these carbon fluctuations in themselves seem not to affect tree growth, they are better indicators of sunspot cycles than the size of growth rings, providing a record of the sun's energy fluctuations as far back as 15,000 years.

Can you really find the end of a rainbow?

Since the dawn of time, people have been enchanted by rainbows. Try as they might, though, no one has ever found the spot where one of these giant, fanciful arches touches the earth. The reason, of course, is that rainbows don't exist—they're an optical illusion.

To see a rainbow, you must be standing with the sun at your back facing a shower of raindrops or mist. The sunlight passing over your head enters near the tops of the raindrops, which act as tiny prisms bending, or refracting, the light and separating it into all the colors of the spectrum. The colored rays are then reflected off the opposite sides of the drops and bent again as they exit and travel toward your eyes.

The angle between the point where sunlight enters the drop and the direction in which it travels toward your eyes will always be 42° for the red band and 40° for the blue one. If any other angles are formed, no rainbow will be visible. Thus you can never run to the spot where the rainbow appears to touch ground: the angles will change and the rainbow will disappear. Since rainbows form only at certain angles, the arch of a rainbow will be higher than a semicircle's when the sun is below the horizon and only a low curve when the sun is high. In fact, if the sun is higher than 42° in the sky, a rainbow cannot form.

➤ *Like a gift from heaven, a rainbow glitters in all its glory at Denali National Park in Alaska. Most of us picture a rainbow as an arch, but the kind seen from a mountaintop at sunset is even harder to chase down: without the horizon to hide part of it, the rainbow forms a perfect circle in the sky.*

~ *No two clouds are exactly alike, and even a single cloud changes its configuration as it drifts across the sky. Shown above are some of the most common types: cirrus (top left), cumulus (top right), cumulonimbus (bottom left), and stratocumulus (bottom right). The lenticular cloud below, seen mostly in mountainous regions, gets its name from the fact that it's lens shaped. It is sometimes mistaken for a UFO.*

Do different parts of the country have different types of clouds?

A meadow without wildflowers, a sea without sails" is how Thoreau described a cloudless sky. If the sky were a giant movie screen, the clouds would stage the drama, setting the mood, serving as characters, and providing the action. Their role, however, goes far beyond entertainment. Clouds cool the earth, bring rain and snow, and help us forecast the weather.

In 1803 an amateur meteorologist from England named Luke Howard developed a classification system for cloud types based on their shapes. It is still widely used today. Cumulus (Latin for "heap") clouds resemble puffed-up cotton balls and are sometimes referred to as fair-weather clouds. Stratus (Latin for "spread out") clouds look like layers of down quilts or gray blankets. Cirrus (Latin for "lock of hair") clouds mimic mare's tails. Modern meteorologists added two specialized terms: alto (Latin for "high") and nimbus (Latin for "dark and rainy"). Combinations of these basic terms give us the 10 specific types that make up cloud nomencla-

ture: cirrus (wispy), cirrocumulus (wispy, puffed up), cirrostratus (wispy, layered), altocumulus (high, puffed up), altostratus (high, layered), cumulonimbus (puffed up, towering rain cloud), stratocumulus (layered, puffed up), stratus (layered), cumulus (puffed up), nimbostratus (dark rain cloud, layered).

The size, shape, and type of clouds that appear in the sky at any given time are determined by a host of environmental factors, including temperature, altitude, wind, and geography. Clouds form when air rises and cools to its dew point, condensing some of its water vapor into tiny drops of water or ice crystals. These particles are so small and light that they float in the air, not quite heavy enough to fall back to earth. When you get right down to it, clouds are wisps of nothing, about as solid as dreams.

While all 10 types of clouds may be found in all parts of the country (depending upon the conditions), some regions favor certain formations. Hawaii and Florida are known for great, billowing cumulonimbus clouds, which are generated when air over land heats up faster than air over the surrounding ocean. When these darkening air ships are spied on the horizon, heavy rain is sure to follow. Towering thunderheads are also the trademark of the Great Plains. A byproduct of the collision between warm, moist air blown in from the Gulf of Mexico and cold, dry air streaming down from the Canadian Arctic, their arrival signals the onset of a drenching storm, perhaps even a tornado.

One of the most distinctive formations is the Chinook Arch, a saucer-shaped cloud created when dry wind blows down the eastern slopes of the Rocky Mountains and meets warm thermal air rising off the plains. Like a pearly portal standing between the desolate prairie and the majestic mountaintops, it's a wonder it isn't nicknamed Heaven's Gate.

Why is the sky blue?

Outer space is black and, as Sir Isaac Newton proved, sunlight is white. It may seem yellow, but it actually consists of all the colors in the rainbow: red, orange, yellow, green, blue, indigo, and violet. So if all this is true, then why do we see blue skies when the sun shines?

Of all the questions posed about our natural world, this one may be asked more often than any other—and not just by children. Early man probably pondered the same notion as soon as he had words to articulate his sense of wonder. Ancient sky watchers insisted that blue ocean waters reflected their color into the sky. Others wondered if something in the earth's atmosphere could be the source of the blue. It took centuries to find that "something," and astronomers still argue over the details. Two hundred years after Newton, scientists proposed that foreign particles, such as dust, made the sky blue by scattering sunlight into its component colors. In 1899 one physicist sug-

gested that foreign particles weren't necessary. Ordinary air molecules, he noted, also scattered the sunlight, resulting in blue skies. So as it turns out, the mysterious "something" is not in the atmosphere; it *is* the atmosphere—the very air we breathe.

Think of sunlight as a large energy wave made up of colors, each having its own length, or specific amount of energy. The shorter lengths at the blue end, having the most energy, are the easiest to scatter. When sunlight hits our atmosphere, the blue light scatters eight times more than the red. Violet, with the shortest wavelength, would be the color of our daytime sky if our vision were more acute. But just as our hearing is limited to certain frequencies (dogs hear frequencies we can't), so too is our vision: our eyes miss most of the violet and indigo while soaking up the blue.

At dusk cobalt blue skies often give way to other hues. When the sun begins to set, its light passes through much more atmosphere than it would at noon relative to our position. Before it reaches our eyes, this light is stripped of its blue color. If the air is filled with dust or other particles, it will absorb much of the yellow and orange colors as well. This leaves only red to capture our gaze as a fiery sunset marks the day's end.

With a ghostly green glow, the aurora borealis, or northern lights, paints the skies over Denali National Park in Alaska. Surprisingly, the best place to view this phenomenon is not the North Pole, but along an oval-shaped band that extends through northern Norway; central Hudson Bay; Point Barrow, Alaska; and northern Siberia.

Why does the aurora borealis occur so far north?

Shimmering like curtains of light rippled by a gentle breeze, the aurora borealis is one of the eeriest and most awe-inspiring sights in nature. As they flicker across the northern sky in pale shades of green, red, blue, or white, these sheets of light move and pulse as though they were alive. The aurora is a polar phenomenon: in the Northern Hemisphere it's called the aurora borealis; in the Southern it's known as the aurora australis. In the high latitudes auroras occur nearly every night, crowning the globe like halos. They appear high in the atmosphere, where charged particles from the sun collide with the earth's magnetic field, releasing energy in the form of light. When the sun's nuclear furnace churns, the auroras may surge far beyond their usual haunts. Every 11 years or so, the sun enters the so-called solar maximum—a period of intense activity blazing with giant flares that blast a powerful "wind" of electrons into space. The electrons transfer their energy to oxygen and other atmospheric gases, which glow like a neon sign. Unlike the normal aurora borealis, these spectacular shows can dazzle observers as far south as the Mexican border.

When are tides the highest?

Since the moon is so close to the earth, its gravitational pull is three times greater than that of the sun, making it the chief influence on the tides. The moon pulls the waters of the ocean nearest to it away from those on the opposite side of the earth, creating bulges—the high tides. The troughs between the bulges are the

How was Meteor Crater formed?

Some 22,000 years ago, a meteoroid (a chunk of iron-rich rock left over from the birth of the solar system) hurtled through space on a collision course with the earth. During the rapid descent through our atmosphere, its surface temperature swiftly increased to a white-hot state, vaporizing the rock and leaving a trail of luminous gases. In its brief but brilliant death throes, it could be called a meteor or, more commonly, a shooting star. Thousands of these metallic objects burn up in the earth's atmosphere every day, but some are massive enough to survive the plunge. This one, a 10,000-ton fireball, crashed into the ground at a speed of roughly 9 miles per second, exploding with enough force to blast out a bowl nearly 1 mile across and 600 feet deep, and instantly killing almost every living thing within a 10 mile radius.

The result of this awesome spectacle—Meteor Crater, near Flagstaff, Arizona—is one of the most dramatic examples of a landform created by the collision of a cosmic body with the earth. (The meteor itself disintegrated on impact, but had a fragment remained, it would be called a meteorite.) Even after many centuries, the site is still impressive, but as cataclysmic events go, this one was relatively small.

Several meteors strike the earth each century with enough force to produce noticeable craters. Large ones form craters much bigger than themselves because their explosive force is dispersed in all directions. Meteorite craters are much wider than deep because there is so much more mass toward the earth's interior to absorb the energy of impact. Most older and smaller craters have been eroded by wind and water or obliterated by geologic or glacial activity, and still others no doubt lie undiscovered on the ocean floor.

↜ Well preserved in the arid Arizona climate, Meteor Crater bears silent testimony to the massive object that created it: a shooting star that hit the earth with a force comparable to that of an atomic bomb. A far greater cataclysm would have resulted if the meteor that whizzed by in May 1996 had been on a collision course with our planet. Missing the earth by 280,000 miles (a whisker in astronomical terms), it would have packed as much power as the combined nuclear arsenals of the United States and Russia.

low tides. As the earth rotates, the bulges travel through the ocean, causing two high tides and two low ones daily on most shorelines.

While the sun is generally of less consequence to the tides, there are four times during the monthly lunar cycle when its role increases significantly. When the moon is in its first and last quarter, it is at a right angle to the sun, causing their gravitational pulls to conflict. This cosmic tug-of-war reduces the height of the tidal bulges to their lowest point. As a new moon or full moon approaches and the moon, earth, and sun align, the height of the bulges gradually increases. When the three are fully aligned, the bulges reach their maximum height. It is then that the highest tides of all, called spring tides, carry the sea onto land that has been high and dry for the previous two weeks.

Why is it so hard to forecast the weather accurately?

When it comes to explaining the challenge of predicting the weather, perhaps Benjamin Franklin put it best. "Some people are weather-wise," said the nation's father of meteorology and author of the first weather guide *(Poor Richard's Almanac)*, "but most are otherwise."

While supercomputers, satellites, and radar imagery have made the process considerably more sophisticated since Franklin's day, weather prediction is still largely a blend of basic science, careful observation, and old-fashioned intuition. Meteorologists base their forecasts on compilations of thousands of readings of air pressure, temperature, wind velocity, humidity, and cloud cover. This information is supplied by a worldwide network of 10,000 weather stations. Five satellites positioned some 22,000 miles above the equator, along with a satellite fleet orbiting pole to pole, also contribute data.

Despite all these tools, however, scientists can predict the weather you will experience in your backyard only three to five days in advance—and even then they are not always on target. The problem is that weather conditions on a given day in a specific place are the result of countless factors, some large and some very small. Variations in temperature of just 1°, for example, can cascade and affect large-scale phenomena such as the path and severity of a storm.

The notion that seemingly insignificant factors can have major consequences has been dubbed the butterfly effect by theorists who developed the mathematical models used in computerized weather forecasting. The implication is that if a butterfly flaps its wings in Shanghai, people in Boston may eventually be shoveling snow.

Which part of the country has the worst thunderstorms?

Like locomotives bound on a collision course, cold, dry air from Canada and warm, moist air from the Gulf of Mexico hurtle toward one another across the vast expanses of the Great Plains. Unlike other parts of the country, the Great Plains offer no tall mountains to derail these powerful air masses. When they crash, the impact eventually results in jagged flashes of lightning that illuminate the skies, and great booms that can be heard for miles around.

Thunderstorms here are at their most frequent and violent during late June afternoons. The long, sunny days heat the flat ground like the bottom of a frying pan, creating thermal currents that lift the heavy, humid air in a rising column. At 10,000 to 20,000 feet, the column meets a current of cool, dry air blowing from the north. At these higher altitudes the water vapor

within the warm, moist, rising air cools and condenses, creating trillions of tiny liquid droplets or frozen crystals. The smallest of these form clouds; the largest fall to the earth. Eventually these particles produce the torrential downpours often associated with thunderstorms.

The friction between the droplets and crystals generates an electrical current marked by near-continuous streaks of lightning that superheat the surrounding air to 54,000°F—more than five times hotter than the surface of the sun. This intense heat causes the air to expand and contract. The resulting shock wave shatters the peace of lazy summer afternoons with one of the most dramatic sounds in nature, the roar of thunder.

Mailboxes stand sentry on a quiet Nevada road as storm clouds loom. Using Doppler-effect radar, scientists can study the anatomy of a storm as it forms, enabling them to gauge its destructiveness and issue early warnings.

237

~ *Air sucked into a tornado funnel rushes upward at over 100 mph, while the walls spin at nearly 300 mph. Such fierce winds can send a grain of sand into a body with the force of a bullet.*

Where is Tornado Alley?

Sweeping across the landscape like a giant vacuum cleaner, a tornado can suck the asphalt off a road, tear houses from their foundations, and whip cars into the air like wind-blown leaves. Yet this same violent whirlwind can be surprisingly merciful, stripping the feathers from a hen without killing it, and snatching a child from its mother's arms, only to set the youngster down six blocks away—unharmed.

The nearly 1,000 twisters that plague the United States each year can strike almost anytime, anywhere, but the majority follow a particular path, dubbed Tornado Alley, that stretches roughly from Texas to Nebraska. In the spring and early summer, warm, moist air from the Gulf of Mexico gets trapped beneath heavier cold, dry air from Canada. Heat and moisture continue to build near the earth's surface until the warm air forces its way up. Buffeted by strong winds, this updraft begins to spin. Gaining momentum, it twirls faster and faster until it spawns a funnel of rotating winds that can suck up everything in its path wherever it touches down. Those funnels that make contact with the ground, however briefly, are officially termed tornadoes, but most never do. The average twister has a lifespan of about 15 minutes—long enough to inflict untold damage on life, limb, and property. One monster in Ohio needed only three minutes to take its terrifying toll: 34 lives and some 3,000 buildings.

What causes our hurricane season?

Each year the red-and-black flags that warn of a hurricane's approach are raised repeatedly along the Atlantic and Gulf coasts. While meteorologists don't fully understand what triggers these deadly pinwheels, they have pinpointed three essential ingredients: heat, moisture, and low atmospheric pressure. This witch's brew is present from late spring to late fall in a belt of easterly trade winds blowing across the tropical Atlantic Ocean. As the sun marches northward, it heats the ocean to the temperature required to whip up a hurricane—80°F or warmer. Add tropical humidity and a zone of low pressure heading north, which produces an upward flow of warm, moist air, and the recipe is complete. Whirled in a counterclockwise direction by the spin of the earth and fueled by heat from the sea, this carousel of winds (which can reach 500 miles in diameter) draws more moisture upward. As it condenses, it releases more heat, which in turn boosts the energy available to the storm. The amount of energy generated by a typical hurricane is prodigious. If it could be harnessed, one day's worth would provide enough electricity to power the entire United States for 200 days.

Where do creatures go during inclement weather?

It's hard to imagine how a delicate butterfly can withstand a strong breeze, much less a raging thunderstorm, but wild animals know where to hole up when nasty weather approaches. At the first sign of gathering clouds, most butterflies head for cover, usually hanging beneath a broad, sheltering leaf, sometimes sliding into nooks and crannies under peeling tree bark or even house shingles. Cavity dwellers like tree swallows seek out hollow trees. Woodchucks and other burrowers tunnel below ground.

Wild animals can even tough out brutal hurricane winds that last for days, taking refuge in dense undergrowth or swimming to safety when a storm floods their territories. When Hurricane Andrew ripped across the Everglades in 1992, conservationists worried about the fate of the 50 or so remaining Florida panthers. Remarkably, all survived by taking cover in dense cypress tree forests, which served as windbreaks against the more than 140-mile-per-hour winds.

Winter's bitter cold can tax animals to the limit. Snow deeper than a foot, for example, limits the mobility of deer and leaves them vulnerable to predators. Some deer compensate by "yarding." They gather together and beat down a large area of snow, providing trails for escape and foraging. For some creatures snow can be a blessing in disguise. Voles, shrews, and other small mammals cover themselves with a blanket of snow that keeps them as much as 50 degrees warmer than they would be in the open air.

➤ *A deer's thick coat is an ideal insulator, retaining so much body heat that the snow the creature sleeps on doesn't even melt.*

Why is San Francisco so foggy?

The dense fogs that are San Francisco's trademark are "current events." They form when the cold California current cools passing masses of warm, moist air, condensing water vapor into cloudy layers of water droplets. Fog, in fact, is really a low altitude cloud. As the fog builds, it hangs over the sea until westerly winds, which generally blow from the afternoon into the evening, push it inland. This soggy mixture dissipates only after the earth's surface heats it sufficiently to make it evaporate—usually sometime before noon the next day.

San Francisco lives up to its reputation as the air-conditioned city. The contrast between ocean and air temperatures is greatest during the summer, making July and August the city's foggiest months. But this also makes for cool midsummer days.

➤ *The thick fogs that play hide and seek with the Golden Gate Bridge above San Francisco Bay also hid the harbor from Sir Francis Drake in 1579. It was finally discovered some 200 years later by Spanish explorers.*

Along the Rockies during the cold winter months, clouds like these often signal the approach of a Chinook. Ordinarily shaped like lenses, these lenticular clouds may be distorted by the Chinook's strong winds.

What is a Chinook?

It has to be one of nature's most supreme ironies: a strong winter wind howling down from the frozen peaks of the northern Rocky Mountains that can send temperatures on the Great Plains soaring and make snow literally vanish into thin air. This wicked wind is called a Chinook, after an Indian tribe of the Pacific Northwest. It is born when a mass of moist air over the Pacific Ocean is swept eastward across the continent to the Rocky Mountains. Ascending their western slope, the air expands as pressure decreases with altitude; expansion causes cooling, which, in turn, triggers condensation. By the time the air has crested the peaks of the Rockies, it is wrung dry of moisture. Roaring down the eastern slope, the air compresses and heats up at a rate of more than 5° for every

1,000 feet of descent. By the time the Chinook swooshes onto the flatlands, sometimes blowing for up to three days straight, it can be 30° warmer than it was before it started its descent from the snow-capped heights.

A Chinook can turn winter into summer in a flash. In Harve, Montana, the mercury once shot up 31°F in three minutes as a Chinook blew through. One February day in Calgary, Alberta, this wind from the west raised the temperature from –14° to 76°F. The hot breath of the Chinook not only melts snow but can actually evaporate a foot of it in about 12 hours. The Chinook's ability to devour snow gave rise, among many of Native American tribes in the West, to various names that share a colorful common English translation: "Snow Eater."

Does El Niño have an effect on our weather?

Every three to seven years in December, the waters off South America warm by as much as 18°F as trade winds that normally blow toward the west across the Pacific collapse in the face of strong westerlies. Winds and ocean currents are intricately tied, and when the wind shifts, the gigantic pool of warm water that is normally held off Australia and Malaysia by the trades sloshes backward to the east. The onset of warm water off the coast of South America at Christmastime led Peruvian sailors to dub this winter phenomenon El Niño, "The Little One," in reference to the Christ child.

When Niño occurs, the change in wind patterns that helped send warm currents eastward also sends heavy rain to some parts of the world while causing scorching drought in others. The largest and most long-lasting Niño on record began in 1982 and continued to influence the weather for 12 years. It was credited with torrential downpours in southern California, record snowfalls in the Rockies, and the worst drought of the century in Australia.

Before the weather system had time to dissipate, a second Niño event began in 1991, unleashing yet another deluge over many parts of the lower 48 states. Some sections of Los Angeles County received more than eight inches of rain between February 6 and 16. More than 25 inches fell between December and February over south-central Texas. In the Midwest rainfall was so heavy at times that it caused the Mississippi River to overrun its banks in several states, leading to the worst flooding in memory.

Can plants influence the weather?

From the smallest mosses to the largest sequoias, plants are natural humidifiers, removing moisture from the ground and releasing it into the air as vapor. On a warm, sunny day, more than 8,000 gallons of water may evaporate from an acre of hardwood trees, feeding cloud formation and producing rain that falls, once more, on plants.

But plants also influence the weather on a smaller scale, shaping so-called microclimates (interactions of humidity, wind, temperature, rainfall, sunlight, and other factors), which may encompass a square mile or just a few square feet. Coastal redwoods, for example, trap fog, increasing the moisture dripping to the ground. They also seal the air beneath their interlocking limbs, insulating against wild swings in temperature. By contrast, the cottonwoods and willows that grow along desert rivers can significantly cool and moisten the surrounding air; their loss, due to overgrazing or timbering, can intensify a drought's grip on the entire region.

How do lakes affect snowfall?

When a dry winter wind passes over a body of water, it is warmed and collects moisture. If the wind's route is across a small pond, the change in temperature and humidity is barely noticeable, but when the body of water involved is one of the Great Lakes, the result is one of the snowiest climates in America.

After absorbing the heat of the summer sun, the Great Lakes remain warmer than the cold air that travels down from Canada in the late autumn, winter, and early spring. As these southbound winds cross the lakes, they pick up moisture. When they collide with the colder air over the far shore, this moisture condenses and falls to the ground in the form of lake-effect snow.

Most common on the eastern and southern shores of the Great Lakes, lake-effect snow helps create the notorious snow cover that regularly blankets the region. The Keweenaw Peninsula of Michigan, which juts out into Lake Superior, averages over 200 inches of snow per year, and New York's Tug Hill Plateau at the eastern end of Lake Ontario once received 466 inches in a single season. In such areas snow can fall for up to 70 days throughout the winter and cover the ground for an average of 150 days.

The largest body of fresh water in the world, Lake Superior covers some 32,000 square miles, providing a vast reservoir of moisture for the lake-fed snow that is unique to the region. In early winter much of this precipitation takes the form of concentrated snow showers, which taper off by midseason, when portions of the lake freeze over.

Continents on the Move *Our restless planet*

Where is it possible to look back 2 billion years in time?

Inspiring awe, exhilaration, and even fear, the vast expanse of the Grand Canyon is truly one of the world's most magnificent sights. Beyond its imposing depths and seemingly boundless breadth, though, this natural wonder boasts yet another astonishing trait: an equivalent immensity in the dimension of time.

The earth's 4.6-billion-year history is told in rocks, and the exposed layers of the Grand Canyon chronicle nearly half of that period. The oldest, lowest layers are ancient schist and granite—dark remnants of mighty mountains uplifted almost 2 billion years ago. The mountains were worn flat by erosion and then submerged under the flood and ebb of a series of shallow seas. Sand and mud deposits from these seas formed the next rocks: strata of sandstone and shale containing billion-year-old plant and invertebrate fossils. The skeletal remains of countless other sea creatures were compacted into thick beds of limestone.

Subsequent cycles of tectonic uplift, erosion, submersion, and deposition preserved a library of evolution in layer upon layer of sedimentary stone—a joy to paleontologists, who have found fossilized trilobites, corals, fishes, and even the footprints of amphibians and reptiles in the canyon's middle-aged rocks. The highest layer consists of 200-million-year-old limestone. Younger rock once topped the canyon walls, but it has long since worn away. The last great upheaval to affect the Grand Canyon was a series of volcanic eruptions 2 million years ago, when hardened lava backed up the Colorado River. In time the tireless river cut through these natural dams and resumed its course.

Despite the antiquity of its stratified walls, the canyon itself was dug only in the last 6 million years, as the surrounding Colorado Plateau

🐦 *Even today the mighty Colorado River shapes the Grand Canyon, scouring out inconceivable amounts of earth as it snakes its way through. By one estimate the amount of sediment displaced during a flood would fill 11 million five-ton dump trucks passing by at a rate of 125 trucks per second!*

was lifted up by tectonic forces. A lesser river might have risen with the plateau, but the stubborn Colorado refused to budge. Carving through the rising rock, the river's elevation remained virtually unchanged as the land around it climbed skyward. Wind, weather, and its own crumbling walls widened the chasm to its current staggering dimensions.

The canyon's appearance of timeless stillness belies the fact that the forces that shaped it are as active as ever. Over one mile deep where its walls are tallest, 18 miles across at its widest gape, the Grand Canyon promises to grow ever greater as time goes on.

How are rocks formed?

Whether it's a sliver of obsidian as black as night, a flaky fragment of shale, or a thick slab of marble, all rocks fit one of three basic types: igneous, sedimentary, or metamorphic.

Many rocks originate deep within our planet, where temperatures can approach those on the sun's surface (around 9,000°F). Here rock flows

in a thick fluid form called magma. When magma approaches the cool surface or erupts from volcanic fissures (at which point it is called lava), it solidifies, forming igneous, or fiery, rocks—abundant in the Pacific Northwest and Hawaii. Shallow streams of lava can cool within hours, forming black volcanic glass such as obsidian. Deeper flows cool over a period of days or weeks into tall, hexagonal columns of basalt. Huge underground pockets of magma may take millions of years to cool, resulting in immense masses of rock, called batholiths, such as Georgia's 800-foot-high Stone Mountain, a once-buried granite mass exposed by erosion.

While igneous rocks are born of fire, sedimentary rocks owe their existence to wind and water. When rocks of any type are pulverized by erosion, they leave behind particles that are blown or washed to the sea as sand and silt. Here they accumulate on the ocean floor in layers. Under their own weight and that of the water above, these sediments are compacted into solid rock: sandstone, mudstone, shale, and when the sediments consist of the remains of sea life instead of rock dust, limestone. One of the world's largest deposits of sedimentary rock is the once submerged Catskill Delta; over two miles deep in places, it stretches from western New England all the way to the Mississippi Valley.

Finally, metamorphic, or changed, rocks are created by pressure-cooking deeply buried rocks of any kind; sedimentary, igneous, or previously formed metamorphic rocks can all be baked by nearby magma or crushed between colliding tectonic plates. Under such enormous heat or pressure, crystals of different minerals form within the rocks, causing changes in their color, texture, and chemical composition. Metamorphic rocks include slate (altered shale) and hornfels (heat-tempered mudstone).

Rocks may be long-lived (the oldest date back 4 billion years), but none are permanent; caught up in a creepingly slow recycling process, new rock is continually created from old. Sinking tectonic plates carry surface stones underground, where some are cooked or crushed into metamorphic rocks; others melt to magma and produce igneous rocks. Eventually the shifting crust of the earth may bring these rocks to the surface, where they will erode and form sedimentary rocks. The cycle grinds on endlessly, at an imperceptible pace barely faster than a rock.

The three faces of rock: a finger of once-molten igneous rock (top) juts into the cool blue water of Lake Superior; metamorphic marble (center), formed from pressure-hardened limestone, adorns Vermont's Mt. Mansfield; and sedimentary sandstone (bottom) is twisted like taffy on the Colorado plateau.

The drifting continents as they stood 250 million years ago (top), 100 million years ago (center), and how they appear today (bottom). The current arrangement is no more permanent than its predecessors: scientists estimate that continental drift will bring the land masses together once again, roughly 250 million years from now.

Slicing across California's Carrizo Plain like a giant, jagged scar, the San Andreas Fault serves as an ominous reminder of the earth's often violent nature.

Was North America joined to Europe?

For all its seeming stability, the earth's surface has an acute case of wanderlust; its history has been one of continental pirouettes, grinding collisions, and sudden partings, all on a mind-boggling time scale that spans hundreds of millions of years.

The continents sit atop large sections of the earth's crust, called tectonic plates, which float on a layer of molten basalt. Circular currents in this liquefied rock cause the plates to move as if riding a vast conveyor belt. Where plates slide apart, magma wells to the surface to form new crust. Where plates converge, the edge of one plate slips under the other and the continents on their backs collide.

This process was at work when a large part of Europe rammed into North America about 400 million years ago; later, parts of Asia came thudding in from the east. The impact crumpled and uplifted the edges of the continents, forming a mountain range that includes what are now the northern Appalachians and the Scottish and Scandinavian highlands. Meanwhile, another partner was approaching from the south—the supercontinent Gondwanaland, with Africa at its prow. The collision between these two great land masses, some 280 million years ago, spawned the Great Smokies and the rest of the southern Appalachians, and formed Pangaea, or "All Land," a single, unified supercontinent surrounded by one ocean. But Pangaea did not last. It split down the middle—creating the fledgling Atlantic Ocean—with the Americas on one side, Europe, Asia, and Africa on the other. The rift continues to widen today, forcing the once-united mountains of North America and Europe ever farther apart. As the Atlantic Ocean grows, however, the shores of the Pacific are squeezed closer together. Eventually the continents will meet again, this time on the other side of the world.

What makes California the earthquake belt?

The Pacific Ocean may have been named for its mild temperament, but its eastern shore is home to a violent geologic conflict between opposing tectonic plates.

When two sections of the earth's crust slide past each other in opposite directions, it is called a transform boundary. Such a boundary is found in California. Most of the United States sits atop the North American plate, but a slice of coastal California from the Mexican border to just north of San Francisco rests on the Pacific plate. (San Francisco proper is perched on the North Amer-

ican.) The boundary between the two plates is full of geological "fault zones," terrestrial gashes that rip through some of the most heavily populated areas of the country.

The Pacific plate creeps in a northwest direction at an average rate of roughly two inches per year—about as fast as fingernails grow—but the movement isn't constant and steady. The plate sometimes surges as much as 20 feet in only a matter of seconds. That jerking motion sends out seismic shock waves that can rumble the surrounding area hard enough to knock down buildings and bridges or cause ripples and splits in the earth's surface.

The most visible sign of California's seismic activity is the 750-mile-long San Andreas Fault. It starts near the Salton Sea, cuts through the San Bernardino Mountains, runs along the San Joaquin Valley, and finally vanishes offshore about 100 miles north of San Francisco. The San Andreas Fault is not the only danger, however: California is rent by dozens of smaller but equally perilous faults, including some near Los Angeles that caused deadly quakes in 1971 and 1994.

Earthquakes originate several miles below the earth's surface. As the plates grind against each other, friction makes them stick together. Tremendous pressure builds up along the fault, and eventually the surrounding rock gives way, explosively releasing its pent-up energy. Gigantic slabs of earth may slide horizontally past each other; two sections may pull apart suddenly; or one slab may be thrust up and over another. Because of its spider web of faults and the continuous stress of the Pacific plate's motion, California has earthquakes nearly every day. Most are too mild to be noticed.

Contrary to the popular notion that a megaquake will someday cause California to fall into the sea, the Golden State is in little danger of meeting such a watery end. Faults usually rupture in only one place at a time, and even in the biggest temblors, the damage is usually localized to within 100 miles of the fault's rupture, or the epicenter of the quake.

Ironically, earthquakes aren't harmful to the natural environment; only structures built by man are in jeopardy. But no matter what's done to predict or prepare for California's quakes, the Pacific plate will continue its inexorable northwest movement. Millions of years from now, Los Angeles—or whatever's left of it—probably will be San Francisco's next-door neighbor.

Where is the world's largest collection of geysers?

Clouds of ash once darkened the sky above the landscape we call Yellowstone National Park, and lava coursed across its face. Just 600,000 years ago, a huge dome of magma lifted the land, then collapsed, leaving behind a caldera nearly 50 miles wide. Yellowstone still seethes above a layer of molten rock just three miles beneath its scenic beauty. This cauldron of magma sends groundwater jetting from the surface in scalding plumes known as geysers.

Nowhere on earth do these fountains exist in such concentration as in Yellowstone, which boasts 300 to 500 geysers, as well as thousands of hissing steam vents, boiling mud pots, and bubbling hot springs. Old Faithful, the park's most famous geyser, lives up to its name by sending 10,000 gallons of hot water arching 100 to 180 feet skyward every 76 minutes or so.

Although you can't set your watch by Old Faithful, it's a marvel of regularity when one considers the volatile forces at work in the land of the geysers. Thousands of tremors too faint to be felt by humans ripple across Yellowstone each year. This underground movement subtly rearranges the intricate plumbing that fuels these natural fountains, shutting off some and bringing others roaring back to life.

Yellowstone's Castle Geyser (foreground, left) resembles a giant whale's blowhole as it spews steam from its massive, blocky cone. One of the park's oldest geysers, Castle erupts every 9 to 11 hours, spouting a 150-foot fountain of water followed by blasts of steam.

Why is New England so rocky?

Two and a half million years ago, the first of a series of four great glaciers descended on New England, covering the landscape in a blanket of ice that reached nearly a mile deep in some places. This glacier and the subsequent slabs of ice acted as vast conveyor belts, scraping away the region's then-deep soil and plucking rocks from the slopes of mountains that once rivaled the Himalayas in size.

These rock-fortified glaciers plowed, grooved, and polished the landscape, forever transforming the face of New England. The ice ground down the once mighty mountains, leaving behind only the worn stumps we know as the Green Mountains of Vermont and the White Mountains of New Hampshire. As the last ice sheet retreated some 12,000 years ago, it ceded its stony armor back to the land, littering the region with rocks ranging in size from a marble to a small truck.

Today these glacial erratics, as geologists call rocks that have been transported by glaciers, are scattered throughout New England—in fields and lawns and along countless streams and road-sides. New England is so rocky, in fact, that some residents coined an appropriately humorous saying: "Maine's number two crop is potatoes. It's number one crop is rocks."

Is the Ice Age over?

Held in the frigid grip of perpetual winter, the North America of 18,000 years ago was a world vastly different from today's. Thick ice sheets sprawled across most of Canada, reaching as far south as Manhattan Island, central Illinois, and Washington State. Beyond the glacial front stunted tundra vegetation and dense spruce forests shook in bitter winds. Great mammals suited to the cold stalked the land: mammoths and American mastodons, saber-toothed cats with canines like scimitars, and short-faced bears that dwarfed modern grizzlies. Eventually the climate began to thaw. The glaciers melted, slowly at first, then with a rush. Retreating north and east over several thousand years, they revealed a gouged, barren moonscape of churned rock and gravel. Most of the hulking Ice Age animals also

Worn smooth by the pounding surf of the Maine coast, these once jagged stones served as teeth for glaciers that gnawed their way across New England during the Ice Age.

vanished, leaving only bones in mute testimony to their once thriving existence.

Yet the Ice Age has not ended. The relatively balmy climate that has held sway for the last 11,000 years is just the latest in a long series of temporary respites known as interglacials. Deep cold and warmth have alternated as many as 20 times since the Ice Age began, some 2.5 million years ago. The current interglacial isn't even the mildest on record; major ice sheets still exist on Greenland and Antarctica, land masses that were free of them in earlier episodes. Scientists believe the current interglacial is more than half over, and barring such man-made changes as global warming, the ice will return.

Why are oil deposits found under seas or ancient seas?

As you pump gasoline into your car, you're actually filling the tank with the chemical residue of marine plants and animals that died and drifted to the sea floor millions of years ago. In Texas, Oklahoma, and other areas once swamped under shallow seas, this organic debris was buried beneath layers of sedimentary sand and mud and broken down by bacteria that thrive in such oxygen-free environments.

Decomposition in this primordial sludge proceeded along different lines than the decay we're accustomed to observing on the surface. In the presence of oxygen, living things break down to form carbon dioxide, water, and nutrients. Covered by silt, however, the ancient marine life did not decay completely. Instead, the resins, waxes, oils, and fats in the material yielded a stew of chemicals that included compounds of hydrogen and carbon. Under the subterranean heat and pressure, these hydrocarbons were transformed into oil and natural gas.

Most of the petroleum left behind by ancient seas found its way to the earth's surface long ago, oozing upward through porous rocks and evaporating into the atmosphere. Today we tap petroleum trapped under rock layers too dense to allow the fluid to pass to the surface. Though our quest for petroleum to fuel cars, jets, and ships may be modern, our predecessors were no strangers to the use of "rock oil" in transportation. Native Americans skimmed oil from marsh water and traded it to settlers, who used the slippery substance to massage their horses' strained limbs and lubricate squeaky wagon wheels.

Land of the Stone Rainbows

Can wood turn to stone? For those with even a shred of common sense, there would seem to be only one answer: "Of course not!" But anyone who visits Petrified Forest National Park in eastern Arizona would find good reason to wonder at nature's wizardry, for within its borders lies the world's largest collection of fossilized wood—transformed into stone by the magic of nature's alchemy.

What makes this place so mysterious is that smack in the middle of a desert, the landscape is confettied with thousands of gleaming, multicolored logs of solid stone, despite the fact that not a single living tree is anywhere in sight. The answer to the riddle dates back 200 million years to a time when this region was a swampy floodplain. Many of the towering conifers growing on nearby hills were toppled by storms, carried into the lowlands by overflowing rivers, and stripped of their roots and branches. Piling up in huge logjams, these trunks were gradually buried under layers of mud, sand, and volcanic ash. Leaving little room for oxygen, this dense mixture preserved them for centuries.

Over the years mineral-rich groundwater seeped into the buried logs. One cell at a time, the original wood was replaced with silica, which crystallized in the form of quartz. Other minerals tinted the quartz with striking hues of red, yellow, orange, purple, blue, and green. After the waters receded and the soil eroded, what remained was a collection of jewels so dazzling that naturalist John Muir called it "a kaleidoscope fashioned by God's hand."

How does water redesign the landscape?

Any plumber will tell you that, sooner or later, the inexorable force of water will win its war of erosion against your piping system. Running water, whether a tiny trickle or a tow-

~ *Despite Indian legend the world's largest natural bridge is not a rainbow frozen in stone. Utah's 275-foot Rainbow Arch was born when a slow-moving stream undercut a sandstone outcropping, tunneling a hole that was further widened by the wind.*

ering tsunami, is one of nature's grandest architects, endlessly altering everything that it touches—building here, demolishing there, shaping and reshaping the landscape.

The changes wrought by water can be instantaneous, as victims who have lost their homes to rain-gorged mudslides can readily attest. More often, however, water works in more subtle ways. Some of America's most fanciful landscapes are

the silent cities of stone—such as the spires and pillars of Utah's Bryce Canyon—sculpted over millions of years as raindrops wore away the softer rock around them. Rain is also behind the sheer cliffs of Half Dome in Yosemite National Park, where water seeped into cracks and froze, causing the rock to split and peel away in layer after layer.

In the West spectacular natural bridges and arches were bored from the rock by rivers, then honed by water's partner in erosion, the wind. Rivers gnaw at soil and rock, carving gullies, valleys, and great canyons. Grains of sand, debris, and even rocks scooped up by the water strengthen its abrasive potency, allowing some fast-moving rivers to obliterate huge boulders in only a few years. Chemicals leached from soil also increase the water's erosive power. Limestone is particularly vulnerable to water that has become acidic from carbon dioxide. This water dissolves buried beds of limestone, creating caves that can stretch for miles, such as Carlsbad Caverns in New Mexico. Sometimes dissolved minerals are redeposited, forming the stalactites that droop from cave ceilings and the stalagmites that spike up from their stony floors.

Water in its frozen form is also an earth shaper. Repeated freezing and thawing of water can pulverize the hardest rock and make the ground bulge, then subside. When this process happens under highways, drivers often experience the destructive power of water firsthand—in the bone-jarring form of potholes.

Why is more gold found in the West than in the East?

While some hearts, as poets sing, may be as pure as gold, no other metal comes close. Like the jewelry from King Tut's tomb, gold forever remains as shiny and lustrous as the day it is plucked from the ground. It is this durability, along with its malleability and rarity, that makes it so sought after.

People have learned that if there is gold in "them thar hills," then those hills are more apt to be in California than in the East. The Golden State leads the country in production of this precious metal, followed by Colorado, South Dakota, and Alaska. That's because granite is nature's Fort Knox, and nowhere in the country is there more exposed granite than in California's 400-mile-long Sierra Nevada.

Granite is an igneous rock, meaning it was once on fire, or molten. In California, where mountain-making is an ongoing process, granitic magma is pushed upward when a jigsawlike piece of the Earth's crust underlying the Pacific Ocean slides beneath the western edge of the North American continental plate. As the magma cools and hardens, cracks, fissures, and faults form. Subsequent subterranean heat and pressure force mineral-rich fluids and gases into these voids in the granite, depositing veins of silver, gold, and other ores.

Not all mineral veins contain gold, however. In fact, the amount of shiny metal found in all igneous rock averages about five ten-millionths of 1 percent. But it doesn't take much to make a deposit worth mining commercially. Prospectors figure a lode that bears one-third of an ounce of gold per ton of rock to be a bonanza.

What makes a stone a gemstone?

Only nature can create minerals and rocks, but it takes the human mind to transform them into gemstones—and human hands to fashion them into precious gems.

To become a gemstone, a mineral or rock must be beautiful—it may sparkle like a diamond, glow like a ruby, or simply startle with color, like a piece of turquoise. Beauty, however, is abundant in nature, so a stone that aspires to gemstone status must also be uncommon. If the land were strewn with emeralds and turquoise, these minerals might be worth little more than colorful pebbles; their relative rarity renders them valuable. Durability is also desirable in gemstones—being hard enough to withstand knocks and blows sets a gemstone apart from an imitation that scuffs and fades over time.

Like most gemstones, those of North America are diamonds in the rough. Agate hides inside dull rocks along beaches in Oregon. Red-brown garnets crop up in rocks from the Adirondacks to Alaska. Orange-pink garnets have surfaced in an asbestos mine in Quebec, while those from Idaho are often aglow with four- to six-rayed stars. In the southwestern United States, chunks and sheets of turquoise emerge from gray rock like patches of blue sky from clouds. Long ago, Zuni Indians kept evil spirits at bay by studding doorways and cradles with bits of this blue mineral—vivid testimony to the power humans confer upon stones that please the eye.

Why is Florida so flat?

Canoeists in Florida may occasionally worry about snakes or alligators—but never waterfalls. Rivers that drop just inches per mile laze along at a few miles per hour. The average depth of Florida's largest lake, Okeechobee, is a scant 12 feet, and Britton Hill, the Sunshine State's Mount Everest, tops out at only 345 feet.

Florida's landscape, however, didn't always resemble the tropical tabletop it is today. Half a billion years ago the Florida Plateau was an arc of volcanoes jutting above the water like today's

Caribbean Islands. Erosion wore down the mountains and they were submerged by the sea. Over millions of centuries, pea-size shells and the skeletons of ancient sea creatures settled to the bottom, where they were compressed into layers of limestone. Eventually the mountain stubs were buried under a limestone platform up to three miles thick.

Meanwhile, a series of ice ages caused global sea levels to rise and fall. The fluctuating waters carved the Florida peninsula into a stack of terraces (each a former beach) ascending like stairs from the depths. When the waters settled at current levels, only the top of the plateau was left exposed; wind and water wore it to the level landscape we now know. Erosion is still at work today, but Florida's lazy rivers flow so slowly it will be thousands of years before gorges and valleys are familiar sights in the state.

The vast flatness of the Everglades stretches to the horizon, never rising more than 10 feet above sea level over its 1½ million acres.

Fountains of Fire *Volcanoes in action*

The 1980 eruption of Mount St. Helens unleashed an explosive force equal to 10 million tons of TNT—500 times the power of the atomic bomb dropped on Hiroshima.

Can we predict when sleeping volcanoes are about to erupt?

The squiggles scrawled by a seismic recorder during the afternoon of March 20, 1980, warned scientists that Washington's Mount St. Helens was going to blow its top, but they were not sure when. Forecasting volcanic eruptions is a tricky business: although volcanoes often alert us when they are growing restless, they may simply toss and turn, then slumber on, while at other times they arise with a violent vengeance.

If scientists know a volcano's past record of eruption, they can often predict when the pressures within are likely to build again. Geologists knew that Mount St. Helens was a young volcano with a violent history, so a decade before the big blowup, they set up seismographs to monitor its activity. As magma pushes its way up through a volcano's interior, it triggers earthquakes. If tremors grow frequent or powerful, as they did around Mount St. Helens in 1980, warning flags go up.

Magma also gorges a volcano, causing it to swell—a process that can happen over decades or, as in the case of Mount St. Helens, only a few weeks. Scientists can measure this swelling and other changes with a variety of devices, including lasers (to spot changes in ground elevation), electric meters (rising magma conducts a discernable electric current), and gas analysis (increases of certain gases can signal an eruption).

Despite such efforts to predict the behavior of volcanoes, these brooding giants still have some surprises in store. After months of telltale grumbling, Mount St. Helens exploded on May 18, 1980, with a fury that stunned experts, instantly transforming over 232 square miles of lush conifer forest into a lifeless landscape.

How many active volcanoes are there in North America?

Volcanoes are the places where the world begins, where its newest earth wells up through the planet's crust. Rivers of red-hot lava burble out of mountains, cool, and harden, altering the terrain for miles around.

For all the effect that volcanoes have had on the face of the earth, there are surprisingly few active ones in North America. Over the last 10,000 years, only 200 or so volcanoes have erupted in the United States and Canada. A volcano can blow its stack more than once, however, so the total number of eruptions is much higher: roughly 800 to 1,000. Currently, the United States is home to only 50 active volcanoes: 4 in Hawaii, 7 scattered throughout northern California, Oregon, and Washington, and 39 in Alaska (including the very active Aleutian Islands). Aside from Mount St. Helens in 1980, notable eruptions in this century include California's Lassen Peak in 1915 and Alaska's Mount Katmai, which exploded in 1912, producing so much ash that decades later astronauts walked across its otherworldly landscape to train for the first lunar landing.

What will the future bring? The restless earth continues to stir, giving rise to new volcanoes throughout the world, including North America. Volcanologists point to Washington's glacier-cloaked Mount Rainier, California's Mammoth Lakes ski area, and Wyoming's Yellowstone National Park as possible sites for near-future eruptions. The earth, however, works on its own timetable, and in geologic time the "near future" could mean 10 years or 10 million.

Will the Hawaiian chain have more islands in the future?

A few hundred thousand years from now, tourists may flock to the southeastern Hawaiian island of Loihi to reenact the 19th-century custom of dipping their postcards into lava to crisp their edges. For now, only scientists can view this future vacation paradise because Loihi is still a seamount, an underwater mountain 15 miles southeast of Hawaii that peaks 3,160 feet beneath the water's surface.

A volcanic island in the making, Loihi is born of the same forces that created the rest of the Hawaiian chain as well as the Emperor Seamounts, a string of submerged mountains 1,500 miles long. Deep beneath Loihi boils a hot spot, a cauldron of magma that remains stationary as the Pacific plate slides above it. Rising plumes of magma force the plate upward, then surge through it, building volcanoes. As the plate travels, though, it carries the fiery mountains away from the source of their power. Eroded by wind and water and carried beneath the waves by the gradually sinking plate, the volcanoes eventually shrink to seamounts once again.

The most northerly seamounts now face the prospect of slipping beneath the Aleutian Trench as the edge of the Pacific plate is subducted into the earth. Meanwhile, at the southernmost end of the Hawaiian chain, volcanoes fueled by the hot spot continue to pour lava onto the island of Hawaii, which formed less than 1 million years ago. Hawaii is home to Kilauea, the state's youngest and most active volcano. Kilauea has erupted regularly since 1983, wiping out nearly 200 homes and increasing the Big Island's size by about 500 acres in the process. But this angry dome, creeping four more inches toward the northwest each year, will one day cede its rage to Loihi, now silently biding its time in the dark depths of the Pacific Ocean.

Streams of molten rock from Hawaii's Mount Kilauea spill into the Pacific Ocean, heating the water to a churning froth. Accumulating igneous deposits from Kilauea's fiery 13-year-long eruption threaten to eventually unbalance the island and topple its lava-heavy southeastern edge into the sea. A diver (inset) examines an underwater eruption at Hawaii Volcanoes National Park.

Can a mountain become a lake?

~ *Shielded from winds by towering cliffs, the waters of Crater Lake have a mirrorlike quality. Though dazzling at any hour, some say the best time to enjoy this giant jewel is daybreak, when it sparkles with an unforgettable shade of vibrant blue.*

This is the tale of a mountain that was pulled inside out, and it begins some 6,500 years ago with the eruption of Mount Mazama, an ancient volcano in the southern Cascade Range of Oregon. Over thousands of centuries the volcano coughed up ash, cinders, and great glowing snakes of lava. As this volcanic effluence hardened, it piled up into a summit over two miles high—a process that accounts for the formation of many large volcanoes, including Mount Shasta, Mount Rainier, and Mount St. Helens. When pressure from yet more magma rising within the mountain caused Mazama to finally blow, its flanks split open, emptying the magma chamber beneath. With nothing left to hold it up, the mountain simply fell in on itself, leaving behind an immense basin measuring six miles across and three-quarters of a mile deep. Unlike a similarly formed crater in Yellowstone National Park, this caldera (Spanish for "cauldron") somehow survived the implosion with its rim intact.

For centuries precipitation that hit the floor of the still-hot crater sizzled before turning to steam. Eventually the surface cooled, and rainwater and melted snow began to collect in the caldera (snowfall in the Cascades often exceeds 50 feet per year). The basin was slowly transformed into a lake—not just any lake, but the deepest body of fresh water in the United States. Since Crater Lake has neither inlet nor outlet, the amount of water entering it roughly equals what is lost through evaporation and seepage. Its water level, therefore, remains fairly constant. The lake's intensely blue hue is a measure of not only its depth but its purity as well. Its waters are so pristine, in fact, that when anglers wanted to stock the lake with fish some decades ago, there was no food supply for them. Freshwater shrimp were added to solve that problem, and today trout and other species abound. Not that Crater Lake needs fish to attract visitors. The secret to its timeless appeal lies, no doubt, in its brilliant sapphire splendor.

What is Devils Tower?

Like a rebellious teenager, the earth is constantly in revolt, its continental plates colliding, tearing apart, or sliding under one another. These subterranean events are, geologically speaking, the greatest of all wars waged on our planet. Volcanoes along the borders of the plates break out like sudden skirmishes, fiery uprisings from deep within the earth. Wyoming's Devils Tower, a gigantic volcanic plug, is a well-preserved monument to one of those battles.

A plug is a volcano in stop-time. It is a remnant of uprising lava that has cooled and hardened inside a volcano, outlasting as much as 50 million years of wind and rain that whittled down the mountain around it. Plugs like this one resist erosion because when magma crystallizes inside the confining pressure of a volcano, the molten materials solidify into minerals that are much harder than anything around them.

Few plugs rise as high as Devils Tower, which resembles the petrified stump of some gargantuan tree. (The name, according to Indian legend, comes from an evil god who so fiercely beat his drums atop the summit that he terrified everyone within earshot.) Visible from as far away as 100 miles, the tower measures nearly 865 feet from its wooded base to its flat-topped summit. No other plug is as wholly formed, which may explain why Hollywood chose it as the landing pad for the alien spaceship in the film *Close Encounters of the Third Kind*. Devils Tower is also unusual because of the tightly packed, fluted columns that extend for much of its height—a result of lava that shrank and fractured as it cooled over the years. In 1906 President Theodore Roosevelt designated Devils Tower America's first national monument, but it has served since long before that as a mighty monument to the awesome power of nature.

Looming high above the Wyoming landscape, Devils Tower dwarfs everything in sight, even the lofty ponderosa pines that ring its base. The polygonal columns of this massive monolith make it an irresistible challenge for rock climbers, who can choose from among 200 established routes.

Urban Wildlife *Nature in your neighborhood*

Why do peregrine falcons like skyscrapers?

Every bird has its own habitat: cattail marshes for least bitterns, shady conifer forests for Steller's jays, rock-strewn seacoasts for purple sandpipers. In a sense the peregrine falcon's habitat is the empty air; this lightning-fast creature is at home at dizzying heights, streaking out of the sky at speeds approaching 200 miles per hour when it dives for prey. The peregrine even nests in high, lonely places, usually on isolated cliff ledges.

Skyscrapers are the man-made equivalent of those cliffs—lofty and, except for the occasional window washer, free of disturbance. What's more, cities offer a smorgasbord of pigeons, fat and for the taking. Before World War II a few peregrines began nesting on skyscraper ledges in Baltimore, Montreal, and elsewhere, but such occurrences have become much more common in recent years as conservationists have worked

to restore this endangered species, once almost wiped out by pesticide use. Young falcons were reared in rooftop enclosures, then released when they could fly; in later years some returned to the cities to nest. In fact, because great horned owls killed many of the young falcons released in wilderness areas, the urban birds had a better survival rate. Urban life, however, is not without its dangers. Inexperienced falcons die from hitting glass-sided buildings (which reflect the sky) and from pollution, a persistent problem for birds and humans alike.

Which trees thrive in cities?

Countless species of trees have been planted in American cities, but just a handful have proven hardy enough to stand the rigors of an urban setting. Air, water, and soil pollution, soil compression from concrete and foot traffic, and lack of water due to pavement and storm drains are only a few of the hazards that a metropolitan life has in store for trees and shrubs.

Most native trees fare poorly under city stresses, but a few do well. Pin oak, silver maple, and box elder are popular urban plantings in the Midwest. Live oak is beloved in the Southeast but is not pollution hardy. Monterey, California, boasts over 30 kinds of eucalyptus, all from the equally warm and dry climes of Australia, but the city's proudest tree is the Monterey pine, its most widely planted native species.

City trees are selected for their ability to tolerate pollution, poor soil, and dry conditions. Some, such as the London plane and honey locust, were specifically bred for hardiness before being imported to North America. Tough and prolific foreign species such as European linden and Siberian elm have also thrived in America's urban areas.

Tree-of-Heaven is another successful visitor from abroad. Originally introduced from Asia, this tree first took root in Philadelphia but soon spread to other cities. While rarely planted, Tree-of-Heaven is so prolific a settler that it dominates vacant lots in many Eastern cities.

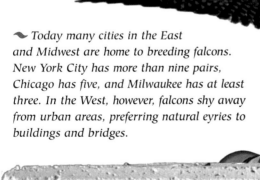
❧ *Today many cities in the East and Midwest are home to breeding falcons. New York City has more than nine pairs, Chicago has five, and Milwaukee has at least three. In the West, however, falcons shy away from urban areas, preferring natural eyries to buildings and bridges.*

What makes city parks so valuable?

Since people began crowding into cities in search of industrial jobs in the mid-19th century, urban parks have offered a substitute for the shaded groves and blooming fields they left behind. Today, harried city dwellers flock to these green preserves to regain a measure of solitude, tranquillity, and contact with nature. Studies have shown that a visit to a park can actually lower a person's blood pressure.

Urban parks, however, provide more than soothing scenery. Not only does the greenery of a park release life-giving oxygen, but it can also act as natural "air conditioning" for a city during the heat of summer. On hot days asphalt and buildings soak up solar energy that they leach back into the night air as heat. When sunlight falls on the green expanse of a park, however, this reheating of the environment does not occur. Instead of reradiating solar energy, plants use it to create food via photosynthesis. Plants also absorb carbon dioxide and other heat-trapping "greenhouse" gases and release water vapor that cools the surrounding area through evaporation.

Parks are also important to a city's nonhuman residents. For animals parks offer islands of green scattered throughout the inhospitable concrete sprawl of a modern metropolis. Some large parks encompass a number of native ecosystems, such as 4,100-acre Griffith Park in Los Angeles. The largest urban wilderness in the United States, Griffith Park covers most of the lower Los Angeles River basin and includes river floodplain marsh and forest, upland oak forest, and manzanita-sage scrub roamed by deer, coyotes, and quails. Smaller cities have also preserved wild lands within parks, such as the 65-acre cypress swamp and marshland of Boerne City Park in Texas.

Other urban parks contain lakes, often former reservoirs, that are now home to native waterbirds, fishes, and aquatic plants displaced by human settlement. As suburbs continue to replace the native ecosystems surrounding our cities, urban parks are more important and treasured than ever before.

➤ Added up, America's urban parkland would fill an area the size of Connecticut. New York City alone boasts over 26,000 acres, including the wildlife-rich stretches of Central Park, where observers have spotted over 175 species of migratory birds during springtime "bird-a-thons."

Are all rodents pests?

There's no such thing as a pest in nature. Every creature is bread and butter to another, a part of the feast that nourishes all life. It's only when animals begin to compete with humans for living space or food that they become pests. Though gnawing mammals called rodents can be formidable foes, they can also be allies. From the lemming to the porcupine, nearly one-half of all mammal species are rodents, and many, like the forest-dwelling red-back vole of the Pacific Northwest, are unsung heroes.

Clearings created by wind, fire, or chainsaws are reforested thanks to the red-backs, which feast on the fruiting bodies of helper fungi called soil mycorrhize. When the voles venture onto open ground, they leave millions of spores in their droppings. These "seeds" grow into a fungal jungle that twines around the roots of seedlings, helping them siphon up nutrients and get a foothold in the opening.

We got our own foothold in North America with the help of a 50-pound rodent: the beaver. Besides providing pelts for the fur trade, beavers made the landscape more suitable for human habitation. For thousands of years, silt collected behind the flood-quelling gates of beaver dams, creating some of the fertile farmland that helped settlers survive in the New World. Beavers, however, were not alone. As these soils tired, they were turned and fertilized by still other rodents, including pocket gophers and woodchucks.

➤ While many rodents are considered helpful to man, the house mouse is not among them. An unwanted visitor in many urban homes, this tiny intruder feeds on scraps of food and even soap and glue. Introduced to America from Asia in the 16th century, the house mouse is a prolific species whose females can produce up to seven litters (of seven offspring each) in a year.

How do wild animals survive in cities?

Scientists studying raccoons near the center of Cincinnati some years ago found that urban raccoons do not have to work as hard as their woodsy brethren to find a meal. The Cincinnati raccoons made nightly rounds of garbage cans near their dens, and since they could always count on this nearby food supply, their home ranges averaged a scant 11½ acres. Wild raccoons, on the other hand, have to search far and wide for food, foraging over as many as 500 acres on a regular basis.

Raccoons are by no means the only wild animals that have learned to survive, or even thrive, in a man-made environment. Some species are

so common in urban areas that people forget they are wild. Mallards that eat handouts of bread in city parks and squawking gulls swarming over garbage dumps are just two species in an ever-growing group of animals that have made the move to a more metropolitan life.

This rise in urban wildlife is due partly to cities spilling into the countryside and infringing on wildlife habitat. As residential developments have invaded brushy canyons on the fringes of Los Angeles, for example, people have found themselves confronted with wild new neigh-

bors, including coyotes and cougars. Ironically, urban sprawl offers advantages for certain species. White-tailed deer benefit from the "edge" habitat created when lawns are placed among woodlands: they find yews and other ornamental plantings simply delectable.

Sometimes people unknowingly invite animals to cities in the most improbable ways. New roads help wild creatures gain access to urban areas as grassy medians become overgrown, providing corridors through which animals can travel from the country to the city. In 1986, after the Congress Street Bridge in Austin, Texas, was rebuilt, Mexican free-tailed bats discovered that crevices in the new steelwork were a perfect place to roost—dark, with optimum temperature and humidity. When they arrived in droves, alarmed citizens called for their ouster. Conservationists labored to calm public fears and save the bats. Bat Conservation International, a group that publicizes the value of bats, even moved its headquarters from Milwaukee to Austin so it could better promote the winged mammals' cause. As things turned out, the bats were allowed to remain, and Austin residents, particularly those who manage hotels and restaurants, have been happier for it. Each year, between spring and fall, an average of 60,000 tourists arrive to watch the bats emerge from beneath the bridge on their sundown forays into the hot Texas nights.

What makes cockroaches so invincible?

The meek shall inherit the earth. If not, it will probably go to the cockroaches. One of the oldest of insects, cockroaches began scurrying over the earth more than 250 million years ago, before the first dinosaur, the first mammal, the first bird, or even the first pine tree. Nobody, least of all man, is about to stop them now.

Cockroaches are the ultimate survivors because they are so versatile. They can live anywhere in the world (except in the polar regions). Our warm homes are ideal for them—even the Pentagon has been invaded. Also, they can eat just about anything: from cheese and leather to toenails, eyelashes, and the dead of their own kind.

🐾 *The Congress Street Bridge in Austin, Texas, is home to over 1½ million Mexican free-tailed bats—the largest urban bat colony in the world. On their nightly forays into the surrounding countryside, these bats consume from 10,000 to 30,000 pounds of insects, many of them agricultural pests.*

Their other survival skills are just as impressive. Cockroaches are able to reproduce in astounding numbers; the American cockroach is particularly prolific, with females able to produce some 500 eggs in a lifetime.

Cockroaches redefine all notions of adversity. They can withstand three months without food, one month without water, and two days frozen stiff. They can also tolerate 100 times more radiation than humans and survive. It's not surprising, then, that attempts to exterminate them often fail. Not only can cockroaches develop a resistance to insecticides, but when exposed to sublethal doses, they learn to avoid treated surfaces and move about elsewhere.

Last, but not least, they're lightning quick. The tiny hairs that protrude from the cockroach's body are sensitive enough to register even the slightest environmental disturbance, enabling the insect to react to a rolled-up newspaper or a rapidly descending shoe in five-hundredths of a second—far quicker than the blink of an eye.

Why do moles and skunks dig holes in our lawns?

Pests they may be, but as moles and skunks make messes of manicured lawns, these determined diggers may actually be doing more good than harm. As a skunk tears up your backyard, it might be hunting Japanese beetle grubs, which, if left to mature, could chew up carefully tended roses. A tunneling mole is likely to encounter and eat cutworms that would otherwise topple tomato plants. Moles also relish those slimy slugs that prowl by night and feast on lettuce leaves. Additionally, as moles dig through a yard, they loosen and aerate the soil, increasing its ability to soak up moisture from rain.

If, despite the beneficial effects of their digging, you want to discourage moles and skunks from invading your property, it is easily accomplished. In the case of moles, simply sink a bottle into a tunnel with its mouth pointed in the direction of the prevailing wind. The reverberations of wind whistling in the bottle will cause moles to quit the premises. Skunks, ironically, are vulnerable through their sense of smell. They detest the odor of camphor—so mothballs scattered over the lawn will cause them to give it a wide berth.

A Call to the Wild

Making your yard a haven for wildlife is easier than you might think. If you provide food, water, and shelter, creatures will flock to your front door. Here are some ways to put out the welcome mat for visitors.

- Favor the native born: landscape your yard with disease-resistant local flowers, shrubs, and trees. Familiar flora make wildlife feel more at home.

- Plants that provide both food (nuts, seeds, and berries) and shelter are ideal. Dogwood, hawthorn, mountain ash, and sumac are pantries that draw hungry animals year-round.

- Butterflies flutter to bright wildflowers. Try purple coneflowers, zinnias, marigolds, and pink swamp milkweed.

- Hummingbirds pollinate some 160 plants. Trumpet honeysuckles, fire pinks, and bee balm are sure-fire lures.

- Don't toss birdseed on the ground. Dampness, mold, animal droppings, and pesticides will spoil your offerings.

- Set birdhouses and feeders at varying heights near sheltering trees (but not so close that predators can reach them).

- Install a birdbath or set out a large pan of water near some trees, and birds will flock to bathe and drink. A larger, reinforced concrete pool ringed with elderberry, crab apple, or winterberry for cover will entice frogs, turtles, dragonflies, and other water-loving animals to make a splash.

- Compost heaps, dead trees, rock piles, and wood stacks are favorite hangouts for groundhogs, rabbits, squirrels, chipmunks, and woodpeckers.

- Six- to eight-inch-high grass will attract mothers-to-be. Spring is "baby time" for most species, so don't mow some patches till late summer.

Into the Woods *Our great green forests*

Do coniferous or hardwood forests have more wildlife?

In the pines, in the pines," goes an old folk song, "where the sun never shines." As much could be said of spruces, firs, and hemlocks; coniferous forests are a bit on the gloomy side, their overlapping evergreen branches shutting out light year-round. Some animals don't mind the dark conifer woods, since their dense greenery provides visual cover and good shelter, especially in winter. Others prefer the brighter realm of the hardwoods, where sunlight supports a greater variety of plants.

Deciduous forests contain more species of trees, and thus a greater variety of seeds, fruits, and nuts—favorites of many critters, including gray squirrels and deer mice. Other key foods are mushrooms and ground herbs, both found in greater abundance in leafy woods. The broad leaves of maple, ash, and oak (more palatable to leaf-eating insects than the needles of pines and firs) support scores of birds.

Despite the variety of ecological roles, or niches, found in broad-leaved woodlands, many animals—including snowshoe hares, red-back voles, and red squirrels—dwell chiefly among the conifers. In many areas conifer and hardwood forests either border each other or intermingle, allowing animals to enjoy the advantages of both. Overall, however, the hardwoods have the edge in terms of the number of different wildlife species that live there.

➤ *The snowshoe hare favors coniferous forests, where in winter it blends in with the snow, and the Eastern box turtle has adapted to deciduous forests, where it feeds extensively on mushrooms (including the poisonous deathcap, to which it is immune). The Cooper's hawk, however, is at home in both habitats and can be seen in most states year-round.*

Are the pine barrens of New Jersey really barren?

Early settlers of southern New Jersey called their home "the barrens." Crops grew poorly in the sandy soil, and about the only wild edibles were blueberries. Though sterile from a human viewpoint, such dry habitats (the Eastern equivalent of Western chaparral scrub) are actually rich reservoirs of wildlife, harboring plants, insects, reptiles, and amphibians found in no other Eastern habitat.

Pine barrens developed after the Ice Age on two kinds of surfaces: outwash plains where sand was deposited as glaciers melted, and deep sand deposited in lakes that dried up as the climate warmed. On these truly barren foundations, most plants could not grow, but pines, oaks, and heaths, which include blueberries and laurels, thrived here. Many pine-barren plants—most notably species such as blue lupine, Indian grass, and little bluestem—moved in from the dry Western prairies along with such creatures as spadefoot toads and tiger beetles. The persistence of such species in the Northeast was aided by a natural force we fear and try to control: fire. It's the lifeblood of pine barrens; without frequent burning, broad-leaved oaks and herbs would push out the pines, which tolerate fire and grow back vigorously.

Paradoxically, rare species abound in pine barrens, among them such wildflowers as sea-blue pine-barrens gentian, white-blossomed pixie, pom-pom–like orange milkwort, and sky-blue wild lupine. The endangered Karner Blue butterfly, whose caterpillars eat lupine, is found only in a few small patches of Midwestern and Northeastern pine barrens. Other species that reside chiefly in pine barrens are the eastern pine snake (a subspecies of the western bull snake) and the pine-barrens tree frog.

Sand barrens have disappeared faster than rock barrens because their loose, grainy soil is so easily bulldozed and landscaped. Of the original estimated 45,000 acres of Albany Pine Bush, the main habitat of Karner Blue butterflies in the East, less than 10 percent remains, much of it in isolated fragments that are too close to houses to allow burning. As pine barrens vanish, so do many irreplaceable plants and animals.

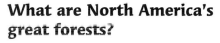

The dazzling diversity of our landscape is vividly illustrated by these tiny but telling portaits of the four major forest regions that are found in North America. Running clockwise from the top left are glimpses of a Western forest in Washington's Olympic National Park, a Northern, or boreal, forest in Montana's Glacier National Park, an Eastern deciduous forest in Vermont, and a Southern swamp forest in Florida's Everglades National Park.

What are North America's great forests?

North America is a land of many trees—and many different kinds of forests. Climate, soil, and geologic history all play a role in determining what grows where. The largest of all woodland regions, the boreal forest, sprawls from northern New England and the Canadian Maritimes to British Columbia and Alaska—a realm of spruces, balsam firs, and hardy deciduous trees like birches and aspens. Needle-bearing trees rule the Western mountains, where the winters are cold, summers are dry, and the growing season short. At lower elevations pinyon pines and junipers dot the landscape, mingling with plants of the desert or shortgrass prairie.

In the Pacific Northwest mild ocean winds laden with moisture have shaped conifer forests of tremendous size and diversity—and astonishing age. Douglas firs, Sitka spruces, western hemlocks, and western red cedars, many of them 1,000 years old, soar to cathedral proportions, bathing the woodland floor with shadows and soft, green light. To the south are stands of red-woods and ancient sequoias, the largest trees on earth, and majestic red and white firs in the Sierra Nevada.

From the fringe of the Great Plains to the Atlantic coast, hardwoods hold sway in the Eastern deciduous forest. The cool North is dominated by sugar maples, birches, beeches, and hemlocks. Come autumn, the mountains flame to orange and red with the colors of the broadleaved trees. In warmer, drier areas, the forest is a mix of oaks and hickories, spreading their nut-rich canopies in a wide swath from southern New England to eastern Texas. Across the Piedmont equal numbers of pines mingle with the hardwoods—straight-trunked loblolly and short-leaf pines, with long-leaf and slash pines taking pride of place along the Southeast coast.

Southern Florida has its own forest type, rich with such subtropical trees as palms, gumbo-limbos, and the strangler fig, which starts as a vine that eventually engulfs its host. Along the shore's edge, mangroves rise from the sea. Trapping sediment among their tangled, stiltlike roots, these salt-tolerant trees build still more land for North America's remarkable forests.

How much rain does it take to make a rain forest?

The recipe for a rain forest goes something like this: First, take plenty of rich, deep soil. Add a generous amount of moisture—rain, fog, and humidity. Simmer at moderate heat (too much will cause the plants to wither; too little will make them freeze). The ingredients are simple enough, but as with any recipe, success depends on how they're combined. In the Pacific Northwest, Mother Nature has once again outdone herself by creating a *pièce de résistance,* the Hoh Rain Forest—one of the best examples of a temperate rain forest in the world, and one of the few coniferous ones in existence.

The forest emerged from a unique set of circumstances. The soil here provides a perfect base. The by-product of glacial action during the ice ages, it is not only deep but loaded with minerals, ideally suited to support lush vegetation. Moreover, the region is nourished by a continuous stream of warm, moist air from the Pacific Ocean. As a result the forest is drenched with up to 200 inches of annual rainfall. Most of this precipitation falls between September and May as clouds blow in from the Pacific, then cool and drop their moisture as they roll up the western slopes of the Olympic Mountains. Only about a foot of rain falls in summer, but fog condensing on needles and leaves ensures that the forest remains dripping wet.

Towering above the forest floor, the conifers that dominate the rain forest are living nurseries that support vegetation so verdant that perhaps a dozen shades of green glow in the soft sunlight. Some 300 kinds of plants abound in this lovely, luxuriant realm, including a wealth of ferns and vines. Seedlings take root in the grooved bark and knotted burls of these giants. Limbs are festooned with lichen, trunks with beards of moss. Fallen trees known as nurse logs serve as nutrient-rich planters for the next generation of evergreens.

➤ *Rain forests are usually associated with tropical jungles, but North America has one of its very own, a temperate rain forest stretching along the Pacific coast from northern California to the Alaska panhandle. Steady, abundant precipitation accounts for the phenomenal growth of western hemlocks and other trees that soar up to 200 feet high.*

Why do so many conifers and so few hardwoods grow in stands of a single kind?

If you were to go hiking on a fall day in the lower elevations of the Rockies or New York's Adirondack Mountains, you would notice patches of deep green scattered among the bright golds and scarlets: stands of evergreens among the hardwoods. Like birds of a feather, spruces, firs, and pines tend to flock together, while broad-leaved trees seem more gregarious, often mixing it up with other species.

Conifers (trees with needlelike leaves and seeds borne in cones) are among the oldest plant groups on earth, dating back 200 million years to the period before the earliest dinosaurs. In their ancient heyday conifers had no competition and ruled the landscape, but today they are restricted to harsh habitats where their hardwood competitors fare poorly: cold Canadian swamps; steep, shaded New England ravines; dry Appalachian ridges; Great Lakes dunes; Southeastern Piedmont sand flats; and dry Western mountain slopes.

Deciduous trees—known as hardwoods because of their stronger wood—evolved features that put conifers at a competitive disadvantage in fertile soils and mild climates. Broad leaves photosynthesize more efficiently, and dropping them before winter reduces the trees' water and energy losses. Once on the ground, these leaves, which decay more readily than the needles of conifers, build a fertile topsoil for spring-blooming wildflowers. The wide crowns and high limbs of hardwoods allow smaller trees and shrubs to grow beneath them, creating ample living space for a variety of animals.

In short, deciduous trees have evolved methods of interaction and sharing, while conifers play the older game of hogging resources and shutting out the competition. Red spruce and balsam fir, for example, have become overspecialized to the point where any infestation of insects or disease will devastate a much larger percentage of the forest. As trees die, more sunlight penetrates the forest, drying out cones and thereby releasing seeds that overwhelm the soil with more conifers. These young trees crowd out other invading plants and eventually create a new forest. By having different survival strategies, these two types of very different tree communities have managed to achieve an enduring coexistence.

What makes the southern Appalachian hollows so rich with plant and animal life?

In the sheltered southern Appalachian valleys known as coves, life runs wild. In spring the ground is carpeted with wildflowers of every description—trillium, fringed phacelia, squirrel corn, and dozens of others—while blooming azaleas and Carolina silverbells illuminate the understory. Warblers, vireos, tanagers, and thrushes sing from the canopy; black bears, deer, and bobcats prowl the shadows. Towering over them is a grand assemblage of trees, more than 100 species in all. No other temperate habitat in North America—and few others in the world—can compare to such richness of life.

These hollows owe their dazzling diversity to a happy conspiracy of climate, geology, history, and topography. The deep, fertile soil is kept moist by abundant rainfall, while the temperatures stay mild in winter and cool in summer. What's more, the southern hollows served as a refuge for many species of plants during the cold of the ice ages, providing an unbroken tenancy by the hardwood forests. The Blue Ridge landscape contributes as well, supplying progressively cooler and wetter environments at higher elevations; mountaintops are clad in spruce-fir forests more typical of Canada. Nor is the diversity confined to plants. The southern Appalachians are home to a host of birds, mammals, insects, reptiles, and amphibians, including many lungless salamanders.

About two dozen varieties of these colorful, secretive creatures live here—more than anywhere else in the world. Some, like the Jordan's salamander, have wide ranges across much of the Blue Ridge, but many inhabit tiny areas. Weller's salamander, a gold-blotched jewel, lives only in high spruce forests around Mount Rogers, Virginia, and neighboring parts of Tennessee and North Carolina. Another species, the Pigeon Mountain salamander, is found only near its namesake summit in northern Georgia.

More varieties of salamander, such as this red eft, live in southern Appalachia than anywhere else. The ancient mountains' many ridges and abrupt rises isolate colonies from one another, allowing separate species to evolve.

From dawn to dusk, the cerulean warbler, one of many avian residents of the Appalachians, sings from treetops.

Is a forest fire always a disaster?

As strange as it may seem, many woodlands stay healthy by falling victim to periodic blazes. This is especially true of Western conifer forests, like the great stands of lodgepole pines that cover much of the Rockies. The thin barks of these trees make them vulnerable to flames, but one of their two kinds of cones rely on these very flames to perpetuate the species. Clinging tenaciously to the tree for up to 10 years, this cone is pried open only by the heat of a fire, after which it spills its contents onto ground cleared of competing vegetation and fertilized by ashes. After an intense blaze, lodgepole pines may disperse nearly 1 million seeds per acre, ensuring a new crop of trees.

By studying historical records and burn scars on old trees, scientists have concluded that fire was a fairly regular occurrence on the Western frontier. Before settlers arrived, low-intensity fires swept through most Arizona woodlands every 2 years or so; in wetter areas like Colorado, the average was once every 66 years. But in the early 20th century, such fires were often doused, breaking the natural cycle. Stands of dry, aging, and diseased trees, along with a buildup of dead trees and woody debris on the forest floor, provided the fuel for unusually hot and extensive conflagrations.

In the summer of 1988, one of these tinderboxes ignited, scorching nearly one-third of Yellowstone National Park's 2.2 million acres. Wild animals all but ignored the flames, feeding near them and moving easily from their path. Surprisingly, only 244 out of more than 31,000 elk were killed. (Unfortunately the fires burned so much forage that almost 40 percent of the elk starved to death the following winter.) Many people mourned the park's loss, but naturalists immediately saw evidence of the forest's resilience. Just as scientists had predicted, by the next summer the charred areas were awash in blossoms of pink fireweed, and up to 400 lodgepole pine seedlings crowded each acre.

➤ *This elk in Yellowstone was spared by the fires, but the winter of 1988 may not have been as merciful. Those animals that migrated out of the park to forage in the grassy lower valleys nearby, however, certainly increased their odds for survival.*

➤ *Fires like this raging inferno that swept through Yellowstone National Park in 1988 can be incredibly capricious. Skipping across the landscape at the whim of the wind, they may char one area but leave the next untouched.*

⤳ *The Great Smoky Mountains National Park (above) is the site of North America's largest stand of old-growth deciduous forest. Nutrients from this toppled giant will fuel the next generation of forest, which will in turn provide food for migrant blackpoll warblers (inset).*

What is an old-growth forest?

Any forest that has grown to a climax state—the point where shade-tolerant trees (such as oaks, maples, and Douglas firs) become the dominant species—is considered old-growth. The hallmarks of such a forest are very old, very large trees; trees and shrubs of different heights and ages, arranged in several layers; clearings where large trees have died and fallen; and underfoot, lumpy ground from the slowly decaying, toppled trunks.

As a forest ages, dead wood and leaves decay, creating deep, fertile soil that nourishes a variety of plants. Unlike the crowded, same-size trees of a second-growth forest, those of an old-growth forest vary in height: a canopy of the tallest trees, such as oaks, hickories, maples, birches, spruces, or firs; a sub-canopy of smaller trees and shrubs, like flowering dogwood, salmonberry, or striped maple; and a ground layer of ferns, grasses, and wildflowers, such as wood sorrel, painted trillium, wild sarsaparilla, twinflower, and vanilla leaf.

Different species of birds live at each level of greenery, depending upon a variety of factors: the size of their bills, the availability of preferred nesting sites, and ease of access to insects or other food supplies. Yellow-throated vireos and cerulean warblers are canopy nesters; scarlet tanagers and wood thrushes like the middle branches; red-eyed vireos and American redstarts nest in low shrubs; ovenbirds take the ground. The broken tops of trees that are dead but still standing are ideal nesting sites for hawks and owls, and the wood of their decaying trunks is home to red-bellied woodpeckers, whose vigorously excavated nest cavities are later taken over by chickadees. Mammals also frequent the different forest layers. The gray squirrel, fox squirrel, and marten climb nimbly about the canopy; chipmunks and weasels scurry furtively across the forest floor.

Many of our native forest plants and animals, such as trilliums and ovenbirds, are disappearing as our woodlands are carved up. Large old-growth forests are reservoirs of wildlife, potentially able to repopulate nearby second-growth woods, but several small forest patches are not the same as a single large one. Smaller forests are more easily invaded by weeds from surrounding areas. These alien plants push out native wildflowers. Also, forest animals in wooded fragments are easier prey for hawks, coyotes, and other predators that prefer to hunt near open areas.

Old-growth forests are less vulnerable to disease and insect infestations than single-aged, single-species stands, in which an insect can quickly multiply and kill all the trees. An insect might decimate one tree group in an old-growth's mix of young and old trees of many species but would not destroy the entire forest.

⤳ *The forest's edge attracts coyotes because of the small prey animals, such as rabbits and hares, that congregate there. Coyotes often hunt in packs, yelping in unison before leaving for an expedition.*

Why are the edges of a forest the best places to spot wildlife?

One forest plus one meadow equals three habitats. It may not add up arithmetically, but wherever two different natural environments meet, they create a narrow transition zone along their borders. These so-called ecotones harbor a wider variety of plants and animals than either of their neighboring habitats.

The reason there are so many animals wherever woods and meadows meet is that these areas are contested boundaries—places where saplings that can grow on open, sun-drenched soil compete with grasses that tolerate some shade. Added to the mix are sumacs, hawthorn shrubs, blackberry brambles, and a host of other plants with sunlight and moisture requirements that are well suited to such in-between spaces. This variety of plants creates a wonderfully rich environment for forest animals, such as woodpeckers and bobcats, and grassland dwellers, including meadowlarks and woodchucks.

Many animals must live along the fringe of the forest because they need more than one habitat to survive. Robins, which nest in trees and feed on open grasslands, thrive there, as well as bluebirds, grouse, and pheasants. Deer and rabbits hide in brush and feed in meadows. Drawn by the abundance of prey, such hunters as weasels and red foxes also find these habitats alluring. They are also the best place to be when you want a close encounter with wildlife.

When a forest is cut down, does one just like it grow back?

If given enough time, yes. Wherever trees are removed, the environment that existed in the shade of their branches is changed immediately. Disaster for one species often means opportunity for another, and altered growing conditions set off a process known as succession, in which different sets of plants displace their predecessors.

The first plants to benefit are low, weedy pioneering species such as grasses and fireweed. Thriving in direct sunlight, these pioneer plants sprout quickly on exposed soil but survive for only a year or two, covering the bare soil and providing shade. This allows longer-lived perennials to grow, shading out the pioneers. These in turn provide the right growing environment for woody-stemmed shrubs, which eventually create a nursery for such sun-loving trees as red maples, aspens, and pines. Soon shade-tolerant species grow until they form an understory beneath the earlier trees. The saplings in this understory are the most long-lived, gradually taking over as they move into the sunlight that becomes available when preceding trees die or are cut down.

Once clear-cut to remove trees damaged by fire or insects, this section of Deschutes National Forest in Oregon shows signs of renewal that are small but sure: seedling evergreens.

❧ *With isolation often comes adaptation. A case in point is the red iiwi (below), among the most vividly colored residents of Hawaii's kipuka forests. Over time this species of honeycreeper developed a long, curved beak that fits into native tubular flowers as snugly as a hand in a glove. Near a kipuka forest (right), a solitary fern has found a foothold atop a hardened lava flow.*

Which virgin forests were preserved by volcanoes?

Lava has no respect for age or beauty. It flows wherever it well pleases, toppling buildings, burning trees, and repaving highways along the way. But just as a tornado may destroy only half of a house, lava can be just as fickle, sparing a patch of forest while obliterating everything around it. On the Hawaiian Islands such an oasis is called a kipuka forest, and several of them were formed when plots of greenery became surrounded by hardened lava flows. Cut off from the rest of the world like remote mountain valleys, kipukas became sanctuaries for the region's unique and spectacular wildlife. They provide a rare glimpse of the pristine forests that once graced these islands—long before humans arrived on these shores, introducing plants and animals that overwhelmed the native flora and fauna.

Among the kipukas' rarities are the mamaki tree, whose inner bark was used to make clothing, and the papala tree, whose branches were used as fireworks by early Hawaiians because they spew sparks when ignited. Of all the sights to be savored in kipuka forests, perhaps the greatest are the honeycreepers, avian treasures found only in our 50th state. About 40 species of these lively little birds once flitted through Hawaii's forests, all of them descended from a few finchlike birds blown off course more than 15 million years ago. Some have parrotlike beaks for crushing seeds; others have evolved long, slender bills ideally suited to probing flowers for nectar.

Today, only about 15 species of honeycreepers survive; at least 8 are highly endangered. Nearly all can be spotted on Kauai's Mount Waialeale, the world's rainiest place. One of the commonest honeycreepers, the scarlet feathered apapane, usually appears wherever ohia trees bloom, dipping its long, curved black beak into their crimson flowers for a sip of nectar.

What makes trees in the Pacific Northwest so large?

Any visitor to the forests of the Pacific Northwest will gain a whole new perspective on what is meant by a "big tree." There, in stands of old-growth forest on the west side of the Cascade Mountains, trees can live up to 1,000 years, soaring more than 250 feet into the sky. Though loggers have felled many of the most magnificent and valuable specimens, about 10 percent of the region's original old growth remains standing, some with trunks so thick that eight grown men with hands linked can't encircle them.

Why these giants evolved in the Pacific Northwest is a question that has long puzzled scientists. Though such factors as abundant rainfall, long summer days, rich volcanic soil, and a climate moderated by Pacific currents certainly play a role, none of them fully explain the mystery, for geographically similar places, like the coastal regions of England, have no such phenomenon.

Some scientists now speculate that these trees have adopted size as the solution to a problem unique to the Northwest. The region's abundant precipitation falls almost entirely in winter rather than summer, when the trees are most in need of water. By growing to an enormous size, however, they develop more space within and between their cells. Cumulatively, these pockets serve as a reservoir for the summer, when as little as 10 percent of the year's rain might fall.

Why doesn't the forest shut down at night?

The forest is like a bustling factory working overtime to fill a heavy order—activity goes on 24 hours a day. Nature abhors a vacuum, and it's not about to let nighttime resources go to waste. Some creatures are active by day and others by night, an arrangement that allows a forest to support more species than if all were going about their business at the same time. Diurnal and nocturnal species can play almost the same roles while avoiding competition. Butterflies, for example, visit flowers in the sunshine, while moths do it by starlight. By day gray squirrels rove the trees as chipmunks scurry over the forest floor. Both critters are hunted by hawks, which rely on keen vision to target their prey, and thus depend on the light of day. After dark flying squirrels glide from branch to branch, deer mice scuffle through the fallen leaves, and owls listen for the tiniest whisper—evidence of a meal on the move.

The Sitka spruce (left), which can live for 800 years and reach a height of 200 feet, is one of several species in the Pacific Northwest that are the tallest of their genera on earth. Among the other champions are the western red cedar and the noble fir.

In deep, swampy forests, the music of the night is marked by the haunting cries of the barred owl, whose raucous repertoire accounts for its nickname: the crazy owl.

The Great Plains and Prairies *America's sea of grass*

➤ *Bison bulls, some weighing as much as 2,000 pounds, plod across a meadow in Yellowstone National Park. Yellowstone's herd has the only free-ranging bison left in the United States. America's largest native land animals, bison can weigh up to twice as much as moose, our second-largest land animals.*

Where can you still see herds of bison roaming free?

Awestruck by the vast numbers of bison they encountered on the shortgrass prairies of Montana in 1805, Lewis and Clark wrote, "We had a very extensive prospect of the surrounding country: on every side it was spread into one vast plain covered with verdure, in which innumerable herds of buffalo were roaming." More than 30 million plains bison roamed the continent then, from the western slopes of the Appalachians to Louisiana, south into Mexico, and northwest to the foothills of the Rockies. A somewhat larger subspecies, the wood bison, ranged in fewer numbers through the mountains from northern New Mexico to the Great Slave Lake in western Canada.

The great bison herds all but vanished in a few short decades, falling before the rifle for meat,

hides, and sport. By the 1890s the plains bison had been reduced to a tiny relict herd of about 20 hiding in the protected fastness of Yellowstone National Park, as well as a small number of captives in private hands. About 300 wood bison also survived in northern Canada. From that meager seed, herds have grown to more than 100,000 bison today—but very few of these are wild, free-roaming animals.

In the United States the 4,000-strong Yellowstone herd is by far the largest unfettered group, while more than 1,000 wild wood bison survive in an isolated sanctuary in the Northwest Territories; thousands of plains-wood hybrids also thrive in Wood Buffalo National Park just to the south on the Alberta border. In these unspoiled surroundings they give a hint of the rumbling, majestic throngs that once ruled North America's untamed grasslands.

ceous growth may soar as high as eight feet. Tallgrass prevails through Iowa and into eastern Nebraska, but a few miles past Lincoln, shorter grasses ranging in height from two to four feet, such as little bluestem and western wheatgrass, and wildflowers such as pasqueflower and golden ragwort begin mixing with the taller ones. By North Platte the taller plants have dropped out. Short ones growing only five inches to two feet high prevail west to the Rockies at Laramie, Wyoming, and to the north even farther westward into Montana and Saskatchewan.

The transition from tallgrass to mixed to short-grass prairie reflects declining rainfall east to west, from an annual total of 40 inches in Indiana to only 12 inches in Wyoming. In northwest Minnesota precipitation is about 25 inches, but tallgrass thrives there because evaporation is low. In shortgrass areas evaporation exceeds precipitation. The plants of this drier climate have small tops to cut moisture loss and huge roots to store water, some extending nine feet deep.

Why did Native Americans set fires on the grasslands?

Indians living on the Great Plains used terms that translate as "red buffalo" to describe the wildfires that routinely raced across their prairie home. Usually the flames were kindled by frequent lightning strikes that accompany the violent thunderstorms common to these parts. Other times Indians torched the grass themselves, either as a way to encircle buffalo during a hunt or to improve pasturage.

Healthy grasslands made for healthy herds of buffalo, and the Plains Indians, who depended on bison for everything from fuel to food to shelter, no doubt concluded that perennial grasses thrive after a fire. Most prairie fires occurred in autumn when the tops of the deep-rooted grasses were dead and dried. When returned to the soil, the burnt plant materials and unlocked minerals, such as carbon, fed the next generation of grasses and prairie wildflowers.

Fire also gives native grasses the elbow room they need by destroying competing shallow-rooted forbs and the ever-invading woody shrubs and trees on prairie margins. Seedling plants and budding trees are easily killed off by fire, while native grasses survive because their roots, rhizomes, and other parts are underground, shielded by a heavy, fire-retardant layer of sod.

Why do wild grasses grow taller in Iowa than in Colorado?

The grasslands comprise our continent's largest natural community, stretching from Indiana and Texas to the California coast, and from Alberta, Canada, into Mexico. Variations in temperature from north to south combined with a decline in moisture from east to west make the grasslands the North American habitat with the widest range of climatic conditions. Low rainfall, high winds, and temperature extremes prevent most trees from growing there.

On the drive west along U.S. 80 from South Bend, Indiana, to Joliet, Illinois, travelers see oak and aspen woodlands gradually give way to tallgrass prairie. Consisting of such grasses as big bluestem and yellow Indian grass, and such lofty wildflowers as prairie coneflower, rattlesnake master, and tall goldenrod, this herba-

What attracts millions of birds to prairie potholes?

Dotted with millions of small glacial ponds, a 300,000-square-mile portion of the northern grasslands produces so many waterfowl that it's often called North America's "duck factory." This area, which stretches from Alberta and Montana on the west to Minnesota and Iowa on the east, contains only 10 percent of the breeding habitat available to ducks on the continent, yet 50 percent of the ducks added annually to the population are born there. Ringed with cattails, bulrushes, reeds, and whitetop grass, the rich, shallow waters of the potholes provide a food bonanza for dabbling waterfowl, while adjacent grasslands offer excellent cover for ground-nesting females. In the spring millions of these birds migrating up from the Gulf Coast and Mexico descend on the potholes to breed.

In a good year as many as 20 million hatchlings, including ruddy ducks, mallards, redheads, and canvasbacks, are fledged across the pothole region. Potholes, most of which are no more than a few feet deep, are so numerous that some parts of North Dakota, for example, have more than 1,000 of them per square mile, and the grand total of pot-

holes for the state is nearly 1.9 million. North Dakota's potholes and the marshes associated with them cover about 3 million acres. While that is a substantial amount of water, it is only half the acreage originally occupied by potholes in the state.

In this century pothole wetlands have been extensively drained, and much of the grasslands where the ducks find cover for their nests has been plowed under. By the mid-1980s habitat loss and drought reduced duck numbers more than 30 percent. By the last half of the 1990s, however, conservation measures, including programs paying farmers to preserve habitat, began to show results, and duck numbers started an impressive rebound.

Why are Midwestern farmlands so fertile?

About 18,000 years ago, during the Ice Age, massive glaciers one mile thick crept from Arctic regions to bury nearly a third of the earth's crust. As the ice crunched down from Canada at an average rate of some 300 feet a year, it scooped basins, hollowed valleys, and crushed hills, bulldozing the soil, gouging out the bedrock, pulverizing boulders into muck.

Then the glaciers halted and slowly began retreating, dumping all that material, much of it mashed to the consistency of flour. Meltwater gushed out from under the ice, spreading the debris onto the plains. Hills of sediment, called moraines, sometimes rose as high as 12-story buildings and extended for miles. Arctic winds, blowing over the ice fields unobstructed by mountains and gathering momentum for 1,000 miles, burst onto the plains at speeds often topping 100 miles an hour. They picked up the dirt and blew it in thick clouds hundreds of miles to the south.

Over the centuries the fine-grained dust slowly spread out across nearly 2 million square miles in the Mississippi River basin, filtering down between the stems of prairie grasses. The soil was loosely packed, mineral rich, and well drained. The grasses flourished. Over countless millennia of growth and decay, the decomposing vegetation built up soil so amazingly thick and fertile that today this fruitful earth helps feed the world with crops ranging from corn to soybeans, from barley to oats.

➤ *Thousands of potholes stretch across the northern prairies. Several small ponds provide much more edge, ideal for nesting birds, than a larger body of water of the same acreage.*

➤ *One of the most graceful of all shorebirds, the avocet nests around prairie potholes and uses its curved bill to sweep for aquatic insects.*

How have animals adapted to life on grasslands?

The basics of survival for animals of the plains and prairies are the same as for creatures everywhere: find a meal and avoid becoming one. To escape being eaten, many grasslands animals rely on running fast or getting underground. Pronghorns can be here one moment and gone the next as their white rumps disappear into the distance at speeds of up to 60 miles an hour. Hooves are an advantage for fast-running animals like the pronghorn because they provide protection against rocks and hard ground.

For bison, locating food isn't difficult, but processing it requires special tools. The bison's lower incisor teeth clip off grass against a hard gum pad that has replaced its upper incisors, and its large molars grind it to pulp.

Many grassland birds such as prairie chickens are cryptically colored to blend with the grass. Some sing territorial songs on the wing because there are no singing perches. Most nest on the ground, but the little burrowing owl has found a shelter solution that perfectly suits the prairies and plains. Despite its name it doesn't dig burrows; it nests in ones abandoned by prairie dogs or other animals that do.

Where are the largest remaining stretches of prairie?

The Great Plains that greeted America's westering pioneers in their prairie schooners appeared like an endless sea of grass. Today with only about 1 percent of the original 142 million acres of grasslands remaining, it's easier to find a virgin grove of redwoods than a virgin stand of prairie.

There are three main types of prairies: tallgrass prairies with grasses four feet high or more; midgrass, or mixed, prairies with grasses two to four feet high; and shortgrass prairies with grasses less than two feet high. Tallgrass prairies are now the rarest. The largest remnant stretches across 37,000 acres of the Osage Hills in northeastern Oklahoma. The Tallgrass Prairie Preserve, located 17 miles north of Pawhuska, features a herd of 300 bison and birds and wildflowers galore. Another large patch of tallgrass prairie is protected in southeastern North Dakota at Sheyenne National Grasslands. Numerous rare plants flourish here, including the western prairie fringed orchid with its delicate feathery white flowers. In the western part of the state, 27,000 acres of midgrass prairie are protected at the Lostwood National Wildlife Refuge.

After feeding, a pronghorn herd beds down on the shortgrass prairie but remains on the alert for predators. If disturbed, the fleet-footed animals will bound away with mouths wide open to gulp air. An unusually large trachea allows a rapid flow of oxygen to the pronghorn's lungs.

Before setting out to feed on grasses and weeds, a family group of four or five black-tailed prairie dogs will often sit at a burrow entrance scanning the landscape for predators. Should one prairie dog spot a soaring hawk or approaching ferret, it will bark a warning, and all will quickly scurry underground.

Which animals of the Great Plains live in "towns"?

Black-tailed prairie dogs, which inhabit the Great Plains from southern Saskatchewan to the northern fringe of Mexico, probably live in colonies called towns for the same reasons people do—because they are gregarious, and living together helps them defend against common enemies. These appealing members of the squirrel family are highly social, communicating by kissing, touching tongues, rubbing noses, and uttering a repertoire of sounds that include the bark that inspired their name.

Early settlers described prairie dog colonies that spread over miles and included thousands, or perhaps millions, of animals. Today, most towns hold fewer than 100 individuals. Each miniature metropolis is a maze of tunnels and portals, which serve as entrances, exits, and observation points. Most entrances are surrounded by circular earthen mounds up to 3 feet high and 10 feet in diameter, where their builders stand on their haunches and gaze over the surrounding plain. The tunnels may extend as deep as 10 feet below the ground and fan out under hundreds of acres of prairie.

Just like people who live together in close quarters, prairie dogs can have their differences. Inside a town the animals are divided into clusters called coteries, each led by a male and including as few as 2 or as many as 35 prairie dogs. These groups engage in spirited confrontations with one another, and while disputes can be frequent, they are usually settled without injuries.

Despite their spats prairie dogs generally get along well with each other. Friendly relations are clearly to their advantage, for the plump ground squirrels have many enemies, including golden eagles, red-tailed hawks, coyotes, foxes, badgers, black-footed ferrets, and prairie rattlesnakes. By sticking together, town residents share the burden of watching out for danger.

How do the prairies survive even the driest years?

Prairie grass is like an iceberg: 90 percent of it lies below the surface. Blades of grass no taller than your kneecap can have root systems that extend up to six feet down and several feet in all directions.

These enormous root systems enable prairie plants to survive some of the harshest and most changeable weather in the world. Temperatures on the Great Plains in June can swing 60 degrees in a day. Violent thunderstorms are common; tornadoes a constant threat. Winters are brutal. Dry, cold winds tear across the prairies at speeds of 100 miles per hour. Droughts can be Biblical in proportion, like the seven-year-long ordeal that produced the Dust Bowl in the 1930s.

Indian grass, buffalo grass, needle grass, and a host of other native species are ideally suited to these climatic extremes. From extensive roots grow stems called rhizomes that snake along underground or just above the surface, producing new stems, rootlets, and leaves as they go.

While underground parts can live 50 years or more, green leaves may sprout only occasionally, usually after a cloudburst in May or early June. By summer's end the blades have dried and died. When the hot winds of autumn blow, they conjure up the image captured by novelist Willa Cather in her book *My Antonia*. The sere brown prairie looks ". . . as if the shaggy grass were sort of a loose hide, and underneath it herds of wild buffalo were galloping, galloping. . . ."

What caused the Dust Bowl?

From 1933 to 1941, black blizzards welled up on the drought-stricken grasslands in a five-state, California-size area centered on the Oklahoma Panhandle. Clouds of dust loomed over parched fields, turning day into night. Crops smothered in dust drifts, cattle suffocated, and thousands of farm families left for California to look for work.

Once the plains were a sea of grasses, rippling in the wind. Not until the 1880s did farmers begin plowing up the sod. In 1894 and 1910, drought sent many packing, but most years brought some rain, and those who stayed wrested a living by planting winter wheat instead of corn. Lured by their successes, others came. Many of these new farmers little understood the pact between wind and grass that gave life to the plains. Grasses defy droughts. Their roots and stems form dense mats to hold the soil in place and prevent the wind from stealing moisture.

When World War I opened a European market for grain, wheat prices soared. Farmers bought more land and tractors to work it. The average farm, 256 acres in 1890, swelled to 800 by 1930. During the Depression wheat prices plummeted. Caught between declining prices and mounting debts, farmers plowed more ground. Soon a third of the plains lay stripped of grass.

The wind picked up the soil, sifting it over Eastern cities. By 1941, when rains returned, such new techniques as contour plowing and planting trees in windbreaks stopped erosion. Still, when higher prices lured farmers into plowing up too much land later in the 1940s and in the 1970s, droughts struck again, and with the ancient balance of wind and grass once more upset, dust clouds blossomed anew.

Why do some birds perform aerial acrobatics or mass dances?

On the great grasslands of North America, birds don't have the luxury of convenient perches for courtship songs as do their forest relatives. Instead, many use the sky itself as an aerial billboard, executing astonishing maneuvers that catch a female's eye from long distances. On the shortgrass prairies of the northern Plains, male McCown's longspurs (sparrow-size birds with black bibs

and caps) pepper the sky with their song flights, vaulting 30 or more feet into the air and descending on stiff, motionless wings, all the time bubbling over with twittering notes. Nearby, male Sprague's pipits soar 500 feet up and descend in a cascade of song.

On the ground males of less agile species gather in strutting, dancing mobs, providing a one-stop-shopping opportunity for females looking for mates. Females assess them on the basis of looks, manner, and social status—and select the most impressive for their own.

➤ *Congregating at mass display grounds known as leks on early spring mornings, male sage grouses inflate air sacs below their white neck ruffs and fan their tails. Males near a lek's center seem to be the most attractive to the watching females.*

Where can you see half a million sandhill cranes in one place?

❦ *A sandhill crane (right) is very finicky about where it will roost along the Platte River. This 3½-foot-tall bird will settle only on sandbars (above) without plants and with water less than six inches deep.*

Wide and shallow, the Platte River drains the central Rockies, channeling late-winter and early-spring snowmelt east across Nebraska's plains in a maze of channels and sandbars. Each spring, sandhill cranes descend upon the river, drawn by its predator-free sandbars and by the availability of food in nearby fields. Here they linger for weeks, refueling by day on a bounty of corn and grain left over from last fall's harvest and roosting by night on the sandbars.

Standing nearly four feet tall, a sandhill crane is the color of a foggy morning, except for the crimson splash on its forehead. Long legs and a supple neck give the sandhill a rangy, almost equine look; their chicks are even called colts. Late each winter, the cranes fly north from Mexico and the American Southwest, their trumpeting *gar-oo-oo* calls echoing like the baying of hounds. Borne by strong wings, the cranes reach the Platte after about a day's flight; the vanguard arrives in late February, and flocks quickly peak at 500,000 by the end of March. An estimated 80 percent of North America's sandhill cranes funnel through Nebraska on their way to Canadian nesting grounds, along with most of the 140 remaining whooping cranes.

Dams now divert up to 70 percent of the Platte's water, and springtime floods no longer create new sandbars. Conservationists, however, are working on water management plans that meet the needs of both cranes and humans in order to preserve one of our continent's greatest wildlife spectacles.

What keeps forests from growing on the Plains?

Pioneer families edging westward beyond the Great Lakes reached a place where familiar forests gave way to a vast treeless grassland, the Great Plains. Viewed from a hill, the boundless grass rippled in the wind like the sea, and people crossing the Great Plains called their wagons prairie schooners.

Why no trees? The answer lies as much in history as it does in prevailing conditions. As an ecosystem the Midwest prairie is only about 7,000 to 8,000 years old. After Ice Age glaciers receded, forests advanced across the exposed land and persisted while glacial meltwaters lasted. As the climate grew hotter and drier, perennial herbs, especially deep-rooted, drought-resistant grasses, took over. Bison, deer, and insects proliferated, living on grasses, whose buried growth tissue allowed their tops to regenerate quickly. Long, unpredictable droughts and frequent lightning storms set the dry turf aflame, killing tree seedlings, except for those along moist riverbanks.

Native Americans living on the Plains used terms that mean "red buffalo" to describe these wildfires. Sometimes they torched the grass themselves, increasing pasturage for the buffalo and extending the reach of the grasslands. Scientists speculate that by the time white settlers arrived, local tribes probably increased the total acreage of prairie in Illinois, at the expense of woodlands, by 20 percent.

At the edge of the Plains, in Illinois and Wisconsin, forest and prairie struggled for territory, the trees gaining ground in wet years, the grasses winning it back in times of drought. Today these battle lines have been obliterated by the artificial human landscape of farms and cities. But in a few remaining tracts of preserved tall prairie and oak savanna, such as in the Minnesota Valley National Wildlife Refuge and Texas's Blackland Prairie Preserve, the quiet struggle between woodland and grassland still continues.

Why are black-footed ferrets so rare?

In September 1981 a ranch dog named Shep startled scientists by bringing home a black-footed ferret, a mammal thought to be extinct. Shep had killed his find, but the discovery led researchers to a colony of the masked bandits living close to Shep's home near Meeteetse, Wyoming—the last known survivors of a species once found throughout the American grasslands.

Ferrets, mainly nocturnal creatures, spend much time underground, hiding from predators or pursuing prairie dogs. A rare sight even in pioneer days, their numbers dwindled further in the 1930s as ranchers exterminated prairie dogs, deeming them destroyers of cattle ranges. Prairie dog towns were plowed up, and the animals were poisoned or gassed in their burrows. Ferrets, who live almost exclusively in abandoned prairie dog tunnels, lost their main food source (90 percent of their diet is prairie dog) or died after eating tainted prey. By the 1950s few ferrets remained.

Even after its reappearance, this dapper member of the weasel family came within a whisker of extinction several times. An epidemic of flea-transmitted plague nearly wiped out prairie dogs sustaining the Meeteetse population in 1985; most ferrets also died. Captured specimens then succumbed to canine distemper. The last 18 survivors rewarded researchers with litter after litter of healthy kits, providing the foundation for an ongoing raise-and-release project. The current population (500 captive animals) is divided among zoos and research centers. Recent breakthroughs with domestic ferrets involving cloning and surrogate mothers raise hopes that the black-footed ferret population can be increased more rapidly in the future. Meanwhile, black-footed ferrets have been reintroduced into the wild in Wyoming, putting prairie dogs on the alert once again for masked marauders slipping through their corridors.

➤ *A black-footed ferret surveys its prairie domain by "periscoping," or squatting on its haunches and stretching its long body*

Desert Domains *Much more than sand*

Are all deserts the same?

Frontiersman Zebulon Pike, who explored the American West in the early 19th century, christened the 440,000-square-mile expanse west of the Rocky Mountains "the Great American Desert." He should have said "Deserts" because there are really four American deserts, each with its own special vegetation: the Sonoran, Mojave, Great Basin, and Chihuahuan.

Extending north from Mexico, the Sonoran Desert reaches into southeastern California and southwestern Arizona. A relatively low-lying desert, no portion of it extends above 4,000 feet, and parts are below sea level. It is the hottest of the four deserts. Summer temperatures often rise above 100°F, and even on many winter days, the mercury can top 70°F. Any Western movie with real saguaro cacti must have been filmed in the Sonoran because this is the only place these distinctive cacti are found.

Northwest of the Sonoran Desert—mostly in southern Nevada and southeastern California—is the Mojave. Though it includes the hot spot of Death Valley, the Mojave is a bit cooler than the Sonoran due to its higher latitude and elevation, which reaches 5,000 feet. Creosote bushes and saltbushes are common, but this desert's most famous plant is the bizarre Joshua tree with its tufts of sharp, daggerlike leaves.

North of the Mojave lies the Great Basin Desert. It covers most of Nevada and Utah and spills over into Oregon, Idaho, and Colorado. Situated mostly between 4,000 and 6,000 feet, it is a cold desert. Winter temperatures can plummet well below freezing, and howling snowstorms can leave several feet of white stuff. Poor in cacti, the Great Basin is abundant in grayish green big sagebrush.

The last of the four American deserts is the Chihuahuan. It lies mainly in Mexico but edges into Texas, New Mexico, and Arizona. Situated at about the same latitude as the Sonoran, it is slightly cooler, being mostly above 3,500 feet. As in the Great Basin, rainfall may exceed the upper limit defining a desert—12 inches annually. Some sections, therefore, can have heavy vegetation, including yuccas, barrel cacti, mesquite trees, and the yellow-flowered agave, considered a Chihuahuan symbol.

Below Arizona's Kofa Mountains (upper right), statuesque saguaro cacti stand like sentinels among clumps of spiny yellow cholla cacti and sprays of wiry ocotillo. The Sonoran Desert harbors a greater variety of plants and animals than any other American desert. Wildlife is much less diverse in the Great Basin Desert (lower right), where big sagebrush and greasewood cover thousands of square miles.

Why are America's deserts located in the Southwest?

A host of geological, astronomical, and meteorological factors keep this region, stretching from Mexico into Arizona and taking up the entire state of Nevada, both hot and dry.

It's no coincidence that America's deserts lie at about the same latitude as the Sahara. In fact, most of the world's deserts are found in the subtropics, north and south, in bands straddling 15° to 30° latitude. Because the earth rotates on a tilted axis, the sun is directly over these subtropical areas during the summer, producing maximum heat.

The sun's heat also creates a pattern of upper atmospheric air currents that help keep the subtropics dry—the other defining characteristic of a desert. When the sun warms the air over the equator, the air rises, then cools, and moisture condenses, falling as heavy rain over the tropics. The remaining dry air masses then descend on subtropical areas, heating up and absorbing any moisture in the lower layers of the atmosphere and on the ground.

Latitude is by no means the only factor involved in the location of America's deserts. If it were, then the Gulf states and Florida would be deserts, too. The reason is really a matter of geology and topography.

The landscapes of the Southwest began to take shape 80 million years ago when the uplifting of the earth's crust created the mountains of the West. Then 60 million years later, the crust began spreading, and the mountain ranges eventually became separated by deep, dry valleys. A relief map of Nevada today looks like a bunch of caterpillars crawling north out of Mexico. The caterpillars are the mountains, and the spaces between are desert valleys.

With the topography in place, the creation of our deserts became largely a question of weather patterns. Moist air from the Pacific smacks right into the Western mountains, beginning with the Sierra Nevada. When a front tries to clear this coastal range, the air rises, cools, and becomes unable to hold its moisture, which then falls as rain on the western slopes. Once the front passes over the mountains, it's left with little or no moisture for the valleys to the east. Because they are, in effect, shadowed from rain by mountain ranges on their western margins, these valleys are known as rain-shadow deserts.

Prickly pear cacti, such as this clump in New Mexico's Animas Mountains (upper left), are scattered across grassy areas at elevations above 3,500 feet in the Chihuahuan Desert, wherever annual rainfall averages about 12 inches. Vegetation is often much more sparse on the Mojave Desert (lower left). Its average elevation, lower than the Chihuahuan's, results in higher temperatures and less rain.

Wind whips over dunes in Death Valley, carrying sand grain-by-grain from the windward to the leeward sides.

How can sand dunes "walk"?

Dunes on the move can sweep across highways, engulf trees, clog waterways, and bury houses. The foot soldiers in this relentless army are tiny grains of sand swept by the wind. Rolling and bouncing, these particles rush up each dune's gentle windward slope and spill down its sharply angled lee side. Tumbling over themselves in this way, the sand piles drift in the direction of the winds that sculpt them.

Wandering dunes can easily "walk" 20 feet in a year and can travel over 100 feet in particularly windy places. Interrupting the flow of windborne sand slows or stops their migration. In coastal areas beach grass and other hardy vegetation can brake the rush of air, forcing it to drop its cargo of sand. Such plants survive repeated burial, poking new growth above the sand and sending out runners to colonize their shifting habitat. Over time dead plant matter helps create a stable layer of soil that may one day support a thicket or forest, forming a living wall against the marching sands.

Planted windbreaks also halt inland dunes, such as those of Nebraska's Sand Hills. When bare patches develop on this wrinkled grassland, ranchers quickly reseed, lest the wind pick up exposed sand and revive the ridges' motion.

Although dunes menace some areas, they also create awe-inspiring landscapes. Mounds over 100 feet tall loom near Nags Head, North Carolina. The mountainous swells of Oregon's coastal dunes tower hundreds of feet high, leaving skeletal trees in their wake. Hikers revel in the splendor of the Great Sand Dunes of Colorado's San Luis Valley, which ripple across the land like colossal waves in a golden sea.

Why is it that some desert plants open their flowers only at night?

The night-blooming cereus, which is also known as queen of the night, is a very inconspicuous cactus. For most of the year, all that can be seen of it are stems that look like a few dead sticks about one inch wide and one to three feet long. But just after sundown on a single night in June, these stems will blossom with radiant, creamy-white flowers three to six inches wide. These flowers are so fragrant that they scent the air for hundreds of feet around with their perfume, but all of them will close as soon as the sun brightens in the morning—and none will be seen for another year.

The spectacular flowers of the night-blooming cereus attract moths and other insects over distances of a mile or more with their strong, sweet scent.

The purpose of the night-blooming cereus's extravagant blossoms and spicy perfume is to attract moths to pollinate the flowers. Like those of many other moth-pollinated plants, the blossoms are highly visible in dim light and are most fragrant during the night when these insects are active.

While other cacti and desert plants, such as the yuccas, bloom at night and are pollinated by moths, the saguaro cactus largely depends upon a different night flier for pollination. Standing up to 60 feet tall, the huge cactus is one of the most recognizable features of the Sonoran Desert land-scape. This spiny plant opens its three-inch white flowers sometime during the month of May at around 10:00 P.M. Its blossoms, which last only to the next afternoon, are pollinated primarily by nectar-eating bats.

The night-blooming cereus and saguaro cactus are well adapted to the arid environment of the desert. By blooming at night, when breezes die down and desert insects and bats are most active, they increase the chances that pollinators will visit them, transferring their pollen to the open flowers of others of their kind. It is an economical way to assure reproduction in a harsh land that quickly winnows out those not making wise use of their resources.

When are desert snakes on the prowl?

Hammered by the yellow fist of the sun, the midday desert sees little movement: a fringe toed lizard scuttles from one patch of shade to another; a small group of pronghorn grazes on bunchgrass; a few vultures rock lazily on updrafts; a tiny Costa's hummingbird, throat glowing purple, zips among the blood-red flowers of an ocotillo. But when the sun goes down, the desert comes to life. Dry and clear, the sky draws off the brutal heat; the air softens with just a touch of moisture. Up from burrows, out of caves, from beneath rocks, and from within sheltering thickets creeps a wildlife menagerie.

Foremost in the night shift are snakes, most of which wait until after sunset to begin hunting. Western diamondback rattlesnakes slide over the still-warm gravel and sand, their forked tongues picking up the scent of food—kangaroo rats and other small mammals. Long-nosed snakes follow the trails of lizards; ground snakes seek out centipedes and scorpions. The desert night snake, its vertical, cat's-eye pupils fully dilated, searches for geckos; once the lizard is grabbed in a lightning-fast strike, the night snake holds tight as toxic saliva oozes down a pair of enlarged, grooved teeth in the back of its mouth. Other desert snakes are similarly rear fanged, including the hook-nosed snake, a hunter of

spiders and scorpions, and the Texas lyre snake. Unlike rattlesnakes and coral snakes, though, these mildly venomous species pose little or no threat to humans.

How do roadrunners cope with temperature extremes?

A roadrunner can sprint as fast as 15 miles per hour, weaving around cacti and bushes in its single-minded pursuit of prey. Whiptail lizards, snakes, and other reptiles form the bulk of this desert speedster's diet. Roadrunner chicks hatch in late spring and early summer—a time of year when heat-loving, cold-blooded animals are abundant.

Roadrunners nest in cholla cactus or shrubs chosen for their access to both sun and shade. During the chilly desert night, they cuddle with their young. In the morning the featherless, shiny black chicks soak up sunlight to keep warm, freeing their parents to hunt before the heat of midday drives prey into hiding. Adult birds also borrow the sun's energy to warm up without having to expend any calories. Branded on a roadrunner's back is an H of black skin—a built-in solar panel, which this sun-worshiping bird activates by standing with its back to the sun and lifting its wings. A fringe of fluffy black down around the exposed skin cuts down on heat loss. This strategy helps the bird boost its body temperature, which may drop 6°F at night—another energy-saving trick.

Keeping warm isn't a problem on a summer afternoon, when temperatures may shoot above 100°F. Baby birds flop into the nest's shady spots, beaks agape and throats fluttering as they "pant" to cool their bodies by evaporation. Adult birds relax in the shade or hop into the nest to shelter their young ones from the sun's burning gaze.

An ability to cope with temperature extremes and a readiness to eat seeds, fruits, scorpions, small birds, and rodents when reptiles are scarce enable roadrunners to be active year-round.

After chasing down a lizard, a roadrunner clamps the reptile in its beak, whacks it on the ground until it stops struggling, and then swallows it headfirst. This energetic member of the cuckoo family can outrun most four-legged predators and rarely flies.

Flowering dune primroses spangle the Mojave Desert in spring and early summer. Quickly taking advantage of rain whenever it comes, these expeditious annuals germinate, sprout, bloom, and set seed for the next generation in a few weeks, filling the air with their sweet fragrance.

What makes the Southwestern deserts bloom?

Visit the American Southwest in April after a particularly wet winter, and you'll never guess that the colorful blossoms festooning the spiny cacti and covering the desert floor are as ephemeral as dreams. That rain can make anything bloom in this brutally hot and dry environment is a testament to the wondrous ways desert plants have adapted.

Scientists use labels that sound more like pop psychology than botany when explaining how Southwestern flora behave in response to long periods of scorching sun and little water. The thousand or so different species are grouped into three general categories: avoiders, tolerators, and escapers.

Avoiders are perennial plants like prickly pear cactus and saguaro that dodge climatic stress by relying on wide but shallow root systems to collect water when it rains, and thick, waxy skins to hamper evaporation when it's dry. These plants have an internal switch that triggers blooming by responding to the right amount of moisture.

Tolerators can survive months or even years of drought by casting off leaves or whole branches in order to reduce their energy intake. Some species, like the palo verde and smoke tree, won't even germinate unless they're guaranteed sufficient water. Their seeds, coated with a tough, thick covering, will wait to sprout until they're dashed upon rocks by a flash flood.

Water-impervious seed coverings are a trick deployed by the escapers—wildflowers such as verbena, daisies, and desert lilies. Their durable seeds can lie dormant for months, even years, before rain rinses away their protective chemical coatings and sets them off on a hurried cycle of germination, growth, and flowering. The plants wither and die in just a few weeks, but not before producing a new batch of seeds that will wait as long as it takes to start the cycle again.

Can fish live in the desert?

The harsh, baked expanse of Death Valley seems the least likely place to find fish. But 10,000 years ago, an Ice Age lake 175 miles long and 600 feet deep covered this now arid land. Fish thrived in its waters until a warming trend dried up their home, corralling the survivors in ponds and puddles.

Today, underground reservoirs still feed small springs and pools, some of which shelter relicts from that vanished lake: the tiny but tough pupfish. Rare and restricted to small habitats, these Ice Age survivors would disappear in an eyeblink without government protection.

Each isolated population of pupfish has adapted to survive the rigors of its particular microcosm: some species flourish in waters that heat up to 100°F, while others cope with water six times saltier than the ocean. Though unimpressive in appearance, this hardy, 2½-inch fish offers scientists a valuable glimpse into the mysterious workings of evolution—and an example to all of perseverance.

Why is Death Valley so hot?

ood-bye, Death Valley," cried one of the first groups of pioneers to cross the lowest spot in North America, a parched desert valley in southeastern California. The name stuck. What started as a shortcut to the California gold fields in 1849 turned into a perilous journey through desolate country. Even when the party discovered water, it often was saltier than seawater and unfit to drink. The oxen grew weak on the sparse and scattered desert forage. Luckily, the pioneers crossed in winter when temperatures were around 70°F. They would not have made it in summer.

The daytime high averages 116°F during July, the hottest month, and night doesn't bring much relief. The average overnight low cools things off to a refreshing 89°F. Rainfall is close to nonexistent, only about two inches per year.

Death Valley's forbidding climate is due to its location. Like most deserts, it lies below a storm-blocking high-pressure zone created by global air currents. When a storm system does slip in off the Pacific and head east toward Death Valley, three mountain ranges intercept the air and wring out its moisture. Little but dry wind remains. Since air slowly heats up as it sinks lower in elevation, the air at the lowest point in the valley—282 feet below sea level—is already prewarmed. Without cloud cover the sun beats down mercilessly. Even after the sun sets, the land continues radiating heat. The record for summer ground temperature is 201°F, only 11°F below the boiling point of water at sea level.

Which animals gather at water holes?

ike the celebrated bar scene in the original *Star Wars* movie, desert water holes attract an amazing array of creatures. Nearly anything that can walk, slither, or fly sooner or later finds its way to water, whether it's a tiny seep, an enlarged rain puddle, or an extensive water hole.

Water holes are the best places to look for big mammals, including mountain lions, bobcats, coyotes, mule deer, pronghorn, and collared peccaries. Though bighorn sheep weigh up to 200 pounds, they need surprisingly little fresh water to survive. Studies of herds living in Death Valley reveal that bighorns wander down from their rocky, precipitous homes to drink at springs every 3 to 5 days in hot, dry weather and every 10 to 14 days in cold weather. Between visits the sheep derive water from the plants they eat. Their pale tan hair also helps to reduce their thirst by acting as a heat shield.

Collared peccaries, on the other hand, rarely live far from water. Also known as javelinas, these sharp-tusked, distant cousins of pigs have an uncanny ability to sniff out water. Even when only a nearly dried-up seep is available, they'll use their hooves to dig out a pool. If forced to go without water for an extended period, peccaries will reduce their urine flow by 90 percent to conserve precious body fluids.

Other animals control their urine flow to save water, too. While the desert tortoise gets a lot of water from vegetation, it will drink freely from rain puddles and springs, storing as much as a year's worth in its bladder. Gambel's quail, another frequent water-hole visitor, will use less water by excreting solid uric acid when its sources of water dry up. The bird's reproductive behavior also hinges on the water supply. Heavy rains produce new plant growth with a high protein content, which in turn stimulates the female's ovaries and the male's testes. In times of drought, their sex tissues do not swell, and the quail wait another year to breed.

Many of the 500 or more species that call the desert home are lizards and snakes. These, too, frequent water holes, but not to drink. Instead, they come to dine on the birds and small rodents that are there to wet their whistles.

A mosaic of polygons rimmed with salt crystals pave Salton Flat in Death Valley, California. After occasional thunderstorms, runoff water bearing dissolved salts accumulates in this playa, a natural basin without an outlet. Subsequent evaporation and seepage remove the water, leaving another layer of salt.

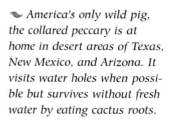

America's only wild pig, the collared peccary is at home in desert areas of Texas, New Mexico, and Arizona. It visits water holes when possible but survives without fresh water by eating cactus roots.

❧ *The austerely beautiful mesas, towers, and buttes of Monument Valley on the Utah-Arizona border are all that remain of a great, elongated sandstone dome created millions of years ago when the earth's crust warped upward. Eventually even these surviving monoliths will be worn down by wind and weather.*

How are mesas and buttes formed?

Some of the flat-topped mesas that dominate so much of the Southwestern deserts tower 1,000 feet or more above the landscape around them. However, mesas and buttes—technically speaking, a butte is a mini mesa, one whose top covers less than one square mile in area—did not rise above their surroundings the way mountains grew out of the earth. To the contrary, the land around them was worn away by erosion. Mesas are the remains of much more expansive tablelands—plateaus of soft rock, such as sandstone, that were carved up and worn down by water and wind. These scattered remnants survived because they were protected by caps of hard, resistant rock such as shale.

The awe-inspiring mesas of red sandstone in Monument Valley, on the border of Utah and Arizona, originated from an ancient seabed that was uplifted into a plateau 65 million years ago. The soft rock was vulnerable to water, which seeped into cracks and crevices and, with the wind's aid, enlarged them. This action created pathways for streams that further ate away the sandstone until only mesas, buttes, and other remarkable rock formations—such as pinnacles and chimneys—remained. The haunting landscape of Monument Valley, crafted by millennia of erosion, serves as a memorable backdrop for many Western films.

🔾 *With an insect in her beak to offer hungry hatchlings, a female Gila woodpecker perches at a nesting hole in a saguaro cactus.*

Where do Gila monsters and other desert animals go to hide from the heat of day?

If animal desert dwellers could hang out signs during the day, almost every one of them would read "Siesta Time." Even the grotesque Gila monster, the world's only venomous lizard, which fears nothing in its path, escapes the heat under a rock overhang or in an abandoned burrow or a tunnel it has dug in the sand.

A central fact of life for most animals is that to stay alive when desert temperatures climb above 100° F, the only option is to go underground. Just a few inches below the desert's sand and rock surfaces, it is cool and sometimes moist. Waiting for twilight to come round again, the desert tortoise retreats into his tunnel, while snakes, lizards, and rodents head for ubiquitous burrows.

For those that don't dig, many of the 1,600 native varieties of cactus provide shade and shelter. For example, the horned toad, a speedy lizard resembling a thorny pancake, often sits in a cactus shadow as it waits for an insect meal.

The most elaborate desert refuges from the searing heat are built by the wood rat, which adores any shiny treasure: lost car keys, marbles, shoelace tips. This enthusiastic collector uses these prizes to decorate a surface structure sometimes several feet high, made of twigs, green shoots, and joints of cholla cactus. Everything is carefully arranged so air can circulate freely in the commodious burrow below—an excavation often expropriated by skunks, raccoons, badgers, and other interlopers.

🔾 *Camouflaged by its disruptive dark markings, a Gila monster rests in the shade of a dead oak branch. During hot desert days this venomous lizard will take shelter in a mammal burrow, such as a wood rat nest, if it happens upon one.*

What birds nest in saguaros?

With their battery of sharp spines, saguaro cacti would seem poor sites for bird nests. Yet hawks build bulky stick nests on saguaros' arms, and Gila woodpeckers put the cacti's spiny defenses to their own use by chiseling nest cavities in the plants.

Gila woodpeckers usually cut a new hole after raising a brood of chicks. Over the winter a layer of sap hardens the walls of the cavity, so it is ready for use by the new hatchlings born in the spring. Ready, that is, if the woodpeckers can chase off claim jumpers. Holes are scarce in the desert, and a host of other birds are always eager to grab one—from elf owls to purple martins, western screech owls, American kestrels, cactus wrens, brown-crested and ash-throated flycatchers, and others. Insulated from temperature extremes, the holes are also choice real estate for lizards, scorpions, rodents, and bats.

Which desert bird hibernates?

To the Hopi the poorwill is Hölchoko, "The Sleeping One," which slumbers through the winter like a hibernating squirrel. Nonsense, snorted early ornithologists, who considered the Indian tale a myth, as unbelievable as the ancient European belief that swallows sleep like frogs in muddy lake bottoms.

Unlike the medieval peasants, however, the Hopi were right. The poorwill, a robin-size bird related to the nighthawk and whippoorwill, sometimes avoids winter hardships by slipping into a torpor similar to hibernation. On a cold winter day in 1946, a scientist discovered a poorwill wedged in a rocky cleft near California's Salton Sea; it had no heartbeat or breath, and its body temperature was only 64° F—roughly half that of an active bird. Taken into a warm room, it revived; banded and released, the bird returned to the same place three winters in a row, sleeping up to three months at a time. Not all poorwills hibernate, and later experiments showed that a lack of food, not cold, brings on the state.

~ *Four young collared lizards sun themselves companionably on a branch. Sharp-eyed and irascible, collared lizards will bite hard if cornered. When fleeing enemies, they run erect on their hind legs, with tails raised, looking very much like tiny dinosaurs.*

Why do lizards like the desert so much?

The farther north you go, the fewer lizards you will find because they fare poorly in areas of prolonged cold. Lizards do, however, have several ways of coping with extended periods of extreme heat, and they are efficient at conserving water. It should not come as a surprise, therefore, that the deserts of the Southwest teem with them. Many desert lizards seldom, if ever, drink because they obtain sufficient moisture from their food: insects, spiders, or succulent plants, such as cacti. Like most other desert animals, they have adaptations that help them retain water: thick scales that reduce evaporation from their skin, feces that are nearly dry, and urine that is a pasty semisolid.

While conserving body water is mostly a matter of physiology, lizards also employ cool behavioral solutions to beat the heat. When the desert surface sizzles, they may head for the shade of a rock or go underground, where temperatures are more moderate and stable than at the sun-scorched surface. Sometimes lizards position themselves head-on toward the sun, so less of their body surface is exposed to its direct rays. The desert iguana cools off by scrunching down and wiggling into the sand, putting its belly in contact with the cooler soil below. When the fringe-toed lizard is too hot, it goes swimming—sort of. Scaly fringes on its toes enable this lizard to swim into the sand to cool off as if it were paddling in water.

What happens after desert rains?

Any fan of Western movies knows a shot in a canteen can be as fatal as one in the heart. So rare is rain in California's Mojave Desert that 25 years may pass without it. When it finally comes, land that once appeared brown and dead becomes green and teeming almost overnight. Shallow basins called playas collect runoff and quickly become nurseries for fairy shrimp hatching from eggs that have lain dormant in the sand for years. Spadefoot toads, stirred from their mud cocoons by water soaking into parched soil, tunnel up to breed in new pools. Mice, jackrabbits, desert tortoises, beetles, and butterflies emerge to partake of explosive plant growth. Larger carnivores such as spotted skunks, coyotes, snakes, and hawks feast on the newly active smaller creatures.

Desert dwellers tend to make the most of a rainy year. For example, Gambel's quails raise young only after rains. In wet years quail couples can fledge 10 or more young, compensating for seasons when no new birds were born.

~ *In the aftermath of a sudden desert thunderstorm, muddy water rushes down an arroyo in Death Valley National Monument. Flash floods are common in the desert, where the ground may be as hard as city pavement.*

Do wild horses still roam the American West?

In the hearts and minds of many, wild horses symbolize the essence of freedom as they race across the desert, tails and manes rippling and nostrils flaring. Yet mustangs haven't always enjoyed such admiration.

Mustangs are descendants of horses that helped shape American history: the fine Barb horses brought to North America by Spanish conquistadors 400 years ago, Indian ponies, and runaway ranch stock. Over 1 million wild horses roamed the nation's grasslands in the heyday of the bison, but as the West became cattle country, their numbers dwindled. Mustangs were driven to forage in increasingly remote areas.

By the 1950s turning mustangs into dog food was big business: horses caught in brutal roundups were shipped to slaughterhouses under shocking conditions. But in 1971 the United States Congress officially recognized the last mustangs as "living symbols of the historic and pioneer spirit of the West," sparking a new era of federal management. Today, excess horses are culled for adoption and relocation.

Remarkably resourceful, mustangs are strong, sturdy creatures that have learned to cope with searing desert heat, freezing winds, poor fodder, and lack of water. No oat buckets or water troughs ease their lives. Nearly 50,000 mustangs range across 10 Western states, with about 35,000 of them eking out a living in Nevada's deserts and mountains. The horses of Granite Ridge in northwestern Nevada have lived free only since the Depression, when desperate farmers turned animals loose to fend for themselves; others, such as the Spanish-type mustangs of the Pryor Mountain National Wild Horse Range in Montana and Wyoming, have been a part of the landscape for over 200 years. Wherever they roam, wild horses offer an echo of the past in the sound of their thundering hoofbeats.

Which hawk hunts in a pack as wolves do?

Most hawks are solitary hunters, fiercely antisocial, but one unusual species shows the kind of sophisticated, cooperative behavior usually associated only with wolves, killer whales, and humans—the sooty black, white-rumped Harris' hawk of the Southwest.

➤ *Sensing danger, wild mustangs look up from grazing grass and warily scan the horizon in southern Nevada's Amargosa Desert.*

Across the deserts of west Texas, southern New Mexico, and southern Arizona, the Harris' hawk constantly keeps an eye out for food—mostly agile, hard-to-catch jackrabbits and desert cottontails. Harris' hawks work in teams that usually number five or six birds, which take turns beating the bushes and perching quietly, watching for prey. If a rabbit holes up beneath vegetation, one or two hawks may walk in to flush it out. When the rabbit bolts for safety, the others then use a relay system to run it to exhaustion. Once the prey is killed, the pack shares the spoils. The younger birds often receive the lion's share, a rare occurrence in nature.

Mountains of Life *Ever-changing peaks and pinnacles*

Which mammals are awake for only three months of the year?

Mountaintop living puts severe strains on animals. It means having to contend with thin air, icy temperatures, battering winds, and (because of a short growing season and poor soil) a limited food supply. Some animals manage to survive the worst of it—the long, brutal winters—by falling into a deathlike slumber known as hibernation.

As hibernators go, the true kings of snooze are the arctic ground squirrel of Alaska and northern Canada and the hoary marmot, the largest member of the squirrel family, which lives high in the mountains of northwestern North America. These miniature Rip Van Winkles can doze through as much as nine months of the year.

During the summer the arctic ground squirrel and marmot engage in many of the same activities as their nonhibernating brethren (albeit on a much shorter time schedule): wooing mates, rearing young, defending territory, and especially, eating. To survive their lengthy hibernation (during which they may lose as much as 40 percent of their body weight), these animals must constantly gorge on food, storing a thick layer of fat for the dark days ahead.

When the first frigid signs of winter arrive, the squirrels and marmots retire to their grass- or fur-lined burrows. There they curl into tight balls and slip into the deep sleep of hibernation: body temperature drops, pulse slows, blood thickens, and respiration falls to a few irregular breaths per minute. In this state of suspended animation, they live off stored fat, safely sheltered from the winter that rages above them.

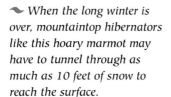

➤ *When the long winter is over, mountaintop hibernators like this hoary marmot may have to tunnel through as much as 10 feet of snow to reach the surface.*

How were the Rocky Mountains formed?

Imagine a car crashing into a brick wall. As the front end makes contact, it crumples, folding like the seams of an accordion. Two or three feet of metal are compressed to inches in the blink of an eye. Extend this process over tens of millions of years, and you have some notion of the forces that forged North America's greatest mountain range.

Stretching from Alaska's Brooks Range south through Canada to New Mexico, the Rockies are part of an even longer mountain chain that spans the length of the western edge of the Americas from the Arctic Circle to the southern tip of Chile. Seen from outer space, this formation looks like a wrinkled fold in the earth's crust, marking the meeting place of two tectonic plates (the Pacific and North American) that slammed into each other some 60 million years ago.

As the two plates collided along the coast of present-day California, the very fabric of the earth was violently rent. The North American plate, the lighter of the combatants, slid over the Pacific, forcing it downward. As the Pacific Plate resisted, the continent buckled, broke, and folded over itself, forming mountains. The greatest disruption occurred along fault lines where smaller pieces of the earth's crust rub against one another. In some places, such as the Lewis Range of Montana, great slabs of crust rose and slid over newer sedimentary rock; in others, one side of a fault rose while the other fell, producing some of the Rockies' most dramatic peaks, including Wyoming's Tetons.

It wasn't until some 2 million years ago—just yesterday in the vast sweep of geologic time—that the most dramatic period of change ended. Ice Age glaciers then set to work, gouging lakes and valleys and buffing the slopes to a fine finish. But still the Rockies weren't complete. Even today, wind and water erosion, plate movement, and fresh volcanic activity continue to shape these rocky giants. Though they seem as ageless and permanent as anything in creation, the Rockies are in fact ever-changing masterpieces of nature.

What are marine fossils doing high atop the Rockies?

➤ *Great slabs of sedimentary rock flank the slopes of the Rocky Mountains. These massive stone layers, once the flat floor of an inland sea, now bear fossils of marine animals. In other areas similar stratified deposits have eroded, exposing the underlying mountain cores of basement rock.*

The region that now contains some of North America's loftiest peaks actually began as a shallow inland sea. Over countless eons sediment washed into this troughlike basin, where it hardened into sandstone, shale, and other stratified rocks. These rocks were later thrust upward when colliding tectonic plates crumpled the edge of the continent.

Trapped in the once submerged stones of the Rockies are the fossilized remains of marine creatures that lived over 700 million years ago. Some of the most interesting fossils were discovered in a Canadian rock formation called the Burgess Shale, nearly 8,000 feet above sea level.

The Burgess Shale is unusual because it preserved soft-bodied animals, some of the rarest creatures in the fossil record. When these creatures died, their boneless corpses floated to the sea floor, where the oxygen-poor water prevented decay. Buried under accumulating silt, the remains were eventually flattened and fossilized.

The most celebrated Burgess Shale creature, hallucigenia, was first depicted as a big-headed bug with seven pairs of stiff, pointed legs and seven tentacles on its back. Later, scientists turned it upside down, and it made more sense—the flexible extensions became legs and the stiff ones protective dorsal spines. Equally bizarre was opabinia, a deadly predator with five eyes, a segmented body, and a flexible snout ending in pincers used to snatch up its prehistoric prey.

A pika (above) harvests plant matter to insulate its winter den. Distantly related to the rabbit, this small animal has earned the nickname whistling hare for its shrill, nasal call. A mountain goat (right) surveys its demanding habitat, where few others dwell. Superbly adapted to this rugged environment, these agile creatures can traverse perilous terrain only a few days after birth.

Can animals live above the timberline?

Where North America's mountains rear their highest, seeming to scratch the cold, oxygen-poor sky, life is a battle with the elements. Only the hardiest of animals can tolerate the constant wind, pervasive cold, and lack of shelter above timberline—a harsh environment where even the trees have surrendered. Most animals seen there are visitors, yet a hardy few—from colorful butterflies to nimble mountain goats—make their home on the high peaks.

In the Shickshock Mountains of Canada, great expanses of mountaintop are bereft of trees, yet they host caribou and, in Newfoundland, burly arctic hares that weigh as much as 10 pounds.

Alpine habitat is rare in the eastern United States, where few mountains rise high enough to leave the forests behind. The high Rockies, Sierras, and other Western mountains, however, provide an abundance of alpine terrain—home to guinea-pig–size pikas, which carefully nip green vegetation and dry it in the sun, building "haystacks" deep in the boulders to tide them through the winter. To mountain goats the rugged

How do fragile flowers survive on windswept mountaintops?

Botanists call mountain flowers "belly plants" because to view them, you have to lie flat. Appearing as dense cushions or spreading mats, alpine plants hide from the wind behind small stones and lumps of dirt. With appealing names like snowball saxifrage and alpine candytuft, these miniature blooms can fit in a circle no larger than a nickel. Mature specimens sprout from big, food-storing rootstocks that may be several years old and a few inches across.

Through the eight- to nine-month winters of the Sierra Nevada, Cascades, and Rockies, these tiny plants ride out subzero temperatures and driving winds entombed in a blanket of snow. For alpine flowers, though, deep mountain snow is a blessing, providing insulation through winter and fresh water in spring. Snow, however, cannot protect high-altitude flora from other adversities, including poor soil, a short growing season, glaring sun, and dry, thin air.

Mountain soil is mostly rock rubble; the wind blows away fine particles, leaving behind almost no nutrients. Worse, alpine plants have only a fraction of the growing season their lowland counterparts enjoy. To accumulate sufficient resources to spare for flowers, a mountain herb like the moss campion may bide its time for a decade or more before blooming, growing just a bit each brief summer.

Thin mountain air holds less moisture and dust, and thus scatters less sunlight. Consequently, light striking the ground is especially intense, boosting plants' photosynthesis but also drying out leaves, disrupting cells, and even mutating genes. The waxy leaves of golden saxifrage and the needlelike ones of sandwort resist desiccation, while the hairy leaves of alpine dryad provide insulation and another advantage: dark hairs retain heat on cold days and light ones deflect harmful ultraviolet rays.

➤ *Low-lying clusters of alpine forget-me-not (blue), pink moss campion (lavender), and compact draba (yellow) grow ensconced by wind-buffering stones in Wyoming's Yellowstone National Park.*

land above timberline provides security, for few cougars dare tackle the precarious cliffs the goats navigate with ease.

Mountaintops also provide a southerly haven for species from the far north. A diminutive brown butterfly called the Polixenes inhabits the alpine meadows of both the Rockies and Mount Katahdin in Maine, hundreds of miles south of its normal Arctic range. Water pipits (slim, sparrow-size birds of the Arctic tundra) nest in the Rockies as far south as New Mexico, sharing their treeless home with white-tailed ptarmigans and rosy finches.

What is krummholz vegetation?

Strong winds are sculptors of trees, and high mountains are where they display the full array of their creations. The crafting process occurs over decades as the wind's rush buffets a tree, bending and pruning the branches on its windward side. Coniferous trees are noticeably sculpted by moving air, and even in mild climates their upper tips are often permanently bent away from the prevailing wind.

As you move up a mountain, wind speed increases, and more branches are frozen, dehydrated, or simply snapped off the trees. The same species of fir or spruce that is cone shaped at the base of a mountain will, at higher elevations, have far fewer branches facing the wind. As you near the upper edge of the timberline—the elevation beyond which no trees can grow—subzero temperatures and gale-force winds stunt the growth of the trees and press them flat against the ground. A forest of these prostrate, miniature trees is known as a krummholz—from the German word for "crooked wood."

The same species of fir that would stand over 100 feet tall and have a 2-foot girth in a valley may, near a mountain's peak, be a ground-hugging trunk only inches in diameter, with branches reaching a few feet high. The trunk itself might crawl along the ground for 30 or 40 feet on the protected side of some rocks, and a few of its branches may have been held against the soil long enough to take root. A krummholz may

appear to be little more than a sparse collection of feeble shrubs, but these twisted trees are in fact hardy survivors that have adapted to life in one of the harshest environments on earth.

Where is the Continental Divide?

Arch forward in the shower and let the water flow down your back. The spray that hits the left side of your back will run one way, the water on the right the other. What keeps it all from falling in the same direction is your spine. The Continental Divide has a similar effect,

➤ *A stand of krummholz, stunted by cold and gnarled by punishing winds, stubbornly hugs a rugged mountaintop. Even these hardy trees, however, cannot survive the alpine winter unprotected: new shoots that poke above the insulating snowfall will die in the icy winter wind.*

though on an infinitely grander scale. This rugged cordillera, or mountain chain, stretches north to south down the length of the United States from Montana to New Mexico, serving as the continent's backbone and separating the rivers of the East from those of the West.

The Continental Divide actually spans two continents: beginning in Alaska's Brooks Range, it winds its way south to the Strait of Magellan at the tip of South America. In this country the divide encompasses the 60 or so mountain ranges known collectively as the Rocky Mountains. With more than 1,100 peaks above 10,000 feet—53 of

them reaching over 14,000 feet—this mammoth expanse of rock began forming roughly 60 million years ago when seismic pressure forced the earth to uplift.

Unlike a dike that separates two bodies of water, the Continental Divide is not a solid, continuous barrier. There are breaks and faults within the cordillera, and in some places the mountains dip and disappear altogether, as in the low-lying, desertlike Great Divide Basin of southern Wyoming. Despite these gaps the only way for water to get from the west side of the divide to the east, or vice versa, is for someone to carry it.

◄ *The Rocky Mountains comprise only a fraction of the Continental Divide. Twisting its way across North and South America, the divide stretches to a total length of nearly 25,000 miles—greater than the diameter of the earth.*

291

◆ *Despite their arid locale the Chiricahua Mountains of Arizona host an unexpected variety of habitats, including stands of pines, aspens, and Douglas firs at their cool, higher reaches; forests of oaks and walnuts on their slopes; and desert scrub at their base. An elegant trogon (above) avoids desert weather by "island hopping" from mountain to mountain as it works its way north from Mexico.*

What are "islands in the sky"?

In a sense climbing a mountain is like taking a trip toward the North Pole. The steadily cooler and wetter climates at higher elevations duplicate conditions farther and farther north. The 6,684-foot summit of Mount Mitchell in North Carolina is dominated by spruces and firs, a distinctly Canadian plant community. Although slightly lower, Mount Washington in cool New Hampshire rises above the timberline, supporting species more at home on the Arctic tundra.

The contrast is even more pronounced in the Southwest. Great mountain ranges form "islands" of forest in a sea of lowland desert and grasslands, home to marooned plants and animals that sought refuge from increasingly arid conditions following the end of the Ice Age. Such mountains are unusually rich in wildlife, blending different habitats and animal populations from both temperate and subtropical realms. The mountains of southern Arizona—including the Huachucas, Chiricahuas, and Santa Ritas—boast the highest diversity of butterfly species in the United States. Other sky island dwellers include rattlesnakes, red squirrels, and voles.

Birders are drawn to Southwestern mountains by such rarities as Mexican chickadees and the aptly named magnificent hummingbird, all green and purple glitter. In the Chisos Mountains of southwest Texas, which punch up from the Chihuahuan Desert in a crown of pine-rimmed peaks, the attraction is the tiny Colima warbler, a bird whose range barely nudges across the Rio Grande from Mexico—one of many surprising animals surviving in these high-altitude oases.

Why do mountains in the East lack jagged peaks?

Time was when the Appalachians had jagged peaks like those of the Rockies, and a time may come when the Adirondacks will, too. The short, rounded summits of the Appalachians are a matter of old age. They last underwent an upheaval about 200 million years ago, and their origins go back 150 million years before that. Although they once rivaled today's towering Rockies (which at 60 million years old are still in their prime), erosion has long since smoothed the ancient Appalachians down to stubs.

The Adirondacks, on the other hand, are still in their infancy. Formed from a nub on the surface of the Canadian Shield (the billion-year-old basement rock of the North American continent), the Adirondacks were long considered to be geologic old-timers. Recent evidence, however, indicates that the Adirondacks bulged out of the shield no more than 15 million years ago, pushing younger, softer rock above them into a dome, which quickly eroded, leaving the basement rock exposed. Moreover, the Adirondacks seem to be still rising. Will they someday resemble the Rockies? Only time will tell.

Did life return to Mount St. Helens after its eruption?

From the Earth to the Moon is one of Jules Verne's most famous science fiction novels. The title also aptly describes what happened to the lands surrounding Washington's Mount St. Helens when the mountain exploded on May 18, 1980, expelling a glowing cloud of 500°F gas and debris at the speed of a fighter jet. Within seconds millions of trees were splintered or blown flat and vast stretches of green forest disappeared under a blanket of mud and gray ash that reached 600 feet deep in places. Nothing, it seemed, was left alive or would live again in this barren landscape. In an instant the earth had become the moon.

Yet the Roosevelt elks returned to Mount St. Helens soon after the eruption. What happened? First the avalanche of mud and rock triggered by the volcanic blast clogged the Toutle River valley, forming a five-mile-long lake and dozens of ponds—water sources for animals wandering into the blast zone. Also, regrowth occurred much faster than expected. Beneath the thick ash, seeds, roots, stems, and bulbs had survived. Aided by erosion from rains and snowmelt, grasses and flowers that elks love soon broke through the surface. Add to nature's resilience an aggressive reseeding program by man, and you have all the food an elk could want.

◥ *The Great Smoky Mountains of North Carolina shimmer like fire in the golden autumn sun. Once barren, rocky peaks resembling the Alps, these erosion-rounded hills have become a showplace of biological diversity, boasting over 100 species of native trees.*

◥ *The elks that ventured onto Mount St. Helens after the eruption quickly adapted to the lack of tree cover—a reminder that they once lived in open terrain before hunting and human population pressures forced them into forests.*

Freshwater Worlds *Lakes, ponds, wetlands, rivers, and streams*

How were the Great Lakes formed?

With horizons stretching away to oceanlike expanses and surf pounding on their rugged shorelines, the Great Lakes certainly live up to their name. Bordering eight states and one Canadian province, Lakes Erie, Huron, Michigan, Ontario, and Superior make up the largest system of freshwater lakes in the world, covering nearly 81,000 square miles.

Lakes are formed in a variety of ways. Some result from natural or man-made dams on rivers. Others take shape when earthquakes create fissures in the land or when water fills the craters of extinct volcanoes. Still others are created when rivers change course, leaving landlocked

⤷ *Taken from a space shuttle in June, this aerial photograph shows a large portion of the Great Lakes region. Partially hidden by the shuttle's cargo door is Lake Michigan with Chicago visible in the lower left. Warm, moist rising air has created clouds over land areas. Cooler air over the lakes remains cloud free.*

oxbow lakes. The majority of them, however, are produced by glaciers.

Valleys, lakes, and other topographical features had long been attributed to the carving effects of catastrophic floods. Then, in 1848, the Swiss geologist Louis Agassiz accompanied an expedition to the north shore of Lake Superior, where he observed bedrock scored with deep lines, and enormous rocks that had somehow been transported hundreds of miles from the north. This led him to propose that glaciers had once covered much of North America and

gradually gouged and sculpted the land like "God's great plow."

Geologists have since confirmed Agassiz's theory. Most agree he was also correct in reasoning that the Great Lakes were plowed by ice not once but many times, during ice ages lasting thousands of years, when advancing glaciers excavated ancient river valleys into huge lake basins. The first of the glaciers, which retreated some 17,000 years ago, was more than two miles thick and so heavy it caused the land to sink 1,500 feet. When the climate warmed and the ice crept northward, the ground began rebounding, a process that continues to this day. Melting ice filled the new basins with water.

Those original basins, now fertile farmland, were located south of what is now Lake Michigan. As new glaciers advanced, they enlarged the first lakes and deposited piles of debris along their southern shores, blocking streams that had previously drained to the Mississippi River. Eventually, as the lakes grew, a new drainage system opened to the east through the St. Lawrence River. When the last glacier receded about 12,000 years ago, the Great Lakes as we know them were left behind.

How do isolated ponds become populated with plants and animals?

Most of North America's more than 2 million ponds began as hollows carved by glaciers, oxbow lakes cut off from rivers, streams blocked by beaver dams, or depressions left in soluble rock. As water from rainfall, snowmelt, or underground springs collects, the first inhabitants to thrive are the food producers—microscopic one-celled plants whose spores are carried to the pond by wind, rain, or runoff.

More complex plants and animals arrive by water in stream-fed ponds and by air, usually courtesy of ducks and other migrating waterfowl, on whose webbed feet seeds and eggs may hitch a ride. Floating plants like duckweed, water lilies, and bladderwort quickly become established in the open water, while shrimp, fishes, and water insects find plenty to eat among the early colonizers or pioneers.

Over time silt, leaves, and other organic materials wash into the pond, and a gentle rain of tiny dead planktonic organisms drifts downward. The bottom of the pond becomes blanketed with a nutrient-rich muck that provides a foothold for rooted plants with woody stems and leaves growing above the water level. As these plants spread and shed their leaves annually, they speed up the accumulation of decayed material covering the bottom, in turn reducing the oxygen level in the water and killing off many animals. They also lower the pond's water level until the once-oozing edges take on the appearance of solid ground. As the pond shrinks, reeds, bulrushes, and sedges advance relentlessly, filling the deeper water as they go. Over hundreds of years, the pond eventually becomes a marsh before drying up altogether.

Are marshes, swamps, and bogs all the same thing?

Although ecologists now use many different names for wetlands, most people still know these soggy areas simply as marshes, swamps, or bogs. While all three habitats are waterlogged, it is their vegetation that distinguishes one from the other.

Like meadows, marshes are covered with grasses and similar plants. Rushes, cattails, sedges, and other marsh grasses grow only in very wet soil or when partly submerged in water. A marsh can be as small as a roadside ditch or as large as the Florida Everglades.

If a marsh is a flooded meadow, a swamp is a water-soaked forest. Characterized by trees and woody shrubs, swamps are usually found in lowlands, coastal areas, or near slow-moving rivers. They can be flooded by either fresh or salt water and may even dry out for part of the year.

Bogs are common in cold, wet climates where retreating glaciers left steep-sided depressions in poorly drained land. Floating mats of low plants growing inward from the water's edge cover the surface, while peat—a thick layer of partly decayed vegetation—carpets the bottom.

❧ *Wetlands can be divided into three general categories: marshes, swamps, and bogs. Marshes like this saltwater one (lower left) at Bass Harbor, Maine, are covered with various grasses. Swamps like Bald Cypress Bayou (below) in Louisiana are dominated by trees. Bogs, such as the New Jersey Pine Barrens (left), may contain grasses and sphagnum moss.*

hollow stems of the lily and breathe through tubes that reach the thin column of air inside. The metallic, half-inch-long adults repay the plant's unwitting favor by crawling inside its unopened flowers and pollinating them. Later, when the blooms open for other pollinators, it is merely as a backup to the beetle's work.

On every side the lily is besieged with attackers. Aphids suck its sap, while another kind of leaf beetle chews meandering trails through its pads. The lily-leaf caterpillar cuts free a circular piece of the lily and binds it with silk to the pad's underside, neatly hiding itself from view. In response the lily casts off old, nibbled leaves and grows a succession of fresh replacements throughout the summer.

Why are bogs nature's time capsules?

Beasts may not rise from bogs, but they certainly are buried there. Because bog water can preserve things that fall into it for hundreds or even thousands of years, plants and animals—among them humans—that end up in a bog become mummified over time.

Bogs are covered with a vegetation blanket (usually sphagnum moss) that emits a bacteria-killing acid and cuts off air. Without bacteria and oxygen, decay is slowed almost to a stop. As plants blanketing the bog's surface die, they do not fully rot but slowly accumulate on the bottom as peat. Some of these peat beds may be over 45 feet thick and thousands of years old.

While hundreds of preserved human bodies have been found in bogs, one recovered in Titusville, Florida, had something unique—a 7,000-year-old brain containing the earliest samples of human DNA ever found. Another extraordinary find was in a mastodon skeleton taken from an Ohio bog. Near one of the ribs were the partially digested remnants of the animal's last meal, and inside these remains were living, 11,000-year-old bacteria. These bacteria are the oldest living organisms ever discovered. They clearly reveal how much the quiet waters of a bog can tell us about the history of life on our planet.

⬧ Among the most populous freshwater microworlds, the undersides of lily pads and their long stems support a variety of tiny life forms, including pinhead-size water mites (inset). Relatives of spiders, these droll vermilion creatures feed on microscopic plankton animals that live in algae coating the submerged portions of lily pads.

What animals live on the water lily?

Rising from the muddy bottom of a shallow lake cove, the heart-shaped, floating leaves and slender stems of the water lily are a universe of life, both visible and invisible. A host of aquatic creatures live on, under, and within the plant—all dependent upon it for their survival.

Some use the lily pad for anchorage: small freshwater sponges; microscopic filter-feeders such as rotifers; hydras, which look like minute sea anemones; and colonies of bryozoans, known as moss animals for their appearance. Green, fuzzy algae growing on the lily's stems provide grazing for pond snails. Within the fuzz bright-red water mites hunt for even more Lilliputian prey, while up on the pads, green frogs keep watch for damselflies and other insects.

For a suite of insects, the lilies are both food and shelter. The grublike larvae of long-horned leaf beetles bury the tips of their tails in the

Why do some rivers abound with trout while others don't?

Born of springs cold as newly melted snowbanks, a mountain stream flows down slopes shaded by thick woodlands, its churning waters home to colorful native brook trout. Yet when the same stream reaches the valley, placidly meandering between pastures and woodlands, the trout disappear, replaced by chubs, sunfish, bullheads, and rock bass. The change from mountain stream to valley creek involves variations in such factors as water temperature, flow rate, and dissolved oxygen level.

Trout, which require cold, clear water in order to survive, are confined to the chillier, shadier headwaters, while more heat-tolerant species such as catfish and bass dominate in the slower, more turbid, sunnier lowland stretches.

The ideal temperature range for brook trout is 55° to 64°F; water much warmer than 77°F will kill them. (Death comes not only from thermal stress but also from reduced levels of dissolved oxygen, which warm water does not hold as well.) Western rainbow trout are somewhat more tolerant of warmer conditions, preferring streams cooler than 70°F, but are able to survive in water as warm as 80°F or so. Brown trout can handle summer water temperatures up to 86°F, which is why this European import is so widely stocked in valley streams, where rainbow and brook trout cannot live.

Can anything live in the Great Salt Lake?

When trappers first discovered the Great Salt Lake of Utah in the 1820s, they assumed it was somehow linked to the ocean, not realizing that they had stumbled upon a remnant of the Ice Age—an inland sea far saltier than the oceans.

This briny body of water, which has no outlet, is actually fed by freshwater streams and rivers bearing snowmelt out of nearby mountain ranges. Once the water reaches the lake's shallow, alkaline basin, much of it evaporates, leaving behind and concentrating dissolved minerals. Over millennia these mineral salts have built up to levels surpassed only by the Dead Sea (bordered by Israel and Jordan).

So saline is the water that only five plants and animals live in it: two species of algae, the Great Salt Lake brine shrimp, and two species of brine fly larvae.

While these are the only species actually living in the lake—the water is much too salty to support even fishes—they're not the only life forms around. The enormous number of brine flies attracts hungry ducks, grebes, gulls, and phalaropes by the thousands at migration time.

Able to tolerate salty water that would kill all but a handful of aquatic life forms, brine flies (below) teem by the millions in Utah's Great Salt Lake (bottom). They feed on microscopic algae, then transform into clouds of tiny flies known as buffalo gnats.

Why does Minnesota have so many lakes?

➤ *From the air northern Minnesota near the Canadian border is a maze of pristine forests, lakes, islands, bays, and inlets. Two-mile-thick glaciers gouged the lake basins out of the area's ancient bedrock, the southern edge of the 2.7-billion-year-old Canadian shield.*

From an airplane on a sunny day, expanses of the state of Minnesota seem more blue than green, more lake than land. This wealth of water today results from the work done by water in its solid form millennia ago. Minnesota's more than 10,000 sparkling lakes were wrought by Ice Age glaciers that plowed their way across the state in fits and starts between 22,000 and 10,000 years ago.

The glaciers formed these lakes in two principal ways. The Crow Wing galaxy of lakes in the north-central part of the state, for instance, formed when huge amounts of ground-up rock and sediment, called outwash, combined with meltwater from a glacier to surround single, huge, broken-off blocks of ice. When they melted, lakes were born.

Much of the state's most spectacular lake region just below the Canadian border, including the Boundary Waters Canoe Area wilderness, was shaped in quite another way. Here the glaciers carved up some of the most ancient exposed rock on earth, grinding it to dust and carrying away pockets of softer rock. Left behind were basins filled with rainwater and runoff from melting glaciers. Today you can crisscross this nearly 1-million-acre wilderness by making brief canoe portages from lake to lake.

Is quicksand really as dangerous as everyone thinks it is?

Its solid appearance is an illusion. So is the idea that if you put one foot in quicksand, you'll be sucked under, never to be seen again. It happens that way only in the movies. In North America quicksand is rare, but where it does occur, it is the result of an underground spring that has bubbled up into sand. Most quicksand is anywhere from just a few inches deep to less than waist deep, so you're unlikely to drown in it unless you fall in head first. Even if quicksand is more than waist deep, you really can't go under all the way—unless you lose your balance and take a header. That's because quicksand is quite a bit denser than salt water, so you'll actually float in it. The only real problem with quicksand is not that it pulls you down, but that the solid ground you might need to help pull yourself out may be out of reach. If you do happen to step in some, don't panic. Just roll onto your back and try to float to the edge.

Why are there so many oxbow lakes along the Mississippi River?

The lower Mississippi teems with oxbow lakes because the river abounds with meanders, those lazy loops that slow-moving rivers like the Mississippi carve from the landscape as they make their way to the sea. When the meander gets too far off course, the fickle waters may take a straighter route, leaving behind a disconnected lake that recalls an oxbow, the U-shaped harness worn by oxen.

Below Cairo, Illinois, the Ohio River flows into the Mississippi. As it spreads out on the great tabletop of the Mississippi floodplain, the river runs out of steam. Instead of hurtling over or cutting through obstacles, it meanders around them. It jogs in one direction for a while until gravity moves it back toward the centerline of the floodplain. Here it may overshoot, meander in the other direction, and then find its way back to the line. From an airplane the path of a meandering river looks like the S tracks of a downhill skier. As the outside banks erode, these tracks spread wider and rounder. Meanwhile, the inside banks fill in with sediment. With time, erosion, and the accumulation of sediment, a loop may pinch itself off from the river, and the resulting bypassed curve becomes another oxbow lake.

What is the "land of the quaking earth"?

The Okefenokee Swamp on the Georgia-Florida border is a place of haunting beauty. Cypress trees, shrouded with Spanish moss, stand in unbroken formation like a spectral army that stretches on for miles. At night the darkness stirs to a cacophony of frog calls and the roars of alligators. Like ships adrift, small islands of plants float aimlessly across marshes and lakes. If you stamp on the ground, the earth literally quakes like jelly, causing small trees several feet away to tremble discernibly. The name *Okefenokee*, in fact, comes from a Choctaw Indian word meaning "land of the quaking earth"—an apt description of this morass of some 400,000 acres.

Backed up behind a ridge that stretches for 100 miles in a north-south direction, the Okefenokee is actually a great bowl full of peat, a squishy turf that is far less firm than ordinary ground. A million or so years ago, when sea levels were higher than they are today, this land was under the ocean. During the Ice Ages the sea retreated, and the Okefenokee was born. Exactly how is a matter of some conjecture. One theory is that seawater trapped behind the ridge became a freshwater lake, which filled in with dead vegetation that turned to peat. Another suggests that when glaciers held sway to the north, the Okefenokee was already a soggy landscape with myriad streams, and its peat was formed when the climate warmed up.

~ *Palmettos and bald cypress trees are reflected in the still waters of Georgia's Okefenokee Swamp. Shakily rooted in peat, even the larger trees vibrate when passersby stomp the ground. The swamp harbors an incredible variety of wildlife, including 210 different bird species, 60 reptile species, and 41 mammals.*

> ～ A 70-foot beaver dam on Minnesota's St. Croix River created a large pond. Built of sticks, logs, stones, and mud, beaver dams are usually located along the narrowest sections of rivers where water flow is relatively fast, the banks are firm, and a number of favorite food trees are nearby. In one year a single beaver may cut down more than 200 trees.

How do beavers alter the land?

Equipped with sharp teeth and superb skills for arranging sticks, beavers are unmatched among wild animals in their ability to mold the environment to suit their needs. A beaver dam turns a fast-flowing stream into a placid pond—a place of refuge for these aquatic rodents, North America's largest (they can weigh up to 60 pounds and measure four feet long). But a beaver dam does much more than that. It radically alters the stream and the surrounding forest, setting off a cycle of change that lasts a century or more.

Built of thousands of logs, sticks, and layers of mud, a beaver dam may stretch beyond a quarter mile in length, but most are less than 100 feet wide. The pond floods the neighboring forest, giving the beavers easy access to such favorite trees as aspen and birch (they eat the juicy inner bark, not the wood itself). At first the pond provides a rich feeding ground for trout, but as the shade trees are cut and the water temperature rises, the pond becomes home to warm-water fish, such as bullheads and sunfish. When enough silt collects behind the dam, marsh plants intrude, attracting nesting waterfowl, rails, and grebes; with time the pond fills completely, creating a wet meadow for grazers like deer and elk. Eventually the forest returns—perhaps to attract a new colony of beavers, which starts the cycle once again.

> ～ A beaver ferries an aspen branch across a pond. In late September and October, beavers drag tree branches close to the entrances of their lodges, piling the branches on top of one another until they sink to the bottom to form a submerged food stash.

Why do some lakes teem with life while others don't?

Fill a glass from a cold, deep lake, and you can see right through it. Try the same at the edge of a warm, shallow one, and you'll think twice about drinking. But this murky water's the real thing to the lake's plants and animals.

Warm, shallow lakes that are the color of tea contain large numbers of phytoplankton, microscopic organisms that carry on photosynthesis. Sunlight (which reaches down to the muddy bottom) and convection currents (which circulate dissolved minerals and carbon dioxide) enable and encourage the phytoplankton to photosynthesize. The more phytoplankton, the more life a lake can support, because these tiny organisms feed larger ones, which, in turn, feed still larger creatures, from insects to fishes to birds. Warm-water lakes, therefore, have a variety and abundance of life, including such species as minnow, pike, pickerel, perch, bass, and catfish.

Cold, deep lakes with sparkling clear water, on the other hand, contain fewer dissolved minerals. The sun warms only the top layer of water, which is separated from the mud on the bottom by cold water. Relatively little phytoplankton grows in these lakes, and thus only a few species of fish—salmon, trout, and whitefish—abound.

What lives in cattail marshes?

To the muskrat, the "little beaver" of the Algonquians, the cattails that grow in freshwater marshes throughout North America are everything in life. Given its choice of food, a muskrat will eat only tender cattail shoots and even build a home from the plant's stalks. Ironically, the muskrat's harvesting of cattails tends to break the plant's usual monopoly on a wetland, creating a more varied landscape of sinkholes, hummocks, and patches of bare soil. This, in turn, transforms the marsh into a home for a variety of plants and animals—animals that don't live by cattails alone.

Only a few other large animals like living among cattails. Eastern redwing and western yellow-headed blackbirds build nests in the upper stems; the least bittern builds a platform nest of old stalks; and the Virginia rail breeds in dense stands. Water snakes use the cover cattails provide when stalking frogs, and they bask for long periods of time in the sunny openings.

How do animals survive in strong currents?

A mountain stream engorged with snowmelt barrels down a hillside with enough force to knock a person down. Life within such a maelstrom seems inconceivable; yet many tiny animals thrive in this tumult. Flattened to a bizarre degree, the nymphs of mayflies scramble beneath rocks. Other aquatic insects, including stoneflies, take a rock-hugging approach, while the maggotlike larvae of blackflies attach to rocks with abdominal suction discs. Caddisfly larvae shield themselves with glued-together cases of twigs or tiny pebbles and cling tenaciously to the bottom; other caddis nymphs cement their homes in place, weaving silken nets to seine food particles from the current. All these aquatic insects benefit also from the boundary layer—a thin zone of quiet water that extends a fraction of an inch above the bottom.

Larger animals take advantage of shelter too. Trout rest behind rocks, fallen trees, and submerged roots—ready to dash into the flow when food washes by, then return to a quiet eddy. But the oddest strategy may be that of the tailed frog's tadpole, which uses its huge mouth as a suction cup, adhering tightly even to rocks of roaring waterfalls.

Caddisfly larva

Caddisfly

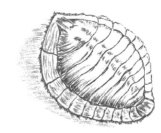

Water penny larva

water penny beetle

A fast-flowing stream (left) appears to be a difficult place to live, but some insects have found ways to survive in strong currents. The larva of the caddisfly (top) protects its soft body in rushing water with a neatly cemented case of sand and small pebbles. The larva of the water penny (above), a small land-dwelling beetle, uses its shell-like body as a suction cup to cling to rocks.

How are waterfalls formed?

To the casual eye, the contest between moving water and solid, impassive stone seems no contest at all. Over time, however, the erosive water always wins—gouging quickly where the rock is soft shale or sandstone, and nibbling slowly where it is hard granite or dolomite. Most waterfalls are born in this manner, from the delicate silver threads that lace the Appalachians to Niagara's tumultuous expanse.

In the Shenandoah Mountains of Virginia, a stream tumbles down a rugged slope in a series of rapids. Beneath the water lies greenstone—a tough, metamorphosed lava that easily resists the stream's erosive force. The water, however, finds a chink in the mountain's armor, a gap where soft sandstone peeks out from beneath the greenstone. Eventually the water wears away the sandstone to form a steadily deepening depression, and so a waterfall is created as the stream races over the lip of hard strata and plummets into the ever-growing "plunge hole" below. Yet waterfalls are not permanent; they migrate upstream as the falling water wears away the softer sediment beneath the falls, eating at the underpinnings of the more resistant rock. Over the past 11,000 years, Niagara has crept 7 miles in this fashion up the Niagara River, and it won't stop until it reaches Lake Erie, 20 miles away.

Some waterfalls have a different genesis. The majestic 2,425-foot drop of Yosemite Falls in Yosemite National Park—the highest falls in North America—was shaped by glaciers, which tore away the side of the mountain. Now Yosemite Creek vaults into the air, shattering into a spectacular mist nearly half a mile below.

At the head of the so-called Grand Canyon of the Yellowstone, the Yellowstone River plunges 308 feet, creating a mist that glimmers with rainbows on sunny days. Spray-nurtured mosses swathe the canyon's perpetually damp lower walls.

Why are the Everglades unique?

Pa-hay-okee, the Seminole Indians called it: "Grassy Waters." Stretching more than 100 miles south from Lake Okeechobee, the Everglades once covered nearly 3 million acres of southern Florida. Through this two-dimensional world of flat horizons and swaying green sawgrass flows a unique river of crystalline water 50 miles wide but only inches deep—a one-of-a-kind ecosystem blending elements of the temperate and tropical worlds, home to animals and plants found nowhere else in North America.

Water is the Everglades' lifeblood, and before humans built levees and canals to control it, the water traveled in a wide, unbroken sheet from the deep interior of the state to shallow Florida Bay. Nonetheless, the Kissimmee River still fills Okeechobee's bowl to the brim, and the water still spills over the shores of the lake. Seeping south and west in a gentle current, it slips noiselessly through head-high stands of sawgrass that thrive in the clear, nutrient-poor liquid.

Apple snails, brown as mud and the size of golf balls, creep through the submerged stems of sawgrass, the only prey of endangered hawks called snail kites, which pry the mollusks from their shells with long, curved beaks. The gangle-legged wading birds known as limpkins also feast on apple snails, making the night shiver with their plaintive, lost-child cries. Like the kite, the limpkin sports a long bill well suited to a diet of snails, its tip curves a bit to the right, a perfect angle for sliding inside a coiled shell.

Where the ground rises just a few inches, the sawgrass gives way to hammocks, islands of Caribbean hardwoods, such as mahogany, festooned with bromeliads, orchids, and other epiphytes—plants that take their nourishment from the rain, air, and sunlight. Along the coast dense tangles of mangroves provide protection for endangered American crocodiles and pastel-pink flocks of roseate spoonbills, one of more than 300 species of birds that nest here. Gentle manatees drift in the warm bay waters, and panthers still prowl the sawgrass and hammocks, which rumble with the throaty bellows of 15-foot bull alligators searching for mates in this wondrously diverse environment.

What draws migrating birds to the Mississippi River basin?

Each autumn, millions of waterfowl—ducks, geese, and swans—fly south above the Mississippi basin, filling the skies with flashing wings and riotous noise. The Mississippi is the most heavily used of the four travel routes, or flyways, followed by North America's waterfowl. (The others are the Atlantic, Pacific, and Central, this last extending down the eastern edge of the Rocky Mountains.) The great river system provides convenient resting sites, wetlands brimming with food, and man-made meals in the form of corn, wheat, and other crops planted on the farms along its banks.

Dozens of avian species use the river basin as a highway. Mallards and wood ducks are among the most common, mingling with blue-winged teal and pintails. Geese abound, including Canada geese, white-fronted geese, and blizzards of snow geese from the Arctic. These and many other varieties throng south along the Mississippi River, ending their journey in the warm winter rice fields, salt marshes, and wooded swamps along the Gulf of Mexico.

❧ Sustained by a slough of fresh water that creeps along at one foot per minute, the Big Cypress National Preserve adjacent to Everglades National Park is part of the Everglades ecosystem—vast grassy flats dotted with cypress hammocks, towering palm trees, pine-shaded sand bars, and mangrove thickets.

Sandy and Rocky Coastlines *Living life on the edge*

How do ocean waves and currents form island beaches?

The barrier islands that fringe much of the coast of the United States, especially those found from Cape Cod to Texas, are the result of an endless game of give and take played between the sea and shore.

As waves crash onto the beach, they scoop up sand, which is then suspended in the churning shallows. If the waves strike the shore at an angle, they create a longshore current when deflected back to the sea, which runs parallel to

~ *Despite their shifting shorelines, sand barriers like Horn Island off the Mississippi coast are stable enough to support a wide variety of residents, including alligators, ospreys, raccoons, bald eagles, and sea turtles.*

the land. This type of current acts as an aquatic conveyer belt, ferrying the suspended sand for miles (a process called littoral drift) and depositing it on sheltered beaches, where the gentle surf cannot whisk it away. Bluffs at the eastern tip of New York's Long Island, for example, supplied the sand that was swept westward to build the beaches of Fire Island, a barrier stretching more than 90 miles. As littoral drift carries away sand, it shrinks, or erodes, a barrier at the updrift end of the current while building one up at the downdrift end. When barrier islands lie in a chain, longshore currents transfer sand from one to another, so one barrier's loss is another's

gain. The traffic in sand along some barriers can be immense. In the Cape Hatteras area, for instance, littoral drift carries as much as 1 million cubic yards of sand per year—enough to erect a sand castle the size of a football field and more than 450 feet high.

Are animals affected by tides?

Standing on its head while kicking food into its mouth, the barnacle has been likened to an upside-down shrimp encased within a cuplike shell. Unlike shrimp and lobsters, which can move about freely to find their meals, barnacles live at the shoreline with their heads firmly affixed to such hard surfaces as rocks, jetties, and piers, and must wait for the tide to bring food to them. Once the tide rises and covers the barnacle with water, it opens the lid of its shell, extends its feathery limbs, and sweeps up the tiny animals and plants on which it feeds. When the tide recedes, the barnacle clamps the lid shut, sealing in water from which its gills can extract oxygen while it remains high and dry.

Many other marine animals also time their lives to the twice-daily rise and fall of the tides. Salt marsh snails, unlike barnacles, get their oxygen from the air, with lungs. When the tide floods the marsh, the snails must ascend tall vegetation to reach a point above high water. Blue mussels, which live exclusively in the intertidal zone, open their shells to feed only if they are underwater: when the tide sweeps in, bringing freshly oxygenated water, and when it retreats, carrying food particles (such as decaying marsh plants). Fiddler crabs, on the other hand, are inactive during high tide—they hunker down inside their burrows on mud flats and emerge to feed when the water ebbs.

Some creatures attune themselves to longer tidal cycles. Horseshoe crabs, not true crabs but relatives of spiders and scorpions, mate on the beach during the high spring tide, leaving their eggs under the sand. The ebbing tide deposits more sand over the eggs, protecting the developing embryos until they are ready to hatch—just in time for the next spring tide, which breaks open the eggs and sweeps the young crabs out to sea.

Can plants help sand dunes grow larger?

It happens twice a day. The tide ebbs and the surf slides down the beach, allowing the breeze to dry the sand and carry the tiniest grains up to the dunes, swirling and skittering. If there were nothing to stop this hopscotch, the "Seaview Drive" along every coast would be covered with sand drifting its way inland.

Fortunately, sand dunes, formed with the help of pebbles and plants, act as barriers. Something as small as a pebble or as wispy as a thin blade of grass can break the stream of wind and cause it to drop its burden of sand. Grain by grain, sand accumulates into a tiny mound on the pebble's leeward side. On this dunelet a seed or a fragment of dune grass finds an opportunity to sink roots—and does so with astounding speed.

The grass grows into a bouquet of pointed, vertical blades that droop to all sides, like a fountain of frozen green water. When the sun is high, each long blade folds along its length, minimizing the area exposed to the baking rays. Long parallel ridges on the inner surface of the blade press together, like the squeezed pleats of an accordion, tightly sealing its moisture-breathing pores from the wind's prying fingers.

Dune grass holds onto the sand with the same tenacity. Like pebbles, though far more effective, the dune grass becomes a wind stopper, preventing the wind from sweeping the sand inland and the dunes into oblivion. As the dune grows, so does the dune grass, snaking horizontal roots every which way beneath the sand and sprouting tufts of grass every few inches. With every new clump there is a fresh rash of roots, until eventually a living lattice stitches the sand in place.

Most dune areas have their own roster of sand-entrenched plant life. Dune grasses' counterpart in the south is the endangered sea oats, a stout-stemmed spikegrass topped with large flowering clusters. Other dune plants include dusty miller, beach heather, seabeach goldenrod, and sea rocket. Together these sand stoppers help make dunes out of pebble-size mounds.

~ *Marsh periwinkles, stranded above the ebbing tide, cling precariously to stalks of cordgrass. This gilled saltwater snail uses a leathery pad at the bottom of its foot (called an operculum) to seal moisture in its shell while it awaits the return of high tide.*

~ *Sea oats is known as a pioneer species because it is often the first plant to colonize and stabilize a sand dune, allowing weaker plants to take root and thrive. The plant's flower heads, which resemble those of cultivated oats, give sea oats its name.*

◆ *Fiery starfish and emerald sea anemones ring a tidepool on the Washington shore. Similar scenes dot the entire rocky West Coast, where tidepools are home to mussels, clams, sponges, and algae. Along the Mid-Atlantic and Southeastern shoreline, where long, sandy stretches dominate, tidepools are much less common.*

What are the risks of living in a tidepool?

Like a soufflé, the sealife contained in a tidepool depends on just the right blend of ingredients and the proper temperature to be successful. Add too much or too little salt or allow the water to overheat or evaporate, and the recipe is easily ruined.

Tidepools are formed along rocky shores when water is trapped in depressions after the tide recedes. Pacific coast tidepools are among the richest in the temperate zone because of their close proximity to upwellings of nutrient-rich bottom waters, freedom from ice in winter, and frequent coastal fogs that shade them in summer. These seaside pockets of salt water support a wealth of ocean species, including hermit crabs, tubeworms, sea slugs, and brittlestars.

Despite these nurturing conditions, tidepools also pose some unique hazards. Changing tides can leave their inhabitants high and dry or drowning in too much water. On a summer's day when the sun beats down, the water temperature in a tidepool can reach 100°F or more. Heat isn't the only problem: as the temperature rises, the oxygen streams out of the tidepool in a trail of bubbles. Without waves to bring in more oxygen, animals risk suffocation. Finally, fluctuating salt levels in a tidepool, due to evaporation or rainfall, can be fatal to ocean creatures suited only to a specific range of salinity.

Many tidepool species have adapted in order to survive. Sea anemones bunch together to reduce their exposure to evaporation. Chitons, periwinkles, and other sea snails draw in their opercula—a hard, tough plug on the foot—to make their shells watertight. An oyster produces some 500 million eggs a year, only one of which need survive the ebb and flow of the tides to guarantee the future of its species.

Is the sea level rising?

Fishermen trawling the cold Atlantic off the coast of New England sometimes find an unexpected haul in their nets: massive fossilized teeth of Ice Age mammoths and mastodons. They are powerful reminders that the world's sea levels were once much lower—back when Asia and Alaska were connected by a thousand-mile-wide land bridge and dry land extended from the Outer Banks to Newfoundland. Just 20,000 years ago ice sheets bound up so much water that ocean levels were as much as 350 feet lower than they are today.

When the glaciers melted, the continental shelf—the gently sloping margin that surrounds much of North America—was flooded. In fact, the sea is still rising, at a rate estimated between half an inch and two inches per decade—whether from man-made climate changes, poorly understood natural cycles, or both, no one is certain. Whatever the cause, the implications for low-lying coastal cities are ominous.

Which plants live between the high and low tide marks?

Although hardy plants such as kelp and surf-grass cling defiantly to wave-splashed rocks along many coasts, one must look to quiet bays and gentle estuaries protected from the battering surf to find the richest examples of intertidal plant life. In these sheltered areas that straddle the sea and shore, salt marshes support vast and varied plant communities. Large marshes can be found along Chesapeake Bay, the Mississippi River delta, and San Francisco Bay.

The dominant plants in most salt marshes are stiff, sturdy cordgrasses, especially smooth cord-grass in the East and Pacific cordgrass in the West. To counter the high salt content of seawater, cordgrass developed glands to excrete the salt, which forms tiny white crystals on its leaves. Another plant, ditchgrass, is so effective at expelling excess salt that it can thrive on tidal flats where evaporation increases the salinity of pooled water threefold or more.

Other marsh plants, especially succulents such as the sea-blite on the West Coast and the seaside orache in the East, are able to tolerate the salt, storing seawater in their fleshy leaves and stems to weather the drought of low tide.

In southern Florida and other parts of the Gulf Coast, ocean shores are occupied by another type of tidal plant community: swamp forests of mangroves. Like some marsh grasses, these tropical trees survive in their seaside habitat by excreting harmful salt. Salinity actually helps mangroves by eliminating salt-intolerant plants that could otherwise outcompete them in the nutrient-rich coastal soils.

Why is life so abundant in salt marshes?

Acre for acre, a salt marsh in Georgia contains as much plant and animal life as an Amazon rain forest. This may seem odd for a landscape of tall grasses that is flooded with seawater twice a day, but the rising tides bring nutrients to plants growing in the area, while receding tides carry out the plant matter to feed the shrimp, snails, crabs, fishes, and other aquatic life that thrive in this ecosystem.

Estimates show that the coastal marshes of Long Island, New York, produce over 100,000 tons of plant life each year. A 10-square-foot patch of salt marsh can contain as many as 4,000 ribbed mussels, 2,000 snails, and 200 fiddler crabs. With so many plants and small creatures to eat, wildlife flourishes. The diamondback terrapin, clapper rail, marsh wren, and rice rat are all permanent residents, as is the muskrat, a stocky, two-foot-long rodent that glides through the marsh with thrusts of its flat, scaly tail. Muskrats use reeds and grasses to construct dome-shaped lodges that rise from the shallows like huge, thatched turtlebacks.

Other animals are only visitors, coming and going with the tide. Crabs and fishes venture into the marsh with the rising water, while shorebirds such as egrets and herons search for food on mud flats exposed at low tide.

⬳ Thick carpets of cordgrass and other salt marsh plants prevent erosion and stabilize shorelines better than dikes and sea walls erected by humans. Instead of stopping the sea in its tracks, tidal plants calm waves by letting the water dissipate slowly around them.

⬳ Coast to coast, the salt marshes of North America echo with the chattering call of the clapper rail, a reclusive bird that is often heard but rarely seen. Aiding the rails' secretive nature is gray-brown plumage that renders the birds all but invisible among the grass and reeds of the marsh.

Haystack Rock, a giant sea stack, looms darkly on Oregon's Cannon Beach. The world's third-largest coastal monolith, it rises 235 feet high. Surrounded by tidepools brimming with barnacles, starfish, and anemones, it is also a designated wildlife sanctuary. Gulls and tufted puffins, colorful birds with white faces and orange bills, nest atop the rock in summer.

Why are sea stacks found off the Pacific coast?

You can see it happen from any vista along California's Shoreline Highway. After a long journey across the ocean, rolling swells of seawater encounter the rising seafloor along the Pacific coast. They rear up until gravity causes them to crest and crash, hurling their fury against the sheer walls of the North American continent. These dramatic cliffs, the result of abrupt faulting and uplift of the land, are kept sheer by the constant assault of foaming waves. Where rocks are softer, the edge of the continent has eroded, or "walked," eastward, and only the hardest igneous rocks, such as granites and basalts, remain to jut into the sea. Sea stacks, those photogenic towers of rock standing separate from the shore, are isolated outposts of this resistant rock, holdouts against the pounding sea.

The geologic carving that produces sea stacks and arches is gradual but grueling. Rocks are continually scoured by sand particles suspended in the water. As waves slap the stone surface, the sheer force of the rushing water can split rocks that have already developed vulnerable fracture lines during previous aquatic encounters. As these cracks widen, whole pieces of rock are plucked out like teeth from a jaw during storms. The loosed rocks, massing at the base of the cliff, are hurled back wave by wave, hammering their way inland. Eventually a horizontal sea cave is formed, causing the overhanging lip of rock to calve like a glacier. Calving creates a large rubble heap at the base, which, over time, will be pounded into sand, then whisked off to a quiet scallop of beach.

The fact that the Atlantic seaboard is dominated by sandy beaches does not mean that the erosion there is in its final stages. Because of the more gradual submergence of the continent's edges, most Eastern beaches have always sloped toward the sea, presenting little resistance to wave action. The mountainous Pacific edge, by contrast, has always been a war zone—a place where surf meets stone, and sea stacks tower, delaying their inevitable surrender to the ocean's relentless force.

How do shorebirds hunt for their food?

While humans flock to the ocean's edge in search of sunny summer fun, birds are attracted to coastlines for other reasons—especially food. For birds, seaside living offers up a smorgasbord of edible delights, and each species joins the feast in its own unique way.

Moving with the mechanical precision of wind-up toys, sanderlings skitter in time with the rise and fall of the waves. These tiny shorebirds favor long, unbroken stretches of sand, claiming the tide line as their favored hunting grounds. There they probe the sand with stubby beaks, chasing the waves to snatch tiny crustaceans or grunion eggs uncovered by the tumbling water.

Along the Pacific and Gulf coasts is an equally interesting seaside diner: the short-billed dowitcher. Despite its name the dowitcher is equipped with a four-inch needle of a beak, which lets it pluck worms, snails, and other creatures from beneath the surface of coastal mudflats. The bird uses its long beak to pepper the ground with a barrage of vertical jabs, loosening the mud and making it easier to remove its wriggling victims. To locate unseen prey, the dowitcher's bill is equipped with sensory organs that allow it to feel animals buried in mud.

Found on rocky beaches along both coasts, the ruddy turnstone earned its name for its unusual hunting method. Aided by powerful neck muscles, turnstones use their stout, pointed bills as levers to flip, or turn over, stones in search of hidden insects and crustaceans. Sometimes a few birds will even cooperate to upend larger obstacles such as dead fish or heavy mats of seaweed. Don't let the turnstone's name fool you, however; these resourceful birds can also use their tough, upturned bills to crack open barnacles and tern eggs or dig for buried prey.

A willet (above) forages for food on the Gulf coast. Named for their distinctive cry, which sounds like pill-will-willet, *willets frequent coastal mud or sand flats, where they often wade stomach-deep into the surf to seek out worms, crabs, mollusks, and small fish.*

Why are beaches different colors?

There are countless types of sand, their nature determined by the minerals of which they are formed—and one of the characteristics that differentiates them is color. The white sands of beaches in the Florida Keys, for instance, are mostly calcium carbonate, from seashells that have been pulverized by wave action.

Quartz also produces white sand—a hard-packed variety that comprises more than half the beaches on the Atlantic seaboard. Surprisingly, the quartz grains in beaches from New England to the Middle Atlantic states originated in the northern Appalachians, while those on the shores of Florida came from the southern Appalachians and the Piedmont region of the Carolinas. Pulverized by erosion aeons ago, the quartz was washed out to sea and carried south by shore-hugging currents before being deposited along the coast.

Sand from other minerals often lace these predominantly quartz beaches with dashes of color: red from garnet and black from magnetite. Both are heavier than quartz, which can be blown about by wind, and so are usually deposited by water below the high tide mark, as were the streaks of red and pink that enliven the beaches of Long Island, New York. Many volcanic islands are ringed with another type of black sand, formed from hardened lava that has been crushed to powder by the pounding surf.

Which animals live in the kelp forests?

Kelp forests are like rain forests; they teem with animal life from top to bottom. Strangely, these fast-sprouting plant giants that can grow 2 feet per day and reach 200 feet in height aren't trees at all—they're algae.

As in many forests, the floor of the kelp forest has the greatest abundance and diversity of inhabitants. Flowerlike anemones, spiny sea urchins, kelp crabs, and snails cling and scuttle among the rocks. The most famous of the snails is the abalone, a shelled gastropod that can reach 11 inches long and whose tasty meat is considered a delicacy by sea otters and humans alike. Abalone come in three varieties—black, green, and red—named for the color of their shells.

Caves and crevices house other residents, including the moray eel. The moray looks like a snake but is really a long, bony fish. Constantly opening and closing its toothy maw has earned the moray a nasty reputation, but the reclusive eel is simply forcing water over its gills.

Bottom fish feed among the rocks and ledges. One of the most colorful is the bright orange garibaldi. This submarine farmer cultivates a favored type of algae on rock gardens, weeding out unwanted varieties with its teeth. Hiding among the kelp blades overhead is the painted greenling, a seven-inch-long fish distinguished by its blood-red vertical bars, and the California sheephead, a bucktoothed spiny wrasse.

Which seashells are you most likely to find where?

For all their fanciful variations in shape, color, and pattern, it's easy to forget that the empty shells that wash up along the shore once served as armor for soft-bodied mollusks. The coastal habitat determines which shells a collector is most likely to find there.

Along open, sandy shores, where the landscape offers little protection from predators, many shelled mollusks make their homes right under our feet. Pastel pink tellins, twisting, tapered augers, and knife-edged razor clams are just a few of the treasures that lie buried beneath the beach, their tide-line hideouts revealed only by delicate feeding tubes that poke tentatively above the sand.

On rough, rocky shores, shells don dark hues to match wave-washed surroundings where the biggest problem is often simply hanging on. Mussels and other bivalves secrete byssal threads (rootlike hairs that anchor them tightly to hard surfaces), while keyhole limpets, resembling miniature volcanoes in their cone-shaped shells, grip rocks with powerful feet. Other mollusks, such as angel wings and piddocks, actually bore into rock, clay, and other materials, making them tricky targets for predators and shell collectors alike.

Warm, southern seas are home to many marvelous shells tucked snugly between knobs of coral. Coming in a vast array of colors, cowries and miters are among the most delightful and abundant of reef shells.

~ *While mollusk shells are found in all the world's oceans, the most exquisite are found in warm, shallow waters—such as these from the coast of Florida. In cold northern waters dull, colorless shells are more common.*

What drowned Maine's coastline?

The jagged coast that Maine presents to the Atlantic Ocean is the result of the heavy hand of ice. The immense weight of Ice Age glaciers, which reached a thickness of 9,000 feet, pressed down upon Maine's mountainous interior, causing the ground to sink more than 1,000 feet and slant toward the sea.

~ *Once perched high atop a hill, these granite slabs now skirt the drowned shoreline of Acadia National Park.*

When the glaciers began to melt about 12,000 years ago, the sea started its steady march inland, creeping up river valleys, isolating mountains from the mainland, and flooding the coastline to a depth of nearly 300 feet. Relieved of its icy burden, the land rose slightly and pushed the sea back, but not completely. The coast was left partially flooded, or "drowned." Granite ridges were now rockbound headlands; former river valleys became fjordlike inlets; and countless hills and mountains formed a maze of islands—all remnants of a landscape once high and dry.

How does shore life hang on in the pounding surf?

Each wave that crashes into the tidal zone is like an energetic catering crew, deluging guests with a smorgasbord of floating plankton and other edibles and then whisking away the leftovers. The feast is fantastic, provided you can keep your place at the table.

One way to stay put is to manufacture your own adhesive, as the acorn barnacle and the blue mussel do. The mussel's adhesive is notable because it works underwater: molecules bond with rocks and other hard surfaces. So strong are these bioadhesives that some chemical companies are researching the possible use of such natural glues in dentistry, boat repair (on the sea), and rust-free car paint.

If a marine creature can't make glue, it helps to own a suction cup. The tortoiseshell limpet uses its suctionlike mouthpart to adhere to a surface while it slowly scours algae off the rock.

When all else fails, some animals duck under tangles of kelp and rockweed for shelter, as does the ocher sea star (a starfish). Keeping the plants in place are rootlike holdfasts that claw their way around rocks, if they can find one. In the scramble for space, an unoccupied rock can be hard to come by. That's why the sea palm often roots down on a mussel shell instead of a rock. If the mussel gets torn loose by the tide, a space opens on the rock, giving the sea palm's progeny (grown from spores) a place to get established.

➤ *Waves, like those that slam into the coast of northern California (top), pose little problem to the clawlike holdfasts of sugar wrack and other kelps (inset). Only the most powerful waves will loosen the plants, which seem to have melted into the rock.*

Why do seabirds nest on remote cliffs and islands?

With tens of thousands of screaming, squabbling birds crammed into every ledge and cranny, a seabird nesting colony looks like a layer cake gone mad. The murres, puffins, kittiwakes, and others that populate these packed avian cities do so not out of sociability but for safety. On the sheer cliffs they are safe from terrestrial predators like foxes, and with a solid wall at their backs, they are more secure from airborne assault by gulls, jaegers, and other egg thieves.

In most huge breeding colonies, each species has its own distinct zone, so neatly segregated that they are easily visible from a distance—the layer of seething white midway up the cliff is composed of the delicate, ivory-colored gulls known as kittiwakes; above is the somber black of the murres and razorbills, looking vaguely penguinlike with their stiff, upright stance and charcoal-and white plumage. (Murres prefer wide, interconnected ledges where they can gather by the hundreds, while razorbills are more stand-offish, taking the isolated knobs and crannies.) Puffins and storm petrels nest at the top, where there is enough soil to dig burrows.

Like their cliff-dwelling brethren, island birds choose nesting grounds for their isolation. Remote offshore islands, free of mammalian predators, provide the ultimate in avian security. Bonaventure Island off Quebec's Gaspé Peninsula supports the world's largest colony of northern gannets, dramatic white seabirds that plunge into the sea like lances, hunting for fish. The Farallons, about 30 miles off San Francisco, harbor more than 2 million seabirds, including the dove-size Cassin's auklet, storm petrels, and murres, while even larger colonies dot the Pribilof and Aleutian islands of Alaska.

Human intervention, however, began to take its toll on these once pristine avian edens. Many Alaskan islands, for example, were stocked with foxes, which in turn decimated bird populations, pushing the Aleutian Canada goose to near extinction. All hope is not lost, though. Since the 1970s a few islands have been cleared of foxes, and the geese were reintroduced. Happily, they are doing well.

◄ *While kittiwakes (left) gather seaweed to build their nests, most cliff dwellers dispense with such luxuries. More typical is the behavior of the common murre, whose single egg is laid directly on the rock; its pronounced pyramid shape helps keep it from rolling off its ledge.*

What creatures make those tiny holes in sand dunes?

Beneath the surf-cooled feet of beach-combers, there is a hidden city revealed only by telltale holes in the sand that pop and bubble as the sea retreats. Along the surf line some of the holes are the hunting lairs of half-inch-long mole crabs. These droplet-shaped crabs stay hidden in their burrows while a wave breaks overhead. Then, as the glassy sheet of water slips back to sea, they make their move. In the blink of an eye, dozens of crabs raise their feathery antennas to "comb" microscopic plants and animals from the spent wave. Mission accomplished, they quickly dig back into the sand, racing to disappear before the beaks of sanderlings pluck them from their hideaways. Their ducking movement is so quick that you may almost think it's an illusion brought on by the sun and salt.

In the sand dunes farther up the beach, another speedster awaits if you are lucky enough to see the shy ghost crab scramble from its hole. This nocturnal four-inch-wide crab scuttles down to the sea sideways, then digs in its heels just above the wave line. Eventually a wave large enough to reach it will coat the crab with water, allowing it to refill a chamber that keeps its breathing gills moist. Carrying this bit of sea inside, it will scurry back to its duneside den.

◄ *A reclusive ghost crab peers over the rim of its burrow with eyes that bob on stalks like living periscopes. If the coast is clear, it will make a break for the surf.*

Wonders of the Open Sea *Exploring the deep*

What kind of animals live in coral reef communities?

A coral reef is "fish city," but the most important animals of the biological community it supports are the creatures that build the reef itself—coral polyps. Reef-building polyps are tiny relatives of jellyfish that secrete lime to form a protective cup around their soft bodies; many are no bigger than the period at the end of this sentence. As polyps die, leaving behind their hard limestone shells, new generations build upon the old, layer after layer, until they form massive underwater structures that provide housing for myriads of marine creatures and, for some of them, a source of food.

and holes, hiding from their arch enemy, the octopus. Small octopuses, in turn, may scuttle into an opening in the coral when pursued by a moray eel, a fish whose snakelike body is perfectly adapted to slithering through the reef. It is the variety of fishes, however, that gives coral reefs their distinctive personality. Hour by hour, squadrons of small fishes—butterflyfish, angelfish, wrasses, and many more—perform a gorgeous aquatic ballet in and around the reef. On a healthy reef such creatures create a constantly moving kaleidoscope of color as they look for food and try to avoid being eaten.

Where does the salt in the ocean come from?

If you could take all the salt in the ocean and shake it evenly across the continents, you would have a layer 500 feet thick. You would also be putting some of it back where it came from. The ocean is a giant catch basin for all rivers; everything that washes downstream eventually winds up there, including salt and other minerals found in rocks. These compounds are released into snowmelt and rainwater when mountains erode. The rocks that lie beneath the ocean bottom are the other principal source of salt.

On average the amount of salt contained in seawater is 35 parts per 1,000, or roughly one ounce per quart of water. Some parts of the ocean, however, are saltier than others. Salinity in the Atlantic near Florida measures 37.5 parts per 1,000, while in the Pacific off Alaska, it averages 34. Water is less salty where large quantities of fresh water are supplied by excessive snowfall and melting glaciers. The amount of salt that enters the ocean is counterbalanced by that which is lost by being absorbed by plants and animals and by being trapped in bottom sediments. So while salt is continually washing into the ocean, the salinity of the sea remains fairly constant.

Reef-building corals live only in warm, crystal-clear water less than 250 feet deep. In North America they concentrate in the waters off southern Florida, where snorkelers may glimpse such aquatic beauties as crinoids, or sea lilies (above), and blue hamlets (right).

Coral polyps are colorful creatures that resemble tiny flowers. As millions of polyps sweep their tentacles through the water in search of a meal, they transform the surface of the reef into a multihued carpet of color. Coral reefs are honeycombed with crevices, tunnels, and caves where a dazzling variety of marine animals takes shelter. Sea urchins nestle in crannies. Spiny lobsters and crabs hunker down in crevices

Which birds spend most of their time over the open sea?

When, after more than five months of adult care, the chick of a black-footed or Laysan albatross opens its 6½-foot wings and rises from the sands of Hawaii's most remote islands, it cuts the bond not only with its parents but with the land itself. For the next four to seven years, the albatross will roam the Pacific, never setting foot on dry land until it returns to these same tiny islands to nest. Its journeys may take it into the cold, fertile waters of the Bering Strait, down the North American coast to Baja California, or west off the shores of Japan. Along the way it will mingle with dozens of other species of birds of the open oceans. Shearwaters and petrels, relatives of the albatross, fly close to the surface and feed on small animals. Tropicbirds and frigatebirds, soaring pelican relatives, catch fishes from the surface of the sea.

The distances covered by pelagic seabirds, as these inhabitants of the open sea are called, are astonishing. In fact, their epic journeys rank as some of the greatest migrations in the animal kingdom. Each year in early May, greater shearwaters leave their nesting islands in the far south Atlantic and head north. Soaring on narrow, four-foot-wide wings, these lithe seabirds arrive off the Canadian Maritimes in early summer, just when the small fish known as capelins are spawning. There they are joined by sooty shearwaters from the Patagonian coast, and Cory's shearwaters from the Azores and other islands off the shores of Africa. One short-tailed shearwater, marked as a nestling on its breeding grounds in Tasmania, was found feeding in the Bering Sea off Alaska—a trip of more than 9,000 miles, accomplished in just six weeks.

Why is the water of the Gulf Stream bluer than water closer to shore?

It isn't always so blue—only on days when the sun is shining. Therein lies a clue. The Gulf Stream, that huge, warm current meandering from waters east of Florida to Newfoundland's Grand Banks, transports 25 times as much water as all the rivers of the world combined. It stretches 30 miles across and sweeps along at nearly 5 miles per hour.

All water—the sea included—absorbs more red light than blue. Since an object acquires the color it reflects, all water in sufficient quantity tends to have a blue cast. But most important to the question of color in the Gulf Stream is what the current carries with it: not much of anything. The stream is extraordinarily pure, nearly free from such suspended matter as mineral bits, dust motes, even animal life.

In contrast, water to the stream's west is full of soil washed in from rivers, matter stirred up by storms, nutrients swept up from the ocean depths. It all supports plankton, which tends to scatter sunlight. So, from above, the rich coastal waters look grayish, even under a blue sky. But the Gulf Stream, fed by pure tropical waters, exhibits a remarkable clarity and reflectivity. Thus, the water mirrors the blue of the sky.

The open ocean holds few terrors for an accomplished aerialist like the tropicbird. Soaring effortlessly on constant trade winds, this graceful glider gleans food from the surface and drinks seawater, filtering out the salt with special glands in its forehead.

315

A humpback whale is caught on film just as it begins to breach—spring above the surface before splash diving. In the vividly blue waters off Hawaii, humpbacks court, mate, and bear their calves each winter, much to the delight of onlookers.

Where are the best places for whale-watching?

Rising from the calm sea, a huge head breaks the surface of the water as an explosion of mist erupts skyward with a loud *whoosh*. A back arches, sliding forward like a moving island, then great flukes spanning almost 20 feet lift above the water for an instant before disappearing. A blue whale, the largest creature on earth, has resumed its deep dive.

Few sights in the natural world can compare with that of a great whale. The privilege of spotting these surprisingly graceful leviathans was once reserved for sailors or researchers, but today whale-watching is a booming pastime, with excursions available along the Pacific and Atlantic coasts. Off the coast of New England, humpbacks, whose courtship songs have become powerful symbols for whale conservation, are the prime attraction. In spring and autumn the Stellwagen Bank and Jefferys Ledge off the Massachusetts coast draw large numbers of whale-watchers, hoping to see humpbacks by the dozen. Spawning fish called capelins attract humpbacks, finbacks, and smaller minke whales to the Canadian Maritimes, thrilling observers around Grand Manan Island in New Brunswick, and off the coasts of Nova Scotia and Newfoundland. One of the more unusual whale-watching opportunities exists in the lower St. Lawrence River of Quebec, where visitors may glimpse belugas, 15-foot-long, all-white whales that are more common in the Arctic.

Some of the finest whale-watching takes place in the Pacific. Gray whales head north from their calving grounds in Baja California in February and March, hugging the shore with their calves on their way to Alaska. Boat operators can get whale-watchers close to the 45-foot behemoths, but many people observe them from headlands along the California, Oregon, and Washington coast. Pick a calm, overcast day, and watch for the blow, or spout of exhaled breath. At times, as many as 30 gray whales an hour can be spotted. To the north, the waters off Vancouver Island in British Columbia boasts one of the world's largest population of orcas, or killer whales. Scientists studying the orcas have learned that they live in stable family groups called pods, which span many generations. In the fjord-rimmed waters of southeastern Alaska, humpback whales put on an unforgettable show with their feeding activity. Diving deep, the whales blow rings of bubbles that "fence in" schools of herring; then they rocket up from below, mouths open, surging halfway out of the ocean with tons of fish-laden water cascading from their mouths, and flocks of greedy seabirds wheeling around them like dust motes.

Which freshwater fish spawns only in the Sargasso Sea?

Many fish, including salmon, shad, and herring, spend their adult lives at sea but return to fresh water to spawn. Only a few reverse that pattern, but none as spectacularly as the American eel, which grows to maturity in rivers and creeks but makes an epic journey to lay its eggs in the Sargasso Sea of the north Atlantic.

Long and serpentine, eels look like snakes but are true fish, with short fins that run the length of the back and belly. Females make tremendous upstream migrations, ascending rivers as far inland as Ontario, South Dakota, and eastern New Mexico. Males, however, do not go as far, tending to stay in brackish estuaries or coastal rivers. Once they reach maturity, the three- or four-foot-long eels turn from yellow to silver and begin moving downstream to the ocean, with the peak migration occurring on rainy, moonless nights in autumn.

From the Gulf and Atlantic coasts, eels converge on the Sargasso Sea, located between Bermuda and the West Indies. Here they spawn—at least, that's what scientists assume happens. No one has ever caught a mature eel in the Sargasso Sea, but careful backtracking of newly hatched eel larvae, transparent and shaped like willow leaves, pinpoints this area as the breeding grounds. From the Sargasso the larvae drift north on the Gulf Stream, joined by the offspring of European eels that also spawn in the same region. After a year or two, the maturing American larvae, now called elvers, begin entering coastal rivers to start their inland lives, while their European cousins will drift for another year or two before reaching fresh water.

What strange creatures dwell in the depths?

Far from the common image of a nearly empty abyss, the deep sea is a realm of dazzling beauty, flashing light, and unexpected life. Scientists now believe that more than 10 million species may reside in the depths of the world's oceans—from exquisite glass sponges that rise like stalked trumpets to diaphanous jellyfish that sparkle with living lightning, and tube worms more than six feet long. In some regions the diversity of life on the ocean floor is even greater than in shallow coastal habitats.

But life in the deep poses some serious challenges. The pressure is literally crushing: 1½ miles down, it is two tons per square inch. The water is numbingly cold (just a few degrees above freezing), and sunlight is virtually absent. Yet light there is. About 90 percent of deep-sea creatures are bioluminescent—able to produce bluish or greenish light from special organs. Lacking sunlight, plants cannot grow in the abyss, and life is largely dependent on the rain of organic matter drifting down from the surface—marine snow, as this gentle blizzard of particles is nicknamed. Yet not all creatures are reliant on leftovers from above. In 1977 scientists

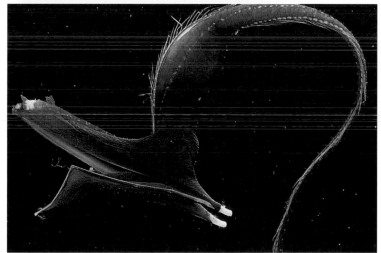

Among the most menacing-looking creatures found in the deep is the gulper eel (below), whose hinged mouth swings wide open to accommodate large prey. Like many deep-sea creatures, the Anoplogaster cornuta (left) is bioluminescent, which some scientists speculate helps to attract food or deter predators.

stumbled on an ecosystem independent of the sun: tube worms, giant clams, crabs, fishes, and other marine animals crowded around volcanic vents thousands of feet deep. Instead of being photosynthetic, these vent inhabitants are part of a chemosynthetic food chain based on bacteria that can consume hydrogen sulfide and are in turn eaten by the other sealife.

Where is the largest population of fish and other marine life?

Americans and saltwater fish have at least one thing in common: the majority of both populations live within 125 miles of where land meets sea. In the case of fish and other marine creatures, home is the water that covers the gently sloping edge of the continent. Known as the continental shelf, this rim of submerged land extends seaward to a depth of about 600

❧ *Named for the season when it migrates to warmer coastal shallows, winter flounder (above), a major commercial fish, can be found along the Atlantic from the Maritimes to Georgia. The American lobster (below) occupies the top of the food chain that depends on plankton, but in its pinhead-size larval stages, it is often consumed by predators along with plankton.*

feet before dropping steeply toward the abyss. Every class of sea creature can be found in this sublittoral zone—from tiny, shrimplike copepods to 150-ton blue whales measuring 100 feet long. More than two-thirds of the world's 20,000-odd species of fish reside here.

Sunlight, abundant food, and a comfortable water temperature are the reasons why. The shelf's relatively shallow, light-filled waters foster food production for fishes and other sea creatures. Phytoplankton (drifting microscopic plants that are the first link in the food chain) are restricted to the sunlit layer of water—the top 500 to 600 feet. Another source of food is underwater plants such as kelp, rockweed, sea lettuce, and other

seaweeds. These, too, can grow only at depths penetrated by the sun's rays.

The most populated places on the continental shelf are found where opposing currents meet head on, creating rising columns of water known as upwellings. In such spots fishes are bombarded by nutrients raining down from above and swirling up from below. One of the richest locations of all is Georges Bank, off the coast of Newfoundland and Maine. Its steady supply of food supports cod, flounder, haddock, fluke, and scores of other species.

Why is plankton so important?

The next time you tie on a lobster bib, remember to thank the plankton that made it all possible. Plankton consists of plants and animals, many near microscopic in size, that float on winds and currents in the sunlit layers of the world's oceans. They exist in a staggering profusion of forms, from diatoms as intricate as snowflakes to diaphanous comb jellies.

The power of phytoplankton (from the Greek for "wandering plants") is their ability to photosynthesize. The sunlit portions of the sea are filled with hundreds of millions of individuals per cubic meter, each one spinning sunlight into carbohydrates. Animal plankton, called zooplankton, is the next step up in the food chain, grazing like cows on ocean pastures. Some of the most abundant zooplankton are called copepods, which resemble tiny wood lice.

Phytoplankton is also relished by larger animals: shrimp, larval crabs, sea clams, and countless fishes, such as anchovies and sardines. These creatures, in turn, are devoured by other ocean predators. Clams, for example, are eaten by moon snails, which are eaten by starfish, which are eaten by lobsters, which are eaten in larval form by cod or in adult form by us. Blue whales don't bother to hunt down individuals; they simply use their filtering baleen mouthparts to consume four tons of plankton-fed krill per day.

Fattening the food chain isn't the only service that plankton provides, however. In the process of photosynthesizing, phytoplankton removes carbon dioxide from the atmosphere while producing oxygen. This oxygen production is vital to the survival of all life on earth as we know it (just as important as the contribution made by land plants), so marine scientists monitor the health of the ocean very closely.

What is the secret of the bluefin tuna's remarkable speed?

With its warm, sunlit shallows, the continental shelf rimming North America bustles with marine life. Clouds of plankton support food chains that end with predators like striped bass and bluefish, which roam the coasts, foraging just beyond the breaking waves. Far offshore, in the colder, deeper waters of the open sea, live even more impressive hunters—giant bluefin tuna, swordfish, albacore, and other incessant wanderers that stitch together the world's oceans with their migrations.

The bluefin tuna is one of the largest and most highly developed species of fish in the world. A mature specimen may weigh 1,400 pounds, yet swim up to 71 miles per hour. Its massive head and shoulders taper smoothly to a crescent-shaped tail that drives endlessly from side to side; its tail powers the tuna on journeys that may stretch from South America up through the Gulf of Mexico and Caribbean to the waters off New England and eastern Canada, then to the mouth of the Mediterranean. Along the way the tuna descends on schools of mackerels, herrings, and squids—quick, agile prey, but not fast enough to escape the tuna, in part because of the predator's unique physiology. Most fish are cold-blooded; their body temperature is close to that of the surrounding water. But a bluefin's circulatory system retains muscular heat deep within the core of its massive body. These giant tuna can maintain a temperature nearly 20 degrees warmer than the surrounding ocean, tripling their muscular power and accounting for their remarkable speed.

Where is the graveyard of the Atlantic?

Shifting shoals and violent weather have earned the coast of North Carolina its much-deserved nickname: the graveyard of the Atlantic. Hundreds of ships and countless sailors have been lost here, starting with a Spanish brigantine and its crew in 1526. The collisions between water currents and between air currents are to blame for such disasters. Warm water pushed north by the Gulf Stream runs head-on into cold water from the Arctic carried south by the Virginia Coastal Drift. The fallout from the impact is sand and shells that pile up in the form of a chain of barrier islands known as the Outer Banks. Treacherous submerged shoals that jut out like fangs from a trio of headlands—Capes Hatteras, Lookout, and Fear—lie in wait to devour any ship that tries to pass.

To make matters worse, corresponding air currents collide overhead, making this stretch of coastline second only to Florida in terms of vulnerability to hurricanes. Devastating nor'easters are common, and thunderheads and waterspouts spawn whenever the warm air from the tropics meets the masses of cold air that build up on the eastern side of the Appalachians. For those at sea, the result can be fatal. In one two-day period in August 1899, a hurricane pushed seven ships ashore here; six more sank without a trace. Throughout much of the 19th century, ships foundered on the Outer Banks at a rate of two per month. It took the development of radar and satellite navigational aids to help stem the tide, but by then, many seafarers say, the graveyard was already full.

Blue sharks (above) are common in the deep sea because they can tolerate lower temperatures than most species. Highly adaptable, they range from tropical to temperate waters around the globe.

A Land Called Tundra *The frigid far north*

Where are most of our glaciers found?

In southeastern Alaska, where the Wrangell, St. Elias, and Chugach mountain ranges converge, lies North America's largest assemblage of glaciers. Everything here is enormous—glacier after glacier, peak upon peak—and the first is the direct result of the second. The St. Elias Mountains are the world's highest coastal range; their height and their proximity to the coast, where rainfall is heavy, allow this region to maintain 70 percent of our glaciers.

Some truly gargantuan glaciers are spawned in this mountain kingdom, North America's greatest collection of peaks over 16,000 feet in elevation. But among the giants—the Guyot, Tana, Hubbard, and Miles glaciers—one dwarfs them all, the Malaspina Glacier. This enormous ice mass covers an area larger than Rhode Island. The Malaspina is a rare piedmont glacier (a glacier that has extended beyond its mountain valleys and spread out onto level land). It flows down from Mount St. Elias, which at 18,008 feet is the second-highest peak in the United States; the ice covers all the territory between Icy Bay to the west and Yakutat Bay to the east and stretches out to the south into the icy waters of the Gulf of Alaska.

Glaciers form on high mountains where snow accumulates and is eventually compressed into ice. Once the ice sheet reaches a critical thickness, about 18 inches, its weight, along with the force of gravity, causes it to expand. Like a slow river, the glacier then flows down mountain valleys and, if substantial enough, fans out over plains and spreads out into the sea.

A slow glacier will move less than 3 feet a day, while a surging one can attain speeds approaching 200 feet. This is the speed of the glacier's surface, which always travels faster than its underside. The bottom of the glacier is slowed as it slides over the land beneath it.

As with armies, the movements of glaciers are spoken of in terms of advance and retreat. Periods of great snowfall cause glaciers to advance, while periods of melting cause them to retreat. The terms *advance* and *retreat*, however, refer only to the terminus, or snout, of the glacier, as even a retreating glacier, which is melting back at its terminus, continues to move downslope.

Glaciers are nature's Rodins, carving out some of the most dramatic scenery on earth. If a glacier's terminus remains stationary over a long period of time, a ridge of till (clay, gravel, and boulders) called a terminal moraine is deposited along the margin of the ice. Some of the world's most beautiful lakes occur in glaciated valleys that are dammed by moraines.

Why do some animals wear winter whites?

Camouflage that craftily conceals in the autumn landscape of browns, golds, and crimsons is positively eye-catching in the white world of winter. This is a serious problem for creatures whose survival requires they remain unseen, but several species have developed the same solution.

❧ *America's largest glacier, the Malaspina, spreads out over more than 1,200 square miles as it flows from Alaska's St. Elias Range to the sea. The glacier's edges carry so much silt that plants sometimes take root and grow on top of the moving ice.*

The willow ptarmigan, a master of disguise, sheds white feathers in spring and dons brown, making it hard to spot among tundra plants.

Around October the snowshoe hare begins shedding its rusty brown summer coat, replacing it with a pure white one (except for black tips on the ears). In March the snowshoe hare molts again, this time changing its white fur to brown. Other animals also use seasonal coloration, blending so well with their habitat that they become nearly invisible. For example, the arctic hare, collared lemming, and ptarmigan all wear winter whites to escape predators. However, some hunters have evolved the same tactics as their prey: the short-tailed weasel (ermine) and arctic fox also don white during winter.

Even during late fall and early spring, when the ground is only partly covered with snow, these color-changing animals remain cloaked in appropriate camouflage. They do this by only gradually changing their brown summer coats to white. For instance, the white hairs of a weasel's winter coat first appear near the abdomen, then move up its flanks, and spread to its legs and face, allowing the animal to blend with fallen leaves covered with snow patches. Later the last brown patches turn white, and even the sharpest eyes may not detect the weasel as it bounds across the snow of a northern winter landscape.

Can anything survive in a frozen tundra pond?

Ice is the enemy of living cells, rupturing delicate membranes and fatally damaging internal structures. Yet some animals living in and around Arctic ponds freeze solid each winter, only to thaw out, unharmed, in spring.

The keys to this seeming impossibility are chemicals controlling where water freezes in the animal's tissues. The wood frog, our continent's most cold-hardy amphibian, can survive in northern Alaska with some chemical sleight-of-hand.

In late autumn, after frigid temperatures reach the frog's hibernation site a few inches below ground, special proteins encourage the growth of ice crystals in minute spaces between cells, where they can do little damage. Moisture is drawn from inside the cells, increasing concentrations of salts in their fluids and lowering their freezing point. What's more, the frog's body pumps the cells full of sugars such as glucose, and alcohols such as glycerol—compounds called cryoprotectants that function as antifreezes. (Glycerol, in fact, is very similar to automobile antifreeze.) Still other proteins regulate freezing and melting rates, so that the frog neither freezes nor thaws too quickly. Slow change is a secret of survival in the cold. These tricks also work for a small Arctic fish, the nine-spine stickleback, and in temperate latitudes for several kinds of frogs, garter snakes, box and painted turtles, and a few lizards.

Why are there so many ponds in the Arctic?

For a brief period each year during the 24-hour daylight of high summer, the frozen Arctic tundra becomes a watery world whose jeweled ponds and lakes dot the landscape from tree line northward all the way to the Arctic Ocean.

The thin soil of the Arctic tundra sits on permafrost—a mixture of frozen earth and ice—which can be as much as 1,500 feet deep. Summer daylight melts the accumulated snow and an additional upper few inches or feet of permafrost, but below the wet surface, the ground remains rock hard. With nowhere to drain, meltwater collects in the form of countless ponds and lakes.

Ironically, for all its standing water, the Arctic receives on average only between 10 and 20 inches of rainfall a year, less than Kansas. Though abundant, tundra ponds are shallow. A wet veneer over iron ground, they freeze quickly as the brief summer ends, and the Arctic once again locks up its treasures in the long night of winter.

Seldom more than 5 to 10 feet deep, Arctic ponds are frequently elliptical in shape, with the long axis often oriented at right angles to prevailing winds. Currents set in motion by these winds contour the ponds' shorelines.

Thanks to thick fur and blubber, young polar bears can spar in springtime, undeterred by frigid temperatures.

Do polar bears seek shelter during the winter?

Unlike most bears, which grow lethargic and search for a warm den when cold weather arrives, polar bears (with the exception of pregnant females) remain active and seldom need cover. With a four-inch-thick layer of blubber and heavy fur providing near-perfect insulation, these denizens of the far north are remarkably unfazed even when temperatures plunge to as low as –70°F.

Few animals can survive in the high Arctic, but neither cold nor scarcity of food presents an unbearable challenge for these huge creatures. Their favorite quarry, the five-foot-long, 200-pound ringed seal, abounds in the waters around ice floes, where the bears spend most of their life. Although polar bears are strong swimmers, they are not as agile as seals and usually do not swim after them. Instead, the bears lie in wait at breathing holes or the water's edge and let their prey come to them, since seals must surface for a breath of air every few minutes.

In the summer, when the ice breaks up and polar bears take to land, the huge carnivores subsist in large part on a diet of berries, grass, and other vegetation. While on land, they sometimes retreat to dens in the ground or in patches of lingering snow. Ironically, they are escaping not the cold, but the relative heat of the brief Arctic summer, when the average temperature is just above freezing.

What animal eats itself out of house and home?

When large numbers of snowy owls turn up during the winter in the lower 48 states, the odds are that on the treeless, windswept Arctic tundra, the number of lemmings has bottomed out. Lemmings are small rodents whose populations peak every three to four summers, then crash by summer of the following year because they have depleted their food supply—green plants and twigs. Snowy owls feed on these little mammals, intimately linking the destinies of furry prey and feathered predator. Boom or

Collared lemmings are normally plant eaters, but during periods of overpopulation when food is scarce, they may resort to cannibalism.

bust for the lemmings is usually followed by the same for the owls.

When lemming reproduction increases, so does that of the owls, which have an overabundance of food for themselves and their young. Lemmings are especially easy to catch after their food supply runs out. Abandoning their shallow burrows in the thin layer of soil above the tundra's permafrost, they spread out over the countryside in a frantic search for forage. Weakened and dying because they lack sustenance, the lemmings are further depleted by the owls and other predators, such as arctic foxes and grizzly bears. By winter it is the owls' turn to wander. Searching for prey, large numbers of them head south, far beyond their normal range. These long journeys take a heavy toll on the owls, and even those that return to the tundra in spring face the threat of starvation. Their nesting success is poor, resulting in fewer owls and, before long, more lemmings. So it will go, as long as owls and lemmings exist.

Why are there so many mosquitoes in the far north?

Above the Arctic Circle, where daylight lingers past midnight in the summer, the sun slowly thaws the topsoil. But since the ground below remains frozen, the runoff—with nowhere to go—creates vast boggy pools that are perfect incubators for mosquitoes. The insects' eggs survive the winter and hatch in peak numbers between mid-June and mid-July, forming hordes that can blacken the sky. Most die within a couple of weeks; indeed, very few survive the first good frost in August. But while they're out, it can be a nightmare.

The demon in this bad dream is the female (males don't bite). During courtship both genders live off fruits and flowers, but once impregnated, the female, who needs a blood meal to feed her eggs, turns into a veritable vampire.

Caribou blood becomes the principal diet of these hungry females, but they will also feed off birds, polar bears, rodents, and of course, humans. Arctic mosquitoes, though they carry no life-threatening diseases, are a ravenous nuisance. Canadian researchers who bared their bodies to them reported as many as 9,000 bites per minute. At this rate it would take only two hours for these voracious little bloodsuckers to drain a human dry.

Where do animals build dens in the Arctic tundra?

The Arctic is as sodden as a place can be and still be called land; less than two feet beneath the surface lies the permafrost, a layer of permanently frozen ground that may extend down for hundreds, even thousands, of feet. In the summer, water pools up at the surface in a kaleidoscope of lakes, ponds, marshes, and bogs; dig down a few inches, and it seeps in immediately to fill the hole. For such mammals as wolves, foxes, and bears, the problem of where to dig a dry den is a difficult one. The answer across much of the Arctic is to dig in eskers—meandering, snakelike ridges of rock and gravel, usually flat-topped or gently rounded, deposited thousands of years ago by melting glaciers.

Eskers are perfect homes for mammals as small as arctic ground squirrels and as large as mature grizzlies. They may rise hundreds of feet above the surrounding tundra, creating hospitable habitats that catch the feeble warmth of the Arctic summer sun on their slopes and, in winter, form deep snowdrifts that insulate hibernating bears. Their soil is porous, well drained, and easy to dig through; it is here that wolves and foxes prefer to give birth, the only time of year they use an underground den. Blown free of the mosquito hordes that plague the region in summer, eskers provide breezy perches for some animals. Caribou, which suffer greatly from biting insects, use the eskers as their favorite migration routes.

In fact, although eskers account for less than 2 percent of the land area in the high Arctic, they are profoundly important to most mammals in the region. Ironically, this very dependence on eskers may place northern wildlife at risk. Geologists have discovered North America's first diamond deposits in the Canadian Arctic, and eskers are being viewed as access roads to planned mines and as the raw material for landing strips and dams. Biologists worry that damaging the eskers may unravel the delicate system that allows life to survive in this unforgiving environment.

The arctic ground squirrel, the only true hibernator in the far north, digs its burrow in a well-drained area above the permafrost and curls up for about seven months.

➤ *The rich golds and crimsons of turning dwarf-birch and dwarf-willow leaves spread across the tundra in late August and early September, signaling the end of the brief summer growing season.*

What happens when summer comes to the Arctic?

An Arctic summer is fleeting as a rainbow, a brief season that lasts only a handful of weeks. But summer crams an amazing exuberance of life into its short span, painting the tundra with a palette of wildflowers. Within the short warm season from June through early August, tundra plants, their growth triggered by snowmelt and lengthening days, accomplish a year's worth of development and reproduction. Hampered by the cold, the presence of permafrost just below the surface, and the constant threat of strong, drying winds, most Arctic plants are dwarfed—although their flowers are frequently large beyond proportion, the better to attract pollinating insects. The woolly lousewort raises a thick column of yellowish blossoms above its four-inch tangle of hairy, ground-hugging leaves. Low mounds of moss campion, growing in sheltered nooks between rocks, cover themselves with pink flowers. Pygmy laurels, tiny gentians, mat-forming blueberries—all take part in the brief, incandescent floral display.

To help them cope with the difficult conditions in the Arctic, where midsummer frosts are common and desiccating winds are rarely stilled, many tundra plants have developed special adaptations such as leaves covered with dense hairs to trap moist air; others bear leathery leaves coated with thick, waxy cuticles to retard evaporation. Even the trees survive by maintaining a low profile. Dwarf willows, just inches high, are among the most common of Arctic plants, raising red bottlebrush flowers above their leaves—ancient survivors that have learned the value of keeping their heads down.

What makes parts of the tundra look like polygon-shaped islands?

From the air much of the tundra looks like a giant's jigsaw puzzle, the pieces spanning many yards and fitting together in a crazy quilt of angular shapes. The pattern resembles the dried, cracked mud of an old lake bottom, only on a vast scale—and the process is similar.

Just below the surface of the ground lies the permafrost, which in parts of Alaska's coastal plain may extend 1,500 feet deep—a zone of perpetually frozen earth. But the upper three feet or so go through dramatic annual freeze-and-

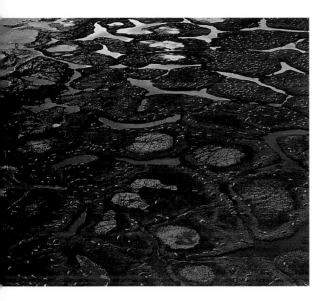

≈ *Thousands of ponds dot the North American Arctic tundra, creating ideal feeding grounds and nurseries for migratory shorebirds and waterfowl.*

thaw cycles. In winter the numbing cold causes the fine-grained soils to contract, forming the broken pattern of polygons; larger stones are pushed to the outside, and water fills the cracks around the edges, freezing into ice wedges that grow each year until they poke many feet deep into the ground. The result is a mosaic of saucer-shaped depressions, raised at the edges and slightly sunken in the middle. Sometimes, if meltwater works its way beneath the permafrost under the polygons, they may slump enough to create ponds and small thaw lakes. This soggy ecosystem is lush with wetland plants, including cottongrass and sedges, and is critically important to breeding waterfowl, such as snow geese, which feed on the vegetation.

How do animals hibernate during the harsh northern winters?

Not many Arctic animals hibernate, but for those that do, it's like crawling into a freezer in October and thawing out in May. The real danger isn't cold, per se, but daggerlike ice crystals that can rupture cell walls and blood vessels.

The tiny arctic wood frog freezes hard as a hockey puck during the winter, but in spring it manages to wake, thaw, and hop away with no apparent damage. Its secret is the massive amount of glucose that floods its body before hibernation—100 times the concentration of glucose normally present in humans. This sugar acts like antifreeze, lowering the freezing point of body fluids. Cells spiked with glucose remain unfrozen. In the watery spaces between cells, some freezing occurs, but the shapes of the crystals are modified. Instead of daggers, the ice freezes in a pattern of feathery branches.

Scientists believe that this same antifreeze is at work in the arctic ground squirrel, the only mammal known to tolerate ice crystals in its bloodstream. During its seven months of dormancy, when temperatures average –4° to –22°F, the ground squirrel lives in a suspended state that falls somewhere between hibernation and freezing. Just as in the wood frog, potentially harmful ice crystals are kept outside delicate cells and organs, proving that it's not whether you freeze but where you freeze that counts.

What attracts birds to the Arctic?

What makes the Arctic so uncomfortable for visiting humans—overwhelming numbers of biting insects—makes it a bountiful place for shorebirds, which seine the larvae of midges, mosquitoes, black flies, and other bugs from the soggy landscape of bogs and marshes. Add to that the nearly perpetual sunlight of midsummer, which allows round-the-clock feeding, and a scarcity of permanent resident species that might compete for nest space, and the tundra is well worth the trouble so many birds take to reach it.

While some songbirds like the wheatear travel to the Arctic each year to nest, the vast majority of the migrants are waterfowl, such as geese and ducks, and shorebirds—strong, fast fliers able to cope with the extended journey. Because many shorebirds winter far below the equator, their twice-annual forays are among the longest migrations on earth. The sandpiper known as the red knot, which turns a lovely shade of robin's-breast orange in spring, is among these champions. The knot commutes between its breeding grounds in the Canadian Arctic islands or coastal Alaska and its wintering grounds in southern South America, traveling some 18,000 miles.

During the Ice Age birds had a much shorter journey to reach the tundra, which covered much of the central United States. But as the glaciers retreated, migratory routes stretched, resulting in today's long-distance marathons.

≈ *One the world's longest migrators, the golden plover nests in the Arctic and winters in South America, flying south from Labrador directly over the open Atlantic.*

Photo Credits

cover Tom Mangelsen/Images of Nature. 1 Daniel J. Cox/Natural Exposures. 2/3 Art Wolfe. 5t Stefan Schott/Ken Graham Agency. 5b Alan & Sandy Carey. 6 Daniel J. Cox/Natural Exposures. 7t Tom & Pat Leeson/DRK Photo. 7b Tim Thompson/Tony Stone Images. 8/9 Daniel J. Cox/Natural Exposures. 10 Renee Lynn/Photo Researchers. 11l Art Wolfe. 11r Fred McConnaughey/Photo Researchers. 12t Art Wolfe/Tony Stone Images. 12m B.J. Spenceley/Bruce Coleman. 12b Sharon Cummings/Dembinsky Photo Associates. 13t Kevin Schafer/Peter Arnold. 13b Barry Griffiths/Photo Researchers. 14t Skip Moody/Dembinsky Photo Associates. 14m M.P. Kahl/Photo Researchers. 14b Gary Meszaros/Dembinsky Photo Associates. 15 Daniel J. Cox/Natural Exposures. 16t Robert Carr/Bruce Coleman. 16m ©1996 Brian Kenney. 16b Jeff Foott/Bruce Coleman. 17t George H. Harrison/Harrison Productions Inc. 17b ©1996 Brian Kenney. 18l Erwin & Peggy Bauer/Bruce Coleman. 18r Jim Brandenburg/Minden Pictures. 19 Jane Burton/Bruce Coleman. 20 Michael Bisceglie/Animals Animals. 21l Hans Reinhard/Bruce Coleman. 21r Harry Rogers/Photo Researchers. 22 Albert S. Grant/Photo Researchers. 23 all Kim Taylor/Bruce Coleman. 24 Jeffery L. Rotman/Peter Arnold. 25 Wolfgang Kaehler. 26/27 Art Wolfe. 28 Art Wolfe. 29 Joel Sartore/National Geographic Image Collection. 30 Michael Sewell/Peter Arnold. 31t Joe McDonald/Bruce Coleman. 31b Suzanne & Joseph Collins/Photo Researchers. 32 Flip Nicklin/Minden Pictures. 33t Anthony Mercieca/Photo Researchers. 33b Aubrey Lang/Valan Photos. 34 Daniel J. Cox/Natural Exposures. 35l Daniel J. Cox/Natural Exposures. 35r Kim Taylor/Bruce Coleman. 36 Larry Lipsky/Bruce Coleman. 37 Robert P. Falls/Bruce Coleman. 38t Donald Specker/Animals Animals. 38b Fred Bavendam. 39t M.P. Kahl/Bruce Coleman. 39b Keith Gunnar/Bruce Coleman. 40 John Shaw/Bruce Coleman. 41t Bruce Watkins/Animals Animals. 41b Ralph A. Reinhold/Animals Animals. 42t Wayne Lankinen/DRK Photo. 42b Holt Studios International/Nigel Cattlin/Photo Researchers. 43t Norbert Wu/Peter Arnold. 43b L. West/Photo Researchers. 44t Adam Jones/Dembinsky Photo Associates. 44b Michael Habicht/Animals Animals. 45t Dwight R. Kuhn/DRK Photo. 45b Flip Nicklin/Minden Pictures. 46/47 Flip Nicklin/Minden Pictures. 49t Jim Brandenburg/Minden Pictures. 49b Erwin & Peggy Bauer/Bruce Coleman. 50t Lior Rubin/Peter Arnold. 50b John R. MacGregor/Peter Arnold. 51 Kevin & Cat Sweeny/DRK Photo. 52t Lee F. Snyder/Photo Researchers. 52b Larry Lipsky/Bruce Coleman. 53t John Gerlach/Dembinsky Photo Associates. 53b Barbara Gerlach/DRK Photo. 54 Art Wolfe. 55 John R. Clawson/Photo Researchers. 56 Daniel J. Cox/Natural Exposures. 57t Gerard Lacz/Peter Arnold. 57b John Shaw/Bruce Coleman. 58t Sharon Cummings/Dembinsky Photo Associates. 58b SharkSong/Marilyn Kazmers/Dembinsky Photo Associates. 59 Pat & Tom Leeson/Photo Researchers. 60 Daniel J. Cox/Natural Exposures. 61t Michael Habicht/Animals Animals. 61m Gregory K. Scott/Photo Researchers. 61b Pat & Tom Leeson/Photo Researchers. 62l Bob Gurr/DRK Photo. 62r James Carmichael/Bruce Coleman. 63 Laura Riley/Bruce Coleman. 64 C.C. Lockwood/DRK Photo. 65t James H. Carmichael/Bruce Coleman. 65b Bruce Dale © National Geographic Society. 66 George J. Sanker/DRK Photo. 67l Jeff Lepore/Photo Researchers. 67r Laura Riley/Bruce Coleman. 68t Sam Abell/National Geographic Image Collection. 68b Mother Nature's Moving Pic Co./Bruce Coleman. 68/69 James H. Robinson/Photo Researchers. 69lb Michael Lustbader/Photo Researchers. 69rb Robert C. Hermes/Photo Researchers. 70l Joe McDonald/Bruce Coleman. 70r Tom Brakefield/Bruce Coleman. 71l Fred Bavendam/Peter Arnold. 71r Skip Moody/Dembinsky Photo Associates. 72t Wayne Lankinen/DRK Photo. 72b Daniel J. Cox/Natural Exposures. 73t Tom Brakefield/Bruce Coleman. 73b Rolf Peterson. 74t Robert F. Sisson © National Geographic Society. 74b Art Wolfe. 75l Jim Brandenburg/Minden Pictures. 75r Daniel J. Cox/Natural Exposures. 76/77 Mike Barlow/Dembinsky Photo Associates. 77r S.J. Drasemann/Peter Arnold. 78t David Cavagnaro/Peter Arnold. 78b Jim Brandenburg/Minden Pictures. 79t Art Wolfe. 79b Robert L. Dunne/Bruce Coleman. 80l John Cancalosi/DRK Photo.

80r Bianca Lavies © National Geographic Society. 81t Karl Switak/NHPA. 81b Norbert Wu/DRK Photo. 82 Frans Lanting/Minden Pictures. 83t Ed Reschke/Peter Arnold. 83b Erwin & Peggy Bauer/Bruce Coleman. 84 Jeremy Woodhouse/DRK Photo. 85lt Alan & Sandy Carey. 85rt Alan & Sandy Carey. 85b Daniel J. Cox/Natural Exposures. 86t John Gerlach/DRK Photo. 86b Stephen J. Krasemann/DRK Photo. 87t Henry Holdsworth/The Wildlife Collection. 87b Art Wolfe/Tony Stone Images. 88 Art Wolfe. 89t Jeff Foott/Valan Photos. 89b Jeff Foott/Bruce Coleman. 90t Jean F. Stoick, Carl R. Sams II/Peter Arnold. 90b Gregory G. Dimijian/Photo Researchers. 91 both John K.B. Ford/Ursus. 92t Nick Caloyianis/National Geographic Image Collection. 92b Don Enger/Animals Animals. 93t Norbert Wu/Peter Arnold. 93b Ann Sanfedele/Animals Animals. 94 Stephen J. Krasemann/DRK Photo. 95t David Hall/Photo Researchers. 95b E.R. Degginger/Photo Researchers. 96 Tom Mangelsen/Images of Nature. 97t Scott Nielsen/Bruce Coleman. 97b Myrna Watanabe/Peter Arnold. 98 Scott Camazine/Photo Researchers. 99t Bev Ford/Ursus. 99b Alan & Sandy Carey. 100 Wendell Metzen/Bruce Coleman. 101 Wayne Lankinen/Valan Photos. 102t Marcia W. Griffen/Animals Animals. 102b Don Enger/Animals Animals. 103 Tom & Pat Leeson/Photo Researchers. 104 Fred Bavendam/Valan Photos. 105t Stephen J. Krasemann/Peter Arnold. 105b Art Wolfe. 106t Skip Moody/Dembinsky Photo Associates. 106mt Marvin L. Dembinsky, Jr./Dembinsky Photo Associates. 106mb Sharon Cummings/Dembinsky Photo Associates. 106b Skip Moody/Dembinsky Photo Associates. 107 John Cancalosi/Valan Photos. 108t Tom McHugh/Photo Researchers. 108b Michael Lustbader/Photo Researchers. 109 Bill Dyer/Photo Researchers. 110 Daniel J. Cox/Natural Exposures. 111 Maslowski/Photo Researchers. 112 Walt Enders/Ellis Nature Photography. 113 Michio Hoshino/Minden Pictures. 114 James Amos/Photo Researchers. 115t Anthony Mercieca/Photo Researchers. 115b Carl R. Sams II/Peter Arnold. 116 Chris Johns/National Geographic Image Collection. 117t ©1996 Brian Kenney. 117b John Cancalosi/Valan Photos. 118 Laura Riley/Bruce Coleman. 119t Howard Hall/Animals Animals. 119b Tom Edwards/Animals Animals. 120t Frans Lanting/Minden Pictures. 120b Ted Kerasote/Photo Researchers. 121 Tom Vezo. 122 Harold Pfeiffer/Tony Stone Images. 123t Gregory K. Scott/Photo Researchers. 123b Jeff Foott/Valan Photos. 124t Leonard Lee Rue III/DRK Photo. 124b J.H. Robinson/Photo Researchers. 125 Jacana/Photo Researchers. 126 Chris Johns/National Geographic Image Collection. 127t Carl R. Sams II/Dembinsky Photo Associates. 127b Joe DiStefano/Photo Researchers. 128t Adam Jones/Dembinsky Photo Associates. 128b Tom McHugh/Photo Researchers. 129t ©1996 Brian Kenney. 129b C.C. Lockwood/DRK Photo. 130 Paul Chesley/National Geographic Image Collection. 131 Daniel J. Cox/Natural Exposures. 132 Charles Palek/Animals Animals. 133 Tom Branch/Photo Researchers. 134t James Carmichael/Bruce Coleman. 134b Glenn Oliver/Ken Graham Agency. 135 Wayne Lankinen/Bruce Coleman. 136l Tom McHugh/Photo Researchers. 136/37 Don & Pat Valenti/DRK Photo. 138/39 François Gohier/Photo Researchers. 140 Joe McDonald/Animals Animals. 141t Leonard Lee Rue/Photo Researchers. 141b neg. no. 5758, photo by J. Beckett, courtesy Department of Library Sciences, American Museum of Natural History. 142 Tee Balog/Photo Researchers. 143 Daniel J. Cox/Natural Exposures. 144/45 Daniel J. Cox/Natural Exposures. 146/47 Wouterloot-Gregoire/Valan Photos. 147b R.J. Erwin/Photo Researchers. 148 Karl H. Switak/Photo Researchers. 149lt Stephen Trimble/DRK Photo. 149lb Simon/Photo Researchers. 149rt D. Cavagnaro/DRK Photo. 149rb Doug Lee/Peter Arnold. 149mb Dominique Braud/Dembinsky Photo Associates. 150 Kim Heacox/Peter Arnold. 151 Ray Pfortner/Peter Arnold. 152/3 Tom & Pat Leeson/DRK Photo. 154t Rod Planck/Dembinsky Photo Associates. 154b Dick Canby/DRK Photo. 155 Art Wolfe. 156 John Gerlach/Dembinsky Photo Associates. 157 Gregory Ochocki/Photo Researchers. 158l Tom Bean/DRK Photo. 158r E.R. Degginger/Bruce Coleman. 159 Rod Planck/Dembinsky Photo Associates. 160 Peter French/Bruce Coleman.

161 © 1996 Brian Kenney. 162 Jeff Lepore/Photo Researchers. 163 Gregory Ochocki/Photo Researchers. 164l D. Cavagnaro/DRK Photo. 164r Pat O'Hara/DRK Photo. 165 Tom Bledsoe/Photo Researchers. 166 Darrell Gulin/DRK Photo. 167 Larry Ulrich/DRK Photo. 168t Dan Suzio/Photo Researchers. 168b Stephen J. Krasemann/DRK Photo. 169 Noble Proctor/Photo Researchers. 170 Darlyne A. Murawski/Peter Arnold. 171t Art Wolfe. 171b Richard Shiell/Dembinsky Photo Associates. 172 John Eastcott/Yva Momatiuk/DRK Photo. 173 Michael P. Gadomski/Animals Animals. 174t John Kaprielian/Photo Researchers. 174b Don & Pat Valenti/DRK Photo. 175 John Shaw/Bruce Coleman. 176lt G. Tomsich/Photo Researchers. 176lb Peter Arnold/Peter Arnold. 176rt Hans Reinhard/Bruce Coleman. 177 S. Nielsen/DRK Photo. 178 David Muench. 179 Stephen Graham/Dembinsky Photo Associates. 180 both John Bova/Photo Researchers. 181 Michael Hubrich/Dembinsky Photo Associates. 182 Nuridsany & Perennou/Photo Researchers. 183t Jeff Lepore/Photo Researchers. 183b Dwight Kuhn. 184 Bill Lea/Dembinsky Photo Associates. 185 Jeff Lepore/Photo Researchers. 186 Michael P. Gadomski/Photo Researchers. 187 Jeff Lepore/Photo Researchers. 188 Stephen Dalton/Animals Animals. 189 Gerry Ellis/Gerry Ellis Nature Photography. 190 Vul S. Maslowski/Visuals Unlimited. 191l Phil Degginger/Bruce Coleman. 191r John S. Flannery/Bruce Coleman. 192 all Dan Suzio. 193 Gary Withey/Bruce Coleman. 194 D. Cavagnaro/DRK Photo. 195 Wendell Metzen/Bruce Coleman. 196t Gary Baker/Dembinsky Photo Associates. 196m J.L. Lepore/Photo Researchers. 196b Wayne Lynch/DRK Photo. 197 Doug Locke/Dembinsky Photo Associates. 198 Dwight R. Kuhn. 199 Gary Withey/Bruce Coleman. 200 S.R. Magilone/Photo Researchers. 201t A. Barbour. 201b D. Faulkner/Photo Researchers. 202 Stephen J. Krasemann/DRK Photo. 203 Zig Leszczynski/Animals Animals. 204 Stephen J. Krasemann/DRK Photo. 205 Fred Whitehead/Animals Animals. 206 Lee Rentz/Bruce Coleman. 207 John Geriacho/DRK Photo. 208 Stephen J. Krasemann/Photo Researchers. 209 Bob Gibbons/Photo Researchers. 210 John Cancalosi/Peter Arnold. 211 Steve Solum/Bruce Coleman. 212 John Shaw/Bruce Coleman. 213t Nancy Rotenberg/Animals Animals. 213b Zig Leszczynski/Animals Animals. 214/15 Tim Thompson/Tony Stone Images. 216 Edi Ann Otto. 217 David Muench. 218t C.C. Lockwood/DRK Photo. 218b David Muench. 219 Pat O'Hara/DRK Photo. 220 Keith Gunnar/Bruce Coleman. 221 Frans Lanting/Minden Pictures. 222l Henry Huntington/Alaska Stock Images. 222r Larry Ulrich/Tony Stone Images. 223t Jim Steinberg/Photo Researchers. 223b Jay Lurie/Bruce Coleman. 224 Kim Heacox/DRK Photo. 225 Soames Summerhays/Photo Researchers. 226t Clyde H. Smith/f/Stop Pictures. 226b David Muench. 227 David Muench. 228 Martha Cooper/Peter Arnold. 229 Stephen J. Krasemann/DRK Photo. 230lt Tom Bean/DRK Photo. 230rt Tom Bean/DRK Photo. 230lm Dick Canby/DRK Photo. 230rm Gerry Ellis/Gerry Ellis Nature Photography. 230b Lee Rentz/Bruce Coleman. 231 G. Alan Nelson/Dembinsky Photo Associates. 232/33 Tom Walker/Tony Stone Images. 233b C.C. Lockwood/DRK Photo. 234 Art Wolfe. 235t Bob Firth/International Stock. 235b Warren Faidley/International Stock. 236/37 Chad Ehlers/International Stock. 238 Warren Faidley/International Stock. 239t Stephen J. Krasemann/DRK Photo. 239b Baron Wolman/Tony Stone Images. 240 Gary Braasch/Woodfin Camp. 241 James L. Amos/National Geographic Image Collection. 242/43 Tom Till/DRK Photo. 243lt Bruce Montagne/Dembinsky Photo Associates. 243rm David Muench. 243rb Adam Jones/Dembinsky Photo Associates. 244l all Dr. Steve Gull/Dr. John Fielden/Dr. Alan Smith/Science Photo Library/Photo Researchers. 244rb James Balog/Tony Stone Images. 245 Daniel J. Cox/Natural Exposures. 246 David Muench. 247 Jack Dykinga. 248 Sylvain Grandadam/Tony Stone Images. 249 Stephen J. Krasemann/Tony Stone Images. 250 Roger Werth/Woodfin Camp. 251t Dan Suzio. 251b Roger Ressmeyer/Corbis. 252 C.C. Lockwood/Bruce Coleman. 253 Andre Jenny/International Stock. 254 Frans Lanting/Minden Pictures. 255t Leland Bobbe/Tony Stone Images. 255b David & Hayes Norris/Photo Researchers. 256 Merlin D. Tuttle/Bat Conservation International. 257 Mike Price/Bruce Coleman. 258l Anthony Mercieca/Photo Researchers. 258rt Art Wolfe. 258rb Zig Leszczyski/Animals Animals. 259lt D. Cavagnaro/DRK Photo. 259lb Werner J. Bertsch/Bruce Coleman. 259rt Art Wolfe, 259rb John Shaw/Bruce Coleman. 260 Ray Pfortner/Peter Arnold. 261t © 1996 Brian Kenney. 261b J. Heidecker/VIREO. 262/63 Craig Fugii/Seattle Times. 263r Jeff Vanuga. 264lt Bill Lea/Dembinsky Photo Associates. 264lb Rob Simpson/Valan Photos. 264r Len Lee Rue III/Photo Researchers. 265 Charlie Ott/Photo Researchers. 266t David Muench. 266b Chris Johns/National Geographic Image Collection. 267r Lynda Richardson/Peter Arnold. 267l Doug Wechsler/Animals Animals. 268/69 Fred Bruemmer/DRK Photo. 270t Jim Brandenburg/Minden Pictures. 270b David Weintraub/Photo Researchers. 271 Victoria McCormick/Animals Animals. 272 Bruce Dale © National Geographic Society. 274t Tom & Pat Leeson/Photo Researchers. 274b Richard Day/Animals Animals. 275 Jeff Foott/Bruce Coleman. 276t David Muench. 276b Galen Rowell/Peter Arnold. 277t David Muench. 277b Steve Solum/Bruce Coleman. 278t John Warden/Tony Stone Images. 278b © 1996 Brian Kenney. 279 Maslowski/Photo Researchers. 280 David Muench. 281t A & L Sinibaldi/Tony Stone Images. 281b Kenneth W. Fink/Bruce Coleman. 282/83 David Muench. 283lb Mickey Gibson/Animals Animals. 283rt Craig K. Lorenz/Photo Researchers. 284t © 1996 © 1996 Brian Kenney. 284b Rosalie LaRue Faubion/Bruce Coleman. 285 Mark Newman/Photo Researchers. 286 Art Wolfe. 287 Paul Chesley/National Geographic Image Collection. 288/89 all Art Wolfe. 290l Jeff Foott/Bruce Coleman. 290/91 John Kieffer/Peter Arnold. 292t P. Betow/Bruce Coleman. 292b Charlie Ott/Photo Researchers. 293t Adam Jones/Dembinsky Photo Associates. 293b Tom & Pat Leeson/Photo Researchers. 294 NASA. 295lb Carr Clifton/Minden Pictures. 295rt E.R. Degginger/Animals Animals. 295rb David Muench. 296t Jeff Simon/Bruce Coleman. 296b Dwight Kuhn/Bruce Coleman. 297t D. Cavagnaro/Visuals Unlimited. 297b John Sohlden/Visuals Unlimited. 298 Daniel J. Cox/Natural Exposures. 299 David Muench. 300t G. Alan Nelson/Dembinsky Photo Associates. 300b Kim Heacox/Peter Arnold. 301 Stan Osolinski/Dembinsky Photo Associates. 302 Gene Boaz. 303 Jeff Greenberg/Photo Researchers. 304 C.C. Lockwood/Animals Animals. 305t Wendell Metzen/Bruce Coleman. 305b David Muench. 306 Darrell Gulin/Dembinsky Photo Associates. 307t Dwight Kuhn. 307b Maslowski/Photo Researchers. 308/09 Michael Hurbrich/Dembinsky Photo Associates. 309r Daniel J. Cox/Natural Exposures. 310/11 Keith Gunnar/Bruce Coleman. 311lb M. Timothy O'Keefe/Bruce Coleman. 311r Willard Clay/Dembinsky Photo Associates. 312t Adam Jones/Dembinsky Photo Associates. 312b David Job/Ken Graham Agency. 313t Lee F. Snyde/Photo Researchers. 313b C.C. Lockwood/Bruce Coleman. 314l Larry Lipsky/DRK Photo. 314r Larry Lipsky/Bruce Coleman. 315 Sandy Spunt/Photo Researchers. 316 Doug Perrine/DRK Photo. 317t © Norbert Wu/Mo Yung Productions. 317b Gregory Ochocki/Photo Researchers. 318 both Andrew J. Martinez/Photo Researchers. 319 Norbert Wu/Peter Arnold. 320 Marc Muench. 321t Charlie Ott/Photo Researchers. 321b Gary Meszaros/Dembinsky Photo Associates. 322 S. J. Krasemann/Peter Arnold. 322b Tom McHugh/Photo Researchers. 323 John Eastcott/Animals Animals. 324 Stephen J. Krasemann/DRK Photo. 325t Michio Hoshino/Minden Pictures. 325b David Weintraub/Photo Researchers. back cover Gerry Ellis/Ellis Nature Photography.

Illustration Credits

All illustrations by Dolores R. Santoliquido, except pp. 22, 55, 138/39, 146, 273, and 301 by Drew-Brook-Cormack Assoc., and p. 155 by Robert Villani.

Key: l = left, r = right, t = top, m = middle, b = bottom.

INDEX

Page numbers in **bold type** refer to illustrations.

Page numbers in **bold type** refer to illustrations.

G

Gambel's quail, 281, 284
Gannets, 25, **25**, 313
Garibaldi, 311
Geese
  Aleutian Canada, 313
  Canada, V formation of, 122, **122**
  colonial nesting of snow, 25
  molting of feathers by, 109
  warning calls by, 54
Gemstones, 249
Geysers, 245, **245**
Ghost crabs, 313, **313**
Giant kelp, 157, **157**
Gila monsters, 129, **129**, 283, **283**
Gila woodpeckers, 283, **283**
Ginkgo tree, Asian, 204
Glacial erratics, 246
Glaciers, 216, 294, 298
  largest, 320, **320**
  moraines, 270, 320
  movement of, 320
Goats
  cliff-climbing mountain, 39, **39**, 288–289, **288**
  licking of young by, 99
Gold, formation of, 248–249
Golden plover, **325**
Golden silk spider, 14
Goosefish, 71, **71**
Grand Canyon, 227, 242–243, **242**
Grass
  cordgrass, 307, **307**
  ditchgrass, 307
  dune, 305
  green color of, reasons for, 179
  Kentucky bluegrass, 204
  scurvy, 208
  types of, in the grasslands, 269, 271
Grasshoppers, 62, **62**
Grasslands
  adaptation of animals to, 271
  fires in, 269, 275
  prairie potholes in, 270, **270**
  See also Great Plains.
Gray squirrels, 56
Gray whales, 111, 121, 316
Great Basin Desert, 227, **227**, 276, **276**
Great blue heron, **17**
Great horned owls
  mating of, 95
  as predators, 78

Great Lakes, formation of, 294, **294**
Great Plains
  adaptation of animals to, 271
  bison herds in, 268, **268**
  dustbowl of 1930s in, 273
  fertility of land in, 270
  grasslands in, 269
  lack of forests in, reasons for, 275
  largest remaining stretches of, 271
  mating of birds in, 273, **273**
  prairie dogs in, 16, **16**, 272, **272**
  prairie potholes in, 270, **270**
  sandhill cranes in, 274, **274**
  survival of plants in, 272–273
Great Salt Lake, 297, **297**
Great Smoky Mountains, **293**
Great Smoky Mountains National Park, **264**
Grebes, **92**
Griffith Park, 255
Grizzly bears
  feeding habits of, 60, **60**
  speed of, 41, **41**
Grouse
  drumming of ruffed, 90, **90**
  feathers in ptarmigans, molting of, 109
  mating of sage, 92, **273**
  migration of, 119
Growth rate of amphibians and reptiles, 108–109
Grunion, 89, **89**
Grunts, bluestriped, **52**
Gulf Stream, color of water, 315
Gulls, urban, 256
Gulper eels, 317, **317**

H

Hailstones, 235, **235**
Half Dome, 248
Hallucigenia, 287
Hammocks, 303
Hardwood forests
  description of, 259, **259**
  growth of, 261
  wildlife in, 258
Hare
  artic, **87**
  snowshoe, 34, 258, **258**, 320–321
Harris' hawk, 285
Hawaiian islands
  formation of, 251

Hawaiian islands *(contd.)*
  kipuka forests in, 266–267, **266**
Hawks
  Cooper's, **258**
  Harris', 285
  hunting by, 67, **67**, 285
  migration of Swainson's, 119
  red-tailed, 67
Haystack Rock, **308**
Heal-all, 211
Hearing, in barn owls, 31
Heartleaf plantain, 164
Heat, adaptations to
  birds and, 117
  desert animals and, 116
  spadefoot toads and, 117, **117**
Helconius butterflies, 170
Hell's Canyon, **226,** 227
Herds
  bison, 268, **268**
  living in, 28, **28**
  regulation of, 143, **143**
Hermit crabs, 19, **19**
Heron, great blue, **17**
Hibernation
  arctic ground squirrels and, 286, 323, **323,** 325
  bears and, 110, **110**
  birds and, 283
  butterflies and caterpillars and, 114–115
  frogs and, 115
  hoary marmot and, 286, **286**
  snakes and, 61
  timing of, 114
  woodchuck and, 114, **114**
Hoary marmot, 54, **54**, 286, **286**
Hognose snake, 83, **83**
Hoh Rain Forest, 260, **260**
Honeybee comb, construction of, 21, **21**
Honeybees. *See* Bees.
Honeycreepers, 266–267, **266**
Honeylocust, 198, 199
Horned lizards
  blood squirting by, 80–81, **80**
  camouflage of, 81
Hornets, bald-faced, 22, **22**
Horn Island, **304**
Horns, difference between antlers and, 85
Horses, 135, 285, **285**
Horseshoe crabs, 89, 140, **140,** 305
Horsetails, 204, **204**
Hot weather records, 222
House sparrows, 146–147
Hover fly, **74**

Hummingbirds
  black-chinned, **33**
  feeding habits of, 58
  movement by, 33
  pollination and, 194, **194**
  territorial defense by, 84
Humpback whales, 51, **51**, 316, **316**
Hurricanes, 220, 239, 319

I

Ice Age, 246–247
Ice pellets, 235, **235**
Ice worms, 134, **134**
Imprinting, 97, **97**
Indian pipe, 180, **180**
Indigo snake, 14, **14**
Insects
  antifreeze production by, 113
  camouflage and mimicry of, 74–75, **74, 75,** 79, 82
  chemicals used for defense by, 79, 127
  life span of, 11
  perfume used for mating by, 45, **45**
  stinging, 124, **124**
  teeth in, 62, **62**
  territorial defense by, 86, **86**
  See also under type of.

J

Jack-in-the-pulpit, 164, **164**
Jackrabbits
  adaptation to heat by, 116
  speed used for defense by black-tailed, 77
Javelina. *See* Collared peccaries.
Jellyfish, 69, **69**, 125
Jet propulsion in sea creatures, 38–39, **38**
Jet streams, 234
Jimsonweed, 192, **192**
Joshua trees, 206, **206**, 276
Jumping spiders, 68, **68–69**

K

Kangaroo rat, 116
Karner Blue butterflies, 258
Kelp
  giant, 157, **157**
  holdfasts of, 312, **312**

Page numbers in **bold type** refer to illustrations.